Looking for Information

A Survey of Research on Information Seeking, Needs, and Behavior

Library and Information Science

Consulting Editor: *Harold Borko*
Graduate School of Library and Information Science
University of California, Los Angeles

Harold Borko and Charles L. Bernier
Abstracting Concepts and Methods

F. W. Lancaster
Toward Paperless Information Systems

H. S. Heaps
Information Retrieval: Computational and Theoretical Aspects

Harold Borko and Charles L. Bernier
Indexing Concepts and Methods

Gerald Jahoda and Judith Schiek Braunagel
The Librarian and Reference Queries: A Systematic Approach

Charles H. Busha and Stephen P. Harter
Research Methods in Librarianship: Techniques and Interpretation

Diana M. Thomas, Ann T. Hinckley, and Elizabeth R. Eisenbach
The Effective Reference Librarian

G. Edward Evans
Management Techniques for Librarians, Second Edition

Jessica L. Milstead
Subject Access Systems: Alternatives in Design

Dagobert Soergel
Information Storage and Retrieval: A Systems Approach

Stephen P. Harter
Online Information Retrieval: Concepts, Principles, and Techniques

Timothy C. Craven
String Indexing

This list of books continues at the end of the volume.

Looking for Information

A Survey of Research on Information Seeking, Needs, and Behavior

Donald O. Case
University of Kentucky, Lexington

ACADEMIC PRESS
An imprint of Elsevier Science

Amsterdam   London   New York   Oxford   Paris   Tokyo
Boston   San Diego   San Francisco   Singapore   Sydney

Academic Press
An imprint of Elsevier Science
525 B Street, Suite 1900, San Diego, California 92101-4495, USA
http://www.academicpress.com

Academic Press
Harcourt Place, 32 Jamestown Road, London NW1 7BY, UK
http://www.academicpress.com

Library of Congress Catalog Card Number: 2002101252

International Standard Book Number: 0-12-150381-X

Printed in the United States of America

02 03 04 05 06 07 MV 9 8 7 6 5 4 3 2 1

Contents

Figures and Tables   xiii
Preface   xv

One
Introduction and Examples

1
Information Behavior: An Introduction

1.1. Introduction   4
    1.1.1. A Bit of Vocabulary   5
    1.1.2. Emphasizing People Rather Than Systems   6
    1.1.3. Ten Myths about Information and
        Information Seeking   7
    1.1.4. When, Why, and Where Information
        Behavior Has Been Studied   9
    1.1.5. The Contexts in Which Information
        Behavior Is Investigated   12
    1.1.6. The Scope of "Information Behavior"   13
1.2. How This Book Is Organized, and How to Use It   14
    1.2.1. Organization of the Chapters   14
    1.2.2. Which Chapters to Read If. . .   16

2

Common Examples of Information Behavior

2.1. Five Information Seeking Scenarios   18
     2.1.1. Buying Products   18
     2.1.2. Finding Information in a Library   22
     2.1.3. Betting on Race Horses   25
     2.1.4. Finding the Law   29
     2.1.5. "I Want to Know More about Cancer"   31
2.2. Summary   33

Two

Concepts Relevant to Information Behavior

3

The Concept of Information

3.1. Searching for a Definition of Information   40
     3.1.1. Explicating "Information"   41
     3.1.2. The Concept of Information   42
     3.1.3. Typologies of Information Concepts   43
3.2. Definitions of Information and Their Problems   45
     3.2.1. The Influential and Restrictive "Information
            Theory"   46
     3.2.2. Five Problematic Issues in Defining
            Information   49
     3.2.3. Uncertainty as a Requirement   50
     3.2.4. Physicality as a Requirement   52
     3.2.5. Structure/Process as a Requirement   53
     3.2.6. Intentionality as a Requirement   56
     3.2.7. Truth as a Requirement   57
3.3. Must There Be a Universal Definition of Information?   58
3.4. Distinctions among Information, Knowledge, and
     Data   61
3.5. Summary   62

4

Information Needs and Information Seeking

4.1.	The Motivational Puzzle	65
	4.1.1. What Is a "Need"?	65
	4.1.2. Needs versus Demands	67
4.2.	Four Scholars Ponder Information Needs	68
	4.2.1. Seeking Answers	68
	4.2.2. Reducing Uncertainty	69
	4.2.3. Making Sense	70
	4.2.4. The Spectrum of Motivations	71
4.3.	The Trouble with Information Needs	73
4.4.	Information Seeking and Information Behavior	75
4.5.	Summary	76

5

Related Concepts

5.1.	Decision Making	80
	5.1.1. Making Decisions	80
	5.1.2. Solving Problems	83
5.2.	Browsing, Etc.	84
	5.2.1. Browsing, Scanning, and Serendipity	84
	5.2.2. Additional Distinctions	86
5.3.	Relevance, Pertinence, and Salience	88
	5.3.1. Relevance and Pertinence	88
	5.3.2. Relevance in Information Retrieval	89
	5.3.3. Salience	91
5.4.	Avoiding Information	92
	5.4.1. Selective Exposure and Information Avoidance	92
	5.4.2. Knowledge Gaps and Information Poverty	95
	5.4.3. Information Overload and Anxiety	98
5.5.	Information versus Entertainment	102
5.6.	Summary	108

Three

Models, Paradigms, and Theories in the Study of Information Behavior

6

Models of Information Behavior

6.1. Models 114
  6.1.1. What Is a Model? 114
  6.1.2. Models of Information Seeking 115
6.2. Examples of Information Seeking Models 116
  6.2.1. Wilson Models 116
  6.2.2. Krikelas Model 119
  6.2.3. Johnson Model 122
  6.2.4. Leckie Model 126
  6.2.5. Comparing the Models 128

7

Perspectives, Paradigms, and Theories

7.1. Perspectives and Paradigms 132
  7.1.1. Perspectives 132
  7.1.2. Paradigms 133
7.2. Theories 135
  7.2.1. What Is a Theory? 135
  7.2.2. Levels of Theory: Grand to Grounded 136
7.3. Sources of Theory in Information Seeking 138
7.4. Some Relevant Paradigms 140
  7.4.1. Zipf's Principle of Least Effort 140
  7.4.2. Uses and Gratifications 143
  7.4.3. Sense-Making 146
  7.4.4. Media Use as Social Action 148
  7.4.5. Play Theory and Entertainment Theory 149
7.5. Other Theories 152
7.6. Summary 153

Four

Methods for Studying Information Behavior

8

The Research Process

8.1. Relating Theory to Methodology   160
     8.1.1. Why We Need Methods   160
     8.1.2. Techniques of Measurement and Analysis   162
8.2. Basic Considerations in Research   163
     8.2.1. Stages of Research   163
     8.2.2. Induction and Deduction   165
     8.2.3. Validity and Reliability   166
     8.2.4. Purpose, Units, and Time   169
     8.2.5. Ethics in Research   171
8.3. Summary   174

9

Methods: Examples by Type

9.1. Types and Examples of Methods   178
     9.1.1. The Case Study: Analyzing an Analyst   178
     9.1.2. Experiments: Shopping for Cars and Cornflakes   183
     9.1.3. Surveys: CEOs and Scholars   190
     9.1.4. Brief Interviews: Studies of Everyday Folks   194
     9.1.5. Intensive Interviews: The Lives of Janitors and Brothers   199
     9.1.6. Focus Group Interviews: Doctors and Nurses Search for Information   202
     9.1.7. Diaries and Experience Sampling   205
     9.1.8. Unobtrusive Approaches: Historical Analysis   207
     9.1.9. Unobtrusive Approaches: Content Analysis   210
     9.1.10. Using Multiple Data Sources in a Single Investigation   211
     9.1.11. Meta-Analysis   213
9.2. Summary   215

Five

Research Results and Reflections

10
Reviewing the Research: Its History, Size, and Topics

10.1. Overview of Part Five   219
       10.1.1. The History of Studying Information
                Behavior   220
       10.1.2. Estimating the Size of the Literature   222
       10.1.3. Contexts and Categories   225
       10.1.4. Choosing Examples of Studies   227
10.2. Summary   229

11
Research by Occupation

11.1. By Occupational Category   232
       11.1.1. Scientists and Engineers   233
       11.1.2. Social Scientists   238
       11.1.3. Humanities Scholars   240
       11.1.4. Health Care Providers   242
       11.1.5. Managers   248
       11.1.6. Journalists   249
       11.1.7. Lawyers   251
       11.1.8. Other Occupations   253
11.2. Summary   255

12
Research by Social Role and Demographic Group

12.1. Two Other Ways of Studying People   258
12.2. By Role   259
       12.2.1. Citizen or Voter   259
       12.2.2. Consumer   262
       12.2.3. Patient   264
       12.2.4. Gatekeeper   267
       12.2.5. Other Roles   269

12.3.	By Demographic Group	270
	12.3.1. Age	270
	12.3.2. Racial and Ethnolinguistic Minorities	274
	12.3.3. Socioeconomic Status	276
	12.3.4. Other Demographic Groups	278
12.4.	Summary	279

13

Reviewing, Critiquing, Concluding

13.1.	Reviewing	281
13.2.	Critiquing	284
	13.2.1. A History of Complaint	284
	13.2.2. Current Criticisms	286
13.3.	Concluding	287
	13.3.1. Eight Lessons of Information Behavior Research	288

Appendix: Questions for Discussion and Application	293
References	305
Index	335

Figures and Tables

Table 1.1: Contrasting examples of information behavior research questions.

Figure 1.1: A continuum of importance.

Table 2.1: Comparison of passenger cars.

Figure 2.1: Portion of an online catalog listing.

Table 2.2: Joe's notes on the three top horses.

Figure 2.2: Excerpt from the *American Law Reports*.

Table 2.3: Comparison of five case studies.

Figure 3.1: Shannon's model.

Figure 4.1: Taylor's typology of information needs.

Figure 4.2: The spectrum of views regarding motivations.

Table 5.1: Examples of browsing goals by domain of interest, goal type, and terminology.

Figure 6.1: Wilson's first model.

Figure 6.2: Wilson's second model.

Figure 6.3: The Krikelas model.

Figure 6.4: Johnson's model.

Figure 6.5: The Leckie, Pettigrew, and Sylvain model.

Table 6.1: Comparing the five models.

Figure 7.1: A hierarchy of theory.

Table 7.1: Some other theories invoked in information behavior research.

Table 8.1: Techniques of measurement and analysis.

Table 9.1: Works reviewed, and related works cited, for methods.

Table 10.1: Early and *ARIST* reviews of information needs, uses, and seeking.

Table 11.1: Works reviewed, and related works cited, for occupations.

Table 12.1: Works reviewed, and related works cited, for role and group.

Preface

This book defines concepts relevant to information behavior, identifies models and theories used in information seeking studies, provides examples of methods for studying information seeking, reviews research findings of the past two decades, and suggests some avenues for future improvement in what we know about the topic. I intend for it to be used not only in schools of information studies and communication, but also in the disciplines of management, business, medicine, nursing, public health, education, and social work.

I chose to write this book for one simple reason: there was no single current and comprehensive text that reflected the full breadth of research on information behavior. By "current" I mean one that reviews the flood of information seeking investigations conducted during the 1990s. When I say "comprehensive text" I mean one that is broad enough in scope to serve as an introduction to the topic for students at the graduate level, as well as a review and handbook for scholars engaged in information behavior research.

I am keenly aware that there may be very good reasons for the absence of comprehensive texts on information behavior. For one thing it is simply a huge literature; I estimate it to number more than ten thousand publications. And it is an unruly literature: publications on information needs, uses, and seeking sprawl across many academic disciplines, using dozens of overlapping concepts with varying definitions that, at times, conflict with one another. The findings of many thousands of studies are difficult to compare, much less to synthesize. Therefore, it is perhaps not surprising that no book attempts to cover the full breadth of the topic — maybe because it is simply too ambitious to even try.

"Perhaps too ambitious" was in fact a gentle criticism that came from two colleagues who read early drafts of this book. I hope that over the last three years I have overcome some of their concerns about summarizing what are indeed very complex issues regarding information and its use. I offer apologies to those many authors whose work I have condensed, or neglected entirely, in an attempt to give this book a digestible form and length. I would rather sketch out a broad canvas that lacks some details than to paint yet another detailed, but ultimately minuscule, portrait of information behavior research.

There is no shortage of specialized books on information. A spate of good texts appeared in the late-1990s, with a focus on information seeking in organizations: Chun Wei Choo's (1998) *The Knowing Organization*, and J. David Johnson's (1996) *Information Seeking: An Organizational Dilemma*. On a more abstract level is Karl Weick's (1995) *Sensemaking in Organizations*. All of these include general material beyond their common domain of interest (organizational behavior) and review hundreds of relevant studies published up to 1996.

I believe a broader approach to this literature is warranted. The prominence given to information behavior prompted by an increased focus on understanding the seeker, the phenomenal popularity of the World Wide Web, and the rapid growth in the number of studies of information seeking argue for a text that brings together key concepts, theories, methods, and findings. That is what I hope I have accomplished in the book you hold in your hands.

Acknowledgments

This book would not have been possible without the support and help of many colleagues and friends. I received helpful comments on selected chapters of the book from Suzanne Allard, Marcia Bates, Christine Borgman, Michael Buckland, Elfreda Chatman, Charles Cole, David Johnson, Carol Kuhlthau, Derek Lane, Ronald Rice, and Tom Wilson. My editor at Academic, Hal Borko, was especially encouraging in seeing this book to fruition and in tolerating my frequent changes in deadline. My colleagues at the University of Kentucky, especially our Director, Timothy Sineath, also deserve thanks for allowing me the time, flexibility, and resources to write and print the manuscript. Finally, I wish to thank Wendy Miller, my muse, for her unflagging moral support during the five-plus years of work that went into this book.

Donald O. Case
University of Kentucky
Lexington, Kentucky
October 2001

One

Introduction and Examples

1

Information Behavior: An Introduction

What you *don't* know has power over you; knowing it brings it under your control, and makes it subject to your choice. Ignorance makes real choice impossible.

Abraham Maslow (1963, p. 116)

Beyond obsessions, curiosity, and creativity, lies a host of motivations *not* to seek information.

David Johnson (1997, p. 70)

Chapter Outline

1.1. Introduction
   1.1.1. A Bit of Vocabulary
   1.1.2. Emphasizing People Rather Than Systems
   1.1.3. Ten Myths about Information and Information Seeking
   1.1.4. When, Why, and Where Information Behavior Has Been Studied
   1.1.5. The Contexts in Which Information Behavior Is Investigated
   1.1.6. The Scope of "Information Behavior"
1.2. How This Book Is Organized, and How to Use It
   1.2.1. Organization of the Chapters
   1.2.2. Which Chapters to Read If. . .

1.1
Introduction

This volume describes common and essential human behaviors: seeking and using information. Noticing a change in the weather, deciding to visit another city, finding out about travel schedules, choosing a departure date, and buying an airline ticket are examples of a range of activities known as "information behavior." These include encountering, needing, finding, choosing, and using information. They are types of behaviors that are basic to human existence.

This introductory chapter describes the scope of the book and what it contains. It says briefly what kinds of concepts, questions, and research have been developed regarding information behavior, and why this topic has attracted attention. I make the case that the nature of this research has changed over several decades, away from an emphasis on institutional sources and searches, and toward a focus on how individuals encounter and make sense of their environment.

The Internet could serve as a metaphor for information behavior and the way our view of it has changed. Think back to a time before the World Wide Web was available. All of the information was out there in individual offices, filing cabinets, minds, and computers. But because it was divided by source, by location, by person, and by channel, it was not always easily located or examined. Making arrangements for *travel* is one comprehensive example: One could hear the weather forecast on the radio, read about a destination in a travel guide, call hotels to make reservations, telephone an airline to learn departure times and fares, visit a travel agent to pick up a ticket, and so on. In terms of research, each of those needs and transactions might need to be conducted (and studied) separately. But now it is possible to satisfy all travel-related requests on a single Web site. Not only have the different channels of communication collapsed down to one, but less goal-oriented behaviors, such as browsing, may play a larger role than ever before. Looking for information becomes more holistic.

The contrast between new and old is even greater when we compare tasks in the office and classroom to their counterparts of 20 years ago. Obscure bits of information—the text of a government regulation, the date of an event, the author of a document—are more easily found in a single "place"—the Web. Both work and school have changed as a result.

In a manner similar to the emergence of the World Wide Web, our view of information behavior has become more integrated and less dictated by sources and institutions. As what we know about these behaviors has grown, so has the vocabulary used to describe it.

1.1.1 A Bit of Vocabulary

In introducing the subject matter of this book I will be using terms like "information," "information need," "information seeking," and "information behavior" without defining them fully until later chapters. For the moment let us assume that there *are* such things as "information" and "information needs" that can be satisfied by "information seeking" or "information behavior." To tide us over until these concepts are fleshed out, here are some brief definitions:

• *Information* can be any *difference* you perceive, in your environment or within yourself. It is any aspect that you notice in the pattern of reality.

• An *information need* is a recognition that your knowledge is inadequate to satisfy a goal that you have.

• *Information seeking* is a conscious effort to acquire information in response to a need or gap in your knowledge.

• *Information behavior* encompasses information seeking as well as the totality of other *unintentional* or *passive* behaviors (such as glimpsing or encountering information), as well as purposive behaviors that do not involve seeking, such as actively *avoiding* information.

The most commonly discussed of these concepts is *information seeking*. It is a behavior so commonplace that it is generally not an object of concern until time pressure makes it so. If we are making a major decision (e.g., buying a house) or finishing a task by a deadline (e.g., writing a report), we might find ourselves in an earnest information seeking mode: talking to others, searching the Web, reading magazines, watching the news, and so on. We may do everything we can to satisfy our desire for input, until either our need is satisfied or we have run out of time. More commonly, it is the latter, as the demand for "information" is usually elastic — there is always more that one could know. After our need is met (or we give up) we return to a more passive state of information seeking, at least as regards the object of our earlier curiosity.

Consider also cases in which the acquisition of information does *not* concern an immediate task like buying or writing something. Our daily life is peppered with instances in which we become interested in learning more about a topic after accidentally encountering some bit of information about it. This sort of curiosity, unmotivated by an immediate goal, is a common aspect of human life.

The situations described above, no matter how familiar to all of us, are much more complex than they may appear on the surface. Information seeking behavior often defies generalization and usually escapes observation. It is difficult to generalize about a behavior that varies so much across people, situations, and objects of interest, and so much of it takes place inside a person's head. This book is about the many ways in which information seeking has been defined, explicated, observed, and measured in studies of human behavior.

1.1.2 Emphasizing People Rather Than Systems

Systematic research on information seeking — at least on the use of sources like books or newspapers — dates back nearly a century. In the first three decades of the twentieth century, studies of information "channels" and "systems" — chiefly libraries and the mass media — accumulated slowly. The 1940s saw the first published reviews of this literature. By the 1960s, such investigations, particularly of the specialized information needs and uses of scientists and engineers, were appearing regularly in a variety of journals and reports.

But much of this older literature was really not about information seeking in the sense in which that concept is discussed in current research. Rather, most of the investigations focused on the *artifacts* and *venues* of information seeking: books, journals, newspapers, radio and television broadcasts, schools, universities, libraries, professional conferences, and the like. What was actually studied were the information *sources* and how they were used, rather than the individual users, their needs (as they saw them), where they went for information, and what kind of results they experienced. Surveys of individuals made such strong assumptions about their needs, motivations, habits, and behaviors that the range of responses they could make was severely constrained; what mattered in these early investigations was how *formal information systems* served the serious (e.g., work, health, or political) information needs of the population studied. Typically this literature was called "information needs and uses" research, or sometimes "user studies" or "audience research." Choo and Auster (1993) call this tradition "system-centered" research; Vakkari (1999) refers to it as "system oriented"; a host of other commentators have applied similar labels.

It was not until the 1970s that investigations begin to branch out beyond the focus on formal channels and task-oriented needs. The emphasis shifted away from the structured "information system" and toward the person as a finder, creator, and user of information. In mass media research the focus shifted to the "gratifications" that users experienced, rather than focusing on "effects" that messages had on people and how to persuade them to do things. Even studies of formal information systems began to consider a wider range of people, more general needs and problems, and the ways in which those systems often failed to serve their publics. The term "information seeking" — and, later, "sense making" — began to be preferred in describing the kind of phenomena that interested a growing number of scholars.

Some observers (see, for example, Vakkari, 1999) have stereotyped the concerns of the old versus the new research on information behavior. Table 1.1 contrasts the person and system orientations by posing some examples of research questions that are typical for each.

The right column in Table 1.1 reflects research questions that have motivated thousands of studies — typically institutionally sponsored evaluations

Table 1.1

Contrasting Examples of Information Behavior Research Questions

	Person Oriented	System Oriented
Task-oriented studies	• How do lawyers make sense of their tasks and environment?	• What kinds of documents do engineers need for their work, and how might the corporate information center supply them?
	• How does a manager learn about job-related information *outside of* formal organizational channels?	• How satisfied and successful are student searches of a university library's new Web-based catalog?
	• What happens when a voter has too much information about a candidate or an issue?	• How much use do medical doctors make of medical databases?
Nontask-oriented studies	• How do the elderly learn about and cope with problems or opportunities that come up in their daily lives?	• How does the public use a library for personal pleasure and growth: what they ask for, borrow, and read?
	• Why do TV viewers choose one program over another, and what satisfactions do they achieve in doing so?	• How do we persuade teenagers to act healthy and responsible ways? What messages about drug abuse do they attend to, in which medium, and why?
	• Why do people browse in stores when they have no explicit need or intention to buy?	• Why do people ignore safety warnings on packages and in advertisements?

of library use, selective dissemination of information (SDI) programs, information retrieval systems, interface designs, information campaigns, advertising effectiveness, and the like. A few of these studies will be discussed in this book, almost exclusively the "nontask-oriented" variety. The left column reflects the emphasis of this volume, and hence, the predominate type of examples used within.

1.1.3 Ten Myths about Information and Information Seeking

A key development in the shift toward more user- or person-centered theories and methods were the questions raised in the early 1970s by several researchers, chief among them Professor Brenda Dervin (Ohio State University). A landmark 1976 article by Dervin encapsulated several years of her work by challenging 10 assumptions that had dominated research on communication and information seeking up to that time. In this article she was concerned chiefly with the everyday information needs of the ordinary, urban resident. However, much of what she says also applies to more formalized needs. Here are the 10 "dubious assumptions" that Dervin (1976a) identified in past writings about information seeking.

1. *Only "objective" information is valuable.* People are rational beings who process data from the environment to analyze alternatives and make optimal decisions. Several problems plague this assumption, including our common tendency to rely on easily available sources of information such as our friends. For most tasks and decisions in life, people tend to settle for the first satisfactory solution to a problem, rather than the best solution.

2. *More information is always better.* Yet too much information leads to overload and thence to deliberate ignoring of inputs. "Having information" is not the same as "being informed,"so increasing the flow of information does not always result in an informed person. Typically there is not a problem getting enough information but rather with interpreting and understanding what information there is — an internal, rather than an external, locus of control.

3. *Objective information can be transmitted out of context.* But people tend to ignore isolated facts when they cannot form a complete picture of them.

4. *Information can only be acquired through formal sources.* This assumption, often made by those in educational institutions, flies in the face of actual behavior. People use formal sources rarely, instead gathering and applying information from informal sources, chiefly friends and family, throughout their lives.

5. *There is relevant information for every need.* The truth is that mere information cannot satisfy many human needs. People may want information in the sense of learning or understanding; more commonly they need the physical and psychological necessities of daily life, such as food, shelter, clothing, money, and love. Information cannot substitute for many human needs, nor even facilitate all of them.

6. *Every need situation has a solution.* Institutions such as libraries, medical clinics, and social service agencies are focused on finding solutions to problems. To do so they attempt to map what the client says — the words they use — onto the resources and responses of their system. But sometimes the client is looking for something — a reassurance, an understanding — that does not come in the shape of a canned response. Nevertheless, the system will usually provide an answer of some type, in its own language and logic, whether it is useful to the client or not.

7. *It is always possible to make information available or accessible.* Formal information systems are limited in what they can accomplish, at least where the vague, ambiguous, and constantly changing needs of the public are concerned. People will continue to come up with their own answers to their own unique, unpredictable questions without resorting to formal information systems.

8. *Functional units of information, such as books or TV programs, always fit the needs of individuals.* Information systems such as libraries or broadcasters define themselves in terms of their units of storage or production: in the case of libraries, this is books, journals, or Web sites; in the case of broadcasters, it is programs, ads, or public service announcements. But the "functional units" of the individual are not often these things; rather, they are responses, solutions, instructions ideas, friendships, and so forth. Thus, client requests for help, action, or resources tend to be reinterpreted by institutions as information needs that can be fulfilled with the units that they provide: books, programs, and the like. The client cannot always effectively use these units of information.

9. *Time and space — individual situations — can be ignored in addressing information seeking and use.* Yet often it is the individual's definition of the situation that shapes his or her needs as much as the "real" situation itself. If individuals perceive a lack of predictability and control of an outcome, then they worry. The worry itself becomes a need.

10. *People make easy, conflict-free connections between external information and their internal reality.* We tend to assume an ordered universe, in which connections exist between the internal and external. In our research, we tend to ask "what" and "how" rather than "why." We ask what people read or view, rather than why they do so. We lack understanding about how people inform themselves, how they make connections *over time,* the sense they make of their world between significant events. Dervin said that instead of studying what "information does... for people" we need to focus on "what people do to information" (p. 333).

Dervin argued that all ten of these assumptions were flawed in the ways indicated. Of course she made these statements about *everyday* information needs, not in the context of highly specific, task-oriented needs like scientific or business data for decision making. There are indeed times when people act mostly rational and optimal in their information seeking and processing. Those situations, too, will be addressed in this volume.

1.1.4 When, Why, and Where Information Behavior Has Been Studied

As a subject of scholarly attention, information behavior has been studied in many different contexts, with a variety of people and a broad array of motives and goals. All people seek information, yet for some people and in some situations the stakes are much higher. Higher stakes are more likely to create situations that attract research.

To illustrate the kinds of people and situations that have been investigated over the last five decades, first let us consider several hypothetical cases. The examples below are constrained by several assumptions. These assumptions are valuable because they will help us compare situations by creating a "standard" set of reactions. However, each assumption has limitations, which will be noted. The assumptions are that information seeking behavior is highly *rational* (which is not often true), that such behavior is oriented toward making some kind of *decision* (a common, yet flawed, assumption), and that it is possible to make relatively simple judgments about the *value* of our decisions (itself a value judgment to which some people would object).

Consider the relative importance of three types of situations and information needs, as located on a hypothetical continuum (Figure 1.1). This continuum reflects the number of people ultimately affected by the search for information and subsequent decisions based on it: at one end are trivial decisions affecting few people, whereas at the other are important decisions that may affect millions of human lives.

Now, one could argue that it is anthropocentric to use humans as the sole benchmark for judging the *importance* of a decision. We could easily imagine real-world problems that involved other sentient beings (e.g., animals) or nonsentient things (e.g., tropical rain forests). If we think through the implications of such problems, we may notice that we tend to judge their importance by their ultimate impact on our own feelings or well-being as humans. So, while recognizing that we could use other real-world objects as benchmarks, for the purposes of this discussion we will consider "numbers of people affected" as a simple indicator of importance.

First, imagine a person trying to choose between different models of a car that vary by features and price; although there are many publications (both printed and electronic) that offer just such information, the outcome of this search is simply not very consequential. Presumably this situation would fall near the "unimportant" end of our hypothetical continuum because it affects only one consumer.

Second, consider a citizen about to go to the polls, choosing among candidates based on information about their positions and past performance; electing public officials is certainly an important decision, and yet this is just

Less Important			**More Important**
One person affected	Thousands affected	Millions affected	Billions affected
◄ - ►			
A consumer gathers information to help in buying a car.	Voters use information to choose among competing candidates for public office.	Medical researchers seek a new treatment for heart disease.	

Figure 1.1
A continuum of importance.

one vote out of many. This situation is more important than the first, but less crucial than others we might imagine.

Third, imagine a biomedical scientist, with years of training and experience, working in an expensive laboratory, developing treatments for heart disease. This scientist must keep abreast of what other researchers are doing in the field, what discoveries have been made, what new equipment and techniques are available, and so forth. (To be more realistic, we could identify just one such need, such as the answer to the question "What are the effects of dietary fish oil on measures of serum cholesterol?") Surely the information needs of this person are important, as judged by the investment society has made in the scientist and the potential outcomes of the work. The scientist's decisions about which research leads to follow could affect millions of people around the globe.

Laying out these hypothetical situations and judging their importance is a precursor to an explanation of why more research has been conducted on some kinds of information seeking and not on other types. We might all agree that the case of the scientist who is working on treatments for heart disease that might affect millions of lives is worthy of study. By studying the information needs of such scientists, and how they go about satisfying those needs, we just might be able to devise a tool or service that would help them reach their research goals a little sooner. In such situations, the potential for public good (and for private profit) is enormous. This is why many of the investigations the reader will encounter in this volume have focused on high-stakes and high-status occupations: research scientists, medical doctors, aerospace engineers, and the like.

And yet many types of information seeking behavior are worthy of study. Sometimes relatively trivial decisions, such as the automobile purchase described above, are the target of expensive investigations due to the cumulative importance of individual decisions. There is an entire industry, commonly called *market research,* that investigates purchase decisions; individual purchases are relatively trivial, yet millions of them add up to significant amounts of money.

We can see a similar logic operating in studies of voting: how a particular individual finds out about issues and candidates may not seem important, but the information-gathering habits of millions of voters may have a crucial impact on a society as a whole. Therefore, there is a sizable literature on political communication, and more specifically on what kinds of information people glean from the mass media. The listening, watching, reading, and learning that takes place in support of buying and voting — and many other daily tasks — is sometimes referred to as "everyday" information seeking. We will learn about that as well in this book.

There is another very important focus of investigation that we have not touched on yet (although the medical study comes close): "basic" research on human information behavior. Ideally, what we would really like to know is how people go about seeking (or avoiding) information in a *generic* way, free of specific contexts like heart disease research or car purchases. Unfortunately, as with other attempts to conduct basic research on human behavior, it is difficult to generalize beyond the specific type of stimulus that prompted the behavior.

There is some doubt as to how deeply researchers can investigate truly basic human behaviors regarding information. Certainly some psychological investigations of perception, human information processing, and pattern recognition are relevant to basic considerations of information seeking. Such studies deal with the fundamental question "What is information?" and are discussed in Chapter 3 of this volume. Suffice to say that, for this book, I am concerned also with a social element: information seeking is *inter*personal as well as *intra*personal.

In the latter sense, perhaps the closest we come to basic research on information seeking are studies of communication in dyads and small groups in laboratory settings. Social scientists conduct these studies to understand how individuals solicit, process, and interpret data and cues they receive from others. Even in closed laboratory settings, the nature of the information itself may intrude. I will say more on this point as we review specific studies.

Finally, one important distinction that is made in the literature on information seeking is between *formal* and *informal* sources of information. The prototypical formal source is a printed one — a textbook, encyclopedia, or daily newspaper — but may also be exemplified by the words of an acknowledged expert on a subject. Informal sources tend to be friends, colleagues, and family, but in the view of some they could encompass what we learn from popular culture as well: TV programs, songs on the radio, Internet mailing list discussions, and so forth. I will make use of this formal versus informal distinction in reviewing some of the findings on information behavior.

1.1.5 The Contexts in Which Information Behavior Is Investigated

The previous section raised the issue of context with considerations such as individual situations, motives for seeking information, the specific activities and kinds of information, the surrounding environment, the types of people, and the size of the social group involved in the investigations. There is no nice, neat, logical delineation of these factors, as human behavior itself is not completely rational or uniform. The examples used later in this volume have been selected with an eye toward the literature that actually *exists* — that is the patterns of studies that have been conducted, particularly since 1980.

There are a variety of approaches that we could use to consider the vast literature on information seeking and related topics. I could, for example, review studies chronologically, showing how they shifted in focus and method.

Or investigations could be selected on the basis of the discipline in which they were published, whether in information studies, communication, management, medicine, and so forth. In fact, both *historical* (in this chapter and the final chapter) and *disciplinary* (in most of the other chapters) categorizations are sometimes invoked in this volume, but they take a back seat to three other ways of considering the literature: by theory, methods, and context.

What is meant by "theory" and "methods" may be obvious to most readers, but "context" warrants some further explanation. For the purposes of organizing this book, *context* will be taken to mean the particular combination of person and situation that served to frame an investigation. In Chapters 11 and 12 I review information seeking investigations under three general categories: the *occupation* studied (e.g., manager, doctor, social scientist, chemist); the *social role* of the persons under investigation (e.g., consumer, voter, student, library user, Web surfer, newspaper reader, television watcher); and the *demographic* groupings (e.g., by age, gender, race, ethnicity, geography). Although a respondent could easily represent an occupation, a role, and a demographic group at the same time, as well as illustrating the use of any number of information sources, investigators typically choose to frame their research questions and respondent samples in terms of one of these three ways. In Chapter 12, for example, I will describe a study of the "urban poor" (a demographic group) that approached its topic by sampling janitors (an occupation). The bulk of investigations that fall under the heading of "information seeking" have concerned the information needs and uses of a specific occupation, role, or demographic group.

1.1.6 The Scope of "Information Behavior"

Information seeking is a topic that has been written about in over 10,000 documents from several distinct disciplines. Because almost everything to do with humans is potentially relevant to this topic, I have trimmed the scope of this book to highlight aspects of information behavior that have become more important in recent years.

For starters, there are two things that this book primarily is *not* about. I refer to the time-honored topics of "library use" and "information retrieval." Both of these (particularly the first) do indeed have strong connections to human information seeking, but each topic has a voluminous literature of its own that is really more about documents (or computer records) than it is about people. One could also say that these have received too much emphasis in the "information needs and uses" literature. Generally speaking, the research described here is *not* well representative of pre-1980 information seeking research, which tended to focus on the use of libraries and paper or electronic documents; I say little about such studies here. Relatedly I pass by the many thousands of studies on the education of students, even though I do treat issues of information acquisition sometimes in passing.

I have also narrowed my review by time period. More than one-third of the publications discussed herein (over 200 items) date from 1990 or later; most of the rest were published during the 1980s. Although I make citations to some earlier, seminal discussions and definitions of the concepts discussed in this volume, those are merely included to ensure proper credit and historical perspective. Most of the examples and references in this book are taken from the last two decades of published literature. As is emphasized here and in the concluding chapter, recent investigations of information seeking focus more on the *seeker* and less on the *sources* or *channels* they use, although it is not possible to ignore the latter entirely.

I have chosen to highlight certain aspects that have received too little attention from mainstream investigators of information seeking; among these less-examined topics are the connection between entertainment and information; passive and accidental information acquisition; and ignoring and avoiding information.

My examples are taken chiefly from the disciplines of information studies, communication, psychology, and professional fields like management, business, medicine, and public health. The investigations used to explain typical findings or methods are taken from a variety of contexts. I am aiming for a multidisciplinary understanding of the concept of information seeking. I hope I have succeeded in reaching that goal.

1.2

How This Book Is Organized, and How to Use It

1.2.1 Organization of the Chapters

This book consists of 13 chapters. I like to think of these chapters as grouped into five segments:

One:	Introduction and examples (Chapters 1 and 2)
Two:	Concepts relevant to information behavior (Chapters 3, 4, and 5)
Three:	Models, paradigms, and theories in the study of information behavior (Chapters 6 and 7)
Four:	Methods for studying information behavior (Chapters 8 and 9)
Five:	Research results and reflections (Chapters 10, 11, 12, and 13)

I have begun by mentioning several basic concepts: *information, information needs, information seeking*, and *information behavior*. Each will be explored in more depth in Chapters 3 and 4. I have sketched out the history and scope of the literature I intend to review.

The second chapter is my attempt to give information behavior a human face by exploring five examples from the individual's point of view. Please do not be misled by the simplistic and everyday nature of these five scenarios. They are here because I believe it is important to recognize that information seeking is something we all do in the course of our everyday existence. It is not a domain of behavior restricted to scientists, engineers, physicians, managers, and the like. We should acknowledge it as a common need before we plunge into the explication of the fuzzy concepts that have tended to plague this research.

Beginning Part Two, Chapter 3 (The Concept of Information) explores the vital notion of *information* and analyzes several problems inherent in its definition. The reader may judge that I say far too much about the definition of information — don't we all know what it is? But I think it is only fair to acknowledge how much commentary this everyday notion has generated. Readers who are new to this literature would be wise to save Chapter 3 for a later time.

The fourth (Information Needs and Information Seeking) and fifth (Related Concepts) chapters continue the review of basic concepts by offering definitions of many other terms frequently invoked in the information seeking literature, such as *decision making, browsing, foraging, encountering, selective exposure, avoidance, overload, information anxiety, knowledge gap, information poverty, pertinence, relevance, entertainment,* and *context.*

In the third segment, Chapter 6 (Models of Information Behavior) and Chapter 7 (Perspectives, Paradigms, and Theories) provide general background about models and theories that have been used to study information seeking. Chapter 8 (The Research Process) contains a brief tutorial about methods of investigation. Then Chapter 9 (Methods: Examples by Type) proceeds to explore methods and techniques commonly used in information seeking studies, providing one or more examples of each approach: laboratory experiment, field experiment, mail survey, e-mail/WWW survey, individual and focus group interview, participant observation, diaries and experience sampling, history, content analysis, meta-analysis, and combinations of these.

In the fourth part of this book, Chapters 10 through 12 identify 14 commonly researched categories of people, and summarize one or more typical studies for each group. Other relevant studies are mentioned in context. First, Chapter 10 explores the history, size, and structure of the information seeking literature. Chapter 11 then examines findings about *occupations* (e.g., doctors). Chapter 12 also reviews individual studies of information seeking, but this time considering investigations of social *roles* (e.g., consumers) and *demographic groups* (e.g., the elderly). Altogether over 100 investigations are cited in Chapters 10 through 12, and 30 are described in detail.

Finally, Chapter 13 summarizes the approaches and findings of the current literature and suggests avenues for future research. The book concludes with a collection of questions for discussion, and a bibliography of over 700 works cited in the text.

1.2.2 Which Chapters to Read If...

This book could be used in several different ways, depending on the needs and goals of the reader. For those who simply want a quick review of the recent literature on information seeking, Chapters 10 through 12 could be read on their own. There has been no general review of this research published during the past decade, so I intend for these chapters to serve such a purpose.

For methods courses in information behavior, Chapters 6 through 9 (covering theories and methods) could be read together, or in combination with Chapters 10 through 13 (reviewing research results). Methodologists interested in the range of concepts that might be measured in investigations should also read Chapters 4 and 5 on relevant concepts; experienced researchers can skip Chapter 8 on basic methods, as this is intended for neophytes.

Finally, students of information seeking, information behavior, and information needs and uses will want to read the book straight through. This text could also be useful in courses on user-centered design of information systems, information architecture, and the like. The appendixes include several questions for each chapter, for use as the basis for classroom discussions or written exercises.

Now let's begin our exploration by looking at some examples of information seeking from the seeker's perspective.

2

Common Examples
of Information Behavior

Information-seeking must be one of our most fundamental methods for coping with our environment. The strategies we learn to use in gathering information may turn out to be far more important in the long run than specific pieces of knowledge we may pick up in our formal education and then soon forget as we go about wrestling with our day-to-day problems.

Lewis Donohew, Leonard Tipton, and Roger Haney (1978, p. 31)

Blood donors often ask, "Will I faint?" Cancer patients ask, "Will I die?" citizens facing everyday situations ask, "How long will it take me to handle this?"

Brenda Dervin (1992, p. 75)

Chapter Outline

2.1. Five Information Seeking Scenarios
　　2.1.1. Buying Products
　　2.1.2. Finding Information in a Library
　　2.1.3. Betting on Race Horses
　　2.1.4. Finding the Law
　　2.1.5. "I Want to Know More about Cancer"
2.2. Summary

In this chapter we will make the case that searching for information is an important part of being human, and it is something that we do on a regular basis. Out of necessity we will encounter concepts and terminology that will be explained fully in later chapters of this book. Consider this chapter to be a preview of what is to come.

Every day of our lives we engage in some activity that might be called information seeking, though we may not think of it that way at the time. From the moment of our birth we are prompted by our environment and our motivations to seek out information that will help us meet our needs.

This chapter will consider five common situations in which information seeking behaviors are in full swing. That is, these are scenarios that face millions of people (at least in developed nations) each year, in which decisions and choices are made that require a great deal of data, information, and understanding. Each will underscore the complexity of information seeking and the strategies we use to make it simpler.

All of the stories here involve not only the search for information but the choice of which data to retain and consider. Four of the tales can be characterized as decision making as well, a narrower type of behavior that is studied in its own right and is not always considered in studies of information seeking.

Let's first consider a very familiar type of activity: shopping.

2.1
Five Information Seeking Scenarios

2.1.1 Buying Products

Few decisions are more common in developed societies than choosing to purchase a product. In our role as consumer we may buy thousands of items a year, mostly foodstuffs, but also intangibles like services and many hundreds of household items. Of the latter, only a few may be considered major purchase decisions: houses, cars, boats, furniture, and large appliances, among others.

From the consumer's perspective it is the expensive, infrequently purchased items that tend to garner the most thought. However, it is important to recognize that many small purchases over the course of a lifetime — such as toothpaste or soft drinks — also amount to large expenditures. The fact that even our most minor needs eventually amount to a great deal of money accounts for the attention paid to the purchase decision from two different perspectives: market research (intended to aid the producers of goods) and product evaluations (intended to aid the consumers of goods).

On the production side, a great deal of thought goes into the design and especially the advertising of items for sale. Advertising is intended to present (and sometimes inundate) the consumer with reminders of the product's existence and with persuasive information about it. Hence, the marketing of products attempts to minimize the effort a consumer expends to search for information.

Indeed, from the marketer's perspective, the information that is put out in print, on radio and television, on the Internet, and on billboards would result ideally in an entirely knee-jerk reaction: the consumer sees the ads, the consumer sees the product, and the consumer buys the product. For those who make and sell products, it is better that the consumer does not engage in a lengthy search for information, but simply buys the product as quickly as possible. Except for those few truly and obviously superior products, the producers are likely to prefer that the consumer does not compare brands at all.

Research on these questions is accomplished by a variety of scientists working in industry and in universities; most have training in psychology or business (or both). When their reports are not proprietary, they may be published in the *Journal of Consumer Research*, the *Journal of Marketing Research*, the *Journal of Advertising Research*, or in more general publications.

Product makers are not the only ones who do research. There are other organizations that, for both profit and public service, provide the research and testing that the consumers do not (and indeed often cannot) do for themselves. The prototypical example is the monthly magazine *Consumer Reports*, published by Consumers Union. A nonprofit organization founded in 1936, Consumers Union reviews goods and services and publishes investigative reports intended to help consumers make intelligent purchase decisions. Consumers Union reinforces its independence (unlike some other "consumer guides") by not accepting advertising and not allowing their published opinions to be used in advertising. Other publications of this type include *Consumer Digest* and *Consumers' Research Magazine*, neither of which undertake the extensive testing programs of *Consumer Reports*.

The publications of *Consumer Reports* offer a prime example of what the consumer needs to know to make an informed purchase. The magazine conducts comparative tests of many brands and styles of a product, presenting the results in simplified tables with accompanying text. No matter whether the cost of the purchase is small (e.g., peanut butter) or large (e.g., a new car), the goal is to reduce the often massive amount of salient information into a few key factors, rated or described in the simplest way possible.

Let's consider a hypothetical review of passenger cars (Table 2.1).

Imagine a consumer (we'll call her Julie) is shopping for a new car. Like many consumers, she already has some background information regarding cars: their makes, models, styles, cost, popularity, and perhaps a sense of their mechanical reliability. She has seen the models that interest her driving about town, and she has shared opinions about them with friends and relatives.

Having two children and a husband to transport, Julie wants a car of intermediate size and good quality. Three sedans made by Mercedes, Volvo, and Lexus interest her, because she has had at least one friend who owned each one of these models and was pleased with them.

Table 2.1

Comparison of Passenger Cars

	Test results for sedans		
	Mercedes E320	Volvo S60	Lexus IS300
Acceleration, 0 to 60 mph	7.0 seconds	8.0 seconds	7.4 seconds
Braking	••••	•••	••••
Ride	••••	•••	•••
Comfort	•••	•••	••••
Controls/displays	••	••	•••
Likely reliability	•••	•••	••••
Required fuel type	Premium	Regular	Premium
Fuel economy	21 mpg	21 mpg	21 mpg

Of course, to completely evaluate a car, one needs to drive it. However, from past experience Julie is wary of dealerships and salespeople, and has decided to go to them only after doing some background research. In fact, she thinks she might ultimately buy the car through a broker, making the deal over the telephone or the Internet after visiting the dealers to test-drive the models.

Julie starts her quest for facts with a review from a consumer magazine. Like many such publications, it contains color pictures of the various models, charts with dozens of facts on each model (e.g., dimensions, fuel consumption, features, prices), comparisons of cars by type (e.g., the best luxury vehicles), and subject ratings and recommendations. What draws Julie to this particular publication is its reputation for objectivity and frequency-of-repair charts, based on hundreds of thousands of reports from owners of the vehicles reviewed and unique to this magazine.

Julie learns several things from the magazine that help her differentiate the three cars. The first thing she notices is that the price range for the Mercedes is several thousand dollars more than the other two, apparently because of the manufacturer's prestige and reputation in North America. Acceleration is considerably slower with the Volvo, as it has a smaller engine than the other two. Fuel economy is the same among the three models, yet only the Volvo can use lower-octane fuel—making it cheaper to operate. The Mercedes and Lexus are rated better for braking ability than the Volvo, while the Lexus and Volvo score better on dashboard design. Turning to the frequency-of-repair charts, Julie sees different patterns among the fourteen "trouble spots" (electrical, brakes, transmission, etc.) but concludes that the Lexus may be more reliable than the other two, which are new models. Julie concludes that, in matters other than the above, the three cars are similar.

Julie is leaning toward the purchase of the Volvo, reasoning that its use of ordinary fuel means a lower cost of operation; compounding those savings over many years of ownership makes the Volvo the least expensive of these higher end sedans. Yet she retains some doubt as to whether the Volvo is truly equivalent in features to the other two. She knows she can get basic price information — dealer costs, sticker price, and the costs of major options — from a variety of sources.

In her office one evening after work, Julie locates the Web site for *Kelley Blue Book*. Here she is able to get price quotes for the three cars with similar options; the Mercedes is considerably more expensive than the other two cars in price, yet the engine (3.2 liters) is only slightly larger than that of the Lexus (3.0 liters). Does the engine size really matter so much, Julie asks herself? Probably not, she concludes.

Armed with this information, Julie heads to the Mercedes and Volvo dealers for test-drives, deciding against any further consideration of the Lexus. She likes the Volvo but finds the salespeople at that dealership to be too persistently aggressive. At the Mercedes dealer, in contrast, the salesman subjects her to less talk, and puts her in a positive mood for her spin in the car; she immediately falls in love with the Mercedes she drives, but realizes that it has many more options than the basic version that she has been considering.

As the week goes by, Julie discusses the purchase with several friends and family members. One friend cautions her strongly against the Mercedes on the basis of maintenance problems she encountered with her own Mercedes, an anecdote that Julie finds persuasive. On the other hand, her husband, who up until now has remained silent on the topic, argues strongly for the Mercedes on the basis of its larger engine capacity. "What if we want to tow a trailer some day?" he asks. That is a scenario that Julie hadn't even thought of, and it causes her to go back to the Internet to find the costs of towing packages for each car. While still convinced that the Volvo would be the more sensible choice, Julie ends up buying a Mercedes through a nationwide car broker. And besides — it came in more attractive colors!

Three common anomalies of information seeking are worth pointing out in this scenario. One, the mysterious influence we call "taste" has a powerful role in the decision process. Two, personal contacts have strong influence, whether they compel agreement (e.g., the advice of a friend or loved one), or disagreement (an overbearing salesperson). Drawing upon basic human emotions, these two influences can overwhelm any collection of facts, no matter how large or persuasive, as noted in the Chapter 1 comments regarding the fallacy of rational decision making. Three, it is useful to keep in mind that affluence and education can make a great difference in both the sources of information available to people and their inclination to pay attention to that information. In this scenario, an affluent (and probably well-educated) shopper both knows about and has easy access to channels of information that a poorer or less-educated person may not be aware of or inclined to use.

2.1.2 Finding Information in a Library

In the widespread literature that could be included under the rubric of information seeking, there is a genre of empirical work that is larger than any other: studies of people finding information in libraries. Most of the publications in this genre focus on "information as a thing" (Buckland, 1991a), that is, use of books, journals, and other "packages" of information.

So let us imagine another information seeker, this one called Leslie. Leslie is writing a paper for her history class on the 1898 war between Spain and the United States. She has gone to the library to gather background data on the role of the United States president, William McKinley, in the decision to declare war on Cuba. Among her questions are these: Had McKinley favored war from the beginnings of his presidential campaign in 1896? Was McKinley reasonably well informed of the facts regarding unrest in Cuba and Spanish military weakness there and on the high seas? Who were McKinley's closest advisors and what was their advice to him regarding intervention? So Leslie has gone to a university library to find answers to these questions. The particular library she has chosen contains roughly 3 million books and subscribes to more than 4,000 printed journals and has electronic access to many more.

Before we begin following Leslie's search, let us consider some tendencies of libraries and their users. First, it is important to recognize that all but the smallest libraries can be complex and intimidating. Although libraries make every attempt to place materials on similar topics in close approximation, this goal is elusive. For one thing it is hard to decide what any one document is "about"; for another, library materials are divided into a multitude of forms — books, journals, computer files (often on CD-ROM), audio recordings (on CDs, tape, or LPs), and loose materials (in file cabinets or special boxes) to name the major categories.

As if it were not difficult enough to classify the content of these different forms of media, sometimes information on the same topic and medium might still be found in different places; background material on international conflicts could be found on the shelves of the main collection, on nearby shelves reserved for oversized books, in the collection that serves the reference desk, or perhaps in a special collection or archive. For example, biographies of American presidents will be found on the main shelves of a library, but the personal documents to which they refer are likely to be held in the archives of a distant library.

Once one considers the various interactions of (intellectual) content with (physical) form, it can be seen why libraries become difficult places to search systematically, even with experience. Many visitors to a library end their search prematurely when faced with a large building full of millions of items and the imperfect tool of the electronic catalog.

Leslie begins by consulting the electronic card catalog, a tool she has used before. Being a regular visitor to this library, she is aware that if she chooses to consider journal articles she will need to consult at least one other electronic index to obtain the specific titles of articles that contain relevant information. She decides to restrict herself to books about the war and McKinley.

First Leslie tries "TITLE = MCKINLEY" and is rewarded with a listing of 12 books. Looking at the book titles, however, she is dismayed to see that few of them are about the former president; rather, they are books that begin with the name "McKinley," whether that is the name of a county or a person. Next she receives a list of four books by typing "TITLE = WILLIAM MCKINLEY." Even though that seems like very little material to browse through, she heads for the shelves. Checking the books in the "E711" section of the Library of Congress system, Leslie immediately sees that there are many more books on her topic than were retrieved in her search — dozens more, in fact. Based on the titles alone, Leslie's first insight is that most of these books are about the life and/or presidency of McKinley, and are likely to contain only brief descriptions of the war with Spain in 1898.

After browsing a while and picking up two books about the McKinley administration and one biography of the president, she heads to the reference department of the library. There she asks why her search of the electronic catalog was so incomplete. The reference librarian shows her that there are such things as subject headings in the catalog records. Returning to a terminal for the online catalog, Leslie enters "SUBJECT = MCKINLEY, WILLIAM". This time, 25 books on McKinley are retrieved, even those that do not have his name in the title (Figure 2.1).

Leslie starts to examine the 25 listings, one at a time. The most promising title appears to be *The Spanish-American War and President McKinley*, a book that she just missed because it was at E715. She makes note of several other McKinley books she missed in her browsing session at the shelf, seeing also that two of the more relevant ones are already checked out.

Now that she knows about subject headings, Leslie sees one that could be useful: "Spanish-American War." Searching that phrase as a subject heading gives her 127 titles. Intimidated by the size of this new list, Leslie slowly pages down through the titles until she just can't read any more. She has jotted down the call numbers of the most promising books, most of which are in the E711–715 range of the Library of Congress system, and a bibliography at Z8561 on the top floor of the library.

```
Search Request: S = MCKINLEY, WILLIAM      University Online Catalog
Search Results: 25 Entries Found        Subject Index
------------------------------------------------------------------------
   MCKINLEY, WILLIAM 1843-1901
 1  COMPLETE LIFE OF WILLIAM MCKINLEY AND STORY OF HIS . . . [1901]
 2  DICKEN TROUTMAN BALKE FAMILY PAPERS [1816] archive-mss
 3  EDWARD HENRY HOBSON PAPERS [1857] archive-mss
 4  FROM MCKINLEY TO HARDING PERSON RECOLLECTIONS OF . . . [1923]
 5  ILLUSTRIOUS LIFE OF WILLIAM MCKINLEY OUR MARTYRED . . . [1901]
 6  IN THE DAYS OF MCKINLEY [1959]
 7  LIFE OF WILLIAM MCKINLEY [1916]
 8  LIFE OF WILLIAM MCKINLEY SOLDIER LAWYER STATESMAN [1896]
 9  MAN WHO SHOT MCKINLEY [1970]
10  MCKINLEYMEMORIAL IN PHILADELPHIA HISTORY OF THE . . . [1909]
------------------- CONTINUED ON NEXT PAGE -------------------
Type number to display full record
NEXT COMMAND:
```

Figure 2.1
Portion of an online catalog listing.

Still carrying her initial three selections, Leslie goes back to the E shelves and an hour later has examined 15 other books, selecting just two highly *relevant* ones to check out from the library and leaving behind all three of the first books she chose. She knows that the bibliography in the Z shelves would help her determine whether she has missed anything—this library does not own everything—but the bibliography is two floors above her and she is tired. "This is enough to finish my paper," Leslie says to herself as she heads to the circulation desk.

In this scenario several lessons about information seeking can be observed. Although perhaps two-thirds of adults in the United States and Canada make some use of libraries in a given year, relatively few (mostly students in universities) search library collections in any degree of depth. Leslie is an untypical user in that she knows how to use a librarian and a catalog; the reluctance of even regular users of libraries to consult these resources is well documented (consider, for example, commentaries by Borgman, 1996; Hancock-Beaulieu, 1990; and Saracevic, Shaw, and Kantor, 1977).

Leslie is, however, typical in her nonlinear search pattern; her search is not a neat one that moves swiftly from catalog to shelf to circulation desk; rather, there is a back-and-forth movement between the catalog and the shelf, with considerable time taken to examine works and reconsider her query. Typical of library users, Leslie takes some shortcuts (choosing to consider only books, not journal articles), reverses some of her early decisions (leaving behind the initial choices of books), and ultimately ends the search process prematurely by not fetching the bibliography and checking that (presumably comprehensive) guide against her search results.

2.1.3 Betting on Race Horses

As in the previous scenario, for horse races the seeker makes a choice. Despite the prevalence of horse-racing language in politics (e.g., "the dark horse candidate" and "backing the right horse" in an election), there are some differences between choosing a candidate and picking a horse. Rather than choosing one candidate from among two or three, in a typical horse race several choices might be made from among roughly 5 to 12 horses, and the type of bet that might be made on the horse(s) multiplies the number of possibilities many times over.

The complexity of horse racing leads to a common, sheepish admission at the tracks: "I choose horses based on their name." That is, if a name like "Gambling Everything" makes one laugh and seems to capture the moment, why not bet on that horse? Infrequent visitors to the race course, attending more for fun than the hope of profit, freely admit the unscientific basis for their choices; if the name is especially clever, reminds them of a friend or circumstance in their lives, then that is a sign to bet on the horse. It is not the only simplified system for betting. Some bet on an animal's color, with the gray horse in a race likely to create odds more favorable than the horse's reputation deserves. Occasionally the gender of a horse will determine many bets, especially in a race in which a talented filly vies with stallions. Races that draw horses from other countries may elicit bets based on nationality. Some wager not on the horse but on the record, gender, or nationality of the jockey (and so on).

Why is properly picking a horse so complicated that people will resort to simple strategies like the above? First, it must be obvious that no matter how much data are considered, horse racing itself is not a science and offers many unexpected surprises. The most dramatic example of this is when a highly ranked horse stumbles in a race, or bumps an opponent in such a way as to be disqualified. Even in the most mundane race, the horse most favored by the bettors wins only one-third of the time (Ainslie, 1986, p. 49).

Serious bettors who gather and use as much information as possible about the horse, the jockey, the trainer, and the track (among other things) are called "handicappers." Handicappers firmly believe that, given enough information, they can swing the odds to their favor in an enterprise where the average bettor loses about 20 cents on the dollar. Not surprisingly, a large publishing industry has grown to serve the information needs of handicappers.

The publications on horse racing are many. Most people who have been to a track are familiar with the racing program sold at the track itself, important for its listings of information about the horses and races to be held on that day at that track. However, a track's own program is just the tip of the iceberg of information about horses. Whatever data a North American track distributes about its own races, that information is overwhelmed by what can be found in the *Daily Racing Form* (published by Triangle Publications, Inc.), which is published every racing day and distributed internationally. The *Daily Racing Form* is in turn dwarfed by the *American Racing Manual*, an encyclopedic by-product of the *Form* that covers an entire year. In addition, there are several (mostly weekly) magazines devoted to racing. Among them are *American Turf Monthly* (advice for handicappers), *The Blood-Horse* (the inside story on horse breeding), and *Turf and Sport Digest* (news for the horsing industry as well as the frequent bettor).

Just what information could merit so many publications? Considering only information about the horse and jockey, there are many items of data to consider. The key category of information is the horse's recent record of racing (the *Form* usually lists the last nine races) and sometimes one to three workouts (trials that were not races). Regarding each race, there are approximately 25 items of information (all on a single line), including the date, length, type, timing, and top three placers of the race, along with the jockey, odds, and weights carried by the horse, and often ending with a subjective evaluation of the horse's performance (e.g., "tired" or "failed to menace"). Elsewhere on the page are summaries of the horse's lifetime earnings by year, and the names of the sire, dam, owner, breeder, and trainer. Altogether, the *Form* typically offers about 250 discrete data items regarding each horse — and there are typically 5 to 12 horses in each race! Even without considering the other relevant information contained in the form about the race itself (e.g., what types of horses can race and how much they can win) and the track (top times for each of up to 16 different lengths that races can run), we can see that each race offers the potential for consideration of several thousand data items.

But humans do not want to digest several thousand items of information and often simply do not have the time to do so. Therefore each handicapper relies on a selection system that eliminates most of this information; typically they focus on just a few dozen data items about each race and sometimes considerably fewer. Less successful but a lot less work are the systems described above, such as "Always bet on the prettiest horse!"

Let us consider the case of an occasional bettor who would like to become a regular handicapper, a common enough circumstance. Joe, our bettor, goes to the track and buys a copy of the *Racing Form*, along with a program of the day's races. It is his first time with the *Form*, and he is at first overwhelmed by the scope and depth of information he finds there. With the first race just an hour a way, he settles into a comfortable spot and starts making notes on what he reads.

Joe has a few rules of thumb in mind to guide his reading. Looking at the listing for the first race, he notes the "morning line" (projected) odds for each of the nine horses that will start that day. Joe can see right away that three of the horses are expected to run at much better odds than the other six; horses one and two are likely to pay $3 for every $1 bet (i.e., odds of 3:1), whereas horse three is expected to run at 4:1. All of the other horses have odds of 8:1 or worse, with one poor horse paying 50:1 for a win. For a moment Joe ponders what he could do with $50 for every dollar he bets, then shakes himself back to reality with a reminder that such horses very rarely win; he also reminds himself that he has to check the TV monitors at race time to see how much the odds have changed as bets are wagered; in parimutuel betting the odds are based on the actual pattern of bets made, rather than the estimates of the *Racing Form*'s handicappers.

Joe decides to concentrate on what are clearly the best three horses in the race and on just three types of information: the horse's performance in recent races, the jockey's record, and something called the "speed rating." He notes that horse one, Entropy, won one of his last nine races, and has placed second (i.e., "placed") in three others. Horse two, Uncertainty, has also won one of his last nine races, and has placed second in two others. The number three horse, Signal, has not won a single race, yet has managed to come in second three times, and has come in third (i.e., "showed") two times as well; furthermore, all of Signal's second-places were in the last three races, indicating an improving performance.

Not seeing a clear pattern in these data, Joe decides to look more closely at each race for further clues. He considers an important question: has the horse won *at this distance* before? Joe knows that distance is an important factor and that an earlier win at the same distance is a strong indicator of potential success today. Races can be a variety of different distances, and many horses excel at the shorter or the longer distances, but not both; in addition, some races are run on the turf (i.e., the grass strip inside of the dirt track), and some horses specialize in such a surface. From the top of the *Racing Form* Joe sees that this is a 1-mile race on the dirt track, and recalls that it has not rained this week; a track muddy from recent rains would require consideration of yet other factors, and Joe feels like he has too much to think about already.

Our bettor happily reads that Uncertainty's win and places have all taken place on the turf, and that may well allow him to eliminate that horse from consideration. His comfort is lessened when he realizes that Entropy's victory was in a race of 6 furlongs (three-fourths of a mile) whereas Signal's near-misses have all been in races of 1 mile. So neither horse has won at this race before, but Signal looks better prepared for this long race.

Next Joe considers the speed rating, which is an objective metric that compares the horse's performance with a rating of 100, meaning that the horse's running time (in a particular race) equaled the track record for that particular distance. Entropy, Joe sees, has a speed rating of 80 for his winning race, indicating a performance 4 seconds slower than the track's record; his places earned similar ratings. Although not usually a dirt racer, Uncertainty is undoubtedly a faster horse at an average rating of 84 for his three best races. Signal begins to look worse with speed ratings between 77 and 81.

So now the picture is looking even more muddy. Joe turns to a separate table in the *Racing Form* that lists the performance records of each jockey, over many races and with different horses. Here, at last, is clear-cut information: Entropy's jockey has won 17% of his races, while the other two jockeys hover near 8%. Joe jots this down on a little table he has been sketching on a notepad (see Table 2.2). This cinches it: Entropy is to be the horse Joe bets to win.

It is now 32 minutes to race time and Joe remembers that he needs to check out the latest information on the track TV monitors. Up to this moment he has been dealing with information that is at least hours, and in some cases months or years, old. It is with a shock that Joe reads on the monitor that Entropy has been scratched from the race, and that Signal has had a change of jockey. Another look at the table in the racing form tells him that the new jockey has a better record—11% wins—than Signal's old jockey. Joe looks at the latest odds and realizes that the turf horse, Uncertainty, is now the crowd's favorite at even odds (1:1) while Signal has crept up to 5:2. "Do the other bettors know something I don't?" Joe wonders.

Joe considers spending more time with the *Racing Form*. He knows that it contains information on the horse's recent condition, class, parentage and so forth, but he is feeling undecided and a bit pressed for time; he needs to place a bet within the next 20 minutes. It is then that Joe recollects a potentially valuable source of information that appears in no published document: the horse's condition at this moment. Walking quickly over to the rear of the racing stands, in a few minutes Joe finds himself at the paddock, where the horses for the first race are being paraded for a large number of bettors crowded around the rails. After a few minutes of craning his neck and standing on his toes, Joe manages clear glimpses of both Uncertainty and Signal; the former animal appears nervous while Signal appears calm and strong. With his mind made up, Joe rushes to the nearest betting window where, after 5 minutes of waiting he bets $10 on Signal to win at the latest odds of 2:1.

Table 2.2
Joe's Notes on the Three Top Horses

Horse	Odds	Wins	Places	Track	Speed	Jockey Won
Entropy	3:1	1	3	dirt	80	17%
Uncertainty	3:1	1	2	dirt	84	8%
Signal	4:1	0	3	turf	79	8%

Ten minutes later the finish line is crossed first by Channel, a horse that Joe had not even considered. Trying to salvage a lesson from this first race, Joe notices that in the last 15 minutes of betting, Channel's odds moved from 6:1 up to 3:1 — a sign that many bettors had begun to favor the horse. "I would have noticed that trend if I had been paying more attention to the monitor," Joe says to himself, and then with a start realizes that he has much less time to do the next analysis: Race Two will begin in only 25 minutes.

We can notice a few principles in this case study: the searcher has much too much data to systematically analyze in the brief time before each race. Hence Joe attempts to simplify the "search space" for a solution by ignoring many categories of information he deems less relevant. Unlike many other search processes that result in some kind of decision, in this case the most important data — the betting odds — keep changing constantly, right up to 2 minutes before the race. Like the opportunity for first-hand observation of additional information (the horse's condition), the need to "monitor the monitor" can be a distraction from further analysis.

2.1.4 Finding the Law

George is spending his Saturday in the law library. A lawyer in a small Kentucky law firm, George has been practicing just 5 months (problem 1) and is overwhelmed by his work (problem 2), which is chiefly tax law (problem 3). Nevertheless, he promised his sister, Edna, to write a legal memorandum on her alimony case even though he feels that he doesn't have the experience, time, or background to do a perfect job of it. The hard fact is that Edna cannot afford a lawyer, is starting to have trouble making her rent, and besides, she's his sister. So even though the course George took in family law is only a dull memory now, today he joins dozens of other lawyers and students in a quest to find the law.

George knows the basic facts of the case all too well. Last year when Edna divorced her husband Fred, the court ordered him to make monthly alimony payments. Three months ago Fred took a new job in another town, moved to an apartment without a phone, and stopped making payments. Fred's only direct communication with Edna was a phone message warning that he would have to skip her next payment to afford the deposit on his new place, and that he would "make it up to her later." The first few weeks Edna was annoyed yet somewhat sympathetic, because she was the one who filed for divorce. But after a month went by with neither the next nor the previous alimony payment, Edna felt foolish that she had not acted more quickly; to make matters worse, Fred has proved to be impossible to contact.

Edna knows that she has legal recourse through the court, but also knows that it could be a struggle to document the facts and recover lost payments. So she turned to George first. George is determined to settle this dispute as quickly as possible, even if it means he has to pay another attorney to follow up his work later; unfortunately he has precious little time over the next few weeks to devote to it. Though George believes that Edna's case is a straightforward one, he wants to check two issues in particular: first, whether a recent raise in Edna's modest salary could reduce alimony or impede collection of what is owed to her; and second, whether Edna's hesitancy to act when the first payment never arrived might allow her husband to argue that she had agreed to the stoppage of payments.

George starts with the index to the *Corpus Jurus Secundum* (referred to as the CJS) and locates the section on Divorce in this encyclopedia-like reference tool. He finds, two subheadings down, a section on "arrears"; he spends some time reading this section of the main body of *CJS*, and also in a newer *Supplement.* As well as reminding himself of the key points of the law in this area, he locates a citation to a recent case decided in Kentucky. George jots down the citation to the Kentucky case, a parallel citation, and a frequently cited decision from New York State. Next George turns to the *Quick Index* to the state volumes of the *American Law Reports* and finds an entry (Figure 2.2) to a discussion of "arrearages" under the heading "Alimony — Delinquent or overdue payments." After reading the discussion in *American Law Reports*, and noting references to yet other cases, George decides to read the cases themselves.

George looks up the Kentucky case in *Kentucky Decisions,* which reports cases for his state, and another in the *New York Reports, Second Series.* For his last task of the day, George uses a public terminal and his office's LEXIS account number to search the online version of *Shepard's Citations* to check on the

ALIMONY — Cont'd
Delinquent or overdue payments
  debt, right of spouse to set off debt owed
    by other spouse against accrued spousal
    or child support payments, 11 ALR5th 259

  laches or acquiescence as defense, so as
    to bar recovery of arrearages of permanent
    alimony or child support, 5 ALR4th 1015

  visitation, withholding visitation rights for
    failure to make alimony or support payments,
    65 ALR4th 1155

Figure 2.2
Excerpt from the *American Law Reports.*

continuing validity of the cases he examined; he finds the most relevant cases are still valid.

George has spent three hours in the library and is tired. But at least he feels grounded in the relevant law and has checked the case updates. Tomorrow George will draft a memorandum on Edna's situation, and the following week he will discuss it with a colleague who practices family law. He knows that it may be hard to get money out of Fred if he continues to avoid responsibility, but George is certain that, should Fred attempt legal resistance, Edna's case would be most compelling to a court.

Given Brenda Dervin's emphasis on "everyday" information seeking, most of her 10 points are not particularly relevant to a highly structured search of formal information sources by an experienced attorney. However, it is worth noting that, although George certainly found "the law" governing his sister's situation, her problems are not over yet! There is much work to be done before the records of law and previous decisions may result in some kind of action in Edna's favor. As Dervin implies, few problems are immediately solved by the discovery of relevant information. And as some psychologists and criminologists have documented, court decisions are not always as rational as we might hope, either.

2.1.5 "I Want to Know More about Cancer"

Let's consider an entirely different kind of desire for information, one in which there is no decision or choice to be made, and in which it is difficult to determine exactly what the "need" is. "Curiosity" is the label that we might apply to the situation described below; according to Webster's *New World Dictionary*, curiosity is a word that is used to indicate a general "desire to know," sometimes "about things that do not necessarily concern one."

It is certainly hard to say what makes us curious about a subject. In a famous article about why and how people ask questions, Robert Taylor (1968) wrote about "visceral needs" of mysterious origins that make themselves known only through a vague uneasiness about not knowing something. The visceral need remains "unarticulated" until we verbalize it to ourselves or someone else. In the process of trying to state what it is we want to know, the information need usually comes out in an imperfect and unsatisfactory statement ("compromised," in Taylor's words). Brenda Dervin's (1983a) investigations into "sense making" employ a similar concept: the information *gap*. That is, until we recognize the existence of a gap in our knowledge—often signaled by a mild anxiety and/or a need to act—we are not motivated to search for information. However, whether we ask questions, read books, or take another kind of action to find something out, it is important to recognize that information often comes to us, fortuitously, in the course of our normal lives. The *serendipity* factor — the seemingly accidental discovery of relevant information — operates more often than we might expect.

Our searcher this time is named Maria. Maria, who is in her early 30s, was never particularly concerned with matters of personal health until a favorite cousin discovered that a firm, red lump on her arm was cancerous. Through several weeks of a successful treatment plan, Maria kept in frequent telephone contact with her worried cousin, who lived in a distant state.

Maria had heard the dreaded word "cancer" her entire life. When she was a teenager her grandfather had died of lung cancer, but other than him nobody close to her had ever been diagnosed with cancer. She knew that many old people died of cancerous growths. Cancer, like death itself, was something that Maria would rather not think about.

Not long after her cousin's discovery, Maria came down with a sore throat and visited a nearby medical clinic. While in the waiting room she noticed a brochure, "What You Need to Know about Skin Cancer," published by the National Cancer Institute of the National Institutes of Health. She took the brochure home to read and was surprised to learn that almost half of all mature adults are likely to have had skin cancer. She had thought cancers were pretty rare, except among the elderly. At least Maria felt confident now that she knew how to spot skin cancer herself and what to do to avoid it. And for a time that was all she wanted to know about cancers.

Some weeks later, coming across the brochure on skin cancer in her living room, Maria found herself curious. What *was* cancer, exactly, and what caused it? The brochure did not say much about the underlying nature and causes of carcinoma, but it listed a toll-free number for further information (1-800-4-CANCER), which she called to request other brochures in the National Cancer Institute series. Later she had coffee with a friend who was a nurse and asked some very basic questions about cancer. Maria didn't understand quite everything that she was told by her friend, but understood enough to know that she wanted to know more. *Why* she needed to know more, she was not exactly sure, but maybe it could be useful in defending herself against future illness.

One day Maria bought some skin cream made by the Avon company. With the skin cream came a list of other Avon products, which mentioned that company's "Breast Cancer Awareness Crusade" and listed a Web site. Out of curiosity Maria used her home computer to reach Avon's Web page, where she found, along with answers to frequently asked questions about breast cancer, some fascinating narratives by women who had survived the illness. She had never thought about using the Internet for this sort of information; somehow it made it easier for her to read about the scary topic of cancer.

Maria noticed that the Avon site did not refer to any other related sites. She decided to do a search on the word "cancer" and was bewildered by the number of sites that contained a reference to the word. Obviously, she had to be more specific. Her nurse friend had mentioned the Mayo Clinic as a good source of information; searching for the words "Mayo Clinic" lead to a site called the "Mayo Health O@SIS" where she found a "Cancer Center" listing that included many pages of understandable text on cancer in its various forms. She printed some pages, and skimmed or read others.

Finding more information on cancer became a kind of challenge. Through the Mayo site she found a link to a page sponsored by the National Institutes of Health. Maria felt like she might be able to trust this information more, because it was provided by the government. However, she found the site somewhat overwhelming—so much information was about government projects or about research projects—and she did not find the sort of common-language explanations she was looking for. She noticed a link to the National Cancer Institute's Web site and there found the same material that she had read in the brochures they had sent her. At this point she decided to call it a day and stop searching.

Maria's interest in cancer did not stop here. At various times she spent hours browsing the personal health sections of a local bookstore and the public library in her town. She talked to her friends about "all this stuff I've learned on the Internet" and became known as somebody who liked to talk about health matters. In turn, Maria learned a great deal listening to the experiences of her friends—their worries about staying healthy, and their stories about relatives who had cancer and heart disease. It seemed like every conversation Maria had with others about health sent her back to the Internet to answer a question, to learn about a disease, or simply to surf.

Maria's case represents one of the squishier dimensions of information seeking: an unquenchable curiosity motivated by deeply held feelings. In situations like Maria's, the urge to find facts and hear personal stories may satisfy some emotional need to be reassured, to be comforted, to *connect* with others. In this sense there is no final answer that will end information seeking—it is the project of a lifetime.

2.2
Summary

We have seen, through five fictitious case studies, the playing out of information seeking in different contexts. Common to them all has been the need to deal with (potentially, at least) great volumes of information, much of it complex. In all cases the searchers have attempted to lessen their cognitive load by jettisoning some types of information, taking a shortcut to a state of satisfaction or decision.

The results of each search, although incomplete and perhaps even resulting in failure (witness Joe's lost bet), were, at the time, *good enough* to satisfy the needs of the seeker, a type of behavior that is called *satisficing*. The seekers of information did *not* make every possible attempt to attain the most complete, accurate, and detailed information available (*optimizing*) but rather gathered just enough data, opinions, and impressions to feel satisfied with the process. When a person reaches such a stage, he or she may end the task with a feeling of closure.

These five scenarios were chosen to provide readers with contrasting elements across different information seeking activities. These contrasts are highlighted in Table 2.3, in which the scenarios are ranked in order of *time pressure*. The primary *motivation* in each of the five scenarios varies widely; two searches are prompted by assignments given to the seeker by other persons, and the rest are personally chosen by the seeker out of self-interest. *Sources of information* used by each person are more homogeneous. Most seekers use a mixture of formal information (e.g., printed publications or electronic sources) and informal (e.g., the opinions of friends); the major exceptions are the two assigned tasks, in which documentation of official sources is important.

Table 2.3

Comparison of Five Case Studies

Seeker and situation	Main motivation	Sources of information	Time pressure	Degree of thoroughness
Julie/car purchase	Optimize functionality and value	Friends, Web pages, salespeople	Low (months)	Low
Leslie/library research	Class assignment; earn credit/ grade	Online catalogs, books, journals, professional advice (on how to search)	Moderate (weeks)	Moderate
Joe/horse race wager	Desire for thrill, to win money	Special journals, observation, intuition	Very high (minutes)	Very low
George/legal research	Work assignment; help relatives	Special databases and publications, professional advice	High (days)	High
Maria/information on cancers	Curiosity; preemptive information search	Web pages, books, brochures, friends, experts	None (lifetime)	Moderate

Time pressure is determined by how quickly a search for information must be concluded: minutes, hours, days, weeks, or months. The *degree of thoroughness* roughly summarizes the ratio of data-actually-gathered-and-considered to all-data-potentially-relevant in a search. The *time pressure* and *required degree of thoroughness* faced by the seekers of information vary the most, as can be seen by examining the more extreme cases.

Maria's interest in cancer-related information comes out of a personal curiosity that may last a lifetime; in her case there is no identifiable time pressure at all. In an optional purchase such as Julie's, the decision could be postponed indefinitely, making the search for information protracted; as well, the number of variables is large and the importance of subjective judgment (e.g., taste) is so important that a relatively low proportion of potentially relevant data are considered in the final decision. In the case of Joe's racing wager, a decision must be made within minutes, and the amount of information of potential relevance is so staggering that only a very selective use of information is possible. Finally, George's legal research requires not only very fast turnaround (days) but absolute accuracy as well; therefore, George must be especially careful to search all of the relevant sources and to do so thoroughly. The other cases lie in between these extremes regarding time and thoroughness.

The cases we have examined represent quite common scenarios: writing a term paper, buying a product, satisfying our curiosity, and so forth. There is one sense in which they are *not* representative, however: most of the academic research conducted on information seeking examines scenarios more like those of George (work in a professional or occupational setting) and Leslie (searching formal sources, particularly in libraries).

In fact, a high percentage of the situations examined in traditional information seeking research have involved either laboratory scientists, engineers in private firms, or university research faculty (in a broad array of disciplines). Because we will be reviewing such cases in future chapters, there is no need to emphasize such complicated research settings at this point in our discussion. The human factors bearing on information seeking are similar with all questions and in all fields of inquiry.

Now that we have grounded the topic in familiar human situations, we will next turn our attention to a basic question: their corresponding definitions and corollary concepts. What is "information"? What is "information seeking"?

Two

Concepts Relevant
to Information Behavior

3

The Concept of Information

Information seems to be everywhere. We talk of its being encoded in the genes ... disseminated by media of communication ... exchanged in conversation ... contained in all sorts of things. ... Libraries are overflowing with it, institutions are bogged down by it, and people are overloaded with it ... [yet] no one seems to know exactly what information is.

Christopher Fox (1983, p. 3)

Information, usually seen as the precondition of debate, is better understood as its by-product. When we get into arguments that focus and engage our attention, we become avid seekers of relevant information. Otherwise we take in information passively — if we take it in at all.

Christopher Lasch (1995, p. 162)

Chapter Outline

3.1. Searching for a Definition of Information
    3.1.1. Explicating "Information"
    3.1.2. The Concept of Information
    3.1.3. Typologies of Information Concepts
3.2. Definitions of Information and Their Problems
    3.2.1. The Influential and Restrictive "Information Theory"
    3.2.2. Five Problematic Issues in Defining Information
    3.2.3. Uncertainty as a Requirement
    3.2.4. Physicality as a Requirement
    3.2.5. Structure/Process as a Requirement
    3.2.6. Intentionality as a Requirement
    3.2.7. Truth as a Requirement

3.3. Must There Be a Universal Definition of Information?

3.4. Distinctions among Information, Knowledge, and Data

3.5. Summary

3.1

Searching for a Definition of Information

"Information" is a fairly old word, making an early appearance in one of Chaucer's tales sometime between 1372 and 1386 (Schement, 1993a, p. 177). One would think that over 600 years of usage would tend to settle a word and result in a consensus on its meaning. This has not been the case with the term "information." Especially in the last five decades, as the various phenomena that people call information began to be objects of empirical study, meanings of the word have proliferated.

One of the problems of studying any phenomenon — or merely talking about a thing — is reaching an agreement on what to call it. Words are ambiguous, the same string of characters often having multiple meanings. Each meaning may identify a distinct concept, in the way that the noun "port" can refer to a fortified wine, the left side of a ship, or a gateway or opening for passage (a harbor, a modem port, a valve port, etc.). The case of the word "information" is much more complex, as it has been used to denote various *overlapping* concepts, rather than neatly distinct phenomena as is the situation with "port."

Unless otherwise stipulated, in this book "information" will be taken to mean *any difference that makes a difference* to a conscious, human mind (Bateson, 1972, p. 453). In other words, information is whatever appears significant to a human being, whether originating from an external environment or a (psychologically) internal world. This definition was chosen by the anthropologist Gregory Bateson, after he had struggled for two decades with the inadequacies of mathematical definitions of information. A *perceived difference*, according to Bateson, is a basic "unit of mind" that can be inferred through study of both humans and animals.

Other authors have employed definitions of information that are similar to Bateson's. A popular version originated with psychologist George A. Miller (1968): information is *any stimuli we recognize in our environment*. Others (e.g., Dervin, 1976a, Farace, Monge, & Russell, 1977; Higgins, 1999; Johnson, 1997; Rogers, 1986) have generalized such statements to mean the *recognition of patterns in the world around us*.

Obviously the characterization of information as a difference implies a very broad definition for a common word that has been defined in several distinct ways — with virtually all other definitions implying more restrictions on meaning. That is, many authors have used other words to define a concept that they have called "information," some of them incorporating specific requirements, such as information must always be *true* or *useful*, or that it must be *embodied* in a form or object, or that it must be *intentionally* transmitted, and so forth.

The reason for adopting this broad (some would say vague) definition is because this book reviews a great many studies from several disciplines, and needs to cover a variety of more restrictive concepts. The reason some other definitions are less appropriate will be made clearer in the remainder of this chapter, which first discusses the nature of conceptual explication, and then examines a variety definitions for "information," each of which identifies a somewhat different concept than the rest.

3.1.1 Explicating "Information"

To discuss and study any concept, we first need to define it. In the process we may identify and define other ideas that are related to (and sometimes derived from) the concept under study. In the case of information, related concepts are "knowledge" and "data." "Information behavior," "information seeking," "information source," and "information use" are among several higher-order concepts that build upon the concept of information.

Social scientists call the process of defining a concept *explication*. As discussed by Steven Chaffee (1991), explication is the intellectual process that relates theory to research, that links a focal concept to the ways in which it is studied. For researchers who aspire to direct observation of phenomena, explication eventually results in an *operational definition* of a concept, a set of procedures used to observe and measure instances of a concept. In this chapter, we will deal only with the initial stages of explication — reviewing and analyzing existing definitions — and leave issues of measurement for later chapters.

The process of explication often starts with a word for which we have only a general meaning. At this stage we have only a nominal, or dictionary, definition for a term — that is, a word is defined by other words. Explication continues by examining what has been written about the concept; we review the publications about it, with an eye toward how different authors have defined and used the concept. In doing this we may not only find multiple definitions for the term, but discover that some authors have studied the same concept but called it by a different name.

The next step in explication is to *analyze the meaning* of a term by one or both of two approaches. The first possible approach is a top-down procedure.

We *distill* the discussions of many authors to their abstract core: what is the heart of what they say about the concept? In the case of information, a core idea may be that it is a message expressed in some medium, and/or that it has the potential of altering a person's consciousness. As Chaffee points out (1991, pp. 26–27), finding a single, central meaning is unusual, particularly when distinct research literatures are examined.

In the second alternative, the bottom-up approach to meaning analysis, we *list* all the subsidiary concepts that make up the focal concept. For "information," we might attempt to list exhaustively all the possible forms that information could take—a Web page, a book, a radio broadcast, a conversation, a handwritten note, e-mail, and so on. This is a massive task that would be subject to change over time as new forms of information appear or are identified. Listing all examples of information has been one way that researchers have guided the *observation* of the concept.

Whichever means of analysis is chosen, the eventual result is a more abstract definition than one defined by near synonyms. The definition may be expressed as a series of critical distinctions between the focal concept and related concepts; for example, what is the difference between information and data? Or instead it may simply identify attributes that serve to identify something as an instance of the concept; for example, a book is an instance of information because it contains symbols that can, or are intended to, inform someone.

The remainder of this chapter will consider, through literature review and distillation, the various definitions of information and their key distinctions.

3.1.2 The Concept of Information

Ordinarily we both use and hear the word "information" without much concern for its definition; *we* know what we mean when we use the word. At first glance the *Oxford English Dictionary* definition seems adequate: "(1) the action of informing. The action of telling or fact of being told of something. (2) That of which one is apprised or told; intelligence, news." This nominal definition reveals at least one important distinction: the term may be used to indicate either a *process* (informing) or a kind of *message* (news).

Further distinctions lay buried in the nominal definition, as a series of publications have made obvious. One explication of the term (Wellisch, 1972) uncovered eight distinct definitions of information, without any common elements. Not long afterward, Wersig and Neveling (1975) identified 17 unique definitions, which they grouped into six broad categories. Summarizing 30 years of commentary, Levitan (1980) declared that 29 different concepts had been associated with the term information. A review by Schement (1993b) includes a selection of 22 definitions written between 1968 and 1989. How has the concept of information been used such that so many definitions have resulted? The central difficulty is that the word "information" has been used to denote several different concepts. The adoption of the term by multiple disciplines is part, but not all, of the problem. The same term has been used to refer to, among other phenomena, sensory stimuli, mental representations, problem-solving, decision making, an aspect of human thinking and learning, states of mind, the process of communication, judgments about the relevance of information to information needs, the content of subject specialties, recorded knowledge, and particular objects that carry information such as documents. It is no surprise that scholars have struggled to come up with a formulation that promises to condense most of these meanings into one universal principle or attribute.

3.1.3 Typologies of Information Concepts

Let's first examine four parallel attempts to identify different "families" of information definitions. Two attempts to distinguish types of information concepts, one from 1976 and the other from 1992, illustrate how periodically we revisit the problem of defining information. Two articles by Brenda Dervin (1976a, 1977) set the stage for the development of the *sense making* school of thought (see Chapters 4 and 7) regarding information seeking. In her articles, Dervin posited three types of information, based on the writings of philosopher Karl Popper (1972):

1. *Objective, external* information is that which describes reality (but never completely so).

2. *Subjective, internal* information represents our picture, or cognitive map of reality, the structures we impute onto reality.

3. *Sense-making* information reflects the procedures and behaviors that allow us to "move" between external and internal information to understand the world, and usually to act on that understanding as well.

Dervin argues that to look at information in such a way has several advantages. For example, it acknowledges that legitimate inputs may come from inside of us, rather than viewing the only important information as arising from external sources. In a similar way this view does not privilege formal information systems (e.g., books) over informal sources (e.g., friends, relatives, or coworkers); consulting the latter is a much more common approach to understanding than are the former channels.

In a manner reminiscent of Dervin, Brent Ruben (1992, pp. 22–24) places information conceptualizations into three "orders." The first of these captures information as "environmental artifacts and representations; environmental data, stimuli, messages, or cues." This *environmental* (Ie) sense of information consists of "stimuli, messages, or cues, waiting to be attended to." Second-order information is that which is "internalized, individualized appropriations and representations." Here Ruben identifies information as something that is "transformed and configured for use by a living system," *internal* (Ii) representations that include "semantic networks, personal constructs, images, rules or mind." And the third type of information is that which is "socially constructed, negotiated, validated, sanctioned and/or privileged appropriations, representations, and artifacts." Third-order information, then, is the *social* (Is) context of information.

Dervin's and Ruben's types are parallel but not identical, especially in the terms and examples they use to describe their third category, which for Dervin is decidedly intrapersonal, abstract, and process oriented. For Ruben, the social context is external, socially constructed, and may encompass physical objects like books (which seems to fall under Dervin's objective category).

Two other typologies, both from the 1990s, are also somewhat parallel, but bear only a modest resemblance to the Dervin and Ruben schemes. Michael Buckland's (1991a) widely cited typology portrays uses of the term "information" as falling into three categories. The first category is *information-as-process*, which refers to the act of informing, the communication of information, and how a person's state of knowledge is changed. A second sense of information is *information-as-knowledge*, a usage of the term denoting that which is perceived in the first category (i.e., the knowledge communicated). The final sense of the term is *information-as-thing*, in which "objects, such as data and documents . . . are referred to as 'information' because they are regarded as being informative."

Buckland takes great pains to explain the difficulties inherent in such a typology, pointing out the intangible nature of the first two categories (which makes them difficult to observe), the issue of intentionality (some definitions of information take for granted an intention to communicate), and the problem that any object in the world might potentially be informative ("if everything is information, then being information is nothing special"). He concludes that it is essential to investigate information-as-process, even though information-as-thing cannot be dismissed as a focus of study.

The second typology is similar to that of Buckland, but breaks out his two categories of information-as-thing and information-as-knowledge into three overlapping conceptions of information. Altogether, McCreadie and Rice (1999, pp. 47–58) identify four distinct "conceptualizations," the first of which is information as a *resource or commodity*. Under this conceptualization, information is something that can be "produced, purchased, replicated, distributed, sold, manipulated, passed along, controlled" — such as a message that travels from sender to receiver, with or without some kind of payment in exchange.

The second type of information is characterized as data in the *environment,* that is, "objects, artifacts, sounds, smells, events" that may be perceived in the environment. This category takes into account the potential for unintentional communication of information, such as when one observes and interprets natural phenomena.

McCreadie and Rice's third type of information concept is that expressed as a *representation* of knowledge, such as that expressed in "documents, books, periodicals." Finally, their fourth type of information is as a part of the communication process. That is, information is meanings that are created as people go about their lives and try to make sense of their world.

While at first glance it may seem that these latter two typologies characterize types of information in similar ways, there are several differences, particularly in the distinctions they make between *representation, thing,* and (in the case of McCreadie and Rice) *resource.* McCreadie and Rice use "documents, books, periodicals" among their examples of representations, whereas Buckland uses those as examples of "things." It seems that McCreadie and Rice are trying to make finer distinctions than Buckland regarding possible embodiments of information.

Ultimately, the typologies of Dervin, Ruben, Buckland, and McCreadie and Rice are each distinct from one another in several ways. At least the distinctions these authors make are useful in illustrating the many ways one could parse the attributes of the information concept.

3.2
Definitions of Information and Their Problems

The typologies discussed above fall short of providing specific definitions of "information." Rather, their intention is to show that there are distinct usages of the term rather than a single universal usage.

Nevertheless, many authors have attempted to create a general definition of information that at least would be adequate for some areas of investigation. As we shall see, many scholars have incorporated into their definitions specific and powerful assumptions regarding the nature of information.

We will begin our examination with the most influential definition of information, one that developed a half-century ago for the study of signal transmission in broadcasting and telephony. Now it might seem odd that a definition for such a mundane concept as information should come to us from a highly specialized field as telephone engineering. In fact one writer (Tor Nørretranders, 1991/1998) jokes that

> there are plenty of grounds for a conspiracy theory of the most devious kind: that the notion of information was invented and developed by engineers from big

private corporations who then made a profitable business out of having the rest of us talk about truth, beauty, meaning and wisdom — on the phone. (p. 96)

In Nørretranders's view, this development was unfortunate because it shifted our attention away from the more important elements involved in information — the senders and receivers of messages — and toward characteristics of the carrier.

3.2.1 The Influential and Restrictive "Information Theory"

The first widely recognized attempt to define information, the misnamed "Information Theory" (properly called "The Mathematical Theory of Communication"), is still frequently invoked to describe the nature of information. The popularity of information theory cannot be overemphasized: a review of two decades (Zunde, 1984) listed over 400 selected citations to this theory; by now the number of references to information theory surely runs into the thousands.

Fifty years ago, the works of Claude Shannon and Warren Weaver (1949) on communication of messages gave rise to a popular conception of information. Shannon, an engineer at Bell Labs, was concerned with the fidelity of telecommunications signals, such as those sent over radio waves, and the determination of the effective capacities of telecommunication channels. It was Shannon who came up with a model of communication as a process of signal transmission. His became the basis for applying measures to parts of messages based on the statistical probability of their appearance — a technique that led to improvements in signal transmission because it helped to predict the likelihood of errors and decide how to correct them, such as the sending of redundant portions of a message.

In Shannon's famous diagram (Figure 3.1), the *source* and *destination* of a message were seen as being at the opposite ends of a chain, linked by a *message* converted by a *transmitter* into a *signal* sent over some kind of *channel* to the *receiver*, which converts the signal back to a message for delivery to the *destination*. The channel was acted on by sources of *noise*, which could disrupt or distort the message.

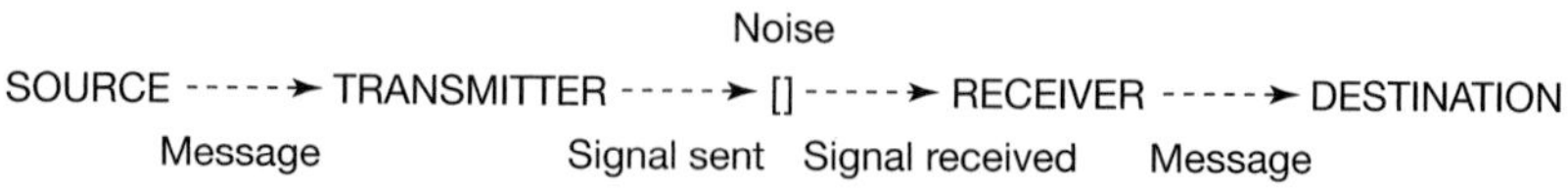

Noise

SOURCE ----▸ TRANSMITTER ----▸ [] ----▸ RECEIVER ----▸ DESTINATION

Message   Signal sent   Signal received   Message

Figure 3.1
Shannon's model.

Along with the diagram came both a definition and measure for the concept of information, as it is encoded in a message. Shannon's definition of information was based on the notion of *entropy*, a measure of the degree of disorganization in a system which reflected a tendency for any state of affairs to lose order and become more random. In signal transmission, *noise* is the vehicle for the effects of entropy, that is, noise degrades the signal to some degree. Messages are organized exchanges (e.g., grammatical sentences) based on *selections* from an agreed-upon set of signals (phonemes, words, letters, etc.). The requirement that the message elements are selected from a fixed universe of possible elements has led some scholars to refer to it as a theory of *"selective information,"* to contrast it with theories of *"semantic* information," that is, theories concerned with the *meaning* of messages.

The effects of entropy lead to more randomness in messages that, in turn, leads to higher levels of uncertainty. In Shannon's view, these *higher levels of uncertainty imply the potential for more information* in the message. At the opposite end of the entropy scale would be messages that are highly organized — and thus familiar to the receiver — but which tend to carry little "new" information.

Such a definition of information is somewhat counterintuitive because we tend to associate information with certainty, rather than uncertainty (Miller, 1983a). In fact, Shannon had been advised by computer scientist John von Neuman to call his concept "entropy" rather than "information" (or "uncertainty," another near synonym) because entropy was a vague term less likely to be confused with the vague, everyday meanings associated with the word "information" (Campbell, 1982, p. 32; Machlup & Mansfield, 1983, p. 48). Indeed, these opposite or "negative" forms of Shannon's definition appeared in the writings of physicist Leo Szilard in 1929 and philosopher Charles Pierce in 1878 (Morowitz, 1991).

To demonstrate how easy it is to misunderstand Shannon's notion of uncertainty when we apply it to human communication, Miller (1983a, p. 495) provides the example of the sentences "Rex is a dog" and "Rex is a mammal." The latter sentence contains terms less likely to appear in everyday usage, so according to Shannon's measure it would carry more "information" that is, a rarer, more surprising, message. But the term "dog" is *more specific* than "mammal" (which could be a dog, a bat, a dolphin, or many other creatures); semantically, therefore, we would judge that "Rex is a dog" carries more information, reversing the logic of Shannon's measure. It is all too easy to misinterpret Shannon's definition of information outside the realm of signal transmission (Losee, 1997).

Common misunderstandings of Shannon's Information Theory are partly attributable to his coauthors and advocates. Warren Weaver, a physicist, was invited to write an introduction to two journal articles by Shannon that the University of Illinois was publishing under the title *The Mathematical Theory of Communication.* In his introduction to Shannon's work, Weaver speculated on how Shannon's model of signal transmission might be applied to *human* communication. Weaver acknowledged in a later publication that the model could be taken too literally: *"Information* must not be confused with *meaning,"* Weaver said (1949, p. 8). Thus he anticipated that some scholars would attempt to extend the theory to the subjective interpretation of signals by humans.

Nevertheless, Weaver's broad-ranging analogies and speculations became conflated with the very limited theorems devised by Shannon, much to the latter's chagrin; according to Ritchie (1986, 1991), it is Weaver's extrapolation of Shannon's model to which most writings refer, not to Shannon's original explanation and theorems. To confuse matters further, Shannon himself was inconsistent in his use of the terms uncertainty and entropy (Cole, 1993).

Despite its flaws, Shannon's simple depiction of *signal transmission* as linear, one-way process was seen by many scholars as an adequate model of human communication. Additional interpretations (e.g., Berlo, 1960) resulted in inevitable simplification and distortion of the model. David Berlo's famous "Source-Message-Channel-Receiver" model (Rogers, 1986, pp. 86–90) dropped the "signal" component of Shannon's model. Conflating the concepts of message and signal ignored an important distinction between meanings (messages) and their encodings (signals).

For several decades, various simplified versions of Shannon's model became the basis for studying the exchange of messages among people (Rogers, 1994). As Jesse Shera and Donald Cleveland put it (1977),

> Everybody tried to get into the act, hopeful that Shannon's magical formula would unlock countless information secrets and give a quantitative measure for laying a scientific theoretical foundation for practically every major field lacking one. Unfortunately this overextension was generally an intellectual get-rich-quick scheme and, in the long run, most of the hopefuls fell to the wayside. (p. 261)

A 1974 article by James Watt and Robert Krull can serve as an example of how some researchers applied Shannon's concepts. In a study of television viewing habits Watt and Krull noted that other researchers had no classification system in common for program contents. Some would use categorizations like "news, mystery drama, situation comedy, quiz-audience," while others used "documentary, crime-detective, comedy-variety, game shows" to cover the same content. Obviously these variations posed problems for researchers trying to test for effects of television viewing, given that the results independent investigations were not directly comparable.

Instead of subjective classifications of content, Watt and Krull argued that "structural or form characteristics of the program may also have an effect on the audience"; therefore, they proposed a "content-free measure of television program form" that applied "information theory entropy terms" to features that appeared on television screens (1974, p. 44–45). In a study of adolescent viewing, they developed several formulas for measuring various aspects of a broadcast. For instance, "verbal time entropy is defined as the degree of randomness of the time of audible behavior on the part of characters in a program"; a formula measured this in terms of a negative, logarithmic function of the time that a series of television characters produced audible sound. I do not need to reproduce Watt and Krull's various formulas to convince you that, although they did indeed carefully measure "nonrandom viewing patterns," their results are difficult to interpret in terms of what normally concerns us about television viewing and its effects.

Nevertheless, Ritchie (1991) describes Watt and Krull's work as among the more successful applications of Shannon's entropy measure, along with Seth Finn's studies of unpredictability in news articles (1985 and 1986). Less successful, in Ritchie's view, were attempts by Garner (1962) and Hsia (1968) to apply entropy to neurologic and cognitive information processing.

Eventually the Shannon and Weaver model came to be seen as inadequate for expressing many of the important features of human communication. As early as 1969, Donald MacKay complained that

> communication engineers have not developed a concept of information at all. They have developed a theory dealing with only one particular feature or aspect of messages "carrying" information — their unexpectedness or surprise value. (pp. 56–57)

Nørretranders (1991/1998, p. 96) observes that Shannon's view of information equated it with "something completely meaningless, something closely related to disorder ... quite unlike what the rest of us understand by the everyday word 'information' — meaning, content, overview, order." It is what Søren Brier (1992) calls a "mechanistic concept of information," which reduces human cognition to the level of computer processing. Shannon's so-called "Information Theory" simply did not adequately reflect the way in which people interpret and assess the "meaning" of messages. As the Canadian sociologist Orin Klapp (1982) concluded:

> Meaning, being subjective, and referring to synthetic or holistic properties that cannot be reduced to the sum of parts, might be called a higher sort of information that does not come easily, let along inevitably, from a growing heap of mere information. (p. 58)

3.2.2 Five Problematic Issues in Defining Information

Despite its popularity, Shannon and Weaver's implied definition of information contains several assumptions and requirements that differ with the ways we usually think about and experience similar phenomena in everyday life. Their definition is useful only in a very limited sense.

The Shannon and Weaver definition is not alone in posing such problems. Most information concepts contain assumptions regarding five issues that often turn out to be problematic when we try to apply their definitions. The five types of assumptions are about the following:

Uncertainty: Does information, in order to be information, have to reduce *uncertainty* about something? A corollary issue is utility: if information does not reduce uncertainty, must it be *useful* in some other way?

Physicality: Must information always take on some physical form, such as a book, the sound waves of human speech, or a natural object that embodies some kind of data? Is it even proper to discuss what people know, or believe, as being information? A related, and perhaps distinct, issue is whether information (or at least its effects) must be directly *observable*. If the effects are not directly observable, then how can it be the subject of scholarly study? This latter question bears on Belkin's seventh and eighth requirements, which he calls methodological, and will be addressed in Chapter 6.

Structure/Process: Must information be structured in some way? That is, must it be composed of elements in fixed relations to one another, or in some way consist of a complex "whole," such as an image? Or is information a *process*, some kind of function, a series of steps — a sort of recipe?

Intentionality: When studying information, is it necessary to assume that someone (or something) *intends* to communicate it to another entity? Or is some information simply out there in the environment, to be perceived and interpreted by a sentient organism? For instance, we can imagine circumstances in which information is not communicated with a *purpose* in mind (requirement 1); a glance at threatening clouds informs us that rain is imminent, but in this case the generator of the message is an aspect of the natural world and has no intentions.

Truth: Must information, in order to be information, be *true*? Is it improper to call something information if it is demonstrably *false*? If so, then we need another term for that which is untrue, such as misinformation.

Let's examine each of these issues in turn, and consider what various authors have written about them.

3.2.3 Uncertainty as a Requirement

From the 1950s through the 1970s, definitions of information proliferated, most of them incorporating one or more aspects of Shannon's model. A review by Bouazza (1989) reflects the majority view regarding the role of uncertainty in these definitions: "The most cited and perhaps the most useful definition of information is '"that which reduces uncertainty"'" (p. 145).

In the interest of brevity we will ignore definitions that try to preserve major portions of Shannon's definition (e.g., those discussed by Artandi, 1973, and Fairthorne, 1975), as in doing so they retain so many restrictions as to make them incompatible with common sense notions of information. The most common drawback of these early attempts is that they insist on defining information in terms of uncertainty reduction — typically in the execution of a choice or decision. For example, Wersig and Neveling (1975) declare that

> The basic term "information" can be understood only if it is defined in relation to ... the information needs of people involved in social labour.... Either as reduction of uncertainty caused by communicated data. Or as data used for reducing uncertainty. (p. 138)

Like many such definitions, Wersig and Neveling's implies that information must be useful ("involved in social labour") and intentional ("communicated").

Similarly, Everett Rogers defines information in terms of reducing uncertainty in a decision task, as "patterned matter-energy that affects the probabilities of alternatives available to an individual making a decision" (Rogers, 1986, p. 85). Other writers leave out the assumption that a task is being performed, but still cling to the uncertainty component, in which information is whatever "removes the doubt, restricts the uncertainty, reduces the ignorance, curtails the variance" (Nauta, 1972, p. 179).

The idea that information must be useful to be information has been undermined in several critiques, most notably by Fox (1983) and Losee (1997). The latter observes that

> a good definition or theory of information ... should bear some resemblance to the natural language notion of information but need not adhere to it when the natural language definition loses its generality and explanatory power. This happens when the common language definition of information, for example, becomes conflated with the notion of *useful* information, that is, information is understood to be in all cases useful. For those accepting this concept of information, if it is not useful, it is not information. Requiring that all information be useful limits the domain of discussions about information to cognitive processes that can "use" something; it excludes the information carried by a subatomic particle which is not sensed by a cognitive process. We try to avoid excluding information phenomena. (p. 257)

Neither must information (intentionally communicated or otherwise) automatically reduce uncertainty. To use an example from Fox (1983), suppose that I tell you something but you do not believe me. I have not reduced your uncertainty. Or suppose I tell you that the stock market crashed this morning. Last you heard, the market was going up, so perhaps I have reduced your uncertainty about the overall direction of the market (assuming you have been wondering about it), and yet I have probably created uncertainty within you regarding collateral knowledge (e.g., the values of your individual stock holdings). As Fox points out, there are other scenarios in which the communicating of information might actually increase uncertainty, rather than decrease it.

Other scholars have also debated the effects of new information on uncertainty. Berlo (1977) notes that information *always* reduces uncertainty in the "now," but in the long term it may have the opposite effect. Yovits and Foulk (1985) conducted an empirical study in which they tested the assumption that information always reduces uncertainty; they found that sometimes new information made their subjects *less* sure that their evaluations of a problem were correct. Similar conclusions are reached by Kellermann and Reynolds (1990) and Robertson (1980).

Although uncertainty is not satisfactory as a basis for defining information itself, it is nevertheless an important concept for information seeking. Even though information can be encountered in a passive way, actively acquiring information implies recognition of uncertainty or anomalies at some level. Kuhlthau (1993b) makes good arguments for considering uncertainty as a beginning stage in the process of finding information, and Yoon and Nilan (1999) demonstrate that one cannot study uncertainty without considering what informants already know (i.e., certainty).

3.2.4 Physicality as a Requirement

Everyone acknowledges that information *can* have a physical form (e.g., see Buckland, and McCreadie and Rice), but few explicitly argue that it *must*. Indeed, many scholars take pains to state that a more useful conceptualization of information is as a phenomenon that exists apart from physical media; that is, that we should *not* think about information as primarily something found in human-created messages like printed texts.

However, as Klaus Krippendorff (1984) has pointed out, at some level information must have a physical form. He argues in favor of information defined as "*a change in an observer's state of uncertainty* caused by some event in his world (sic, p. 49). This, of course places Krippendorff's definition in the "uncertainty requirement" camp we have already discussed. But the interesting aspect is how he analogizes information to *energy*:

> First, neither energy nor information exists in a vacuum. Both are embodied in material processes to which one must refer. Just as one can speak of energy only in conjunction with some specific resource, fuel or storage capacity . . . so one can speak of information only in conjunction with a physically identifiable source, a message or a situation as described by an observer, and relative to what he already knows. Second, energy and information are measures of work . . . information is a measure of the (intellectual) work required to distinguish, to a degree better than chance, among a set of initially uncertain possibilities. (pp. 49–50)

Certainly information in the sense of *thoughts* has a physical dimension: the electrical impulses of a human nervous system. In any event, it does not pose much of a restriction to contend that information must have a physical component, in the sense that energy does. In Krippendorff's case it is much more of a restriction to require that information reduce uncertainty—as his Shannonesque conceptualization makes clear.

3.2.5 Structure/Process as a Requirement

Other families of definitions avoid the uncertainty concept through use of analogy—typically to a structure or process—and sometimes require intentionality to do so. Kenneth Boulding (1956) used the analogy of an *image*, or a "picture in our head" in his popular characterization of messages and meaning. In Boulding's view (1956, p. 7), "the meaning of a message is the change which it produces in the image"—that is, the image of reality (or a portion of it) that exists in someone's mind. This conception of information is similar to the one offered by Bateson at the start of this chapter, defining "change" as "difference which occurs across time" (1972, p. 452).

Expanding on Boulding's analogy, Pratt (1977) defines information as an *event:* "That which occurs within the mind-upon-absorption-of-a-message" (p. 215). That is, information (or an "informative event") is what we call a change in one's mental image. For Pratt, then, information is the event that changes someone's image of reality. Like those of Boulding and Bateson, Pratt's definition has ties to the "Internal Information" described by Dervin and Rubin earlier in this chapter.

The "image" metaphor is evoked by Donohew and Tipton (1973) as well. But for them the idea of "image" is not something like a holistic picture but rather a complex mental structure of parts and subparts:

> An individual's "image of reality" is divided into three parts. First are the goals, beliefs, and knowledges [sic] which an individual has compiled as a result of his lifetime of experiences. These cognitive "objects" are defined as any concepts, issues, material objects, or ideas which exist psychologically for a person ... The second part of an individual's image or reality is the concept of self. This includes an evaluation of his ability to cope with various situations ... The third part of the image of reality is an information-handling "set" developed out of past experiences. The "set" probably controls the selection of information used by the individual to cope with the environment. here we are talking about an individual's information-seeking and processing "styles." (pp. 246–247)

Other authors have conceptualized information as a *structure* or *organization* of experience and sensory data, for example, Thompson (1968) and Belkin and Robertson (1976). Following Thompson's definition, Belkin and Robertson

(1976) state that "information is that which is capable of transforming structure" (p. 198)–in other words, it changes the knowledge state of the recipient. A parallel characterization comes from MacKay (1969), in which information is "that which does logical work on the organism's orientation" (p. 95).

Belkin (1978) notes that characterizing information as something that transforms knowledge structures has its problems, but that it relates well to information as it has been defined in a variety of disciplines. Given that information-as-process assumes that a process has an effect on some entity—as an alteration of a mental image, or the creation of meaning in a human mind—the process and structure views of information are analogically similar. In some definitions of this type, individual authors have added one or more restrictions to serve their purposes. Belkin and Robertson (1976), for example, are concerned with document retrieval systems and therefore assume that messages are intentional and that messages are represented by *texts:* "a collection of signs purposefully structured by a sender with the intention of changing the image-structure of a recipient" (p. 201).

Charles Cole (1994) notes a dilemma that accompanies the assumption that information changes a cognitive structure: if "new" information can modify knowledge structure, then it must be so that "old" or "expected" information does not modify knowledge structures in the same way, or at least at the same time. New, or "pure," information must be extremely rare because such information is completely unanticipated, and there is a natural tendency not to recognize, see, or perceive that which is unanticipated. Information, then, has the quality of being unexpected and expected, old and new, at the same time. Therefore, for information to be unexpected and expected, old and new, at the same time, information must enter the perceptual system in at least a two-stage process.

More recently, Robert Losee (1997) has advanced a general and coherent definition of information. He attempts to resolve some of the conflicts between definitions of belief, knowledge, information, and misinformation by viewing information generically as processes that produce outputs. The processes, or functions, may be invoked by humans, or machines, or other entities. The inputs into the process can be perceived from the environment or retrieved from human memory. The output of the process (e.g., the value taken on by a variable) is informative about both the original inputs and the process that produced the output from those inputs. Thus, Losee defines information as "the values of characteristics in the processes' output" (p. 256).

In Losee's view, by examining any output we can usually infer something about the process that created it. Examining a tree, for example, informs us about its origins, soil, moisture, and growth process. Or a cake, which is created through a procedure that includes ingredients, instructions, and heating, may be inspected to determine some, but not all, of the ingredients and process by which it was created.

Defining information in terms of the output of a process, Losee concludes, moves beyond discipline-specific definitions (such as the tendency for decision theorists to define information in terms of uncertainty reduction) and provides a link between various studies of information. Yet while Losee's definition sidesteps some of the criticisms of Fox regarding information-as-process, it substitutes the vagueness of "process" with a mysterious "function" that takes input and returns a value to be attached to variables (or "characterizations"). This in turn begs the question of how variables emerge in the first place, and what determines the nature of the functions. These are not necessarily questions that Losee is responsible for answering, but rather problems to be faced by researchers trying to apply his definition of information.

Fox (1983) criticizes all structure-based definitions as failing to provide a clear definition of "structure" itself. Fox also makes compelling arguments that information cannot be considered either an event or a process—although he also provides counterexamples supporting the process view of information.

Fox himself favors defining information as a type of "telling," as represented in propositions. It would be impossible to fairly convey Fox's arguments in any shorthand version, presented as they are in 213 pages. It may suffice to say that his is the most extended dissertation on the subject thus far. Fox summarizes his conclusions in this way:

> Information need not be true, though misinformation must be false; information need not be believed by anyone; information need not originate with a reliable informant, but is must originate with someone in an appropriate position to know. Ontologically, information is propositions [the identification of which] depends on contextual factors. (pp. 212–213)

Fox admits that his conclusions leave several issues unresolved, including the

> crucial notion of the *amount* of information carried by a set of sentences remains unanalyzed. The notion of *informativeness* remains unanalyzed. . . . The details of how meaning determines propositional content as a function of context is not well understood. (p. 213)

In the intervening years since Fox's book, Tor Nørretranders has published (in 1991, translated into English in 1998) a text that addresses the relation of context to content. Nørretranders introduces the term *exformation* to describe the ways in which messages may refer to a "mass of information" that is "not present" and "explicitly discarded" but nevertheless is understood to be relevant by the receiver and is used in construing the meaning of a message (p. 92).

Nørretranders provides two examples to illustrate the concept of exformation, one involving an extremely short message and the second no message at all. The first example is Victor Hugo's famous query to his publisher regarding the appearance of his latest novel, *Les Misérables,* in 1862. On vacation and out of touch with news about public reaction to his work, Hugo mailed a letter consisting of a single character: "?" His publisher replied, simply, "!" Without prearrangement, both parties understood these exchanges to mean something like the question "How is my book selling?" and the response, "Surprisingly well!"

Nørretranders's second example corresponds to the saying "no news is good news." When parents do not receive a phone call from their son away at college, they assume that he is OK and that things are fine. Information has been conveyed without sending a message at all. This example echoes Cole's (1994) observation about "new" information versus "old" or "expected" information: can "no news" be viewed as merely preserving the original knowledge structure — or does it still modify the structure, but in a different way?

3.2.6 Intentionality as a Requirement

The manner in which Fox characterizes information has a critical limitation. His analysis is based, by necessity, on propositions expressed in the form of sentences. ("In this work I deal *only* with information carried by sentences," 1983, p. 7). Fox notes that his propositions represent "*what is asserted to be the case by (someone who writes or utters)*" (p. 77). One problem with this limitation is that it takes us back into the assumption of a message intentionally sent by a sender to a receiver.

We could call this type of intentionality the "communication assumption" — that information necessarily involves communication, and hence, intention to communicate. Bowers and Bradac (1982) see the presence of intentionality as a key dividing point in among rival definitions of "communication." Their examination of 27 metatheoretical discussions of communication finds that 18 of their authors hold that intentionality is a requirement for communication to exist. Few of those theorists have an unusual definition for "intention"; most mean the concept in its usual sense: a "purposeful activity . . . [that] must be explained by 'in order to' as well as 'because' statements" (Bowers and Bradac, p. 7).

Although the restriction of *intentionality* may hold true for what is the most important sense of information — the exchange of information between humans (e.g., see Buckland, 1998) — it does not apply to all senses in which we use the word. Information may originate outside of natural language propositions, for example, as signs occurring in our environment. Whether we are viewing the natural world (e.g., trees, animals, rocks) or the human-made world (e.g., what people are wearing and doing, or a printed sign that says "exit"), we can take in stimuli that have meaning. The only way to retain the notion of intentionality is to assume that it can refer to *either* a "sender" ("someone who writes or utters") or "receiver"(the viewer of the world), but does not necessarily involve both ends of a communication process.

If we believe that people must *intend to receive* in order to take in information, then information is, in this more limited sense, intentional. Intentionality solely on the part of the receiver was suggested by Westley and Maclean in 1957, and in a discussion of news-seeking behavior, by Westley and Barrow (1959). The latter described "the need of the selecting receiver to be oriented in his extended environment" (p. 431); this assumption would take in the kind of "viewing" that I discussed previously. Theirs was a rather radical conception of communication, because it did not assume that a sender's intentions were involved; hence, Bowers and Bradac count it among the "nonintentional" definitions of communication. However, it *is* an intentional view of information behavior.

3.2.7 Truth as a Requirement

Losee (1997) also considers the notion of "misinformation." He notes that information can have various flaws, including inaccuracy, incompleteness, lack of justification, and intent to deceive. Do we need a special label for information that is so flawed as to be untrue?

Traditionally, philosophers have made a distinction of this type regarding *knowledge,* the common stance being that knowledge is "justified true belief." In this definition belief is taken to be "the most elementary of our opinions . . . characterized by two qualities: . . . either true or false . . . arrived at either rationally or nonrationally" (Cherwitz & Hikins, 1986, p. 31). By *justified* is meant that the believer has *sufficient, relevant evidence* that his or her belief is true. The "justified true belief" definition of knowledge has been criticized since the analyses of Russell (1959) and Gettier (1963), but continues to have many advocates. More to the point, no major philosophers have extended the requirements of truth and justification to the concept of *information.*

Patrick Wilson's quote at the beginning of the next chapter suggests that the truth or falsity of information is something that we can ignore in discussing information in the abstract sense. For one thing, it could be argued that we rarely know for sure if something (a statement or perception) is true or not; even if a "fact" is demonstrated to be true at this moment, it may be possibly proven wrong a few moments later. Fox (1983, p. 212) and Derr (1985, p. 496) also hold that information need not be true, based upon analyses of usage of the term in ordinary discourse. Buckland (1991b) concludes that

> the question of whether specific bits of knowledge are true is not central to our concerns. We adopt the position that the process of becoming informed is a

matter of changing beliefs. Whether these beliefs are held or denied by others and whether they are compatible with some *a priori* or fundamental assertion need not detain us. (p. 43)

Some would disagree with this point of view and instead argue that a true–false distinction is worth keeping in defining "information." Frické (1997), for example, argues that information should be "truthlike" in order to "fit the world" so that we can "succeed in our interactions with the world" (p. 888). Dretske (1981, 1983) makes a similar case, that information must tell us truly about a state of affairs, such that we can learn from it; he concludes that false information and misinformation cannot be considered to be varieties of information, but rather distinct concepts.

However, we are concerned here with a broad view of information phenomena that fits both real life and empirical studies of real life, not with establishing a philosophical distinction. Studies of information seeking provide many examples in which people value information that they know not to be entirely true. For purposes of this text, then, we will generally ignore any distinction between the truth or falsity of information, unless such is the focus or finding of a given investigation.

3.3
Must There Be a Universal Definition of Information?

All of the definitions we have examined have taken a stance on one or more of these issues. The distinctions and disagreements among reviewers of definitions are too many to resolve; in short, there is as yet no single, widely accepted definition for the concept of information. At least among recent reviews, however, there has been some agreement on the *types* of definitions of information that exist.

To summarize the chapter thus far, we can see that there have been many attempts to characterize information, some of them quite broad (e.g., the Image/Event/Structure/Process definitions), while others have been very narrowly focused (e.g., the view of information as a selection of signals from a well-defined set of symbols, the reception of which may reduce uncertainty for the receiver of the signals).

Narrow definitions assume one or more of the restrictions discussed earlier in the article. They hold that information must be *useful*, or that its transmission is *intentional*, or that it must be *represented* in an recordable medium (in written or spoken language, or images), and/or that information must be *true* (or at least easily verifiable). Shannon's model contains examples of all of these assumptions. The vast majority of the early definitions and investigations of information seeking include at least the first three of these assumptions.

Before we go any further, it is important to note that defining information in an absolute and final sense is not entirely necessary for the study of information phenomena to proceed. As Artandi (1973) and others have pointed out, all we need are *useful conceptualizations* of information. Belkin (1978) makes this point most effectively when he says,

> we are not concerned with *definitions* of information, but rather with *concepts* of information. The distinction is that a definition presumably says what the phenomenon defined *is*, whereas a concept is a way of looking at, or interpreting, the phenomenon. . . . by accepting the idea of a concept one becomes free to look for a *useful* concept, rather than a universally *true* definition of information. (p. 58)

Carl Hempel (1952) notes that there are some terms in any conceptual scheme that are so basic that they need not be fully explicated. Hempel calls these basic concepts "primitive terms." Primitive terms are simply accepted as they are commonly understood. Chaffee (1991, p. 7) provides the example of the concept of a "person," or a "human." Perhaps there are some fields in which the concept of a human needs to be carefully defined and is subject to debate — in zoology, for example. But for most purposes of study we do not need to dig deeper into that particular concept. It is when we deal with concepts that *build upon* the notion of humans — family, community, society — that we are in need of careful definitions for those concepts.

Information can be, and has been, treated as a primitive term as well. In commenting on a variety of recent studies, Pertti Vakkari (1997) notes that

> one of the striking features in many studies was the use of the central concepts, like information, knowledge, information need, seeking, and use as primitive concepts, i.e., without definition. (p. 460)

Can we reconcile the various definitions of "information" with one another? It does not seem so, and perhaps it is not necessary. Although there is scholarly disagreement over the "most rigorous," or "most easily quantifiable," or "most productive," or "most parsimonious" meaning of "information," these debates have done little to promote a fuller understanding of the concept among a community of scholars. In fact, if anything such discourse has resulted in a fracturing of scholarly effort in studying the phenomenon of information; it has resulted in too many definitions that defy comparison and that provide no common basis for understanding.

Therefore, let us treat "information" as a primitive term, as a phenomenon that we all recognize when we see it in its various forms (Fox, 1983, p. 16). Information would then be treated as "anything that exists psychologically for a person" (Carter, 1965; Chaffee, 1991, p. 9). We have only to look around us to establish the fact that information exists in the form of physical objects (what Buckland, 1991a, calls "information-as-thing"); and hundreds of studies have documented that people believe that information exists as a psychological object as well—a disembodied result of "becoming informed."

Fox (1983) observes that the "ordinary notion of information" is one through which "information scientists apparently do succeed in communicating with one another quite effectively regarding information and related concepts" (p. 5). However, allowing a broad definition of information poses problems for operationalization and measurement of concepts, as shall be seen as individual studies are reviewed in later chapters. Yet to argue for any tighter definition of information would be to limit the scope of this book, which is intended to review a broad spectrum of investigations having to do with information seeking and sense making.

Therefore, in this text we allow for any definition of information, however vague or difficult to study. Where more restricted definitions of information apply in the review of individual theories, methods, or studies, they will be made explicit.

It should be noted that the definition "any difference that makes a difference" places at least *one* important restriction on the scope of information: it rules out the possibility of information existing independently of a knowing mind. For the purpose of this text, we will assume that a conscious brain must be engaged *at some point* for information to be said to exist. Otherwise, we are back to the unhelpful stance that "*everything* is information."

Two examples, the first suggested by Fox and the second by Buckland, will help to make the restriction clear. First, Fox provides the example of someone who keeps a secret diary that no one else is ever allowed to read. Some definitions of information would imply that, since the content of the diary was never *communicated*, that it cannot be considered information. (Fox uses this straw man to defeat the requirement that a message *must* be transferred—i.e., received—to qualify as information.) Of course, a diary is a clear example of information-as-thing, and the symbols written in the diary are an expression of a human mind—it is some kind of message, even if never received by any other than its creator. So, yes, a secret diary (an unviewed, human-created record) can be safely considered to be information.

In the second example, trees could be viewed as carrying information in the form of their growth pattern of rings, which among other things tell us about the amount of rain that fell in a past season. Even if no person has viewed that information, is it not it still information? For our purposes, the answer is "no." It is nothing more than wood until someone both encounters *and* makes some sense of it. So, if a tree falls in the forest and there is no one there to see it, then it conveys no information.

To conclude this portion of the chapter, it bears emphasizing that in this text we will consider only *human* information seeking and sense making, and therefore we interpret information as requiring the involvement of a *human* mind. (It could be easily argued that *animals* seek information, but they are simply outside the scope of this book.) As will be seen in later chapters, a broad conceptualization of information is in keeping with the way the term has been employed in studies of information needs, uses, seeking, and sense-making.

3.4

Distinctions among Information, Knowledge, and Data

A side issue as regards information seeking research is worth noting. Much attention has also been granted to defining the concepts of "data" and "knowledge." Machlup (1983) examines the issue of whether *information* is synonymous with *data* and *knowledge*, noting that there has been a tradition to treat the three as a hierarchy, with data at the bottom and knowledge at the top.

Machlup holds that historical usage of the three terms does not fully justify the distinction that information is data that has been processed and/or organized. The origins of the term in the Latin *dare*, "to give," along with the history of its usage, imply that the word data ("the givens") can be assumptions, facts, measurements, and so forth, expressed in either words or numbers. As Machlup points out (p. 647), many writers claim that data are a "raw" type of information, while a few others see information as a type of data. Machlup concludes that there is neither precedent nor need to establish a hierarchy between the two words.

The common notion that knowledge is information that has been sifted, organized, and understood by a human brain is on firmer ground. Brown and Duguid (2000) complain that the two concepts are unfortunately conflated:

> People are increasingly eager that their perfectly respectable cache of information be given the cachet of knowledge. Such redefinitions surreptitiously extend the overlapping area where knowledge and information appear as interchangeable terms. Nevertheless ... there do appear to be some generally accepted distinctions between knowledge and information. ... For example, it sounds right to ask, "Where is that information?" but odd to ask, "Where's that knowledge?" (p. 2)

Machlup (1983) makes the useful point that "information is acquired by being told, whereas knowledge can be acquired by thinking" (p. 644). Through our inner experience of thought, we can form new knowledge without taking in new information from the external environment. Information implies *transfer*, says Machlup, while knowledge is a *state* ("knowing"). Knowledge and information are therefore not usually the same, except that "information in the sense of that which is being told *may* be the same as knowledge in the sense of that which is known, but *need not* be the same" (p. 644). Robert Hayes (1993) makes a somewhat different point when he says that "knowledge is internal; it cannot be received but must be internally created" (p. 5).

In this book, the usage of the terms *data, information,* and *knowledge* will generally be used synonymously, because they are usually not clearly delineated in studies of information seeking. Knowledge, however, is strictly a phenomenon of the human mind, whereas data and information are often represented by tangible, physical objects. That information usually has a physical manifestation has often been the key consideration in past studies of information seeking. The way that information seeking is typically approached under the new paradigm, though, is in the sense of knowledge — something in someone's mind — not primarily as a physical object.

The usage of data, information and knowledge outlined above represents a necessary simplification of the many definitions and examples that have been discussed in dozens of scholarly works. However, the fine distinctions made between data, information, and knowledge are of little value in most studies of information seeking. This book will treat information as a broad concept, encompassing instances that would be considered unusual by some scholars.

3.5

Summary

This chapter has explored the central concept employed in studying information seeking: information. We have seen that there are widespread disagreements about what would constitute a general definition of information. Most of these disagreements concern the issues of truth, physicality, intentionality, uncertainty, and utility. The most common types of definitions that have emerged assume that information is something that either reduces uncertainty or changes one's image of reality. In this chapter I provide examples that suggest that a truly universal concept of information would need to fulfill at least the following requirements:

1. allow for common sense notions of information used in everyday discourse;

2. allow for unintentional origins of information (e.g., observations of the natural world) as well as for purposeful communication among people;

3. allow for internally generated information (e.g., memories, constructions) as well as externally generated information (e.g., reading a text);

4. allow for types of information beyond that needed for "solving a problem" or "making a decision";

5. admit the importance of informal sources (e.g., friends) as well as formal sources (e.g., data or documents); and

6. involve the human mind, either in the creation, perception, or interpretation of information; to leave out such a requirement is to declare

that anything is information and that would leave us with no focus in our investigations.

I have considered numerous distinctions made over the years, but I argue in favor of treating information as a primitive concept that is so basic to human understanding that it does not require a tight definition. To the extent that information needs a definition it must be a broad one, such as "any difference that makes a difference" — in essence, implying a change to the structure of a human mind. Such a characterization, vague though it is, would allow us to consider what many authors have said about information seeking without having to worry about whether they restricted their observations to phenomenon that must be true, observable, physical, intentional, and so forth.

In the next chapter I will build on the initial discussion of information to define information needs. Following that, Chapter 5 ventures farther afield to consider more peripheral concepts and behaviors related to information seeking. A review of these other concepts is important in addressing several vexing questions about information-related behavior:

- Why do people seek information?
- What makes information relevant?
- Can information be found without intentionally searching for it?
- Is it possible to have too much information?
- Why do people sometimes avoid information?
- How does information differ from entertainment?

These and other issues are taken up in Chapters 4 and 5.

Recommended for Further Reading

Belkin, N. J. (1978). Information concepts for information science. *Journal of Documentation, 34,* 55–85.
   This lengthy article explains Belkin's view of information and articulates his concept of the Anomalous State of Knowledge (ASK) and how it is resolved.
Boulding, K. (1956). *The image: Knowledge in life and society.* Ann Arbor, MI: University of Michigan Press.
   An oft-cited book by the unconventional thinker Kenneth Boulding. Boulding uses the analogy of an "image" to discuss how we come to know our world.
Schement, J. R. (1993). Communication and information. In J. R. Schement & B. Ruben (Eds.), *Information and behavior* (vol. 4, pp. 3–33). New Brunswick, NJ: Transaction Books.
   Jorge Schement examines a variety of definitions of information. A companion article in the same volume supplies the history of the word itself.
Thayer, L. (1987). How does information "inform"? In B. D. Ruben (Ed.), *Information and behavior,* (vol. 2, pp. 13–26). New Brunswick, NJ: Transaction Books.
   Lee Thayer's amusing essay considers several problematic aspects of information as the term is commonly used. He convincingly makes the point that information is always "from the perspective of some observer."

4

Information Needs
and Information Seeking

Need for information consists of the process of perceiving a difference between an ideal state of knowledge and the actual state of knowledge.

Lidwien van de Wijngaert (1999, p. 463)

Information seeking is the behavior that is the directly observable evidence of information needs and the only basis upon which to judge both the nature of the need and its satisfaction.

Bryce Allen (1996, p. 56)

Chapter Outline

4.1. The Motivational Puzzle
    4.1.1. What Is a "Need"?
    4.1.2. Needs versus Demands
4.2. Four Scholars Ponder Information Needs
    4.2.1. Seeking Answers
    4.2.2. Reducing Uncertainty
    4.2.3. Making Sense
    4.2.4. The Spectrum of Motivations
4.3. The Trouble with Information Needs
4.4. Information Seeking and Information Behavior
4.5. Summary

4.1

The Motivational Puzzle

Not only has a definition of "information" proved difficult to establish, describing exactly how it influences human behavior has also been controversial. Several authors complain of lack of consistent definitions. Krikelas (1983) suggests that there are at least as many definitions of subsidiary concepts — including *information need* — as there are for information itself. Forsythe, Buchanan, Osheroff, and Miller (1992) say that

> no explicit consensus exists in the literature regarding the meaning of the central concept of "information need.". . . In effect, "information need," has been defined according to the particular interests and expertise of various authors. (p. 182)

What do we mean when we say that people "need" information? This concept is the next most fundamental, building on a primitive notion of "information." In this chapter I will consider how various scholars have defined the concept of *need* and *information need*.

4.1.1 What Is a "Need"?

It is fitting to begin with a definition of what we mean by a human "need," because it is upon this hook that most writers hang the motivations for information seeking. "Needs" are typically characterized as an "inner motivational state" (Grunig, 1989, p. 209) that brings about thought and action. Other "inner states" may include, for example, wanting, believing, doubting, fearing, or expecting (Liebnau & Backhouse, 1990; Searle, 1983).

The distinctions made among varieties of "need" can be bewildering. An essay by Andrew Green (1990) describes debates over the nature of "needs" that have taken place among political philosophers and social policy advocates. Green identifies four general conclusions about the concept of need (pp. 65–67). First, a need is always *instrumental*: it involves reaching a desired goal. If I "need to know" the chemical composition of heroin, it is typically because I desire to accomplish something with that information. That "something" may be to answer a test question, to write about narcotics for a class assignment, or simply to satisfy my curiosity. It is also the case that my need in those examples is based on some preexisting need: to pass a class, to get a degree, to be a knowledgeable person, and so forth. The key factor is that knowing it will put me at, or closer to, an end state that I want to achieve.

Second, according to Green, "needs are usually contestable. In this they differ from wants." That is, if I say that I *want* to know the chemical formula for heroin, you could hardly argue with me about this odd desire. However, if

I say I *need* to know what heroin consists of, you might ask me why; if I replied that I need it to write an essay on drug addiction for an English course, you could perhaps reasonably argue that I don't really "need" to know that fact to write a good essay on addiction (or to pass a writing test, either).

Third, need is related to the concept of *necessity* in such a way as to carry, at times, more moral weight. That is, we use phrases like "human need" or "basic need" to refer to goal states (e.g., to be safe or to be loved, in the view of Abraham Maslow) that everyone agrees are good. Doyal and Gough (1984) say that basic human needs include "health, autonomy, learning, production, reproduction, communication and political authority"; Lederer, Galtung, and Antal (1980) suggest that hypothesizing any needs beyond "primary" ones like food and shelter is problematic. Distinctions among primary versus secondary needs have led some information seeking scholars (e.g., Wilson, 1981) to argue that information is clearly a secondary, rather than a basic, need. Yet some psychologists (e.g., Cacioppo & Petty, 1982; Cacioppo, Petty, Feinstein, & Jarvis, 1996; Cohen, Stotland, & Wolfe, 1955; Petty & Cacioppo, 1986) have treated a closely related concept, "the need for cognition," as though it were a basic, rather than a secondary need.

To *deny* a life-sustaining need (e.g., for medical care) would be morally wrong. Yet even regarding such a basic need we might make distinctions; if I said to you that I *needed* narcotics, that statement may be true in the sense that drugs are *necessary* to accomplish my goal — to satisfy my addiction. But it would probably not motivate you to help me satisfy those needs. You might judge my felt need to imply such a "bad" purpose that, even while acknowledging the truth of my need, you would feel comfortable in denying me your help. Perhaps you would rationalize by saying that I really need something else such as a drug treatment program.

This line of thinking leads to Green's fourth point: that need is not necessarily a state of mind, and it is possible to be unaware of one's *true* needs. For example, I may *think* I need to scan every psychology journal in the library to find information about recovered memory syndrome. But an experienced librarian might judge that what I *really* need to do is to search *Psychology Abstracts* on the Internet.

So this leads us back to the distinction between needs and wants. Others have needs that we may judge to be "merely" desires, not needs. Obviously it is more difficult to find evidence of needs than it is of wants, because wants more typically result in observable behaviors. We can also ask people what they want, but people may not be able to articulate their needs so easily — this is certainly true if they are not even aware of their needs.

Green suggests that, within the study of information behavior, most attempts to define "need" faded away after some initial attempts made during the 1960s and 1970s. According to his view, most subsequent writers simply took for granted whatever definitions had been derived to that point, such as those discussed by Michael Brittain (1970), Maurice Line (1974), and Herbert Menzel (1966a). One exception is Richard Derr (1983, 1985) who made notable attempts to define information and information need during the 1980s.

4.1.2 Needs versus Demands

Brittain's book ventures into the realm of need by first noting that most research upto that point had instead concerned the concept of *demand* — the requests made to an information system, such as a library or database. Data regarding demands were readily available from (or at least easily collectible in) information agencies that supported studies of their users. Demands are relatively easy to measure. Investigations of information demands supported the goals of libraries and vendors to improve their services. So, according to Brittain, "most studies which have purported to be of information needs have in fact been of information uses or, at best, demands" (1970, p. 3).

Another writer, John O'Connor (1968), has suggested three "possible meanings" of information need: [1] a "negotiated" (and thus, refined) version of the *initial* question or demand stated by the inquirer; [2] whatever information provided that actually "helps" the work of the inquirer; or [3] giving the inquirer documents that he or she judges to be "pertinent" on the basis of a comparison with their internal need. O'Connor finds problems with all of these possible meanings, as they may involve differing standards of judgment. That is, different people (e.g., the inquirer, the provider, groups of colleagues) use varying criteria, at different point of times (e.g., immediate versus long-term effects). Much of O'Connor's concern with the relativity of judgment could be summed up by Michael Ignatieff's comment that

> there are few presumptions in human relations more dangerous than the idea that one knows what another human being needs better than they do themselves. (1984, p. 11)

Few investigations of information seeking delve very deeply into the issue of what human "needs" really are. Not many even question the notion of "information needs." Rather, most writers assume that information needs exist and are relatively unproblematic. When information seeking researchers *do* refer to more fundamental discussions of how information needs arise, they typically cite one or more of four authors in doing so: Robert Taylor, Charles Atkin, Nicholas Belkin, and Brenda Dervin.

4.2
Four Scholars Ponder Information Needs

4.2.1 Seeking Answers

The earliest of the popular depictions of how information needs arise is that of information scientist Robert Taylor. Taylor discussed the origins of information needs in 1962, and his 1968 article holds the distinction of being one of the most frequently cited items in the information seeking literature. Taylor's characterization of the origins of information needs provides a particularly useful frame of reference for the concepts discussed in the subsequent chapter.

Taylor focuses on how and why people come to ask questions at library reference desks. He describes a series of four stages or levels that began with a "conscious or even unconscious need for information . . . a vague sort of dissatisfaction . . . probably inexpressible in linguistic terms" (1968, p. 182). Taylor calls this unexpressed need for information the *visceral* need. The next level a person reaches is "a *conscious* mental description . . . an ambiguous and rambling statement" which sometimes results in talking to another person about it.

At this point the inquirer may be able to construct a *formalized* ("qualified and rational") statement of the need. However, the person is not aware whether the need could be answered in that form by any available person or information system. In the fourth and final stage, "the question is recast in anticipation of what the files can deliver." This *compromised* need may be a question asked of a librarian, or a search statement entered into an information retrieval system. At this point the question also reflects the kinds and forms of data that may be available (such as books, images, or tabular data) and the ways in which they are organized or indexed. Essentially, the final stage is a *compromise* between how the requester originally envisions the query and how the query must be restated to match the language used by the source.

In summary, Taylor says that our chain of cognition and communication often proceeds as shown in Figure 4.1.

The implications of this conceptualization of information need are several. A perception of need may differ greatly from its ultimate expression in words. There may be "unconscious needs." Recognition of uncertainty does not always lead to action. And central to the entire process is the ability to communicate one's thoughts, to "negotiate" questions and answers.

Visceral need - - ▶ **Conscious need** - - ▶ **Formalized need** - - ▶ **Compromised need**

Figure 4.1
Taylor's typology of information needs.

Let's look at an example of how this typology can relate to a real-life situation. A patron asks a librarian, "Do you have books on philosophy?" It may be that the inquirer in this case actually wants to understand the traditional distinction philosophers have made between "truth" and "truthfulness." She may start with a broader request that she hopes will orient the librarians to what is coming: a more specific statement about her needs. A helpful response to such a question would not be one of the obvious ones ("yes," "no," or "I don't know") but rather a request for clarification ("What is it you'd like to find out?"). The inquirer might then follow with a more specific request ("I need a dictionary that would explain the difference between . . ."), or instead might settle for directions to the philosophy section of a library. Thus, Taylor's typology helps to explain why people seeking help in libraries may ask questions that are overly general.

4.2.2 Reducing Uncertainty

The notion of *information as uncertainty reduction* is one that dates back to at least to the nineteenth century (Morowitz, 1991). In the late 1940s Shannon and Weaver popularized this connection between information and uncertainty, although in a counterintuitive way (see Chapter 3). By the 1970s, reducing uncertainty was firmly cemented in scholarly dialogue about motivations for information seeking.

For example, in 1973 Charles Atkin (1973) offered a definition of *information need* as "a function of extrinsic uncertainty produced by a perceived discrepancy between the individual's current level of certainty about important environmental objects and a criterion state that he seeks to achieve" (p. 206). The "environmental objects" in his definition refer to people, things, events, or ideas that possess psychological importance for the individual. In Atkin's view, humans sense differences between what they know and what they want to know as regards a salient "thing" in their mental universe. Thus, they constantly compare current levels of knowledge against goal states that they wish to reach (presumably "perfect knowledge" of all those things that concern us), and react by seeking information whenever they sense uncertainty.

We should also consider the work of Nicholas Belkin and his collaborators (1976, 1978, 1982, 1985) as advancing the view of information as uncertainty. In terms of its vocabulary and sources, Belkin's writings most reflect Taylor's concept of "visceral need." To Belkin the basic motivator of information seeking is an "anomalous state of knowledge" (ASK). An ASK exists when a person recognizes that there is an anomaly (i.e., a gap or uncertainty) in their state of knowledge regarding a situation or topic. Faced with an ASK, individuals may attempt to address their uncertainty by requesting or consulting information.

The person will then judge whether the anomaly has been resolved; if it is not resolved, another ASK may be generated, or the motivation to address it may be exhausted.

To illustrate these last two stages of ASK, consider our earlier request for philosophy books. If indeed the hypothetical inquirer is directed to shelves filled with hundreds of philosophy texts, she may very well decide to give up and ignore her anomalous state of knowledge. Alternatively, she might be handed a dictionary of philosophy that contains a discussion of the concept of "truth"; reading what the dictionary says, she decides whether the text resolves her uncertainty, or whether she needs further explanation. Her anomaly might well change in the process of seeking: now she realizes that it is the nature of "belief" that she doesn't understand. Again she must decide whether to continue until her information needs are met, or be satisfied with what she knows now. In a sense, an inquirer always "gives up" eventually, because there is always more that could be known regarding a topic. The question of "when" is determined by available resources and the inquirer's level of motivation.

4.2.3 Making Sense

The most ambitious attempt to explain the origins of information needs lies in the work of Brenda Dervin and her colleagues (1982, 1992) on "sense-making." This line of inquiry has been applied widely in the context of what Savolainen (1995) calls "everyday life information seeking," rather than traditional research on the use of factual information from libraries, television, newspapers, or other sources. Perhaps for that reason, sense-making tends to emphasize the *feelings* rather than cognitions "in situations where humans reached out for something they called information" (Dervin, 1992, p. 68).

Brenda Dervin believes that we have a need to "make sense" of the world. Dervin believes that it is safe to assume that need

> implies a state that arises within a person, suggesting some kind of gap that requires filling. When applied to the word information, as in information need, what is suggested is a gap that can be filled by something that the needing person calls "information." (1983b, p. 156)

Dervin prefers to define information needs as a need to *make sense* of a current situation:

> The individual, in her time and place, needs to make sense.... She needs to inform herself constantly. Her head is filled with questions. These questions can be seen as her "information needs." (p. 170)

In the sense-making characterization, a search for information starts with questions directed at making sense of the situation; communication is central to the process of "bridging the gap" to reach some kind of information or help desired. The strategies employed are shaped by the searcher's conceptualization of both the gap and the bridge, and by the answers, ideas, and resources obtained along the way. They are engaged in a search for meaning (Cornelius, 1996; Wilson, 1984). As others have noted (Kuhlthau, 1991; Mellon, 1986), emotions are at least as important as cognitions in "gappy" situations: searchers may be intent upon reducing their anxiety as much as their uncertainty.

4.2.4 The Spectrum of Motivations

That people have information needs is a fundamental assumption regarding information seeking. Taylor, Atkin, Belkin, and Dervin all provide frameworks to discuss a phenomenon that remains beyond our observation: the activity in human minds that leads to an individual recognizing an information need.

The work of all four scholars has been widely applied and continues to be cited. Robert Taylor's writings have been used in the training of public service workers such as reference librarians. Charles Atkin's research on the effects of mass communication continues to be used in public information campaigns about important issues regarding health and political affairs. The work of Nicholas Belkin has been widely applied in the development of information systems, in which the emphasis is on the way that queries evolve as the answers they generate are evaluated.

Dervin's work has been, like Taylor's, used to understand what takes place in question-answering arenas like the library reference desk. Dervin's "neutral questioning approach to the reference interview" (Dervin and Dewdney, 1986) advocates asking open-ended questions (e.g., "What are you trying to understand?" or "How are you planning to use this information?") to better understand the questioner's situation and needs. Because of sense-making's emphasis on emotions as well as cognitions, it has also inspired a broader audience of professionals involved in human services, such as specialists in health care and in social welfare.

What scholars say about information needs can be illustrated on a continuum that reflects their assumptions about the nature of information, *why* people seek it, and what they *use* it for. We might call one end of the spectrum the *Objective* pole and the other the *Subjective* pole (Figure 4.2).

At the Objective end of the continuum are those who view information as reflecting an objective reality, and information seeking as driven primarily by a rational judgment that some uncertainty exists that would be resolved by specific information; emotional motivations of the search process, such as anxiety, tend to be set aside. The prototypical search from the Objective

Figure 4.2
The spectrum of views regarding motivations.

point of view is one in which there is a well-defined need to retrieve a specific fact to make a decision or solve a problem. From this perspective, information needs are thought to be relatively fixed. The early writings of Charles Atkin (1972, 1973) best illustrate this view; he acknowledges "non instrumental" information seeking motives, but he defines them as out of his scope (1973, p. 205).

In contrast, the Subjective pole represents the idealized view that many (and perhaps even the majority of) searches for information are prompted by a vague feeling of unease, a sense of having a gap in knowledge, or simply by *anxiety* about a current situation. This view does not deny that purposeful thought leads to information seeking, but rather emphasizes that humans are often driven to "make sense" of an entire situation, not merely its component "data," and that rational goals are often overstated. Under such a view, information needs are highly dynamic. Brenda Dervin's work is an exemplar of the Subjective view.

Of course, saying that there are two views of information needs makes an artificial distinction. The differences between the Objective and Subjective camps are not all that great; there are many examples of overlap and agreement. But proposing these stereotypes helps to explain why different approaches to studying searches and sense-making have evolved. The Objective school tends to focus on the psychological aspects of processing information; it tends to view some types of information seeking as trivial or irrational — particular in cases in which people do not use the most authoritative sources of information or in which they ignore seemingly relevant information. The Subjective camp holds that an understanding of the receiver as "making sense" of the world leads to more accurate picture of when and how messages are "received" — and when they are not.

In ending this section I must note two facts. First, that in labeling the work of these four authors as being about "answers," "uncertainty," and "gaps" I am grossly oversimplifying their respective works. My stereotypes are simply meant to make their ideas both more digestible and more comparable. The reader is urged to follow up with the Recommended for Further Reading suggestions for this chapter.

Second, neither do I mean to suggest that these characterizations of information needs — as answers, as uncertainty reduction, or as gaps — belong exclusively to the four authors mentioned. Rather, it is merely that these four authors are frequently cited in discussions of how information needs arise and are attended to in certain kinds of information seeking.

Connections between information acquisition and the concepts of uncertainty, ambiguity, and curiosity, in particular, were widely explored by psychologists from the 1940s through the 1960s such as Allport and Postman (1947), Berlyne (1960), Driscoll and Lanzetta (1965), and Miller, Galanter, and Pribram (1960). Many other authors in the last half-century have invoked the idea of uncertainty reduction as a prime motivator for information seeking. The notion of "making sense" also has roots in the work of sociologists like Cicourel (1964), Garfinkel (1967), and Schutz (1962, 1964, 1967).

4.3

The Trouble with Information Needs

Wilson (1981, 1997) says that, while researchers fret over a definition of information *need*, much of the time they are really studying information seeking *behaviors*. Belkin and Vickery (1985) point out that observing an information need is problematic, because it exists inside someone's head and must be inferred by any interested observer while a search is in process, or after it has taken place:

> Less tractable is the issue of why people look for information at all; that is, what is the status of the concept or category of *information need*?... [I]s there such a thing as a need for information, which can be considered on its own ... or is information-seeking behaviour contingent upon the desire to satisfy other types of needs, or to resolve situations which are not in themselves information-dependent? (p. 6)

Indeed, other scholars (e.g., Wilson, 1981, and Poole, 1985) believe that the notion of an information need is a unrealistic concept, as most information needs could be said to be accounted for by more general needs, and in any event they cannot be observed. An example of their first type of objection would be that our need to know the prices of items (e.g., milk) may be driven by our need to eat (surely a more basic human need), or our need to conserve our resources (less basic, but compelling to most humans). Bosman and Renckstorf (1996) point out the circular nature of assumptions about information needs as a distinct motivator:

> it is in fact an *ad hoc* notion created for practical purposes in order to predict information-seeking behaviour and information consumption. It is rather obvious that people who consume much information on a certain subject will also state that they have a certain need for this information.... However, if one wants to explain why some people do and others do not consume certain information, the information needs concept is as elucidating as, for instance, explaining criminal behaviour on the basis of hypothetical "criminality needs." (p. 43)

In reviewing issues surrounding human motivations, Hirschman and Holbrook (1986) say that "action theorists" (e.g., Goldman, 1970; Hampshire, 1982) generally argue that wants and desires — when coupled with beliefs about the relationship between means and ends — provide *reasons* for actions. However, these theorists are divided about whether such reasons could be said to *cause* actions.

In the case of information, Bosman and Renckstorf see three overlapping motivations that determine a need for it:

> social utility (e.g. in order to have topics of conversation), instrumental utility (e.g. in order to decide whether to buy something) and intrinsic utility (e.g. the entertainment value of the information offered). (p. 46)

The first (social) and last (intrinsic) of these "utilities" are not always counted as "real "information needs. Bryce Allen (1996) points this out when he says

> there may be a variety of gratifications that are provided by the information-seeking process that cannot be considered meeting a specific information need or solving a particular problem. Another way of looking at these information activities is that they meet needs (such as the need for entertainment or companionship) that are not classified as information needs. (p. 56)

Given the multidimensional nature of such needs, how are we to describe them? Harter (1992) argues that to talk about an individual's "information need" is virtually the same as describing his or her "current psychological state," because needs shift stochastically as each relevant piece of information is encountered. One bit of knowledge may raise questions, lead to another fact or to a new conclusion, and so forth, which changes one's knowledge state and hence what one finds relevant and worth seeking. At least Wilson, Pool, Bosman and Renckstorf, and Harter would agree that, however information needs are characterized, they are not something fixed and long-lasting.

Most of what I have said (and quoted) thus far has downplayed the idea that having information is a "basic" human need. Many psychologists would disagree. George Miller (1983b), for example, described information gathering in instinctual terms. Another psychologist, Abraham Maslow (1963), said "I am convinced that man *does* have a need to know," describing it as "instinct-like," even though he admitted that he couldn't prove its existence (p. 111). Wendell Garner, who wrote extensively on the role of information in forming cognitive structures, believed that "the search for structure is inherent in behavior. . . . People in any situation will search for meaningful relations between the variables existing in the situation" (1962, p. 339). Milton Rokeach's view was that "we are all motivated by the desire, which is sometimes strong and sometimes weak, to see reality as it actually is" (1960, p. 400). To "see reality," we *need* information about it.

4.4
Information Seeking and Information Behavior

We come, at last, to information seeking. It may seem counterintuitive, but researchers have had less to say about this concept than they have about needs. Perhaps the meaning of the term is thought to be obvious. Most accounts of empirical investigations do not bother to provide a definition of information seeking, taking it for granted as what people do in response to a need for information. It could be said that information seeking is more closely tied to the concept of "need" than it is to the notion of "information" itself. For instance, Tom Wilson has said that information seeking is "the purposive seeking for information as a consequence of a need to satisfy some goal" (1999b).

The few authors who state an explicit definition of information seeking typically describe a process of either *discovering patterns* or *filling in gaps* in patterns previously recognized. Garner (1962), for example, implies that it is the search for relationships among stimuli. Likewise, Zerbinos (1990) says that

> information seeking takes place when a person has knowledge stored in long term memory that precipitates an interest in related information as well as the motivation to acquire it. It can also take place when a person recognizes a gap in their knowledge that may motivate that person to acquire new information. (p. 922)

The basic notions behind what Garner and Zerbinos describe date back to John Dewey's (1910/1933) characterizations; Dewey saw *inquiry* as motivated by recognition of a problem—of something lacking in a situation. Gary Marchionini's definition of information seeking is problem oriented: "a process in which humans purposefully engage in order to change their state of knowledge" and which is "closely related to learning and problem solving" (1995, pp. 5–6). Also in this vein is Brenda Dervin's definition of sense-making in terms of confronting problematic situations; indeed, for some investigators information seeking has come to be synonymous with sense-making.

Johnson offers one of a few definitions that are more restrictive than those above: "Information seeking can be defined as the purposive acquisition of information from selected information carriers" (1997, p. 26). In this case there is no reference to the "purpose" itself, or to what motivates a person to select a "carrier" and acquire information from it. Krikelas (1983) describes information seeking in like terms.

The reader may have noticed that the definitions of information seeking quoted above emphasize *purposive activity*. There is a broader term that encompasses information seeking yet also includes behaviors that are passive: "information behavior." Tom Wilson (1999b) defines this term as:

> the totality of human behaviour in relation to sources and channels of information, including both active and passive information seeking, and information

use. Thus, it includes face-to-face communication with others, as well as the passive reception of information as in, for example, watching television advertisements, without any intention to act on the information given. (199b)

Although it has not yet widely used, the concept of "information behavior" is a useful one that I hope will catch on. As it is defined above, it captures a broader range of information-related phenomena, some of which are receiving fresh attention in recent research (see Chapters 10, 11, and 12 for examples). It is a term whose time has come.

In conclusion, information seeking is a taken-for-granted concept, a catchall phrase that encompasses a variety of behaviors seemingly motivated by the recognition of "missing" information. Although it is the most common term in use, information seeking is typically defined strictly in terms of active and intentional behavior, which limits its applicability to the broad range of research currently being conducted on human use of information.

4.5

Summary

In this chapter I have explored the notion of information need. I have pointed out, as have many others before me, that "need" is an awkward concept, particularly in that it is not easily observable. Rather, needs are more typically inferred post hoc, after some action or request has been made manifest.

The notion of an information need is rooted in more basic human needs. The extent to which humans have a "need to know" is disputed, with most scholars identifying it as a secondary need that is much less important than the need for food, shelter, or companionship.

I described four oft-cited conceptions of how information needs arise: models by Taylor, Belkin, Atkin, and Dervin. Each of these is similar in that they all point toward feelings of uncertainty, ambiguity, or uneasiness as the root cause of information needs. You will read more about these authors — particularly the work of Brenda Dervin — in future chapters. For now, here is a brief comparison of what they say about the origins of information needs.

Robert Taylor talks about a series of stages in which "vague sort of dissatisfaction" may (or may not) become "an ambiguous and rambling statement" that in turn may (or may not) become an articulated question. Taylor's examples suggest that his main focus is the situations in which one person asks another person a question, as occurs at a library reference desk. Taylor's work helps us to understand the nature of human questioning or, as Taylor calls it, "question negotiation."

Charles Atkin uses "uncertainty reduction" as the key motivator in sparking the search for information. His research is helpful in understanding why and when people choose to expose themselves to messages from the mass media.

Nicholas Belkin emphasizes the notion of anomaly and the uncertainty that accompanies it. He also invokes the idea of a "state of knowledge" that is being constantly updated and compared with earlier states to judge whether or not an anomaly has been resolved. Although Belkin's concepts are very general, his work lends itself to the modeling of information retrieval systems. In such systems the results retrieved are evaluated and may result in additional query statements if the results are judged to be inadequate, or if the retrieved information results in a "shifting" of the focus and vocabulary of the question.

Brenda Dervin freely acknowledges the overlap between her ideas and those of Taylor and Belkin. Like Belkin she invokes the idea of a "gap" in life's experience as a motivating stimulus for seeking information. However, Dervin is concerned with a broader issue than simply getting answers to questions. Her writings emphasize basic issues in human welfare, such as the goals of feeling secure and self-actualized. For Dervin, looking for "information" is only *one* response to a "gap"; other responses could include seeking reassurance, expressing feelings, connecting with another human being, and so forth.

Many writers on the topic of information needs suggest that it is not a basic human need, comparable to those for food, shelter, security, or companionship. Information needs are said to change constantly with new, relevant sensory inputs. In other words, new questions emerge as old ones are answered or even partially satisfied. Yet some psychologists with existential leanings see information processing as a basic aspect of being human; they are inclined to see information as a basic human need after all.

Finally, I addressed the concept of "information seeking" itself, pointing out that researchers rarely bother to define it explicitly. When it is defined at all, it is described as a reaction to the recognition of an information need — a somewhat circular definition. I make a case for use of the term "information behavior" as better suited to characterizing a broad range of relevant human behaviors dealing with information.

Information needs and information seeking are related to a host of other notions, some of them tightly coupled and others more peripheral. In the next chapter we will explore these related concepts and see where and how they fit in.

Recommended for Further Reading

Allen, B. (1996). *Information tasks: Toward a user-centered approach to information systems.* San Diego, CA: Academic Press.

Although directed at the design of information systems, Allen discusses many aspects of information seeking, including the concept of "need." His book contains many examples of how social relations and context influence the seeking of information.

Dervin, B. (1983). Information as a user construct: The relevance of perceived information needs to synthesis and interpretation. In: S. A. Ward and L. J. Reed (Eds.), *Knowledge structure and use: Implications for synthesis and interpretation* pp. (153–184). Philadelphia: Temple University Press.

A well-written explanation of Dervin's earliest views on the subjective nature of information.

Green, A. (1990). What do we mean by user needs? *British Journal of Academic Librarianship, 5,* 65–78.

Green's article is broader in scope than either its title or journal of publication would imply. His topic is human "need" and how it has been defined by political philosophers and social theorists. The concept of need is a slippery one, and even more so when we discuss the need for information, which is even more subjective than needs for physical things and states.

Morris, R. C. T. (1994). Toward a user-centered information service. *Journal of the American Society for Information Science, 45,* 20–30.

Morris compares the ideas of Brenda Dervin to those of Carol Kuhlthau, Robert Taylor, and Nicholas Belkin. She attempts to synthesize a "conceptual base" that could serve as the basis for a redesign of information service delivery.

Taylor, R. S. (1968). Question-negotiation and information seeking in libraries. *College and Research Libraries, 29,* 178–194.

Taylor's observations about how a reference question is negotiated between librarian and client still seem fresh after many years. In this piece he suggests how information needs arise and are satisfied.

5

Related Concepts

Though we speak of knowledge, it is to be remembered that we are not distinguishing among knowledge, belief, opinion and information. We are not concerned with whether a man's image of the world is correct, whether his beliefs are true, whether his information is information or misinformation.

Patrick Wilson (1973, p. 462)

We are not, can not, be moved by the "truth" of information. We can only be moved by its *relevance*.

Lee Thayer (1987, p. 18)

Chapter Outline

5.1. Decision Making
    5.1.1. Making Decisions
    5.1.2. Solving Problems

5.2. Browsing, Etc.
    5.2.1. Browsing, Scanning, and Serendipity
    5.2.2. Additional Distinctions

5.3. Relevance, Pertinence, and Salience
    5.3.1. Relevance and Pertinence
    5.3.2. Relevance in Information Retrieval
    5.3.3. Salience

5.4. Avoiding Information
    5.4.1. Selective Exposure and Information Avoidance
    5.4.2. Knowledge Gaps and Information Poverty
    5.4.3. Information Overload and Anxiety

5.5. Information versus Entertainment

5.6. Summary

We will now consider some other concepts that are closely related to information seeking. Among these highly relevant notions are *decision-making, relevance, pertinence, salience, selective exposure, browsing, serendipity, knowledge gaps, information poverty, information overload, information anxiety,* and *entertainment.* This chapter will explore these concepts in the context of what people think and do when they are looking for that thing we call "information."

5.1

Decision Making

Donohew and Tipton (1973, p. 251) point out that "much information seeking research is intertwined with decision making." A great deal of the information seeking literature indeed refers to decision making and problem solving. Although they are not universal aspects of information seeking, solving problems and making decisions and judgments are undoubtedly important in life. Herbert Simon and his associates go so far as to say that

> the work of managers, of scientists, of engineers, of lawyers — the work that steers the course of society and its economic and governmental organizations — is largely work of making decisions and solving problems. (1992, p. 32)

Because so many information seeking studies are concerned with the first three of the professions mentioned by Simon, it is no surprise that seeking of information has often been characterized in terms of the problems and decisions seekers face.

5.1.1 Making Decisions

Reviews of the decision making literature by Abelson and Levi (1985), Goldstein and Hogarth (1997), March and Shapira (1992), March (1994), and Zey (1992) point out that decision making research has a long history and a considerable number of dimensions, applications, and offshoots. Two major distinctions are whether the decisions are made by individuals or by groups, and whether these are one-time decisions versus repeated choices. Abelson and Levi, for example, focus on *one-time* decisions by *individuals,* acting on the basis of *preferences.*

Most reviewers rule out special uses of the term "decision," such as when it refers solely to when an experimental subject identifies the presence or absence of an attribute (e.g., a tone) in a stimulus (e.g., a sound). Goldstein and Hogarth (1997) refer to this latter branch of investigation as research on *judgment*, to distinguish it from research that focuses on choice and decisions.

Some areas of decision making research are unlikely to hold much relevance for information behavior that takes place in real-world contexts. For example, many normative models (how people *should* choose among alternatives) seem invalid outside of highly specialized contexts (such as games of chance in which exact probabilities can be calculated). Descriptive models, focusing on how people *actually* choose, have been examined in both highly structured and ill-defined problem situations. It is the latter that more closely resemble most circumstances studied under the rubric of information behavior.

Normative models and highly structured problems have been extensively studied by economists and psychologists operating under well-defined paradigms of experimentation and mathematical modeling. In contrast, poorly structured problems (e.g., management decisions about strategy) typically involve information that is lacking or unreliable, unclear goals, inadequate measures of success, and short supplies of time, money, and attention. Poorly defined problem situations have attracted attention from a number of disciplines, including management, sociology, and psychology, using both experiments and more qualitative methods like protocol analysis.

"Decisions" are typically characterized as choices made from among alternatives; that is, at least two options are, available and the decision-maker may select only one of them. Faced with such a situation, the decision-maker must gather information that allows each potential choice to be evaluated and compared to the alternative(s). A typical example of such decision making is the car-buying scenario discussed in Chapter 2, in which a consumer gathers information to make a purchase decision. Whether the decisions are purchases or other kinds of choices, they can be looked at as comparisons of alternatives (e.g., a particular model of car; an information source) across their attributes (e.g., price; accessibility).

Uncertainty is a key concept in decision making research, as it has been in information seeking (Atkin, 1973; Belkin, 1978; Kuhlthau, 1993b) and communication (Berger, 1997; Kellermann & Reynolds, 1990; Stewart, 1997). It is typically assumed that whether we are reading or conversing, we are at least partially engaged in an attempt to reduce uncertainty. Decision making research also assumes uncertainty reduction as a key process, even though it cannot be assumed that possessing more information always reduces uncertainty (e.g., Yovits & Foulk, 1985).

A frequent concern in decision making research is the degree to which our rationality is bounded. It is obvious that we have limits to both our attention and our ability to process information. For example, there are fairly consistent experimental findings about information overload, expressed as the number of alternatives that need to be examined, multiplied by the number of their attributes, which are the ways that things can differ from one another, such as the features of a car.

We tend to be more sensitive to increases in the number of attributes than we are to increases in the number of alternatives we must examine. Once the numbers of alternatives and attributes each gets above 10, individuals are likely to experience overload. As the number of information items increase—or as the amount of available time decreases—people resort to simpler and less reliable rules for making choices to shorten their search time (e.g., Brucks, 1985; Ozanne, Brucks, & Grewal, 1992; Urbany, Dickson, & Wilkie, 1989). Much psychological research on decision making focuses on examining the *rules* that people use to make choices. For example, in applying the lexicographic rule, a person would decide which attribute is most important (say, a car's fuel economy) and chose an alternative only on that basis; in the event of a "tie," they would consider the next most important attribute to resolve their choice.

Much of information behavior literature considers essentially unique searches—deciding how to address a health problem, or finding relevant articles for a paper. However, much of our everyday activity involves *repeated* behavior. Long ago, Cyert, Simon, & Trow (1956) discussed why routine (programmed) choices are much easier to make than novel (nonprogrammed) decisions. Langer (1978) refers to the former as "mindless" decisions while Steinbruner (1974) calls them "cybernetic." Both authors provide examples of just how common such decisions are in everyday life, for example, in feeding oneself or walking to work. The notion of cybernetic decisions—in which "standard operating procedures" are established by prior experience and altered only in the event of negative feedback—is highly relevant to everyday information seeking. This concept of feedback and its importance in information behavior has been recently reviewed by Newhagen (1997) and Spink (1997).

For instance, Savolainen describes his Everyday Life Information Seeking model (ELIS) model as reflecting Bourdieu's concept of *habitus*, "a relatively stable system of dispositions by which individuals . . . evaluate the importance of different choices" (1995, p. 262). While Savolainen's investigation was aimed at examining "nontrivial issues such as unemployment or health problems," there is much about his framework that captures routine choices regarding many types of actions and the information on which they are based. One category of life experiences has to do with "consumption of goods and services" (Savolainen, p. 263; Hirschman & Holbrook, 1986; Sheth, Newman & Gross, 1991). Therefore, some of the many approaches to decision making are surely relevant to consumption-related information behavior, even though "consumers ... are not merely decision makers" but rather people "emerging into being" (Hirschman & Holbrook, pp. 215–217).

5.1.2 Solving Problems

Simon (1992, p. 32) makes a distinction between problem solving and decision making when he says that *problem solving* has to do with identifying issues worthy of attention, setting goals and designing suitable courses of action. In contrast, *decision making* is the activity of evaluating and choosing among alternative actions to take in response to a problem. Together the two activities form a sequence that begins with focusing on a problem and ends with selecting from among various choices.

James March (1994) agrees that decision making is a separate and narrower activity than problem solving, and further emphasizes that the *search* for alternatives and the choice of which to pay *attention* to are the key components of decision making. According to March (1994, p. 23), "The study of decision making is, in many ways, the study of search and attention."

However, definitions by organizational theorists like Simon and March may not be universally held; some authors from other fields collapse together goal-setting and searching and call it all "problem solving." This is because the solving of problems has been investigated primarily by psychologists, while decision making has been studied mostly by economists, operations researchers and organizational theorists. Interestingly, the organizational theorist's view, with its emphasis on attention and search, is readily congruent with the usual focus of information seeking studies. Therefore, in this review I set aside the usual preoccupation of problem solving studies with problem identification and the setting of goals; instead I focus on decision making—which is to say attention management and search processes.

Some writers assume that information seeking is always motivated by a need to solve a problem. Yet Sperber and Wilson (1995) point out that problem solving does not fit all situations in which humans are "informed":

> Most discussions of information processing ... have been concerned with the realisation of absolute goals. "Problem solving" has become the paradigm of information processing. The problems considered have a fixed solution; the goal of the information-processing device is to find this solution; efficiency consists in finding it at the minimal cost. However, not all cognitive tasks fit this description; many tasks consist not in reaching an absolute goal, but in improving on an existing state of affairs. (pp. 46–47)

In other words, information seeking is not always motivated by the need to "solve a problem" or "make a decision"—activities that have a clear-cut and short-term end. Sometimes it is a desire simply to have *more or less* of some quality: more information, stimulation, or assurance; or less uncertainty, boredom, overload, or anxiety.

5.2
Browsing, Etc.

5.2.1 Browsing, Scanning, and Serendipity

As shown in the scenarios presented in the second chapter of this book, information does not always result in either a decision or the reduction of uncertainty. Sometimes the receipt of information causes us to reassess the state of our ignorance (thereby increasing uncertainty), as one thinks "I know so little about this!" At other times we can be so overloaded with information that further progress toward a goal becomes (cognitively or emotionally) impossible to make. At times information is merely sought for stimulation or entertainment value. And sometimes information is encountered without being sought.

Some writers on information seeking assume it to be an *intentional* action; that is, for information seeking to take place, the individual must be consciously and actively looking for information. Most other scholars (e.g., see the review by Chang & Rice, 1993) allow for the possibility of "unintentional communication," such as when we notice data in the environment (objects or events, whether of human or nonhuman origin). Such accidental or incidental encounters with information (Williamson, 1998) may either trigger a preexisting interest or cause a new interest to arise. The most common terms used to describe such phenomena are "browsing" and "scanning." A closely related concept is "serendipity."

Browsing is certainly the central (and oldest) concept among a variety of terms used to denote informal or unplanned search behaviors. As an English word, "browsing" itself derives from old French and refers to the way that animals feed upon the young shoots of trees and shrubs (Cove & Walsh, 1988). Since at least 1823, the word has been applied to reading habits, and thus *Webster's Third New International Dictionary* includes among its meanings "to look over casually (as a book).... To skim through a book reading at random passages.... To look over books (as in a store or library)...." (Chang & Rice, 1993). Browsing has come to refer to a wide range of information behaviors, ranging from aimless scanning to goal-directed searching. Chang and Rice note the bifurcated nature of the concept as it is commonly used: it may refer to purposive, goal-directed actions, or it may imply nonpurposive, unplanned behavior. Perhaps the very vagueness of the term has encouraged the proliferation of alternate terminology during recent years.

Long a consideration among librarians, the use of browsing by scientists as a topic of empirical investigation was first discussed by Saul Herner in 1954. Since at least the mid-1960s, the concept has appeared regularly in the general literature (e.g., Gerstberger & Allen, 1968; Herner, 1970; Levine, 1969; Overhage & Harman, 1965). An allied notion, *scanning,* has been employed in studies about as long (e.g., Aguilar, 1967; Duncan, 1972). Enough publications on browsing had accrued by 1985 to occasion a 112-page report (Ayris, 1986). The most recent comprehensive review of the literature (Chang & Rice, 1993, which featured 164 references) states that "we do not have a good vocabulary to describe and discuss various forms or degrees of browsing" (p. 233). Since then, the vocabulary to describe browsing has expanded to include terms like scanning and encountering.

Many authors consider browsing to be a type of information seeking, even though the browser may be seeking nothing in particular. Apted (1971) makes the point that accidental discovery of information is a special case of browsing that we should distinguish as *serendipity.* Although most studies of information seeking have chosen to ignore instances of encountering information by serendipity, it is obvious that such circumstances are fairly common. The role and value of serendipity in scientific investigation has been much discussed (Roberts, 1989; Shapiro, 1986).

Boyce, Meadow, and Kraft (1994) link serendipity and browsing when they say that

> people find valuable information on subject B when searching for subject A, a phenomenon often called *serendipity.* The very act of browsing allows a user to recognize information of value in other contexts than that in mind when the search was started. (p. 177)

At times individuals simply engage in scanning their field of vision without a particular goal in mind (e.g., when we browse a magazine rack). A childhood fascination with certain objects in the environment—such as coins—may result in a perusal of magazines about coins in a bookstore; the browser may admire photographs of coins, glance at articles about specific types of coins, and so on. Only later might this half-formed interest lead to a complex of learning and actions that we call a "hobby," a work–like activity that is done for pleasure, without external rewards. Similarly, an adult's curiosity about a social issue such as drug abuse may result in sustained reading on the topic without any particular plan of action.

Yet we can also "find" information without premeditated action (i.e., without conscious browsing), as when we glance at an advertising billboard that pictures an attractive product—say, a new car that we now learn is a Lexus. Therefore, it is safe to claim that at least the *absorption* of information may not be overtly intentional. An early review of the concept of browsing (Herner, 1970) described it as a mechanism that we could not stop even if we wished to:

Continually, awake or asleep, consciously or unconsciously, we rummage through our minds, reviewing the data we have collected and stored within them. . . . [W]e know, or our minds store memories of, what interests us, and we match the contents of what we sense, regardless of where it occurs, against what interests us. (p. 408)

A study of browsing by Elaine Toms (1999) contains an extensive review of what psychologists have had to say about our *motivations* for exploration, curiosity, and the like. She reviews theories (e.g., uses and gratifications theory, play theory, and expectancy-value theory, as described in Chapter 7 of this book) that have been used to explain browsing behavior. Toms's own results suggest that browsing is more closely "connected to satisfying human curiosity than to resolving a predetermined information gap or need" (p. 204).

5.2.2 Additional Distinctions

Distinctions among degrees of browsing — some of which go back many years — have led to a proliferation of terminology to describe individual behaviors. The most distinctive (Choo, 1998, following Saunders & Jones, 1990) considers scanning of the environment to have four modes, the lowest effort of which is the sort of "undirected viewing" that results in the serendipitous discovery (or "sensing") of what information exists in the environment. This seems to correspond to Erdelez's (1997, 1999) concept of "information encountering," which she equates with "accidental discovery," serendipity, and "incidental learning." In Choo's typology, "conditioned viewing" or *browsing* results from a higher level of effort, the goal of which is increase understanding and make sense of the environment. It is only with still greater effort that focused "searches" are evident, according to Choo, and this level of seeking can be either informal or formal. Informal searches are those that examine relatively few sources and aim to increase knowledge within narrow limits, with the goal of simply learning; formal searches involve both more effort and more sources, and are tied to an impending decision or action.

To make the vocabulary issue even more complicated, additional terminology is used in specific domains in which browsing phenomena are studied. Studies of organizational information seeking and use favor the descriptor *environmental scanning* (Keegan, 1974; Kefalas & Schoderbek, 1973). The concept of browsing is widely employed in investigations of the interface for electronic information systems, where the word *navigation* is sometimes used to indicate a movement through search space in graphic interfaces (e.g., Canter, Rivers & Storrs, 1985; Thompson & Croft, 1989). Proper and Bruza (1999) use the phrase *information discovery* to apply solely to the identification and retrieval of relevant content from electronic sources. In studies of television viewing, the terms *grazing* and *zapping* indicate the frequent scanning or browsing of multiple channels that is enabled by the remote control (Heeter & Greenberg, 1985; Perse, 1990). Some investigations of document retrieval also invoke the grazing metaphor (e.g., Bates, 1989; Cove & Walsh, 1988; O'Connor, 1993). Finally, the uses and gratifications line of research (see Chapter 7) distinguishes "instrumental" use of media (a parallel to "searching") with "ritualized" use which "suggests utility but an otherwise less active or less goal-directed state" (Rubin, 1994, p. 427), which is similar to browsing.

In only two contexts does the primary term, browsing, still seem to suffice on its own: *shopping* (e.g., Bloch & Richins, 1983; Bloch, Ridgway, & Sherrell, 1989, Salomon & Koppelman, 1992; Schmidt & Spreng, 1996) and *book usage within libraries* (e.g., Baker, 1986; O'Connor, 1993). Even in the latter we have seen recent variance in terminology though, as in discussions by Sandstrom

Table 5.1

Examples of Browsing Goals by Domain of Interest, Goal Type and Terminology

Example Domains	Distinction Made, with Associated Terms			
	Well-defined	Semidefined	Poorly defined	Undefined
	(Formal Search & Retrieval)	(Browse, Forage, Scan)	(Browse, Graze, Navigate, Scan)	(Encounter, Serendipity)
Library or bookstore	Find material by a particular author or on a specific subject	Find books, tapes or articles on a general subject	Find any material of potential interest	Discover previously unknown interests
Electronic information resources	Find specific pages or records using controlled terms or attributes	Find records or pages matching general, natural language terms	Follow links to pages that pique interest	Accidently encounter pages of interest
TV/radio	Locate specific program, e.g., *Cheers*, on a specific channel, e.g., WTBS	Choose a specific TV channel (4) or radio frequency (FM 88.4)	Watch or listen to whatever catches attention, purposefully	Serendipitous viewing or listening, unintentionally
Shopping	Find an item of a particular brand in a category, e.g., Kellogg's Cornflakes	Find items in a category, e.g., breakfast cereals	Find something to eat, e.g., packaged foods	Pass by/see items for sale without intent to buy

(Adapted from Figure 3 on page 262 of Chang & Rice (1993), Browsing: A multidimensional framework. In Williams, M. E. (Ed.), *Annual review of information science and technology* pp. 231–276. Medford, NJ: Information Today, Inc. Used with permission of Information Today, Inc., 143 Old Marlton Pike, Medford, NJ 08055; tel:609-654-6266; Web:www.infotoday.com.)

(1994) and Cronin and Hert (1995) of scholarly *foraging*, which corresponds more closely to the notion of a formal search as described by Choo (1998). Chang and Rice (1993) tease out the origins and research usages of these terms in their comprehensive review of browsing concepts.

Table 5.1 combines and adapts distinctions made by Saunders and Jones (1990), Chang and Rice (1993), and Choo (1998) to illustrate browsing terminology.

5.3
Relevance, Pertinence, and Salience

5.3.1 Relevance and Pertinence

The topic of browsing provokes us to consider how one recognizes something of interest, and, by extension, the general problem of *relevance*. Relevance is a concept that extends well beyond browsing. A great deal has been written about it in the information science literature and most of that concerned with technical measures of document retrieval. The latter topic is of minor interest to this discussion; of greater importance is the general issue of what we *mean* when we say that information is relevant to a person.

Much commentary and some empirical investigations regarding relevance—and the related terms of *pertinence* and *salience*—are to be found in literature on perception, attention, memory, attitude and belief formation, and persuasion. Psychological investigations of these phenomena have been extended in the direction of speech, mass media studies, and information retrieval. Besides their import to basic research on human psychology, mechanisms of attention and attitude have great practical applications in everything from learning and healing to publicity and advertising.

The dictionary informs us that "relevance" means to have a close, logical relationship to a matter, topic, thought, remark, or question. Ritchie (1991), striving for a definition consistent with those for the term "information," says that

> relevance has to do with meaning and describes the relationship of patterns and whatever patterns indicate to the cognitive environments of the originator and perceiver of a message. Patterns with communicative potential are data, and data with relevance are information. (p. 20)

In their book on the concept of relevance in communication, Sperber and Wilson (1995) imply that any pattern (e.g., a message in a conventional form) that attracts our attention calls for interpretation by us. Our interpretation must take into account the *context* of the message—the background of time, place, persons, and recent ideas, statements, and events. "Relevance" is the interpretive connection that is made between the observed pattern and the context of the observation (Ritchie, 1991, pp. 16–20).

Sperber and Wilson see relevance as a key aspect of efficiency in human information processing. Our long-term goal is to improve "one's knowledge of the world as much as possible given the available resources" (p. 47). We always face two problems in processing information efficiently: First, the environment contains much more information than our senses can process; second, we have "plenty of unfinished business" in our minds. The unfinished business may run the gamut of time and importance from "Is there a God?" and "Am I a good person?" to "Should I lose weight?" or "Where will I vacation this summer?" or "What should I have for dinner tonight?"—plus a few thousand other questions and concerns.

In information science, relevance is used in a different sense than the characterization of Sperber and Wilson; that is, relevance is equated with *aboutness* and *topicality*. A document is relevant to an information need if it is judged to be "on the topic" (Harter, 1992). Topicality serves as the basis for measures—the most common ones being precision and recall—of the effectiveness of a document retrieval system. We will take a short detour to consider briefly the substantial literature on relevance in the context of information retrieval.

5.3.2 Relevance in Information Retrieval

In its most common form, relevance measures are operationalized as a document retrieval system user (or some other judge) declaring a document to be either "relevant" or "not relevant" to a specific request for information. Thus, relevance measures are based on the relationship between an information request and the content of a collection of document records — or more usually document *surrogates* (e.g., author-title-keywords) rather than the complete text (Belkin & Vickery, 1985). Investigators have sought an *objective* measure of relevance for this particular situation of information transfer.

Even though a narrow definition of relevance enjoyed wide acceptance during the 1950s and 1960s, there was a growing recognition that it left out important aspects of information seekers and their situation. Rees and Saracevic (1966) and Cuadra and Katter (1967), for example, were among the earliest critics of objective definitions of relevance, and by the mid-1970s the criticisms were widespread.

The main problem facing an objective operationalization of relevance is the contextual nature of human judgment. Even when the terminology of the request maps neatly onto the terms of a document index, there may be reasons why a such a match may not be judged truly relevant. Setting aside the obvious problem that words can have multiple meanings and varying interpretations, it has been effectively demonstrated that relevance assessments can shift, depending on the order in which retrieved documents are presented to a judge. There is considerable variation among judges as to the point at which a document starts being relevant and ceases to be nonrelevant (Eisenberg, 1988; Eisenberg & Carol, 1988; Janes & McKinney, 1992).

Harter (1992) describes a number of examples in which relevance is clearly not judged on the basis of topicality. A common case is one in which a user judges information to be relevant even though it is not strictly "about" the stated information need; such judgments are in tune with the everyday, dictionary sense of relevancy as "bearing on or relating to the matter in hand." For example, when searching for information on the Peruvian economy we may encounter an article about the global effects of El Niño, which may lead us to wonder what effects that weather phenomenon will have on the fishing and farming sectors of the Peruvian economy; the article is not "about" the topic of our interest, but nevertheless we see it as relevant to our information need. Harter (1992) goes so far as to suggest that *"references on the topic may be less important than relevant references not on the topic*—references that allow the making of new intellectual connections" (p. 612).

Accordingly, since the 1970s the information science literature has shifted toward a definition of relevance that is based on the knowledge state and intentions of the user rather than a logical match of terminology by the information system—toward a *subjective* view (Mizzaro, 1998). The subjective characterization of relevance is most commonly called *situational* relevance (Barry, 1994; Bruce, 1994; Carter, 1965; Dervin & Nilan, 1986; Schamber, Eisenberg, & Nilan, 1990; Wilson, 1973) or sometimes *pertinence* (Belkin & Vickery, 1985; Howard, 1994; Kemp, 1974) or *psychological* relevance (Harter, 1992). Belkin and Vickery (1985) make a neat distinction between objective relevance and situational relevance (i.e., pertinence) by saying that "relevance is the property that assigns an answer to a question and pertinence is the property that assigns an answer to [an] information need" (p. 46).

Froelich (1994), in fact, points out that what most people mean when they use the word "relevance" is actually "pertinence": "bearing on or connected to" an information *need*, rather than a stated *question*. In other words, they mean subjective relevance. In Froelich's view, this meaning of relevance forms a "natural category from cultural experience," in reference to Eleanor Rosch's theory of prototypes and basic level categories (in Rosch & Lloyd, 1978). Rosch demonstrated that people divide up (categorize) their perceptual world according to certain principles. Basic level categories (such as "bird") are usually the first learned by children, and they gradually come to organize the contents of this category around the most "typical" example (which functions as a prototype) of the category. Thus, in North America either the sparrow or American robin comes to be the central example to which are all other birds are compared. Not surprisingly, birds like pelicans and storks are regarded as peripheral examples of the bird category, as not being "typical" enough even though they have the logical, defining characteristics of "birdness": feathers, wings, beaks, and the ability to fly. Flightless birds, like the penguin or ostrich, may be judged as even poorer examples of birds, depending on one's origins.

Froelich is saying, then, that subjective relevance (pertinence) is the core meaning of a cluster of related concepts. Other concepts include germane, material, apposite, and apropos (Froelich, 1991). The cluster of overlapping meanings has, at its center, the everyday sense of "relevance," while at the periphery is the technical sense of relevance as answers (or documents) that logically match a formal, stated query — the technical view of relevance.

Whatever we call it, the subjective view of relevance argues for the importance of the user's knowledge state and intentions at the time of encountering information. For example, a document might be retrieved by a system on the basis of a logical match between words in a query and words in a title. However, it may be that the user has previously read that document. The mere fact that the information is *not novel* is likely to cause users to judge it as *not relevant* to their needs; presumably the information in the document is already a part of the context of their information seeking. In keeping with this view, some psychologists note that pertinence (situational relevance) is determined by *context* and guides selective attention to information (Lachman, Lachman, & Butterfield, 1979, pp. 194–197).

5.3.3 Salience

A related term less frequently discussed is *salience*. Something that is salient "stands out," is vivid, unexpected, notable, conspicuous, prominent, or "unpleasant, deviant, extreme, intense, unusual, sudden, brightly lit, colorful, alone" (Kiesler & Sproull, 1982, p. 556). Salience evokes the figure/ground distinction in gestalt psychology, in which certain principles (e.g., proximity, similarity, closure) tend to account for which elements in an image stand out from the others (Glass, Holyoak, & Santa, 1979). What is it that grabs our attention when we look at a scene? What stands out as the "figure" and what is perceived as mere background? Salient items of information are more easily recalled later, perhaps because they are coded more effectively in memory (Abelson & Levi, 1985, p. 282).

A salient stimulus is not necessarily relevant to one's current information needs. Witnessing a car accident as a pedestrian certainly raises one's interest and potential for taking action. ("Should I call for an ambulance? Help the victims exit their vehicles? Offer to serve as a witness? Get out of the street?") Yet if the scenario does not map on to preexisting interests, sympathies, intentions, or plans, no action may be taken and the incident may pass from the mind of the witness minutes later. ("I must be on my way. I don't want to get involved.")

Correspondingly, potentially relevant sources of information may not appear particularly salient at the time an information need begins to emerge. Our need for the exact location of a new movie theater may not occur to us as we pass by the phone book on our way to the front door, or as we drive by the neighbor who first told us about it. It is only later, when we can't find the theater, that every phone booth stands out like a beacon on the horizon. ("I' check the phone book, or call directory assistance. Or call my neighbor!)" Sometimes we pass over the easy sources of information because we do not see them in that context at the time; later those sources may be highly salient and we may be willing to be much more active in our search for information.

Johnson (1997) sees both salience and beliefs as a part of "personal relevance factors" that are antecedent to any information seeking activity. That is, before one begins to consider the characteristics of an information source and its usefulness, an interaction occurs between a gap in knowledge, beliefs about that topic of knowledge, and the import or "standoutedness" of it. We pay attention and render action to those things that are salient to us. Later we will examine Johnson's model that describes the sequence of events and factors that lead to information seeking. For now, the cluster of concepts we call relevance, pertinence, and salience give rise to another question: When do we decide *not* to pay attention to information? This is a phenomenon known as "selective exposure."

5.4
Avoiding Information

5.4.1 Selective Exposure and Information Avoidance

It is widely believed that humans tend to seek information that is congruent with their prior knowledge, beliefs, and opinions, and to avoid exposure to information that conflicts with those internal states. In contrast, a high level of interest regarding a certain topic will tend to increase exposure — interested people are motivated to acquire more information about a topic that fascinates them.

An early look at selective exposure to information was that of Hyman and Sheatsley (1947), who invoked selectivity as a reason why attempts to use the mass media to change attitudes or behavior (e.g., in political campaigns) often fail. In addition to the general tendency to reinforce preexisting knowledge, beliefs, and attitudes, Hyman and Sheatsley observed several other tendencies. First, some people are chronically ignorant in relation to the topic of the information campaign and there is something about the uninformed that makes them harder to reach.

People who are interested in a topic tend to acquire more information about it (Chew & Palmer, 1994; Reagan, 1996). There are also differences in the ways that people interpret the same information: their perceptions and memory are distorted by their individual motives and attitudes. Finally, receiving information does not necessarily change attitudes or behavior. For all these reasons, simply increasing the flow of information does not automatically attain the desired result.

Twenty years after Hyman and Sheatsley published their observations, a critical review by Sears and Freedman (1967) raised questions about the phenomenon of selective exposure, and clarified its nature. Sears and Freedman noted that experimental evidence showed that people do not always prefer information that agrees with their opinions. In cases in which discrepant information might be highly useful, or where an individual already had a great deal of information on the topic, a person was open to dissonant (i.e., contradictory) information; and the tendency to openness was more common among educated individuals. Later experiments (e.g., Frey, 1982; Frey & Rosch, 1984) that used better measures of information seeking and information avoidance confirmed that we often seek dissonant information in cases where it might improve future decisions we make, and even in some cases where it might not. Yet, in general, such research still demonstrates a preference for supportive information in most cases.

More to the point, Sears and Freedman also noted a sense in which selective exposure is common: while there are *instances* in which we may welcome contradictory statements, *in the long-term* we drift toward information that supports our point of view. In other words, we tend toward a usual diet of information that is *mostly* congruent with our beliefs and opinions.

Over the five decades that selective information seeking has been discussed, many others have pondered the implications of selective perception and attention for the next step: using information. Thayer (1987), for example, notes that knowledge often does not result in changes of behavior. We tend to think that acquiring information obligates one to think, feel, or do something about it. But *informed behavior* does not always result from exposure to information. Not only are people *told* that taking drugs and smoking are ultimately bad for their health, they can observe this fact in the world around them; those observations, however, often do not result in less consumption of harmful substances. As Sears and Freedman pointed out, failure to act on information is often due less to selective exposure than to a *rejection* of information with which we disagree: "Perhaps resistance to influence is accomplished most often and most successfully at the level of information evaluation, rather than at the level of selective seeking and avoiding of information" (p. 213).

Zillman and Bryant (1985) observe that we tend to think of preference for entertainment content, for example, to be fairly stable, a matter of a deeply ingrained "taste" of unknown origin. These authors, however, believe that "the choice behavior in question grows from a situational context [in which] affective and emotional states and reactions play a key role" (p. 157). Charles Atkin (1985) agrees, to the extent that selection (and sometimes, avoidance) of entertainment seems to be motivated by both affective and utilitarian concerns — that is, seeking both emotional gratification and the means to reach some goal.

Reviewing a number of studies in which individuals were placed in either boring or stressful conditions, then allowed to select entertainment programming, Zillman and Bryant found support for "therapeutic" uses of media. That is, one of the ways people cope with negative affect is to choose materials that may diffuse such feelings: arousing programming (if bored), calming music (if stressed), or simply messages that comfort or distract. Zillman and Bryant regard this "selective behavior to be intelligent in that messages are exploited for their therapeutic value" (p. 186), even though such selections offer only short-term relief to emotional problems. This tendency to use various media — especially television — to ameliorate stress has been noted for many decades (e.g., from Pearlin, 1959, to Henning & Vorderer, 2001).

The notion of *selecting* inputs can also be applied to *avoiding* them. Noted Yale sociologist Charles Perrow, in his essay "On Not Using Libraries" (1989), discusses the *avoidance* of information. Perrow reverses the typical view of libraries when he says that

> I require libraries to *hide* most of the literature so that I will not become delirious from the want of time and wit to pursue it all. There is just too much material. The problem is not access, it is the reverse, containment.... Were I now to browse the stacks ... I would drown, or panic, and certainly lose my way." (pp. 29–30)

Perrow says that, as most of what he reads is determined by the demands of others (students, colleagues, journal editors) and he has adequate ways of keeping up with the literature in his field, he is rarely motivated to seek library materials. When he *does* need a book, article, or chapter from the library, his way of coping is to send an assistant to get it so that he will not be distracted by adjacent materials. Perrow's strategy is an extreme example of *filtering,* justified by his belief that most of the literature in his area is redundant and of low quality.

Patrick Wilson (1995) points out that filtering behavior (or "nonuse," as he calls it) is both efficient and perfectly rational if it is a matter of conscious *policy:* being presented with more information than one could absorb ... being burdened by a large supply of relevant information, that is, forced to spend more time and energy on assimilating new information than one would like to do ... information one thinks to be probably relevant but does not use because of lack of time. (pp. 45–46)

In a later publication Wilson (1996) provides a scenario of how a nonuse policy might be implemented for interdisciplinary researchers, faced as they are by many documents from the multiple literatures they monitor:

> Large literatures may be cut down drastically: one may ignore the past, ignore "foreign" contributions, ignore contributions from identifiable schools and traditions of thought (e.g., no Marxists, no deconstructionists, no positivists, etc.), ignore work done with certain techniques or in particular styles or with particular approaches. (p. 199)

Most of the time, then, information is not avoided but rather simply not *used*. This applies to the average person as well as the scholar. Dervin (1983b), for example, criticizes the tendency for studies of information usage to blame the public for not taking more advantage of authoritative information — typically in the form of documents or expert advice. Dervin takes the counter view that most "canned" information is not relevant to the needs of most individuals in the general public:

> When you listen to people's reasons for not using or rejecting information ... what you hear them say most often is, "It didn't fit my circumstances," or "It arrived too late," or "I couldn't make it work for me." (p. 170)

When, for whatever reason, entire groups of people do not get the same information as other groups, we speak of them as having a "knowledge gap" or as being "information poor" — the subject of the next section.

5.4.2 Knowledge Gaps and Information Poverty

Earlier when we considered the concept of a "gap" it referred to an *individual's* encounter with a discrepancy or lack of "sense" in their environment. When such gaps are differential and persistent, they are called "knowledge gaps" (Chatman & Pendleton, 1995; Chew & Palmer, 1994; Tichenor, Donohue, & Olien, 1970). That is, when one human group (whether defined by income, education, location, or other variable) persistently differs from another human group in *what they know*, a knowledge gap is said to exist.

Knowledge gaps are often discussed in the context of public information campaigns (Rice & Atkin, 1989, 1994; Rice & Paisley, 1981), which are attempts to inform mass audiences of some facts or practices. Information campaigns are often conducted with the intention of improving health practices, such as publicity aimed at encouraging people to avoid illegal drugs, stop smoking, eat less fat, get more exercise, and so forth. Public information efforts can also attempt to inform people about matters of fact, such as public television programming (typically aimed at children) intended to increase literacy or knowledge of language, science, history, and geography. In the United States, programs like *Sesame Street* and *3-2-1-Contact* are of this type.

One of the problems with such well-intentioned programming is that some segment of the intended audience may not watch at all, or may watch but learn less than other audience segments. When that happens, disparities in knowledge may actually be created among groups by a program intended to reduce them. A particular concern is when an already disadvantaged group, such as lower-income persons ("the poor") do not get the message at all, either through nonexposure or through exposure without learning. This, of course, is not a new phenomenon, but merely an extension of an old observation as rephrased by Brenda Dervin (1989, p. 219): "the informationally rich get richer, the poor get poorer."

A basic example of "the poor get poorer" mechanism is *literacy*. If one never learns to read, the potential for learning is greatly diminished and others who can read will more steadily increase the amount of knowledge they possess. Recently this concern has been extended to those who never learn to use computers and telecommunications networks. People who do know how to use computers (and have access to them—a separate issue) have both additional means of learning and more stores of information available to them.

The tendency of information campaigns to perform poorly, or to fail altogether, was noted by Hyman and Sheatsley as early as 1947. Later scholars outlined how such attempts to inform and persuade could be successful (McCombs, 1972; Mendelsohn, 1973), and recent reviews of decades of campaign evaluations outline the circumstances that can lead to persuasion and change (Friestad & Wright, 1994; Hornik, 1989; Viswanath & Finnegan, 1996).

Cecile Gaziano's recent (1997) review of 97 knowledge gap studies claims that inequalities are increasing, especially in public affairs and health knowledge. Her analysis points out the many "barriers to knowledge acquisition" that have been blamed for gaps among both individuals and groups: attitudes, beliefs, values, (domain, accuracy, and/or breadth of) knowledge, family socialization, community identity and connectedness, socioeconomic status, ethnic or racial group stratification, behaviors, media use, and media exposure. It is these latter two variables—media use and media exposure—that seem to explain the largest effects in most studies of knowledge gaps. She concludes that information sources are often linked to socioeconomic status (SES):

> If knowledge is distributed equally within a social subsystem, equal knowledge acquisition within the system is not assured. Exposure to information sources, especially to print media, frequently correlates with SES and having a greater number of information sources often correlates with knowledge gaps.... [G]reater

access [by the most advantaged] to an array of economic and financial information sources, especially in newspapers, subscription newsletters, and computerized databases, greatly increases their ability to maintain and increase their privileged position, relative to that of the less advantaged. (p. 254)

When some segment of a population seems to be permanently ignorant, their state is labeled *information poverty*. Childers and Post (1975) define information poverty as a "culture" marked by three characteristics: [1] A low level of processing skills, marked by reading, language, hearing, or eyesight deficiencies; [2] Social isolation in a subculture, leading to unawareness of information known to a larger public, reliance upon rumor and folklore, and dependence on entertainment-oriented media like television; and [3] A tendency to feel fatalistic and helpless, which in turn reduces the likelihood of active information seeking. According to Childers, the prototypical member of the information poor

does not know which formal channels to tap in order to solve his problems . . . watches many hours of television daily, seldom reads newspapers and magazines and never reads books . . . does not see his problems as information needs . . . is not a very active information seeker . . . [and] is locked into an informal information network that is deficient in the information that is ordinarily available to the rest of society. (pp. 42–43)

Wilson (1983) says that

information poverty is a typical soft concept, and there is no way of saying what its incidence is; but certainly there are many for whom the world is a tiny place and the supply of second-hand knowledge a very small one. Information poverty can be a self-selected condition freely entered into and willingly endured. (p. 151)

We might question the validity of the information poverty concept as described by Childers and Wilson, because it seems to encompass such a broad swath of human groups and behaviors, most of which could be described more parsimoniously by the word "ignorance." To a degree Dervin (1989) clarifies the concept in discussing "how research categories perpetuate inequities" in society by defining "users" in terms of *systems they are supposed to use*; that is, if the "have-nots" do not use the information sources designed for the "haves," it is their own damn fault.

Whatever the applicability of the term "information poverty," the basic concept underlying it has been invoked and enlarged in a number of books and articles on the information society (e.g., Gandy, 1993; Murdock & Golding, 1989; Schiller, 1996).

The underlying reasons for selection, rejecting or avoiding information, often have to do with "information overload" and the feelings of anxiety that too much input may give rise to. Those are the topics of the next section.

5.4.3 Information Overload and Anxiety

In contrast to a state of ignorance about something, it is also possible to have too much information. According to Everett Rogers (1986, p. 181), *information overload* "is the state of an individual or system in which excessive communication inputs cannot be processed, leading to breakdown." Sociologists and political scientists (e.g., Karl Deutsch, 1963) tend to discuss overload in the "systemic" (or global) sense, in which such a flood of messages proliferate in the in urban environment that many are ignored.

In contrast, the psychological viewpoint on overload (as represented in the writings of James Grier Miller, and Henry Mintzberg, for example) are prone to characterizing it as an *individual* factor. J.G. Miller (1960, 1978), a psychiatrist, attributed some aspects of schizophrenia to information overload. Similarly, management theorist Henry Mintzberg explored the problems created by overload in decision making, noting that

> brains have difficulty processing all the relevant information — there is too much, it may not fit with expectations and previous patterns, and some of it may simply be too threatening to accept. (1975, p. 17)

When too much information confronts us, we cease to pay prompt and careful attention to some of it. It would be wrong to characterize this "editing" of reality as *always* problematic, because we naturally treat information selectively, choosing only a small portion of all possible inputs for our attention. We mark the difference between what we "need to know" versus what would be merely "nice to know" (Paisley, 1993). Such selective attention to environmental inputs is called "filtering" by psychologists Miller, Galanter, and Pribram (1960), who point out that it is often necessary for humans to filter their experience.

Miller classified possible responses to overload into seven categories:

1. Omission — failing to process some of the inputs
2. Error — processing the information incorrectly in some way
3. Queuing — delaying the processing of some information with the intention of catching up later
4. Filtering — processing only that information identified as having "high priority"
5. Approximation — lowering standards of discrimination by being less precise in categorizing inputs and responses
6. Multiple Channels — splitting up the incoming information in order to decentralize the response
7. Escaping — giving up the burden of attending to inputs entirely

A review of voter reasoning by Samuel Popkin points out that voters in United States presidential elections commonly use shortcuts in obtaining information, shortcuts in evaluating information, and shortcuts in storing and recalling information about parties, candidates, and issues. (1993, p. 19)

But we employ these filtering strategies at our peril. Katz and Kahn's (1978) analysis of Miller's strategies points out that most of them have the potential to be maladaptive. Omission, error, and escape are by definition dysfunctional, they point out, whereas queuing, filtering, and approximating *can* be maladaptive if not based on well-considered priorities. In other words, people who use these strategies in their jobs or personal life are likely to make serious errors.

One is reminded of Abraham Maslow's connection between knowledge and avoidance of responsibility (1963, p. 122): "we can seek knowledge in order to reduce anxiety and we can also *avoid* knowing in order to reduce anxiety." Sometimes we would rather not know that we are at high risk for a disease or natural disaster. Public health campaigns that attempt to encourage safe practices by emphasizing potentially harmful effects are often "tuned out" by readers, viewers, and listeners who simply would rather not know. We often think of information as *reducing* anxiety, but such is not always the case. A recent study of the effects of a consumer health information service (Pifalo, Hollander, Henderson, DeSalvo, and Gill, 1997) found that 52% of the people who received information said that it reduced their anxiety about a health concern; yet for another 10%, having the medical information *increased* their anxiety!

George Miller's categories reflect the ways that people *adjust* to having too much information. When adjustment is not possible — where the mechanisms above do not work, and when a person does not have the freedom to abandon a task (such as is the case with students and school assignments) — the result is stress and *anxiety*. If one cannot address the anxiety by taking action, a typical result of anxiety is lowered performance and less enjoyment, whether on the job or in one's personal life. We often feel that way about information because we do not control its production and dissemination, and the environment bombards us with plenty of it. The psychologist William Garner (1962) believed that finding a pattern in information was necessary to maintain peace of mind:

> The search for structure is inherent in behavior.... People in any situation will search for meaningful relations between the variables existing in the situation, and if no such relations exist or can be perceived, considerable discomfort occurs. (pp. 339–340)

Graphic designer and architect Richard Saul Wurman (1989) coined the term *information anxiety* and devoted an entire book to the notion. He defined it as a condition "produced by the everwidening gap between what we understand and what we think we should understand. *Information anxiety* is the black hole between data and knowledge" (p. 34). His definition does not emphasize information overload as a cause of anxiety, but portions of his book do so. It is not merely the huge amount of information that we perceive in our environment, Wurman implies, but also an accompanying feeling of being unable to keep up, no matter what strategies we employ.

The idea that information can cause anxiety and dysfunction is an old one, particularly among scholars of management and human factors. Organizational theorist Karl Weick (1970, 1995) considered information *load* to be one of the crucial properties of the work environment that determine how well people perform on the job. A relevant example of task-related anxiety comes from Meier (1963), who documented a case in which psychological stress and service failures resulted when requests for service exceeded the capacity of a library staff to accommodate them.

Several investigators have identified library research as a producer of anxiety among students. Constance Mellon (1986, p. 162) describes how university students are sometimes stymied in their library research by feelings they described as "scary, overpowering, lost, helpless, confused." Mellon studied 6,000 students and found that about 80% of them associated their first experiences with academic libraries with anxiety. Jiao and Onwuegbuzie (1997) have demonstrated that negative perceptions of the library, library staff, library devices, and one's own abilities predict less library usage, as do certain demographic variables. Kuhlthau (1988a) sees the ubiquity of confusion and anxiety among novice library users as confirming psychologist George Kelly's view of behavior as the *testing of constructs,* in which encounters with new situations frequently begin with negative feelings (Kelly, 1963).

Not surprisingly, Batson, Coke, Chard, Smith, and Taliaferro (1979), and other psychological studies, have found that people are more prone to seeking information when they are in a good mood. We would naturally expect information seeking to be less likely when conducted under a cloud of negative feelings.

How often do searches for information end in failure due to heightened anxiety? Probably a great many. It is easy to imagine calling a halt to research when one is faced with an overwhelming number of information sources and an uncertainty about their relative quality. "Giving up" evokes both the remarks of Charles Perrow and the predictions of cost-benefit analysis: when the effort of gathering information seems too great, we make do with what little information we have. And yet when one stops searching before one has found much of anything, the result may be a complete failure to meet task goals. For this reason, encouraging success in task-related information seeking has been a major concern of information literacy advocates (e.g., Adler, 1999; Breivik, 1998).

In some ways the phenomenon of overload is paradoxical, because humans also seem to have a need for stimulation. Kuhlthau (1993a) notes that while the arrival of new information may cause anxiety, the failure of new information to appear may cause boredom. Zillman and Bryant (1985, p. 158) observed the same pattern in their experiments, writing that "extreme understimulation (boredom) and extreme overstimulation (stress) constitute aversive states." Both understimulation and overstimulation are uncomfortable, but the latter is surely harder on our mental health.

Overload can appear in a number of contexts, work settings being the most common. In studies of office workers O'Reilly (1980) discovered that too much information appeared to degrade the job performance of these workers while it *increased* their satisfaction; in contrast, white collar workers reporting "underload" (too little information to perform their task optimally) also reported lower levels of satisfaction than those workers with too much information.

But everyday tasks also present overloads. Over a quarter century ago, Jacoby, Speller, and Berning (1974) pointed out that the typical American supermarket displayed more than 8,000 unique items—a number that has surely grown much larger in the intervening years. Experiments with hundreds of consumers have confirmed that they use only a limited amount of information—typically just three or four product attributes—in making purchase decisions. Since the early investigations that established overload effects in shopping, market researchers have been studying how this phenomenon differs among subpopulations (e.g., the elderly, children, the poor), whether there is an optimal information load, and which kinds of information should be provided for a given product type (Jacoby, 1984).

Newspapers contain much more information than readers care to digest; two-thirds of the stories they contain are ignored by the public (Graber, 1984). Television stimuli may overload the viewer, at times intentionally in the case of ads and entertainment programming. Yet even watching the news on television may burden the processing powers of the viewer when

> the brevity of information-heavy presentations, and the lack of stopping points to allow reflection and internalization of the story make it almost impossible for average viewers to process more than a fraction of this overload of information (Graber, 1989, p. 148).

Given the proliferation of media in our time, with the World Wide Web now competing with television in the degree to which it juxtaposes strange images on a screen, it is inevitable that overload will become an ever more present distraction in making sense of the world. A January 1999 feature in *Inc.* magazine claimed that there had been over 3,000 newspaper and magazine articles on "information overload" published in the previous two years, and that there were over 15,000 Web sites that mentioned that concept. What irony: even our awareness of overload is overloaded!

In addition to the sheer amount of information in the world, Donnelly (1986) complains that overload has a *qualitative* dimension as well:

> What the rhetoric, fantasy, unrootedness, and unrelatedness of much of our communications images have in common is not what is put into them, but what is left out. They are as light as confetti . . . the problem with this type of information overload is not simply quantity, but the unconnected, excited nature of the images that package and distribute this information, whether it be news of the world or stories of human interest. (p. 186)

Donnelly's complaint is an old one, advanced by critics of television over several decades. The paradox is that at times *we cause our own overload* by choosing to attend to many messages or other stimuli. Our need for stimulation highlights the close link between the concepts of information and *entertainment*.

5.5
Information versus Entertainment

One of the unfortunate blind spots in the study of information seeking has been the artificial distinction between "entertainment" and "information." It is as if the two had nothing to do with one another. And yet they clearly represent, for individuals, some kind of continuum; entertainment clearly has more to do with the subjective end of the continuum posited earlier in this chapter.

Part of this bias against entertainment undoubtedly comes from our tendency to overrationalize human behavior. We prefer to see people primarily as *thinking* beings. Hence we emphasize cognitive factors in behavior rather than affective influences. As will be seen in the review of literature on decision making that follows, it is tempting to overemphasize (and even reify) rationality in human behavior.

Zillman and Bryant (1986, p. 303) define entertainment as "any activity designed to delight," observing further that "no culture of which we have an adequate accounting has been entirely without it." In their historical overview of the topic, Zillman and Bryant (1994) note that early Western philosophy (beginning with Plato), as well as religion, tended to disparage entertainment as morally unfit or stemming from human failings. For example, in his work *Pensées* Blaise Pascal stated that humans have an "instinct which impels them to seek amusement . . . [arising] from the sense of their constant unhappiness" (1670/1941, p. 50). It was not until the 19th and early 20th centuries that amusement began to be studied in a serious, nonmoralistic fashion (for example, by Sigmund Freud, 1905/1960).

Zillman and Bryant conclude that "media idealists" believe that only "serious" uses of information channels are worthy of study, leading to an unfortunate state of affairs in which "effects of entertainment, presumably because of the ready condemnation of entertainment as cheap escapism, have received very little attention from researchers" (p. 321). Intellectual snobbery may be partly to blame. Murray Davis (1986) claims that one predictor of a successful social theory is its invocation of "high-status" explanatory factors, such as "rationality" or "the division of labor." Those that invoke other factors, such as the influence of communication media or information sources, tend to fail:

> few would rank McLuhan in the same league as Marx, Durkheim, Weber, Simmel or Freud. . . . the factor [McLuhan invokes] is anathema to many intellectuals and social scientists who regard television as merely kitsch. (p. 299)

Serious investigation of the utility of print and electronic entertainments (e.g., Radway, 1985, and Rosengren, 1974) are less than three decades old. It was not until a 1981 essay by William Safire (cited in Bogart, 1983) popularized the term "infotainment" that closer attention began to be paid to the ways in which fact and fiction, news and dramatic programming, influence one another. University of Denver professor Harold Mendelsohn (1966) wrote an entire book on the use of the mass media for entertainment. Early in the volume he rails against the cultural bias against the use of entertaining materials:

> the investigator of entertainment is immediately struck by the ascriptive language that is used by layman and scientists alike, by theologian and social critic, by educator and moralist, by legislator and social commentator. For the most part, the language about entertainment emanating from these sources is equally highly negative, disparaging, and admonishing. In short, entertainment is relegated to those rubrics that are ordinarily reserved for the "evils of society.". . . (p. 18)

It is not merely popular society but scholarly discourse that tends to shove entertainment under the rug. In the case of information seeking research, any content that is potentially diverting has often been defined as "out of scope." The information scientist Bryce Allen (1996) argues that the human "need for entertainment" is not even "classified as an information need" because it is commonly assumed that a

> search for information is purposive and thus can be analyzed as a kind of problem solving. These narrow assumptions exclude a range of information behaviors that are not associated with information needs and do not appear to fit the problem-solving perspective. It is quite possible for someone to search for information, not because of an information need, but for some other motivation. People who watch television programs may do so because they need to know what is going on in the world, or they may just want to be entertained and diverted. (p. 55)

Brenda Dervin, too, challenges the artificiality of the information–entertainment distinction made by "experts":

Experts make judgments as to how their "information" will help. They deem some observations as "information," others as "entertainment," some as "factual," others as "opinion." (1983a, p. 27)

In other words, we have a tendency to dichotomize (fact versus opinion, information versus entertainment) phenomena that are really not really that discrete. Making distinct categories of information and entertainment inevitably results in a focus on utilitarian behaviors — as anything labeled as "entertainment" by definition cannot inform anyone and is thus not worthy of our attention. Another commentator, Patrick Wilson (1983) points out the folly of reifying this view of information when he observes that

> for many of us, a good deal of time is spent gathering information in the activity best described as simply watching the world go by. The world is a spectacle, a great show, and watching it is an endless source of entertainment and instruction. We can do it seated in a café, watching television programs, looking out the window, reading newspapers, or traveling. It is a frequent complaint by critics of the mass media that television news is treated by its producers as a form of entertainment, not as a serious instructional form. The charge is correct but the blame is undeserved. (p. 142)

The tendency to treat news as entertainment has received much attention in studies of journalism, whether in print or electronic formats. For instance, Levy and Windahl (1984) found that TV viewers actively seek news (for specific information and general surveillance of the environment), but that they did not actively seek entertainment programming. Rather, entertainment-seeking is more of a *ritualized* behavior that is less goal-directed and more habitual than instrumental use of media (Dozier & Rice, 1984). Cutler and Danowski (1980, p. 269) note that television viewing may be "more for process than content," and can be used to spark interaction with others. It appears that people differ widely in the degree to which they actively seek involvement with media, and that their degree of effort is partly related to the information versus entertainment dichotomy.

In the print realm, Donohew, Nair, and Finn (1984, pp. 279–280) suggest that news reading is preceded by a desire for entertainment seeking; that is, that readers have a need for novel stimuli that first draws them to certain articles, and it is only later that what they read is integrated into their personal cognitive structure. The irony in this is that readers may be drawn toward novel (i.e., entertaining) information that, upon reading, becomes threatening to their belief structure, resulting in increased uncertainty and anxiety, and possibly more seeking of information as a further outcome.

Holmöv (1982) goes even further, claiming that the amount of news reading is largely unrelated to actual knowledge of particular news topics, and that readers of serious news may be reading entirely for the fun of it. An alternative explanation, according to Holmöv, is that readers are programmed to read for the sake of "learning," even though they may not absorb or remember what they read. In any event, it is clear that the desire to be stimulated plays a prominent role in the seeking of "news" (Finn, 1985, 1986).

Brenda Dervin's (1983b) view of the mass media as information sources resembles that of Wilson:

> The picture that emerges is one that shows most citizens, educated or otherwise, essentially relying on close friends and relatives for their information. Media, primarily so-called entertainment television, make up the major portion of the information day. Use of books, newspapers, and magazines is typically low. People seek formal information sources only in a small subset of situations — when all else has failed in coping with a situation or when outside factors force them to. And current efforts to make the information more palatable evidently do not override this essential picture of a "law of least effort" operating. (p. 158)

One has only to consider what actually happens in publishing and broadcasting to realize how artificial and unfair is the sharp distinction between information and entertainment. Most books published are fiction, and just one fiction genre alone, "romances," accounts for perhaps 40% of all mass market paperback sales (Linz, 1992, p. 11). Some estimate the content of broadcasting media to be even more slanted toward fiction: Leo Bogart (1983) estimated prime-time television in North America to be 85% entertainment programming, but with a trend toward more news shows.

Communications researcher Byron Reeves (1989) points out the difficulty of dichotomizing the content of information, whether in print or broadcast media:

> New information cannot be prejudged just because we are aware of the message genre it represents. It is still reasonable to assume that people judge some information as factual, some as lies, and some as fantasy; however, it is likely that these evaluations do not exactly overlap content genre. There is fact in fiction and vice versa. (p. 195)

Catherine Ross (1999) points out that the 10% of the North American population who are "heavy readers" (one or more books a week) read mostly fiction, and primarily for "pleasure." Likewise, a Gallup Organization poll found that 52% of adult Americans read as many, or more, fiction books than nonfiction books (Carlson, 1999). So it is not surprising that most of what public libraries circulate is fiction. Richard Rubin (1998) explains why when he says that

> the public good implies that the citizen has a right to good entertainment, that people have a right to enjoy life, and that the library has a role in promoting pleasure. Certainly the presence of copious fiction, romance, travel, and popularized science and history attests to the strong feelings that librarians have about this dimension of library service. (p. 258)

Public libraries provide fiction because that is what their clients want, despite some ambivalence about devoting scarce resources to nonfactual materials (Rubin, 1998, p. 313). Whether library clients use fiction to complete an educational assignment or for personal growth, entertainment, or to escape an unpleasant reality is not a part of the library's consideration. Fiction plays a key role in attracting people to many libraries in the first place, and that effect in itself has value.

One might imagine that university libraries eschew entertainment materials, and this is largely true. Yet consider that, at least in North American higher education, students choose academic majors based on a mix of practical ("work") and gratifying ("play") considerations. Students who choose to major in the literature of their native language do not always do so to prepare for a particular career. The minority who hope to become a faculty member in, say, English literature, face intense competition for a very few positions. Most students major in literature because the subject matter is interesting, personally satisfying, may provide an insight into human affairs, and so forth—more for reasons of personal satisfaction than for strictly utilitarian purposes.

As Spacks (1985) points out, "Fictional characters and actions, comprehended, may teach us to understand better ... characters and actions that comprise our real-life experience" (p. 23). Ross's (1999) extended interviews with 194 heavy readers uncovered a variety of motivations having to do with personal growth: awakening to new possibilities, finding a role model, confirming self-worth, connecting with the experience of others, accepting one's self and situation, getting the courage to make a change, and so forth. Most of the motivations for reading fiction are affective, rather than cognitive, according to Ross; relevant information tends to be encountered in the text by accident, rather than design.

Although the university library provides many materials that are of an obviously factual nature—most science and mathematics fall into this realm—some portion of academic "information" certainly has "entertainment" content. Recent popular novels, for instance, might be useful for their literary or social content. Even a work of dubious literary value might be acquired if it becomes controversial. For example, two novels by Bret Ellis, *Less Than Zero* (1985) and *American Psycho* (1991) are widely found in university library collections. Yet reviews of these novels have described them as "pointless," "sensationalist," "juvenile," "boring," "mediocre," and "lame." On the other hand, some critics came to their defense, including Norman Mailer. Were the Ellis novels selected for research collections based on their literary value, their controversial history, their entertainment potential, their popularity, or what? Or, more likely, was it related to some combination of those factors? Curry (1994), in fact, uses Ellis's second novel as vehicle for exploring how public libraries deal with the issue of adding controversial books to their collections, noting the interplay among the deciding factors of publicity, popular demand, and reviewers' opinions. These are also factors in university library collection decisions. We might erroneously assume that loftier educational criteria trump all of them, but they do *not*. It is too difficult to judge where information ends and entertainment begins.

Perhaps more obvious instances of the mixing of information and entertainment are media *forms* that deliberately do so to capture audience attention. Film documentaries strive to be interesting and provocative as well as informing. Educational television programming for children (e.g., *Sesame Street*) strives for visual variety to keep the young viewers' attention long enough for the *content* to be be absorbed by them. Public health advocates (e.g., Brown & Walsh-Childers, 1994, p. 407) speak frankly of the need for "edutainment" approaches to antismoking and family planning information campaigns; embedding persuasive messages in dramas, soap operas, and music videos is more likely to capture the attention of the intended audiences, and to hold them long enough for the message to have an effect. The question for information campaigns is "What is the proper mix of education and entertainment?" (Rice & Atkin, 1994). Another example is the increasingly ubiquitous "infomercial" that tries (or at least pretends) to teach us something while selling us a related product or service.

The newspaper *USA Today* has been nicknamed "McPaper," on the grounds that, analogous to fast food, it is popular but not as nourishing as we would hope. Among the criticized aspects of *USA Today* are its colorful graphs, which often convey surprisingly little data; many of these charts use the shape of objects rather than a conventional line to represent trends in data; thus, the upward slope of a whale's back might represent increases in whale populations. The use of such graphics in the business world has provoked Edward Tufte (1983) to condemn them as "chart junk." Tufte even attributes the loss of the *Challenger* space shuttle to a "cute" but misleading chart and a faulty graph that were influential in the decision to launch the shuttle at a low temperature.

It is not merely reading or viewing in which a mix of information and entertainment (or, as Stephenson puts it, "work and play") is to be found. Consider this quotation from a *Wall Street Journal* article in which various financial experts explain to the reporter why money from small investors has been leaving mutual funds and going into individual stocks:

> And don't forget the entertainment value. For many, trading stocks is a source of both pleasure and profits. "The press has played up the dot-com stocks," says Scott Greenbaum, a financial planner in Purchase, N.Y. "People want to participate. Mutual funds are pretty boring by contrast." (Clements, 1999, p. c1)

We would think that investing money and saving for retirement are behaviors too important to approach with anything less than cold-blooded rationality—but apparently they are not. Other types of purchasing behavior are also regarded as providing "psychological gratification" by those who study them (e.g., Bloch, Ridgway, & Sherrell, 1989; Salomon & Koppelman, 1992)

The confluence of information and entertainment is so ubiquitous that we hardly notice it. This is not a new phenomenon, but rather is simply one we have typically chosen to ignore in studying information seeking. Maybe the "most authoritative source" is not what many people prefer when seeking information; maybe they would rather have the most entertaining one. Of course, when "hard facts" are presented in an entertaining manner, we have the best of both worlds.

5.6

Summary

In this chapter we have explored several peripheral concepts and behaviors, including decision making, browsing, relevance, information anxiety, information overload, knowledge gaps, information poverty, and entertainment seeking.

I first discussed the relationship of the decision making and problem solving literature to information seeking, finding some parts of it relevant. Then I moved on to consider the burgeoning number of discussions of browsing and its sibling topics, foraging and encountering.

Whenever information is actively sought, issues of relevance, pertinence, and salience arise. "Context" — a person's situation, background, and environment — partly determines one's perceptions during information seeking. Context will affect the choice of sources that are attended to and meanings that are derived.

Conditions or distractions may also emerge in the information seeking process. There is, for example, a tendency for uncertainty to make us anxious; a feeling of uncertainty comes not only from having too little information, but from having too much information as well. In a behavior possibly related to anxiety (as a relief mechanism), or possibly unrelated (as a result of a human need for play and creativity), people tend to seek out entertainment as well as information. Often they prefer to mix fact and fiction to some degree. The desire to be entertained in turn strongly affects the type of sources to which people turn for their information.

Now that we have been introduced to the principal notions that come into play in discussions of information seeking, we can turn to the theories and models that make use of them. The following chapters consider the models, paradigms, and theories under which information seeking has been investigated.

Recommended for Further Reading

Dervin, B. (1999). On studying information seeking methodologically: The implications of connecting metatheory to method. *Information Processing & Management, 35,* 727–750.

In this rather abstract essay, Brenda Dervin considers the boundaries between metatheory, methodology, and method. A highlight of this interesting article are her comments regarding how her views regarding constructionism have changed over the years.

March, J. (1994). A primer on decision making: How decisions happen. New York: Free Press.

An interesting summary of several decades worth of research on decision making, with special emphasis on the seemingly subjective and irrational aspects of decisions.

Wurman, R. S. (1989). *Information anxiety.* New York: Doubleday.

The influential graphics designer Richard Saul Wurman is noted most commonly for his Access series of travel guides. Those guides emphasize certain principles that Wurman has identified as making information easier to find and digest. For instance, the guides exploit the human preference for spatial analogies, and also make highly effective use of color-coding in presenting information. In this book, Wurman explains how "data glut," and the confusions and anxiety it provokes within us, have made his philosophy of design necessary.

Zillman, D. and Bryant, J. (1994). Entertainment as media effect. In J. Bryant & D. Zillman (Eds.), *Media effects: Advances in theory and research* (pp. 437–461). Hillsdale, NJ: Erlbaum.

Zillman and Bryant have spent much of their careers advancing a rigorous agenda for the investigation of entertaining content in the mass media. This chapter provides a brief history of moral judgments against entertainment in human affairs, which partly explains why it has not been treated as a serious research object until recent decades. They then describe how the concept has been, and might be, approached by investigators of this characteristically human activit.

Three

Models, Paradigms, and Theories in the Study of Information Behavior

6

Models of Information Behavior

Theoretical models of information seeking must address three key issues. First, models should provide a sound theoretical basis for predicting changes in information-seeking behaviors. . . . Second, models should provide guidance for designing effective strategies for enhancing information seeking. . . . Third, models should explicitly conceptualize information seeking behavior, developing rich descriptions of it. Finally, models should answer the "why" question, they should explicitly address the underlying forces that impel particular types of information seeking.

J. David Johnson (1997, p. 104)

It is a widely shared notion that the aim of INS studies is to build models of information behavior which show how different factors or variables influence information seeking.

S. Talja, H. Keso, and T. Pietiläinen (1999, p. 753)

Chapter Outline

6.1. Models
    6.1.1. What Is a Model?
    6.1.2. Models of Information Seeking
6.2. Examples of Information Seeking Models
    6.2.1. Wilson Models
    6.2.2. Krikelas Model
    6.2.3. Johnson Model
    6.2.4. Leckie Model
    6.2.5. Comparing the Models

6.1
Models

In this chapter I highlight five of the best-known, general models of information seeking. Each of them resembles a conventional flow-chart and suggests sequences of events. They all aim to describe and explain circumstances that predict actions by individuals to find information of some kind. Following a bit of background information regarding models, each of the five models will be depicted and explained.

6.1.1 What Is a Model?

Models typically focus on more limited problems than do theories, and sometimes may precede the development of formal theory, which is a reason for discussing them before I address theories used to explain information behavior. An example of a limited model would be one that depicts how research subjects typically navigate through a series of Web pages; such a model may not address how *all* people find information on the World Wide Web (much less how humans find information in multiple circumstances), and yet it might eventually *lead* to a theory of electronic information seeking. An instance of this is Claude Shannon's model of signal transmission (see Chapter 3); it led to both explicit theories of the information content of messages and to vague theories about how mass media had effects on its viewers (so-called hypodermic needle theories; Klapper, 1960).

Models are often defined in relation to theories. For instance, a methods text by Simon and Burstein (1985, p. 53) calls models "minitheories." More will be said about theory in the next chapter; for now let us say that a theory is a set of related statements that explain, describe, or predict phenomena in a given context. Both theories and models are simplified versions of reality, yet models typically make their content more concrete through a diagram of some sort. By illustrating casual processes, models make it easier to see if hypotheses are consistent with what we observe in real life (Reynolds, 1971). Like a theory, a model describes relationships among concepts but is tied more closely to the real world: one changes a model only after first comparing it against the real world and confirming that modifications are warranted (Cappella, 1977).

Models range from the purely pragmatic and descriptive (e.g., a flowchart of how a document moves through a bureaucratic process), to formal models that combine mathematical and pictorial logics (as found in statistical path analyses, such as that used by Lin in 1993 to explain and predict television viewing). Simulations, such as the use of algorithms in artificial intelligence to model certain behaviors (e.g., the perception of shapes in studies of computer vision), are also models (Capella, 1977). Some disciplines have made extensive use of complex models; the study of consumer behavior, which is of some relevance to information seeking, developed and tested four distinct models of consumer information search and decision processes within an eight-year period (Walters, 1974).

As a means of representing and organizing complex processes, models have strengths and weaknesses (Johnson, 1997, pp. 112–113). On the positive side, the depiction of key elements make clear the investigator's approach and selection of explanatory factors. The strength of a model to simplify one phenomenon can become a weakness when it is overgeneralized to another, dissimilar phenomenon. Shannon's model is again an apt example, as it has been applied much more broadly than was intended by its creator.

6.1.2 Models of Information Seeking

Wilson (1999a, p. 250) points out that models of information seeking typically do not embody fully formed theories:

> A model may be described as a framework for thinking about a problem and may evolve into a statement of the relationships among theoretical propositions. Most models in the general field of information behaviour are of the former variety: they are statements, often in the form of diagrams, that attempt to describe an information-seeking activity, the causes and consequences of that activity, or the relationships among stages in information-seeking behaviour.

Many models of information seeking exist, but this chapter will focus on five models from four publications, roughly in chronological order: Wilson (1981, 1999a), Krikelas (1983), Leckie, Pettigrew and Sylvain (1996), and Johnson (1997). Wilson has published several versions of his model, of which I will use the earliest (1981) and latest (1999a; originally published 1996) to show how his thinking has developed.

I have several reasons for focusing on five particular models in this chapter. These models chosen for discussion are more fully developed than most others. A major criterion for inclusion here is that the model *attempts to depict and explain a sequence of behavior* by referring to relevant variables, rather than merely indicates a sequence of events. For instance, the "flow model of information seeking, avoiding, and processing" by Donohew and Tipton (1973) — perhaps the earliest attempt to model information seeking — depicts sequences of events but does not identify important influences (e.g., demographic, task, or psychological variables). The authors explicitly say that their model was not intended to be used for designing investigations of information seeking.

A second criterion is that the models *indicate something about information needs and sources*. The models of search processes by Ellis (1989) and Kuhlthau

(1991) are universally applicable to any domain, each depicting a series of cognitive (and, in Kuhlthau's case, affective) stages or behaviors through which people are thought to move as they find and evaluate information. But their models make no claim to consider many of the factors and variables generally considered in information seeking research: the type of need and what sort of information or other "help" might satisfy it; or the availability of sources and their characteristics. Savolainen's (1995) depiction of "components" important in the study of "everyday life information seeking" also lacks these elements of information needs and sources.

As Wilson (1999a, p. 254) points out, both Ellis's and Kuhlthau's models attempt a different level of analysis than the models in focus here. The Ellis model has been nested in Wilson's (1999a) update of his 1981 model. Kuhlthau's "Information Search Process" model, based as it is on theories of *learning*, is mentioned elsewhere in this book.

I emphasize *general* models. It is often the case that information seeking models are narrowly focused along some dimension — usually by task, discipline, or job. For example, the models proposed by Ingwersen (1996) and Marchionini (1995, p. 59) are meant to apply to a particular *task*, typically searching electronic information in databases or online library catalogs. The models of Voigt (1961), Menzel (1964), Paisley (1968), and Orr (1970) were intended specifically to portray the information seeking of scientists. Among the newer publications, the "addressing information needs" model of Hernon (1984) and the search model of Ellis (1989) were intended to apply to social scientists; the latter was later extended to some physical scientists (1993), while that of Baldwin and Rice (1997) was meant to apply to security analysts — surely a tiny population. I do examine one such restricted model below (by Leckie Pettigrew, and Sylvain, 1996) because the population it applies to is rather large ("professionals") and I judge it to be more general than the authors imply.

In keeping with the theme of this volume, I will consider general models of information seeking, applicable in multiple contexts, occupations, roles, and knowledge domains. The models by James Krikelas (1983); Leckie, Pettigrew, and Sylvain (1996); David Johnson (1997); and Tom Wilson (1981, 1999a) meet these criteria. I will begin with Wilson's first model, published in 1981.

6.2

Examples of Information Seeking Models

6.2.1 Wilson Models

A series of models by Wilson (1981, 1994, 1997, 1999a) reflects trends in the theory and practice of information seeking research. Their evolution makes them particularly interesting to analyze and compare with those of other researchers.

The Wilson models examined here have appeared in their current forms fairly recently, even though they are based on diagrams originally published in 1981. The first model (Figure 6.1) identifies 12 components, starting with the "information user" — although Wilson makes clear that he is interested in much more than "use" itself.

Wilson's information user has a need, which may (or may not) stem from his or her level of satisfaction (or dissatisfaction) with previously acquired information. Wilson suggests that the perceived need then leads the user into a cluster of activities, the most straightforward of which is to make direct demands on sources or systems of information. The results of these demands lead either to success (in which case the information is "used") or to failure, which is presumed to be a dead end, as information that is not "found" cannot be used. It is odd, however, that "failure" of "demands on other information sources" are not depicted as directly feeding back to "need" by way of another arrow.

An important aspect of Wilson's model is the recognition that information is exchanged with other people (a process he calls information transfer) in the

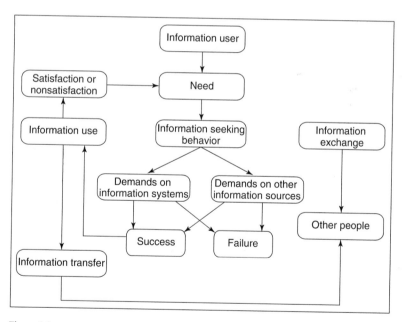

Figure 6.1

Wilson's first model. (Adapted from figure on page 257 Wilson, T. D. (1999). Models in information behaviour research. *55(3)*, 249–270. Used with permission of Aslib and the *Journal of Documentation*.)

course of information use and seeking behaviors. As he points out, relatively little attention has been paid to informal transfer of information among individuals. But other people are an important source of information in many circumstances, even during direct interaction with a formal system such as a library.

In describing his model, Wilson acknowledges its limits:

> [I]t does little more than provide a map of the area and draw attention to gaps in research; it provides no suggestion of causative factors in information behaviour and, consequently, it does not directly suggest hypotheses to be tested. (1981, pp. 251–252)

The second of Wilson's models (1999, pp. 256–257) presented here is based on another of his diagrams from 1981, this time emphasizing the complex *context* of information seeking (à la Dervin). Wilson identified the factors in this model in research from other fields, including "decision making, psychology, innovation, health communication and consumer research" (p. 256).

Wilson's second model is a complex one (Figure 6.2). It invokes explicit theories at points to explain the following three aspects of information seeking:

• Why some needs prompt information seeking more so than others (stress/coping theory, from psychology)

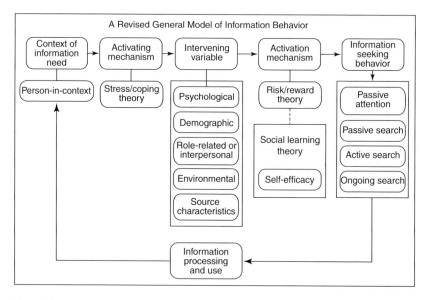

Figure 6.2
Wilson's second model. (Adapted from figure on page 257 Wilson, T. D, (1999). Models in information behaviour research, *55*(3), 249–270. Used with permission of Aslib and the *Journal of Documentation.*)

• Why some sources of information are used more than others
(risk/reward theory, from consumer research)

• Why people may, or may not, pursue a goal successfully, based on their
perceptions of their own efficacy (social learning theory, from psychology)

We might think of Wilson's "activating mechanisms" as motivators:
What motivates a person to search for information, and how and to what
extent? These motivators are affected by intervening variables of six types:
psychological predispositions (e.g., tending to be curious, or averse to risk);
demographic background (e.g., age or education); factors related to one's social
role (e.g., whether one is acting as a manager or a mother); environmental
variables (e.g., the resources available); and characteristics of the sources (e.g.,
accessibility and credibility).

An important aspect of Wilson's new model is that it recognizes that
there are different types of search behaviors: passive attention, passive search,
active search, and ongoing search. These differentiations parallel comments
made earlier in the book regarding different modes of information seeking:
simply being exposed to relevant information versus actively looking for it.
By "information processing and use" Wilson implies that the information is
evaluated as to its effect on need, and forms part of a feedback loop that may
start the process of seeking all over again if the need is not satisfied.

6.2.2 Krikelas Model

Perhaps the most widely cited model is that of James Krikelas (1983). The
Krikelas model contains 13 components. The causal process generally flows
downward, with some provision for feedback loops. In describing his model,
Krikelas asks us to

> imagine a situation in which a person becomes aware of a state of uncertainty
> about a problem (question, issue) and attempts to reduce that state of uncertainty to
> an acceptable level. The cause of that uncertainty may be a specific event or simply
> an ongoing process associated with work, ordinary life, or both. Naturally, for many
> issues much of the information required would already exist in the individual's
> memory; only a small part of a person's ongoing needs would produce an outward
> behavior that we might identify as information seeking. Furthermore the level of
> "urgency" and the perceived importance of the problem ... would influence the
> pattern of information seeking.

The Krikelas model (Figure 6.3) thus claims to be a general one that would apply
to "ordinary life"). At the top of the model (implying a beginning) are the twin
actions of "information gathering" and "information giving." The activities of
information gathering come about in response to deferred needs, which in turn
have been stimulated by an event or the general environment of the seeker.

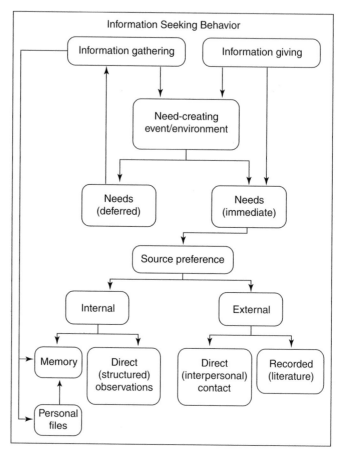

Figure 6.3
The Krikelas model. (Adapted from Figure on page 13 of Krikelas, J. (1983). Information seeking behavior: Patterns and concepts. *Drexel Library Quarterly, 19*, 5–20. Used with permission of the College of Information Science and Technology, Drexel University, Philadelphia, PA.)

Krikelas sees any attempt to isolate individual elements of the environment as "hopeless." The results of information gathering are directed to memory or, in physical form, to some kind of personal file or other storage mechanism. Thus, information gathering is the acceptance and holding of "stimuli . . . in storage to be recalled on demand. Such efforts may have a purpose (directed but not problem-specific)" (p. 9).

Yet, as revealed in his discussion, what Krikelas mainly has in mind are efforts to keep up with literature relevant to one's work — which is a more specific, occupation-oriented version of information seeking than we would prefer to see. But his model at least does not restrict itself to one type of occupation. For Krikelas, information gathering *does* have a more general and less formal purpose too, which he describes as "an attempt to continually construct a cognitive environmental 'map' to facilitate the need to cope with uncertainty" (p. 9). Hence Krikelas identifies uncertainty as a key concept.

Information giving is defined as "the act of disseminating messages [which] may be communicated in written (graphic), verbal, visual, or tactile forms" (p. 13). About *information giving* Krikelas says little, except to point out that individuals are typically both senders and receivers of information, and that neither role is independent of the other.

As mentioned earlier, information gathering comes about because of an environment or event that creates needs. Some of these needs can be deferred, which leads to storage in memory and/or physical media, while other needs are immediate, or at least are dealt with as though they were urgent. To meet an information need, the searcher is assumed to consciously select a source. As Krikelas describes in his scenario, the source could be *internal* (i.e., oneself) or *external* (other people — communicated with through some kind of medium).

Although Krikelas makes a hard distinction between "direct (interpersonal) contact" and "recorded (literature)," it is important to realize that today's expanded media environment blurs such boundaries. Although the main and preferred source of information for people is still likely to be face-to-face conversation, "direct contact" could occur over a telephone or a videophone, or by way of e-mail, voicemail, or a videotape as well. Krikelas undoubtedly had in mind the main kind of "recorded" material one found in libraries two decades ago (books and journals), but the increased ease of asynchronous interpersonal communication makes the distinction between "recorded" and "live" difficult. Even the issue of what kind of human communication is truly interactive is a complex one (Durlak, 1987).

One appealing aspect of the Krikelas model is its simplicity. The model is a simple, one-dimensional flow-chart in which all of the arrows travel in one direction (i.e., there are no two-way influences among the boxes) and no one part of the process encompasses another.

Of course, simplicity implies oversimplification, and leads us to some comments and questions about the model. The environment could be depicted as surrounding the other factors, rather than appearing as a box in the middle of them. The manner in which "information giving" is depicted as separate from "sources" seems odd. Wouldn't those persons and objects that impart information be considered sources? Likewise, it is unclear whether "personal files" can also include "recorded literature" as well as notes made by oneself— one would assume so. Therefore, it seems like a distinction is being made between a formal information system (such as a library) and an informal one (such as the contents of an individual's home or office). It is also notable that *characteristics of the seeker* are not considered in the model. Demographic variables such as age or education might affect information seeking; perhaps these could be considered to be a part of the "need-creating environment."

Although the Krikelas model could be applied to ordinary life, it nevertheless retains the flavor of a "library search model" in the way it seems to depict the decision points along the path to either the reference desk (Immediate Need → External Source → Librarian) or the library collection (Immediate Need → External Source → Stacks). Perhaps it is more applicable to the information seeking of students or professionals in some work-oriented context. The Krikelas model *does* have the virtues of simplicity and comprehensiveness: it emphasizes the important roles of own's own memory and of information received from others, along with the formal sources typically emphasized in such models.

6.2.3 Johnson Model

Johnson's model contains seven factors under three headings. It is pictured as a causal process that flows from left to right (Figure 6.4), beginning with four "antecedent" factors under two categories. The significance of Johnson's model components is not obvious in its depiction, but rather is explained in

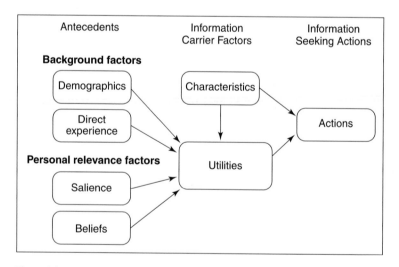

Figure 6.4
Johnson's model. (Adapted from figure on page 34 of Johnson, J.D. (1997), *Cancer-related information seeking*. Used with the permission of Hampton Press of Cresskill, NJ.)

depth in his writings (e.g., 1997). Therefore, I will need to say somewhat more about this model than the others.

In Johnson's model, it is the antecedent factors that motivate a person to seek information. The first two are grouped together under the label of *background* factors. One factor is *demographics*: one's age, gender, and ethnicity, along with socioeconomic variables like education, occupation, and wealth. Historically, such demographic variables are the mainstay of social research, which tries to find patterns among the behaviors, beliefs, and attitudes of populations based on correlations with such demographic variables. In any consumer-oriented research, dividing a population by such variables is referred to as *audience segmentation*.

In certain contexts such information may be useful in characterizing and predicting information use, such as gender differences in the context of health information. However, Johnson points out that characterizing information usage on the basis of ethnicity is problematic, because of both overlapping group membership and within-group differences. Dervin's (1989) arguments also cast some doubt on the usefulness of any demographic categories in stereotyping the search for information.

A background factor far more difficult to characterize is one's *direct experience* in relation to the domain of interest. The concept of experience brings us into issues of knowledge representation and memory that are too complex to consider here; suffice it to say that typically one starts out knowing *something* — perhaps little or a great deal — about the phenomenon of interest, as well as about the ways in which one can find out information about it. Thus, a key concept under the heading of experience is the *social network* of the individual with an information need: who do I know who might know the answer to my questions, or know how to find out? For example, Johnson focuses on information about cancer, and thus a prime determinant of knowledge is "who do I know who has had cancer?" A majority of families are touched by the disease in some way, and the occurrence of cancer in one member of the family often motivates other family members to seek information about treatment, so cancer information has high levels of social significance.

Just as the first and second factors are grouped together, the third and fourth fall under the heading of *personal relevance*. These include *beliefs* about the topic and the *salience* of information about the topic. Both are dependent on a person's degree of knowledge — or, conversely, on their state of ignorance — about the topic.

Johnson makes an important distinction about ignorance when he asserts that it is different from "ignoring, which often happens when an individual consciously knows that a problem exists, but chooses not to confront it" (p. 56). This is because ignorance by itself is not typically a motivator for information seeking. People are only motivated to seek information when they both know that they are ignorant *and* the missing information becomes salient. As noted earlier, sometimes people prefer to be ignorant, particularly in matters of health. A confounding problem is that we often believe information that turns out to be flawed; these kind of *false truths* can suppress or distort information seeking.

The concept of *salience* implies that information is not only perceived to be relevant to a need, but that it is also applicable. In Dervin's terms, information that is salient is that which could be used to bridge a gap, solve a problem, or resolve a troublesome ambiguity. Thus salience is the key motivator in deciding to look for information (Johnson, p. 72).

Beliefs are important in information seeking because they constrain the individual's thinking and level of motivation regarding information seeking. The beliefs that people have has about the world and their selves determine the answers to questions like: "Is there is a problem?" "Is there a solution?" and "Can I change my situation?" Beliefs are not only about facts, but also about our relation to the current situation: our degree of control over events, our self-efficacy. If we do not believe that knowing more about a topic will allow us to affect a change, then we are not likely to seek information. Conversely, feeling that we can solve a problem will motive us to find the means to do so — which includes gathering information.

The second column of Johnson's model, *information carrier factors*, encompasses the factors that have preoccupied many older studies of information seeking: the *characteristics* and *utility* of the information channels selected and used by seekers. As Johnson highlights (p. 101), what information seekers are concerned about is the content of the information, not the channel through which it arrives. So the academic preoccupation with the nature of sources and why people select them has been criticized by Dervin (1989) and others as distracting attention from the user of information and their particular needs, which typically do not map neatly onto individual channels or sources. To make matters more complicated, channels (in a narrow sense of the term) have proliferated greatly due to the application of computers and telecommunications to older media.

The literature that defines a "channel" is often confusing. The primary distinction usually made among the older typologies is between interpersonal (face-to-face interactions with other people) and mediated (print and mass media). Where something like e-mail would fall within such a dichotomy is debatable: it is mediated by a technology, yet can be very much like a personal conversation. In a similar vein is the telephone, which Johnson discusses as a "hybrid" of interpersonal and mediated channels. We will examine the channel classification problem further in other chapters.

For now it is important to note that in almost any information seeking context there is a strong preference for information that comes directly from other people. Use of other channels tends to be predicted by the *social presence* they offer, that is, how much they are perceived as being like a face-to-face conversation with another person, or as Johnson puts it "the extent to which they reveal the presence of other human interactants and can capture the human, feeling side of relationships" (Johnson, 1997, p. 92).

Johnson says relatively little about the *utility* of channels. His main point is that channels are selected on the basis of their match with the seeker's needs, and with expectations regarding likely satisfactions to be obtained. For research on the choice of print media, potential utility is equated with "interest, usefulness and importance for achieving one's goals" (p. 100). One might choose to read a book for advice on health, for example, because it is expected to offer information that friends are unlikely to have. Johnson cites studies suggesting, however, that ease of accessibility often wins out over authoritativeness (the latter implying, apparently, better utility); the public still receives much of their health information in watered-down form from the mass media, despite the availability of health professionals to answer their questions and despite the general preference (noted earlier) for interpersonal channels.

The final component of Johnson's model is *information seeking actions*. Searches for information involve conscious choices among channels and sources, but also imply processes, feelings and a whole host of other behavioral and cognitive elements. Even simple choices among channels and sources may be characterized by the number chosen and the depth to which they were examined. Thus, the study of actions taken by any one individual in quest of information is likely to be involved and result in a unique case study from which generalization is difficult.

Johnson seems to adopt a sense-making perspective when discussing information seeking. He describes, for example, how all information seeking takes places within a context and must be understood as influenced by context. He also notes the fuzziness of the concept of *context* itself. Following Dervin, Johnson asserts that information seeking begins only when a person perceives a gap in his or her existing knowledge. At that point, seeking actions begin and the factors in the model begin to apply.

Johnson's empirical tests of his model in both health and decision making point out both the importance of context and the difficulty of modeling information seeking. With some audiences and tasks, for example, the antecedent variables had little influence on actions taken; in others their effects were significant. Data gathered on channel selection suggest that in many cases one channel may substitute for another; thus the characteristics of channels may be less important than scholars have previously thought. Among a group of engineers the motivational issues are perhaps less driven by problem than by role: information seeking is an end in itself because it is an activity expected of certain individuals in a social system.

Johnson also notes that among the more general difficulties inherent in studying the actions people take when they look for information is a distinction between *active* and *passive* acquisition. It is difficult, if not impossible, to know whether someone has found information in their environment (active acquisition) or, instead, has retrieved it from memory (passive acquisition).

Johnson concludes that his model may be improved through the inclusion of feedback loops between actions and antecedents. Antecedent factors continue to shape the searching actions as they proceed, while actions may simultaneously modify the nondemographic antecedent factors of experience, belief, and salience. That is, "information seeking is clearly a dynamic process, with an individual's level of knowledge changing as it goes on," along with the perception of the gap.

An important consideration in Johnson's model is that it is intended to be the basis for empirical research, and is currently being used in a series of health care studies funded by the National Institutes of Health through the University of Kentucky. Although it is a very general model intended to apply to adult populations, it is less applicable to *work* situations. However, another book by Johnson (1996) discusses information seeking research within work organizations and suggests ways that his model can be used in such settings.

6.2.4 Leckie Model

The model by Leckie, Pettigrew, and Sylvain (1996) resembles Johnson's model in its surface format yet is more like the Krikelas model in its limitation to a range of people — in this case, "professionals." It features six factors connected by arrows, all but one of them unidirectional (i.e., "outcomes" and "characteristics of information needs" influence each other in mutual fashion). The Leckie model is depicted as flowing from top to bottom (Figure 6.5). The causal process begins on the top with "work roles," which in turn influence "tasks."

The meaning of some of the terms is not explained in very much depth in the accompanying text, although some of their significance can be inferred from the authors' review of other studies (seemingly the main objective of their article) and their discussion of commonalities among those studies.

Given that the Leckie model is restricted to "professionals" (such as doctors, lawyers, and engineers), it is not surprising that "work roles" and "tasks" are thought to be the prime motivators for seeking. Although individual demographics (age, profession, specialization, career stage, and geographic location) are not depicted in the model itself, they are said to be "variables that influence or shape the information needs," along with certain aspects of the need itself. The later include the context, frequency, predictability, importance, and complexity of the need situation. Because the emphasis is on the facts

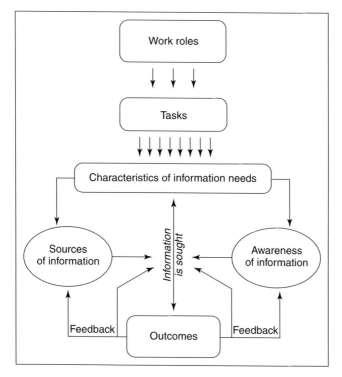

Figure 6.5
The Leckie, Pettigrew, and Sylvain model (used with permission of the publisher.)

of working life, *beliefs* or *attitudes* are seemingly less relevant than they are in the Johnson model (which considers health information among the general population), so their role is not discussed.

In the Leckie model, needs create an awareness of information sources and/or content, and thus motivate a person to examine those. Here, the most important variables are thought to be the familiarity and prior success with the source (or the search strategy employed), along with the trustworthiness, packaging, timeliness, cost, quality, and accessibility of the source(s).

The Leckie model depicts information seeking behavior itself as a two-way arrow labeled "information is sought." The end results of information seeking, labeled "outcomes," affect most other aspects of the model through feedback loops to "sources," "awareness," and "information is sought."

The diagram by Leckie, Pettigrew, and Sylvain is clearly intended to feature *work-related* processes. Thus, it has somewhat limited applicability to everyday life information seeking.

6.2.5 Comparing the Models

Given their differences in vocabulary, emphasis, and age, the five models we have reviewed are difficult to compare in great detail. Obviously they differ in many respects from one another. To start with, four of them (Krikelas, Leckie, and the two by Wilson) come from the literature of information studies, whereas the other one (Johnson) originates from the discipline of communication. There are other differences that stem from the intended applications of the models.

The Krikelas model shows its age in the way that it privileges document and/or library usage ("recorded literature"). Its value was in placing the use of literature in the context of other sources of information, such as other people and one's own observations and memories.

The first Wilson model, in contrast, does not explicitly refer to documents as sources but rather refers to "systems," "sources," and "people" — making it somewhat more general than that of Krikelas. Beyond those notions emphasized by Krikelas, Wilson's 1981 model introduces the concepts of the results of seeking (i.e., success or failure), and the degree of satisfaction of a need. It ignores questions of source characteristics and personal preferences among them.

Wilson's second model introduces factors that his first model ignored. It identifies not only potential personal variables and modes of seeking, but also suggests relevant theories of motivations behind search behaviors.

The Johnson model is much more general than the earlier three. Like that of Krikelas, this model has the virtue of simplicity: it moves in a chain-like sequence in one direction, with only one of the factors possessing more than one arrow (suggesting direct causation). It lumps together potential intervening variables as "antecedent" factors, emphasizes source characteristics, and does not attempt to spell out the various forms that "actions" might take. (Of course, these aspects *are* spelled out in texts that accompany the model.)

The Leckie model is the only one deliberately limited in scope to a range of people — in this case, "professionals." It features six general factors, most notably "work roles"and "tasks." Given its emphasis on tasks, the model by Leckie, Pettigrew, and Sylvain emphasizes *work-related* information seeking and so is limited in its applicability to the behaviors of a general population in everyday activities.

All five models suggest useful insights for analyzing the studies described in the following chapters. Table 6.1 compares several aspects of the five models. The Krikelas model is simple, straightforward, and is widely recognized. The Wilson model was intended to illustrate the broad scope of information behavior, and is thus both more general than that of Krikelas and more useful as a heuristic diagram for designing empirical studies of information seeking; the

Table 6.1
Comparing the Five Models

Author(s) of Model	Number of Factors/Boxes	Main Antecedent[a]	Main Factors or Variables[a]	Main Outcomes or Behaviors[a]
Wilson, 1981	12	Need	Seeking; purchase	Demands; success; failure; use; transfer; satisfaction or nonsatisfaction
Wilson, 1996	14–20	Context; Person-in-Context	Psychological; demographic; role-related; environmental; Source characteristics	Passive attention; passive search; active search; ongoing search; Seeking, use and processing
Krikelas, 1983	13	Need-creating event or environment	Internal and external sources	Observations; interpersonal contact; use of literature, memory, or personal files; giving; gathering
Johnson, 1997	7	Demographics; direct experience; salience; beliefs	Information carrier utilities and characteristics	"Actions"
Leckie, Pettigrew, & Sylvain, 1996	6	Work roles; tasks	Needs; sources; awareness	"Outcomes"

[a]These compare the vocabulary used by the model-builders, not necessarily the meaning of their terms.

model itself was an outcome of several years of field research. Wilson's model is also fairly specific in its reference to applicable theories regarding motivations and behaviors. The Leckie model is obviously useful for studying the work of professionals, and although the explanations behind it are somewhat brief it concisely reviews many relevant studies that invoke some of the variables included in the model.

Among all five, Johnson's model has the most extended (book-length) explanation and by far the most references to theories and empirical studies on the affects of certain variables in information seeking. As a diagram, however, it is somewhat cryptic.

Earlier it was noted that models sometimes lead to theories. None of the authors of these models have claimed, as yet, that their efforts have led to an explicit theory of information behavior. In the next chapter we will consider what explicit theories *have* been invoked in information seeking studies.

Recommended for Further Reading

Johnson, J. D. (1997). *Cancer-related information seeking.* Cresskill, NJ: Hampton Press.

This 239-page volume examines the information seeking literature from the perspective of health communication. With over 600 references, many of them to more general literature on the topic, Johnson's book makes a useful reference resource.

Leckie, G. J., Pettigrew, K. E., & Sylvain, C. (1996). "Modeling the information seeking of professionals: A general model derived from research on engineers, health care professionals and lawyers. *Library Quarterly, 66,* 161–193.

The authors review dozens of studies of the information needs, uses, and habits of medical doctors, nurses, other health professionals, engineers, lawyers, and other professionals.

McQuail, D., & Windahl, S. (1993). *Communication models for the study of mass communication* (2nd ed.) New York: Longman.

As the title implies, this book focuses on models used in research on mass communication. It contains several models relevant to information behavior as well as a wide range of other examples and explications of models.

Wilson, T. D. (1999). Models in information behaviour research. *Journal of Documentation, 55*(3), 249–270.

Wilson explains the evolution of models of information retrieval and seeking research, with many cogent examples.

7

Perspectives, Paradigms, and Theories

The word "theory" threatens to become meaningless. Because its referents are so diverse — including everything from minor working hypotheses, through comprehensive but vague and unordered speculations, to axiomatic systems of thought — use of the word often obscures rather than creates understanding.

Robert Merton (1968, p. 39)

Unfortunately, so much work has been done without reference to any theoretical framework that it must either be ignored completely or the "miscellaneous" category would be very large indeed.

Tom Wilson (1994, p. 17)

Chapter Outline

7.1. Perspectives and Paradigms
    7.1.1. Perspectives
    7.1.2. Paradigms

7.2. Theories
    7.2.1. What Is a Theory?
    7.2.2. Levels of Theory: Grand to Grounded

7.3. Sources of Theory in Information Seeking

7.4. Some Relevant Paradigms
    7.4.1. Zipf's Principle of Least Effort
    7.4.2. Uses and Gratifications
    7.4.3. Sense-Making
    7.4.4. Media Use as Social Action
    7.4.5. Play Theory and Entertainment Theory

7.5. Other Theories

7.6. Summary

Just as a pyramid depends on its foundation to provide stability for the rest of the structure, scholars rely on basic assumptions regarding the nature of reality and the purposes and methods of investigation. This chapter introduces the basic building blocks of inquiry and examines their relationship to specific traditions of social research.

Obviously the topics in this chapter could constitute a book in itself. I hope this brief overview of perspectives, paradigms, and theories will enable those readers unfamiliar with such issues to better grasp the concepts associated with information seeking and how they have been studied.

7.1

Perspectives and Paradigms

7.1.1 Perspectives

We live in a time of intellectual ferment. For those who study the ways in which people act and think, there are a variety of perspectives available for the taking. Dervin, in an introductory chapter to a volume of studies of information seeking "in context," identifies some of these perspectives and methodologies:

> symbolic interaction, pragmatics, system theory, qualitative studies, cultural studies, hermeneutics, political economy, phenomenology, constructivism, interpretive anthropology, transactionism, contextual psychology, ethnography, perspectivism, situationalism and postmodernism. (1997, p. 15)

Dervin consciously chose the words "perspectives" and "methodologies" because her list consists of a mix of labels for different philosophies, methods, research traditions, and in only one case, something explicitly labeled as "theory." Dervin's list reflects the situation surrounding information seeking research, in which there has been relatively little direct usage of formal theory; instead, more emphasis has been placed on schools of thought (e.g., "postmodernism") and methodologies (e.g., "qualitative studies"). Where theory *is* invoked, it tends to be borrowed from other disciplines.

Fifty years ago there was little diversity in most social scientific and humanistic investigations of human behavior and cognition. North American psychology, for example, was in the grips of a behaviorist paradigm of research that strongly restricted what could be taken as evidence regarding the mind (Gardner, 1985). Most disciplines in the "human sciences" (Foucault, 1972) had a fairly restrictive range of theories and methods that were widely accepted by research practitioners, particularly those influential in determining the publication of study results.

The good news is that we now have a much more diverse array of assumptions, approaches, theories, and methods from which to choose. However, that is also the bad news, because there is disagreement on what kinds of perspectives or actions are most appropriate when doing research that involves people. Questions of the importance, purpose, ethics, and meaning of research abound.

For example, there are those who argue that people (e.g., their observable behaviors) should be the object of our study; others say that we can be more objective by observing only the artifacts of human behavior (e.g., the traces or records that people leave behind); yet other researchers say that there is no such thing as "objectivity," because the investigator is inextricably bound to the "object" of their study, and the best we can do is collect "contextualized" narratives or discourses in the domain of our interest.

Perhaps most unsettling is that there is seemingly widespread disagreement about the philosophical underpinnings of research on human behavior (Budd, 1995; Dervin, 1997; Lincoln & Guba, 1985; Pavitt, 1999; Sandstrom & Sandstrom, 1995; Slife & Williams, 1995). Often debate about philosophical foundations centers on simplistic dichotomies, such as "explanation" versus "understanding" (Stewart, 1997), "quantitative" versus "qualitative," "positivist" versus "naturalist," or "empirical" versus "interpretive" (Pavitt, 1999). Some seasoned researchers are reconsidering their assumptions regarding ontology (the nature of *reality*), axiology (the nature of *values*), epistemology (how we *know*), and methodology (how we *find out*).

It is not the goal of this volume to enter into an extended debate about the nature of reality or knowledge. I will assume that ontological and epistemological differences exist among researchers of information seeking (whether or not they are discussed in their publications) and instead will focus on the choices of topics, theories, models, and methods they have made in their studies. For further background, the reader is encouraged to explore some of the sources mentioned above.

7.1.2 Paradigms

One of the difficulties in discussing the concept of theory is that it has layers of meaning. That is, that there are not only different *levels* of theory but there are also overarching concepts like "paradigm" that are sometimes conflated with the notion of theory. I will discuss paradigm and theory in the context of a hierarchy that places paradigm in the most global and encompassing position, and "observations" at the bottom — the most limited and narrowest context (Figure 7.1):

Paradigm/Perspective/Tradition
Grand/Formal Theory
Middle-Range/Grounded Theory
Observations

Figure 7.1
A hierarchy of theory.

"Paradigm" is a term popularized by the work of the historian of science Thomas Kuhn, a historian of science, who wrote the influential book *The Structure of Scientific Revolutions* (1962). Kuhn has been criticized for using "paradigm" in as many as 21 different ways (Masterman, 1970). Nevertheless, the term has become immensely popular as a way of describing (among other things) the various points of view that researchers take in their search for explanations.

We might, for example, speak of a "conflict" paradigm that theorizes that conflicts among individuals or groups underlie much of social interaction; many social theories, such as that of Karl Marx, share this view. Alternatively, the "exchange" paradigm says that much of life is based on individual calculations of the costs and benefits of undertaking a certain action, whether the action is speaking to a stranger or getting married. Or we might speak of a "sense-making" paradigm that stresses how people create both meaning and social structure in their lives through their interactions with others. Thus, asking another person for help in solving a personal problem may reveal a solution merely by sharing views of the problem; it may also create friendship or dependency.

However vague the definition of a paradigm, it is an essential concept for describing research on information behavior. For one thing, it is not possible to talk about competing theories, or schools of theories, in information seeking research. The field is simply too diverse for that, and formal theory is invoked relatively rarely. Second, the notion of paradigm highlights the connections between research and the purposes and beliefs of the investigator. For example, a distinction has been made between "critical" and "administrative" research traditions (Lazersfeld, 1941; Rogers, 1982). Let us consider two different cases. One researcher's worldview may be that it is not up to him or her to question the nature of power relationships in the world, but rather to investigate "administrative" problems that appear. Perhaps the researcher's focus is why more people do not make use of a social service agency, and their goal is to explain such behavior and perhaps even to make things run more smoothly.

In contrast, another investigator may feel compelled to challenge and expose what they judge to be an unfair social relationship — the failure of a government agency to provide the kind of services that most people need — with the intention of raising public awareness of an injustice and perhaps, in so doing, to change the world. Although these two researchers might choose similar methodologies to address the research problem as they have defined it, they would be using dissimilar theories and operating under quite different paradigms.

Some researchers prefer to avoid the term "paradigm" as much as possible. Anthony Giddens (1989) prefers the word "perspectives," Hans Gadamer (1976) "traditions," and Brenda Dervin (1991) "analytics," when referring to strategies that guide research. Yet others may use the term "approach" to describe both assumptions and the range of methodologies employed in investigations.

I will employ the word *paradigm* in the Kuhnian sense of a "tradition" for the practice of research (Masterman, 1970, p. 62); "perspective" will be taken to mean the same thing. Traditions, perspectives, and paradigms then subsume models and theories.

7.2
Theories

7.2.1 What Is a Theory?

Theories are explanations. They are generalizations. Theories are statements that try to explain relationships among various phenomena (Baker, 1999; Mullins, 1973) and from which one can make inferences and deductions. Theory results from an interplay among ideas, evidence, and inference (Chaffee, 1991, p. 14).

Beyond these simple statements, more formal definitions of "theory" show wide variance in usage among researchers. Kerlinger (1973), for example, defines theory as

> a set of interrelated constructs (concepts), definitions, and propositions that present a systematic view of phenomena by specifying relations among variables, with the purpose of explaining and predicting the phenomena. (p. 9)

Simon and Burstein (1985, p. 52) adhere to Kerlinger's complex definition when writing of disciplines like physics and economics, pointing out that "there is no theory unless it is a *body of theory*," a set of well-established definitions, assumptions, and systematically organized propositions. Nearly all explanations of theory invoke the idea that it must be systematic — relying on more than just a single, simple statement. Yet Simon and Burstein also note (as did Merton, quoted at the beginning of this chapter) that theory

> has a looser meaning; it often refers to a loosely organized collection of hypotheses ... and sometimes is even used to refer to almost any speculative thinking offered as an explanation. ...

Many examples of this "looser" invocation of theory can be found in everyday life, such as when a friend asks "What's your theory about the

Kennedy assassination?" But such vague use of the term also abounds in scholarly discourse. Without passing judgment on whether the author's usage met formal definitions of theory, Pettigrew and McKechnie (2001) examined 1,160 information science articles that invoked theories, hypotheses, frameworks, principles, approaches, conceptualizations, or models as explanations. The results ranged from single concepts (e.g., "relevance" and "information needs") attributed to particular authors, to formal theories identified with major figures like Dewey, Freud, Giddens, Habermas, and Merton. Only a minority would probably meet the formal criteria for "theory."

Reynolds (1971) points out that the term theory is commonly used in at least four different senses: [1] A set of "laws" that are "well-supported empirical generalizations"; [2] An "interrelated set of definitions, axioms, and propositions"; [3] "Descriptions of causal processes"; or [4] Vague concepts, untested hypotheses, or prescriptions of desirable social behaviors (pp. 10–11).

Each of these descriptions has its place, and for this chapter I will mainly assume Reynold's second definition, which is the *vade mecum* (received or "handbook") view of theory more typical of social research: as an "interrelated set of definitions, axioms, and propositions." Human behavior is seen as complex and requiring a special vocabulary to describe it. Statements about phenomena (e.g., propositions and hypotheses) are used to guide observation and the development of theories. Claims about human behavior are recognized as being probabilistic or conditional (e.g., time and context bound), rather than deterministic.

The first notion — that of theory as a set of laws — is not very satisfactory for the study of human behavior, in which relatively few absolute regularities have been found to exist. That the social sciences see themselves as uncovering universal and absolute laws regarding people is a claim that few, if any, contemporary social researchers would make.

The third conceptualization of theory — as causal processes — will only be used in the limited sense of a *model*, as discussed in the previous chapter. It is difficult to establish causation in human behavior, especially a phenomenon such as information seeking in which many important aspects cannot be observed. However, it is certainly possible to identify key factors and their likely sequences and interactions in the process of information seeking. Models make these aspects explicit and thus guide research design and theory development.

7.2.2 Levels of Theory: Grand to Grounded

A theory is something more specific than a paradigm; the question is, How specific? In a quotation at the beginning of this chapter, the eminent sociologist Robert Merton complains that social scientists do not always share the same definition for *theory*, much less the same goals regarding the kinds of theory to construct. He was particularly concerned about continued attempts to create "grand" theories that tried to explain large segments of human behavior in a universal way. In their emulation of major social theorists like Karl Marx, Herbert Spencer, and Talcott Parsons (Merton, 1968, p. 44), other scholars have tried (and failed) to predict actions and tendencies across too many individuals, cultures, and societies. Recently Skinner (1985) has pointed to a "return of grand theory" in the work of still-living scholars like Jürgen Habermas and Anthony Giddens, who refuse to restrict theory to limited questions, methods, and evidence.

Davis (1986) describes how "successful" (i.e., both famous and widely applied) social theories addressed major problems (e.g., economic change) and also overturned previous assumptions about the topic (e.g., that religion is largely unrelated to economic activity, a view challenged by Max Weber). Davis examines the grand theories of Karl Marx, Emile Durkheim, and Max Weber, among others, to show how broadly they were applied to explanations of behavior. For example, Durkheim's theory that the "division of labor" played a primary role in social organization has been used to study phenomena in government, law, religion, science, and the arts, as well as to explain the very notion of individuality among humans. His notion that intermediate social groups, such as occupations, helped to hold society together in the face of declining community and family ties could be considered a "grand theory."

Rather than trying to reinvent or replace the broad theories that emerged during the 19th century, Merton argued that we should concentrate on the development of limited, "middle-range" theories; such theories function at a higher level than a testable hypothesis, but deal with limited settings, remain close to the level of observable phenomena, and offer the potential for aggregating findings.

To illustrate the middle-range, Merton offered the example of "reference group theory," the idea that individuals judge themselves by referring to the standards of significant people in their lives, rather than to some absolute criteria that apply to all humans. Referential judgments constitute a phenomenon that can be readily observed in many social settings and across cultures, such that results can be compared and related to other sociological concepts, such as class.

Theories tied to observation and meant to apply in a particular area of application are called "grounded" by Glaser and Strauss (1967). In their study of the awareness of death, Glaser and Strauss demonstrated middle-range theory is constructed by "grounding" it in observation—that is, building a theory by relying more on observed data than on abstract ideas. However, the so-called "grounded theory" approach does not rely entirely on *induction* (reasoning from particulars to generalizations), but rather moves back and forth from data-gathering to *deduction* (reasoning from generalizations to particular cases) to test the theory.

   Grounded theories may serve as building blocks for formal and grand theories, while remaining close enough to real-world observations as to give us confidence in their validity. An example from information seeking would be Kuhlthau's (1993a) model of the search process. Kuhlthau's model was developed through close observation of the ways that information seekers construct knowledge by tying it to what they already know, as they pass through various stages of uncertainty and understanding. Itself derived from a general, psychological theory (i.e., Kelly, 1963), Kuhlthau's model could be expanded into a more general theory of information seeking through further observation and development. To see how these ideas evolve, let's begin by looking at the foundations of information seeking theories.

7.3
Sources of Theory in Information Seeking

   Krikelas (1983) merely states the obvious when he says that there is no single theory of information seeking that would make possible easy comparisons among studies. Similarly, Chatman (1996, p. 193) laments that

> we have no central theory or body of interrelated theories we can view as "middle range."... it would appear we are currently focused on the application of conceptual frameworks rather than on the generation of specific theories.

   Most studies of information seeking (and indeed virtually all of those studying information *use*) have made no explicit claims to theory. Instead, most of them have been administrative in nature, concerned with collecting data for the purpose of improving operations in information agencies such as libraries. Despite this, there is no shortage of theory from various disciplines that might be applied to the search for, and use of, information.

   Zweizig (1977) says that theories applied in information seeking studies tend to come from three disciplinary sources: sociology, mass communication, and psychology. Zweizig does not provide examples, but the first two sources can be readily seen in the work of a single researcher: Elfreda Chatman. Chatman (1990) invokes Durkheim's sociological grand theory of the division of labor, in particular the concept of *alienation* as it was articulated by Durkheim and related social theorists (e.g., Weber and Merton). Chatman studied the flow, expression, and use of information among janitors, relating their responses to indicators of alienation such as anomie (i.e., normlessness), powerlessness, meaninglessness, isolation, and self-estrangement. In other works she has made use of Rogers's (1983) diffusion of innovation theory, stemming from both sociology and communication (Chatman, 1986) to describe the diffusion of job information among workers, and uses and gratifications theory (e.g., Katz & Foulkes, 1962), also from mass communication (Chatman, 1991), to explore how janitors used the mass media, and other sources, for information and entertainment.

Some kind of psychological theory is implicit in much of information behavior research. Many of the studies of individual use of information retrieval systems (e.g., Daniels, 1986) and libraries (Mellon, 1986) assume a psychological (or cognitive) perspective, whether or not they cite a specific theory or theorist. Indeed, much of information seeking research could be said to relate to, if not descend directly from, a single psychologist: Sigmund Freud.

Freud's (1922) "pleasure principle" encapsulates the view that both social and psychological activities stem from a need to reduce emotional tension — a type of "drive reduction." People seek pleasure to alleviate unpleasant internal states — painful feelings or felt desires — and thus reduce tension (McQuail and Windahl, 1993, pp. 288–289). Donohew, Nair, and Finn (1984), for example, believe that the acquisition of information is an automatic response in us, and typically brings pleasure. Because information seeking implies that people take action in response to some disquieting internal state (e.g., an "anomalous state of knowledge" or "visceral need"), the pleasure principle could be said to apply universally to information seeking.

Perhaps because it is common sense that people seek pleasure and avoid pain, Freud is rarely cited in information behavior research. Among those psychologists who *are* cited at times are Bruner (1973, 1990), De Mey (1982), Kelly (1963), Miller (1968, 1983a, 1983b), and Piaget (1952). Some of the work of John Dewey (e.g., *How We Think*, 1933) could be included among the psychologists, even though Dewey is more noted for his contributions to philosophy and education.

Besides sociology, psychology, and communication there are other disciplines that either build on those above (e.g., management and business, especially consumer research) or that have closely related theories (e.g., economics and linguistics). In short, there are a number of academic fields that serve as sources of paradigms and theories for the study of information seeking and some of their theories have been actively used in such research.

In the way of theory "native" to the study of information seeking, we have Chatman's own theory-building efforts. The first was her "theory of information poverty," based on her experiences in studying aging women in a retirement community (1992). This theory consists of six propositions, such as "people who are defined as information poor perceive themselves to be devoid of any sources that might help them" (1996, p. 197). Lately Chatman has developed a complementary theory of "life in the round" (1999).

It would be nice if theories and their paradigms could be sorted into neat typologies so that we can compare them. Some typologies have been devised, particularly in sociology—see, for example, Burrell and Morgan (1988), Little-john (1983), Mullins, (1973), and Rosengren (1989)—but without much agreement. Where information seeking is concerned, the sheer diversity of theoretical borrowings makes a single, comprehensive comparison impossible. Therefore, the remainder of this chapter describes a selection of paradigms and theories that have been, or could be, applied to the investigation of information behavior.

7.4
Some Relevant Paradigms

In addition to the social and psychological theories already mentioned in this chapter, there are a number of paradigms that have been, or could be, used in information seeking research. At least the first three of these might be grouped together under the general heading of "psychological perspectives." However, most of them retain some measure of both psychological and social aspects, and overlap to such a degree that it is difficult to categorize them fairly. They will be discussed, therefore, under the following headings:

- Principle of Least Effort
- Uses and Gratifications
- Sense-making
- Media Use as Social Action
- Play Theory

7.4.1 Zipf's Principle of Least Effort

Several authors (e.g., Bierbaum, 1990; Buckland & Hindle, 1969; Gratch, 1990; Hardy, 1982; Mann, 1993; Poole, 1985) have pointed out that a body of work by philologist George Zipf (1949) functions as a paradigm or grand theory for studies of information seeking. Poole's (1985) analysis of the information seeking literature found that 40 of the 51 studies he sampled lent their support to Zipf's Principle of Least Effort. Although Zipf did not claim that his principle was a formal theory, Poole demonstrates that it has the earmarks of a general theory, and that propositions may be derived from it.

According to Zipf (1949), each individual will adopt a course of action that will involve the expenditure of the *probable least average* of his work—in other words, the least effort. Zipf supports his theory with evidence from various aspects of human behavior, most of it based on studies of language usage.

For example, the statistical distribution of words in the text of James Joyce's *Ulysses* follows the kind of pattern on which Zipf based his theory.

Ranked by frequency of appearance, the 10th most common word in *Ulysses* appears 2,653 times; the 100th most common word, 265 times; and the 1,000th, 26 times. The result is a distribution of data in which the number 26 appears as a constant. Another example comes from the 1930 U.S. census, in which a ranking of the 50 most populous cities revealed that the second-largest had one-half the population of the first, the third-largest one-third of that population, and so forth, down to the 50th-largest city. Again, a suspiciously nonrandom distribution.

Zipf called such relationships "harmonic distributions" and posited that any human allocation of resources (words in documents, documents in files, or people in cities) tends to fall into such arrangements. The reason has to do with economy of effort; humans tend to use short, common words whenever they can (leading to highly frequent usage of just a few words) rather than longer words that take more effort. Zipf used the analogy of an artisan seated at a desk; while working, the artisan would tend to pick up tools and lay them down in order of how frequently they were used, with the most frequently used ones kept closest at hand (Kenner, 1986).

A corollary is found in both libraries and office filing systems, in which people tend to use, borrow, or cite the same documents again and again; this has become known as the "80–20" (or sometimes "70–30") rule: 20% of the documents account for 80% of the use. Communication media (e.g., phones, e-mail) exhibit a similar phenomenon: a minority of the population of users (20–30%) tends to account for the majority of messages sent (70–80%). Studies of prominent scientists by Robert Merton and others (summarized in Merton, 1973) found that just a few of them received a disproportionate amount of citations, funding, and other resources (the so-called "Matthew Effect"). And to echo the first example, in Henry James's novel *The Ambassadors*, 75% of the text is composed of 27% of its vocabulary (i.e., 176 of the 665 unique words that make up the entire novel) — again, an approximation to 70–30.

Internet Web sites exhibit harmonic relationships in two ways. First, Broder *et al.* (1999) have found that about 28% of all Web sites are more "central" in terms of the strengths of their links to other Web sites — approximating the 70–30 ratio. Second, it is clear that just a few sites have vastly larger numbers of visitors, while the rest taper off in a harmonic distribution (Huberman, Pirollis, Pitkow, & Lukose, 1998).

Evidence for the Principle of Least Effort can be found in other realms of information behavior. Like links to Web sites, requests made in libraries also seem to exhibit harmonic relationships: Dorsch and Pifalo (1997) demonstrate that just 25% of medical journals accounted for 74% of the requests in their state of Illinois. The same is apparently true of citations among authors. Howard White (2001) has invoked Zipf's principle to explain patterns of citations that authors make to the works of other authors, based on the notion that supportive (i.e., positive, agreeing) references require more explanation (i.e., effort) than citations that are critical of the works of others. That would explain the relative rarity of critical (i.e., negative) citations.

In the practical realm, the human tendency toward economy of effort is often exploited by systems designers. Indexers of documents, whether working by instinct or with term rankings, may establish cutoff points to determine which words are indexed and which are not. Very common words like "and" and "the" are not indexed; rarely occurring words like "onomatopoeia" or "calliope" or "sesquicentennial" will not be indexed either, unless they have some central relationship to the theme of the text. What are indexed are the words in between the common and the rare—the so-called "middle-frequency" terms (Salton & McGill, 1983)—identified by a derivative of Zipf's research, the Rank-Frequency Law of document vocabulary. Similarly, some office managers arrange files by frequency of use so that the most frequently used files are at the front of each drawer, rather than filing them alphabetically or in some subject arrangement. System designers sometimes refer to "Mooer's Law," (1960) which suggests that no one will use an information system if using it is more trouble than it is worth.

An oft-cited example of Least Effort at work is when a professional asks the nearest coworker whether any new reports have been published on a topic, rather than conducting a thorough search of the literature in question. As Joan Durrance put it,

> research on information seeking has consistently shown that people prefer interpersonal over print sources. That finding came as a surprise to researchers 30 years ago when they looked at information seeking among scientists. An appropriate research question might be: "Why do information seekers choose oral channels first?" People may simply take the path of least resistance. (1988, p. 161)

Another example is when the professional consults last year's handbook simply because it is in her office, when the latest version exists just down the hall. Allen's (1977) study of 19 research and development engineers found that they operated on Least Effort basis when selecting information channels, and easy accessibility was more highly related to the frequency of use than was the quality of the information. Rosenberg's (1967) study of industrial personnel found patterns similar to those observed by Allen. Orr (1970) makes comparable observations about scientists. And decades of reviews and studies (see, for example, Chen & Hernon, 1982) document a strong preference among information-seekers for interpersonal sources, who are typically easier and more readily accessible than the most authoritative printed sources. Similarly, Dervin (1983b, p. 158) refers to the tendency of people in "relying on close friends and relatives for their information" as demonstrating a "law of least effort."

However, here we are concerned with theory rather than practice. Zipf notes that the importance of his Principle of Least Effort lies in its universality in regards to human behavior. Over the long haul, humans tend toward a surprising efficiency in their allocation of effort. This tendency has enormous implications for studying the use of information.

A related approach has been called the *cost−benefit paradigm*. This perspective attempts to explain behavior in terms of a tradeoff between the effort required to employ a particular type of strategy (e.g., eliminating choices by looking at their worst possible outcomes), and the quality of the resulting action. The notion of a cost−benefit trade-off in information seeking is similar enough to the Principle of Least Effort that the two paradigms are sometimes conflated. There are differences between the two, however, not the least of which is that Least Effort claims to be a *descriptive* principle that applies across many aspects of human behavior, whether goal oriented or not. The cost−benefit approach is more *normative* in its assumptions, and is applied toward conscious decisions regarding the expenditure of effort to achieve some goal.

According to Andy Hardy (1982), the cost−benefit paradigm proposes that as people seek information they select information channels based on their expected benefits weighed against likely costs. Under this paradigm, information seeking is highly rational and emphasizes a calculation of the benefits to be gained from obtaining the most complete and accurate information. An example is the doctor who considers whether she can render an immediate diagnosis based on the symptoms that are presented by the patient, or whether it is worth the time and money (assuming the patient must pay expenses) to run further laboratory tests before deciding on a treatment plan. The doctor must estimate the likely value of the information yielded by the tests versus the monetary cost and any potential dangers due to a delay in treatment.

In contrast, the Principle of Least Effort, which is chiefly pragmatic and not at all optimal, predicts that seekers will minimize the effort required to obtain information, even if it means accepting a lower quality or quantity of information. Hardy's study of 968 U.S. Forest Service professionals found that they were oversensitive to the costs involved in acquiring information and undersensitive to issues of information quality. On average, Hardy found, the Forest Service workers held acquisition costs twice as important in their decisions as they did the quality of the outcome (i.e., the benefits to be derived from reliable information).

7.4.2 Uses and Gratifications

Elihu Katz, Jay Blumler, and Mickael Gurevitch, in their preface to 1974 collection *The Uses of Mass Communication,* describe a "perspective," "approach," or "model" that has come to be known as "Uses and Gratifications." This paradigm is concerned with

- the social and psychological origins of *needs*;
- the way in which needs generate *expectations* regarding *sources* of information and entertainment;
- the resulting manner in which people *expose themselves to media*; and
- the resulting *gratifications* of needs, along with other *consequences*, many of which may be unintended.

The Uses and Gratifications approach to research has several characteristics that distinguish it from other approaches to the study of mass media (see Levy & Windahl, 1984, and Palmgreen, 1984). First, it is assumed that the media audience plays an *active* role in the selection of sources to attend to, rather than being the passive target of messages. Second, it is the person who uses the medium, rather than the medium that uses the person. That is, if media have "effects" it is at least partly because people choose to be affected by them. Third, the various media are merely a portion of the range of options individuals may have for fulfilling needs, in a universe dominated by interpersonal contacts and intrapersonal activity. Thus, if one has a need for "entertainment" one could just as well play a card game — whether by oneself or with another individual — rather than watch TV or read. Fourth, media use can be studied by asking people directly about their interests and motives, rather than collecting data surreptitiously and/or inferring motives to observed behavior. Finally, it is best to suspend value judgments about the significance of various media and their content until the users of the media are studied on their own terms; dismissive judgments about the value of certain kinds of magazine, books, films, or television programs do not lead to a better understanding of what those sources *do* for people, and why they choose one source over another.

McQuail and Gurevitch (1974) point out that the Uses and Gratifications perspective can be approached via three research traditions: functional, structural–cultural, or action–motivation. In keeping with theories of drive-reduction (like Freud's Pleasure Principle, discussed previously), the seeking of gratifications clearly has a functionalist flavor: audiences choose among media and content to accomplish the goal of gratification. People actively invoke that function of the mass media — usage doesn't just "happen" to them. An example comes from Cutler and Danowski (1980), who demonstrated that as people got older they watched election coverage on TV less for the content and more for "process gratifications" — to engage their senses, to connect with the culture, and so on. Actual interest in political "facts" may decline, but not the watching of election news.

The structural–cultural tradition emphasizes the media environment that a culture has created, and how those limit choice and invoke trade-offs in uses and gratifications. For example, Williams (1987, p. 224) suggested that differences in gratifications found in two national studies of political news is due to "structural differences in the ownership, operation, programming, or content of newspapers and television in Great Britain as compared to the United States." Another key consideration is the role that media choices play in the forming of one's personal identity. Here Williams cites results suggesting that the unavailability of the telephone may move some individuals to make more use of television content to form their personal identity.

The action–motivation tradition is found in the application of expectancy models such as that of Fishbein and Ajzen (1975). In fact, Rayburn and Palmgreen (1984) say that these two research traditions have enough in common to be merged. Expectancy models assume that beliefs and evaluations partly determine the gratifications sought, which in turn influence how media content is chosen and consumed. Williams (1987, p. 225) characterized the expectancy model as saying that

> either behavior, behavioral intentions, or attitudes [are] a function of (1) expectancy — the perception of an object's possession of a particular attribute or that a certain behavior will lead to certain consequences — and (2) evaluation — that is, the degree of "effect, positive or negative, toward an attribute or behavioral outcome" (Palmgreen, 1984).

Some information seeking research lends itself to more than one of these approaches. Dervin's sense-making research, for example, involves expectations about the utility of various sources for reducing uncertainty and bridging gaps in daily experience. It also concerns the way that information needs are affected by a changing environment (Williams, 1987, p. 226).

The uses and gratifications perspective has been criticized on several grounds. Most fundamentally, concepts like needs, uses, motives, and gratifications lack some clarity, and may be used somewhat differently across investigators (Rubin, 1994). Uses and Gratifications is not yet well connected to other theories of beliefs, attitudes, motivations, and behavior, many of which are surely relevant and could serve to ground these central concepts. Uses and Gratifications offers a rather simplistic explanation of why we choose certain media and content, namely "we use X because X gratifies us" (Williams, 1987). The studies themselves tend to be very individualistic, making it difficult to explain more than the behaviors and reports of those persons studied.

Investigations conducted under the Uses and Gratifications perspective tend to be compartmentalized by audience and/or medium, without many syntheses across studies. For example, Rubin's 1983 study of the uses of television found five common motivations: information, entertainment, escape, habitual passing of time, and companionship. Would these uses apply equally to fiction-reading? "Companionship" would seem to be less plausible, as nearby TV viewers are more open to interaction than nearby readers.

But a few studies make comparisons among such behaviors, across media. Eugenia Zerbinos (1990), for example, invokes Uses and Gratifications in her study of the uses of newspapers versus videotext, finding more specific information seeking and better recall of facts from the electronic news, but she discusses only the surveillance functions of these media. Kirsty Williamson (1997, 1998) employs the theory to study a wide range of personal, institutional, and mass media sources used by the elderly.

Another difficulty with Uses and Gratifications lies in its assumption of a universally *active* audience. Experience sampling studies by Csikszentmihalyi (1990; see Chapter 9) find little evidence to support the notion of an active television audience, finding instead that TV viewers report feeling relaxed and relatively inattentive.

Despite these possible shortcomings, Uses and Gratifications is highly relevant to the study of information seeking. Elfreda Chatman (1991) offers an example of an application of this approach. Chatman conducted interviews with janitors to test six propositions about the activities and gratifications of the working-class poor, including their use of the media. She concluded that a theory of gratification was applicable to the study of information seeking. In particular Chatman found that a focus on gratifications helps us to understand how the poor define and deal with problems in their lives, and why it is that they are not more active in seeking information. Two important reasons for this seeming passivity were that [1] respondents tended to see problems as being resolved by "luck" rather than their own efforts, and [2] they failed to see external sources of information, including libraries, as relevant to their everyday problems.

7.4.3 Sense-Making

Whether sense-making constitutes a paradigm, a theory, or a methodology—or all of these—is open to question. Brenda Dervin, the primary proponent of this approach to information seeking and use, notes that "some people call sense making a theory, others a set of methods, others a methodology, others a body of findings" (Dervin, 1992, p. 61). This text will treat sense-making primarily as a paradigm that emphasizes naturalistic methods (Dervin & Nilan, 1986; Park, 1994) and that has theoretical grounding in the constructivist learning theories of John Dewey (1933, 1960) and Jerome Bruner (1973, 1990). Dervin acknowledges additional intellectual debts to many other scholars, including Richard Carter (1965, 1973), Clifford Geertz (1973), Anthony Giddens (1984, 1989), Jürgen Habermas (1979, 1984), and Robert Taylor (1962, 1968), to name a few.

A main tenant of sense-making is that information is not "something that exists apart from human behavioral activity." Rather, information is "created at a specific moment in time-space by one or more humans" (Dervin, 1992, p. 63). Unlike other approaches to information seeking that see information as something "out there" that is transmitted to people (as Dervin says, an information "brick" that is put into a human "bucket"), sense-making sees information as something that is constructed internally in order to address discontinuities in life (see the earlier discussion in Chapter 3 of "gaps"). This approach uncovers the problems that people experience in life and how they face those obstructions.

The core of the sense-making research could be said to derive from the philosophy and learning theory of John Dewey (1960). Dewey's philosophy of instrumentalism emphasized pragmatic problem-solving through actions carried out in the real world. He saw both science and individuals as cycling through five phases of reflective operations: suggestion, intellectualization, hypothesis, reasoning, and then testing a solution by action. Conscious connection and interaction with objects and ideas led on the collective level to productive science, and on the individual level to thinking and learning.

George Kelly (1963) advocated similar views in his theory of personal construct formation, a key component in his Theory of Personality. Kelly saw a person's behavior as strongly shaped by their mental constructs of the world and how it operates; constructs are knowledge structures that "enable us to anticipate events and predict outcomes" (Kuhlthau, 1988a, p. 233). Kelly's construction of knowledge also hypothesized five phases in thinking: encountering a new experience; initial feelings of confusion that result; the formation of a working hypothesis; taking actions that result in either reconstruing a (faulty) hypothesis or validating a (true) one; and, finally, assimilation of the findings with previous knowledge, resulting in changes of behavior. Jerome Bruner's (1990) phases of interpretation and perception parallel, to a large degree, those of Dewey and Kelly.

Sense-making has incorporated Dewey, Kelly, and Bruner's notions of life as an encounter with problems and discontinuities in knowledge, and also the view that information is something we create through our interactions with the obstacles in our progress through life. It is an active, process-oriented view of learning and being. The end-product of the process—sense—is equated with knowledge but also with opinions, intuitions, evaluations, and (effective) responses.

An example of sense-making research is reported in Dervin, Nilan, and Jacobson (1982) and Dervin, Jacobson, and Nilan (1982). Donors of blood were asked to describe the process of donating: what happened, what questions they had, and how they hoped the answers to their questions would help them. By documenting a time-line of the steps in the process and analyzing responses to the interview questions, the researchers were able to demonstrate that each step in the process had a distinctive pattern of questions and information usage. The results were used to create a touch-activated, question-answering computer screen that would address donors' information needs at each stage in the process. The answers given included not only the perspectives and responses of the medical personnel, but also those of previous donors, another useful outcome of the research.

In summary, the sense-making research agenda produces detailed knowledge of the strategies by which individuals cope with problematic situations. In doing so, sense-making research places a high value on the insights gained by the persons under study, as they reconstruct their solutions to past problems.

7.4.4 Media Use as Social Action

Closely allied with sense-making, and building upon the Uses and Gratifications approach, is an allied perspective in communication studies: Media Use as Social Action (abbreviated as MASA in Renckstorf & McQuail, 1996), also known as Renckstorf's Social Action Model (McQuail & Windahl, 1993, p. 143). Like sense-making, MASA differs from Uses and Gratifications research in downplaying the idea of "normative" (or objective) behavior that can be used to judge an individual's actions. Like sense-making it borrows from symbolic interactionism and phenomenology a microsociological perspective with an emphasis on interpretation. Proponents of MASA are clear, however, that it "maintains a commitment to the possibility of scientific generalization about patterns of audience behavior" (Renckstorf & McQuail, 1996, p. 13).

The MASA perspective involves three primary assumptions. First, "the mass media, by distributing messages, can only offer information about things, actions and/or events to their audiences: information that may be accepted by individuals as objects of their environment that need to be perceived and thematized — or not. Thus, mediated messages are not viewed here as stimuli causing responses [but rather] as environmental objects, requiring interpretations." Second, that information is assumed to be part of a "sense-making symbolic environment" in which the relative importance of a message "is determined by social situations and circumstances as well as ... individual characteristics and personality." Third, "viewers, listeners and readers are seen here as the factual creators of messages" not "pure recipients" (Renckstorf & McQuail, 1996, p. 15).

MASA theorists see the phenomenological sociology of Alfred Schutz (1964, 1967) and Berger and Luckmann (1966) as a source of method, along with borrowings from the symbolic interactionism of Blumer (1986), Becker (1970, 1982), and Goffman (1956, 1975), the ethnomethodology of Garfinkel (1967), and the ethnographic methods of Spradley (1979). In its adoption of Schutz's assumptions and methods, MASA is similar to the long-standing research programs of Dervin, Wilson, and others.

As yet not many studies have been conducted under the MASA rubric, and most of these are assembled in a volume edited by Karsten Renckstorf (1996).

MASA researchers tend to highlight regularities in the use of media, particularly television viewing, for various purposes. For instance, can we generalize about how television is used by viewers living alone, versus those with housemates? Housemates influence not only what is viewed but *how*. Television programs become the basis for social interaction in multiperson households, in that they are used as vehicles for conversation and information exchange. MASA researchers make a basic distinction between such "social" uses of media and "instrumental" uses (such as deciding what car to buy), and the "intrinsic" use of media for entertainment.

The tie to information seeking lies in the *motivations* for media use, according to Bosman and Renckstorf (1996). They describe a study that asked 950 respondents what they were currently "worried about." Their answers, coded as "interests," correlated highly with consumption of certain kinds of programming. Bosman and Renckstorf conclude that "solving problems" is a key motivator, just as it is in Dervin's sense-making approach. "Having a problem" was a determinant of information consumption, contingent upon whether respondents believed that information could really help them address the problem. Respondents who reported "financial worries" did *not* believe that information alone could help them with their money problems.

MASA — and the sense-making and Uses and Gratifications approaches as well — are concerned with entertainment in the context of what it *does* for people. Another paradigm focuses more centrally on entertainment: Play Theory.

7.4.5 Play Theory and Entertainment Theory

As noted in earlier chapters, the artificial distinction between information and entertainment masks an area of investigation that, although it is clearly relevant to information seeking, has not been fully addressed. Thus, it would be useful to have a theory that addresses both phenomena. Stephenson's Play Theory does just that.

Stephenson (1967) launched a research program based on the notion that humans manipulate their intake of entertainment and information to serve their emotional needs. What makes an input "pleasurable" is subjective, however; one person may enjoy reading today's stock market results (whether or not it is their duty to do so), while another person may find such content unpleasant to some extent. Most messages contain some elements of both pleasure and pain, play and work, depending on the perception of the individual recipient. As Mendelsohn (1966) noted, when we have a choice we tend to choose entertainment over information. Even while engaged in serious work we may prefer to have our information presented in a stimulating format and style — "sugar-coated" to some degree.

Play Theory is more applicable to the viewing of entertainment media than to the usual concern of the information seeking literature with factual information; nevertheless, such theories have been usefully invoked to study events like newspaper reading as a quest for both facts and amusement (see Dozier & Rice, 1984).

At the heart of Play Theory is not only the idea that humans tend to seek pleasure and avoid pain, but also that they tend to mix work with play. Stephenson lamented that the study of communication media had been preoccupied with persuasion, public opinion, and social control; rather, he saw media as used for satisfying individual "wants," and hence a need for "a play theory and not an information theory of mass communication" (p. 3).

An example of pain-avoidance can also be found in newspaper reading; Stephenson quotes findings from a study of reader motivation that suggest "people feel lost and anxious without a newspaper ... fearing the worst, they are reassured to read each day that everything is well" (p. 147). The newspaper may have been replaced to a large degree by electronic media, but the hypothesis is still valid: we are reassured to learn that no major disaster has occurred, particularly one that might directly affect us.

Similarly, Kay (1955) noted that the reader of a newspaper may obtain the immediate satisfaction of a vicarious experience (i.e., reading about the good or bad things that happened to others) and/or the delayed reward of learning how to avoid or "handle" certain kinds of situations in their own lives. Kay also thought that news offered the challenge of "intellectual puzzles" — such as trying to understand *why* something happened — and might offer an escape or catharsis (abreaction) from the pressures of the day; both types of motivation help explain why people may read about the same things (or even the very same text) over and over again. Shepherd, Duffy, Watters, and Gugle (2001) have reviewed decades of research on newspaper reading and invoke Play Theory to describe human behavior in this arena.

Stephenson devotes an entire book to elaborating his Play Theory and the Q-sort methodology used in its application; however, relatively few other studies have been conducted using his framework explicitly. Stephenson does report several of his own studies that documented the entertainment functions of newspaper reading. A fresh investigation in this vein by Elaine Toms (1999) invokes Play Theory (along with other theories of motivation) in describing her experimental results on electronic newsreading. Toms finds support for a curiosity- or play-driven interpretation of browsing text:

There was no "need," no anomalous state of knowledge and no knowledge gap evident. This was simply an information gathering experience without expectations or predicted outcome . . . novelty stimulated curiosity (and thus exploration). (p. 202)

Studies of "creativity"(e.g., Getzels & Csikszentmihalyi, 1976; Ghiselin, 1952; Mansfield & Busse, 1981; Weisberg, 1986) also consider the nature of play. Creativity investigations have their own identity and yet overlap with information seeking studies; they interview some of the same categories of people: writers, painters, sculptors, musicians, and scientists.

The applied literature on how to encourage creativity contains concepts and language that should be familiar to students of information behavior. Robert Fritz (1989), for example, emphasizes the ability of creative people to break away from commonly held views of reality. Fritz says, in essence, that what keeps most people from behaving creatively is the "reactive-responsive orientation" that we all develop as children in the normal course of socialization. In brief, we learn to follow the "path of least resistance" (the title of Fritz's book) by avoiding "trouble" — chiefly conflict with others. Creativity springs from an ability to abandon, at least temporarily, the *problem orientation* of the reactive-responsive mindset. Creative behavior comes from deep within, an urge that transcends the situations facing us and makes us *go beyond our current context*. Theories that attempt to explain creativity and imagination (e.g., Johnson, 1987) are well worth exploring in relation to information behavior.

A final play-related research agenda is that of University of Alabama professors Dolf Zillman and Jennings Bryant. Zillman and Bryant have advanced a related theory of deliberate media exposure that is well-supported by experimental results. Variously called "Entertainment Theory," "Mood Management Theory," or "affect-dependent stimulus arrangement" (Bryant & Zillman, 1984; Zillman & Bryant, 1985, 1986, 1994), it has been used by those authors and many others in various experiments and observational studies.

Mood Management Theory hypothesizes that people use entertainment sources (particularly television programming) to relieve stress by replacing anxious thoughts with positive (or at least distracting) stimuli. Anderson, Collins, Schmitt, and Jacobvitz (1996), for example, applied it in a three-part study that found some effects for families and differential effects for men and women, depending on the study design. For example, stress and TV viewing were more highly correlated among men, while among entire families stress was associated with watching more comedy and less news. Potts and Sanchez (1994) also found their subjects watching less news programming when they were depressed. Other researchers (e.g., Kubey & Csikszentmihalyi, 1990) have found that the mood-altering effects of TV tend to be less positive and shorter in duration than activities like reading or playing games with others.

Many investigations that highlight entertainment also fall under the Uses and Gratifications paradigm. One example of such entertainment-oriented research is that of Carolyn Lin (1993), who investigated what pleasures teenage television viewers hoped to obtain from viewing, and what gratifications they actually obtained, as mediated by their viewing situations and degree of involvement with the content. Lin found that teenagers obtained five types of gratifications from TV. Obviously, both entertainment ("excitement, fun") and diversion ("helps me relax, forget about my problems") were important gratifications. TV viewing also gave the respondents fodder for conversations (thus enhancing "interpersonal communication"), and opportunities for "parasocial interaction" (identifying with TV characters and talking back to the TV to express their feelings). Yet TV viewing also imparted "information" in the form of advice about how to make friends, get along with family members, and solve the teenagers' own personal problems.

In agreement with a central theme of this book, information and entertainment are often inextricably entangled. It is difficult to say where "information" stops and where "entertainment" begins. Yet they are typically treated quite separately in reviews of relevant literature, and it is evident in the work of most authors that entertainment is not worthy of scholarly consideration — an attitude that deserves rethinking.

7.5
Other Theories

It is difficult to know where to stop in discussing the use of theory in information seeking. As mentioned in the introductory discussion about theory, I have taken a fairly narrow definition of the term. Many theories or principles have been invoked in information seeking research, although some of them appear in relatively few studies. Depending on what passes for theory, and how many uses of it must occur before we take it to be generally applicable, there are other candidates that could be discussed as theories relevant to information seeking.

Anderson et al. (1996) and Pettigrew and McKechnie (2001) offer a number of examples of potentially relevant theories, paradigms, or frameworks in their analyses, many of which have not been described earlier in this volume. In Table 7.1 I expand upon their examples and add some of my own. I include examples of theories invoked in discussions of information behavior, for which I found at least two recent examples. This list is meant to be illustrative, rather than exhaustive, of theories used in information behavior research. These theories are, of course, in addition to, the theories discussed earlier. Nearly all of the publications cited are empirical investigations; however, a few merely discuss how the theory might be applied to study information behavior.

Table 7.1

Some Other Theories Invoked in Information Behavior Research

Theorist(s)	Theory	Authors Who Cite the Theory
Bandura 77	Social Learning Theory/Self-Efficacy	Papa 00; Wilson 99a
Bourdieu 84, 90	Theory of Taste	Savolainen 95, 99; Van Snippenburg 96
Dunn 83; Granovetter 73, 82	Social Network Theory/Strength of Weak Ties	Erdelez 00; Pettigrew 00; Savolainen 01; Wicks 99
Fish 87; Iser 78; Suleiman & Crosman 80	Reader Response Theory	Ross 99; Scott 94; Stern 92
Foucault 72, 80	Power/Knowledge/Discourse	Talja 97; Olsson 99; Tuominen 97; Radford 01
Folkman 84;	Stress and Coping Theory	Anderson 96; Bryant 84;
Fishbein & Ajzen 75	Theory of Reasoned Action (Expectancy-Value Theory)	Leung 99b; Toms 99
Goffman 56, 83	Presentation of Self	Chelton 01; Radford 01
Habermas 84, 87	Theory of Communicative Action	Benoit 00; Cornelius 96; Hagen 97
Kelly 63	Personal Construct Theory	Kuhlthau 91, 93a,b, 99
Rogers 83	Diffusion of Innovation	Chatman 86; Case 87
Smith & Winterhalder 92	Optimal Foraging Theory	Sandstrom 94; Williamson 97, 98
Zillman & Bryant 85 86 94	Mood Management Theory	Kleiber 95; Stone 92; Wilson 99a

Note: Studies are listed by first author only, plus year See the references section.

7.6
Summary

I began this chapter by discussing the nature of paradigms adopted by researchers. These are difficult to place in a single framework, both because they overlap and because they operate at different levels of generality. I noted that various words may be used to describe much the same thing regarding research: perspectives, traditions, or approaches. I use the word "paradigm" interchangeably with these.

I discussed the nature of theory, describing it as a generalized explanation of the relationships among various phenomena. I described the confusions that arise with varying usage of the term "theory." One implication of that confusion is that theories also vary in the degree to which they attempt to generalize; theorists and epistemologists refer to this as the issue of "levels of theory." In this chapter a "theory" is assumed to be a closely related *set* of definitions and propositions, rather than a simple statement like "people seek information when they are uncertain." The latter declaration, though perhaps true, needs to have a supporting set of concepts and hypotheses to result in a useful series of investigations that we can all make sense of.

Next, I explored a number of paradigms that have been employed in research on information seeking. These included Zipf's Principle of Least Effort, the Uses and Gratifications tradition, sense-making (as advanced in the work of Brenda Dervin), the Media Use as Social Action perspective, and Play Theory.

Finally, I closed with a list of other theories that have been applied in information seeking research. These included Social Learning Theory, Theory of Taste, Theory of Reasoned Action, Theory of Communicative Action, Personal Construct Theory, Diffusion of Innovations, Optimal Foraging Theory, Social Network Theory/Strength of Weak Ties, Reader Response Theory, and theories of Power, Knowledge, and Discourse.

Most of these theories have origins that are decades old. They are likely to continue to attract adherents, as no comprehensive theory of information behavior has emerged. A recent trend among information behavior researchers has been to embrace theories originating in the humanities. This represents a break from the past, when social science disciplines (chiefly psychology and sociology) provided, almost exclusively, the theoretical basis for empirical work on information needs and uses.

Recommended for Further Reading

Chatman, E. A. (1990). Alienation theory: Application of a conceptual framework to a study of information among janitors. *RQ, 29*, 355–368.

Chatman's study is a fine example of the use of theory in information seeking research, and it makes fascinating reading, too.

Dervin, B. (1992). From the mind's eye of the user: The sense-making qualitative-quantitative methodology. In J. Glazier & R. Powell (Eds.), *Qualitative research in information management* (pp. 61–84). Englewood, CO: Libraries Unlimited.

Dervin is a prolific author and has published several explanations of her sense-making research. This is one of the most accessible.

Dozier, D., & Rice, R. (1984). Rival theories of electronic newsreading. In R. Rice (Ed.), *The new media* (pp. 103–128). Beverly Hills, CA: Sage.

This study contains a capsule explanation of Stephenson's Play Theory as well as a brief critique of Uses and Gratifications research. Although the technologies it discusses are now old hat, this work contained a prescient discussion of a still-valid question: What motivates people to read text on a computer screen?

Rosengren, K. (1989). Paradigms lost and regained. In B. Dervin, L. Grossberg, B. O'Keefe, & E. Wartella (Eds.), *Rethinking communication: Paradigm issues* (vol. 1, pp. 21–39). Newbury Park, CA: Sage.

Rosengren discusses the ways in which communication scholars — and other social scientists — have been divided by different philosophical and epistemological assumptions. This chapter contains a version of Burrell and Morgan's thoughtful typology of sociological schools.

Weick, K. E. (1995). *Sensemaking in organizations.* Thousand Oaks, CA: Sage.

Weick takes a different perspective from the usual information seeking authors — who tend to focus on the sense that individuals make of their world. Here the emphasis is on the responses that social groups and institutions make in the face of ambiguous situations. Weick's fascinating explanations range from the reasons that battered child syndrome took decades to be recognized, to why it is that soldiers in battle often fail to fire their guns.

Four

Methods for Studying Information Behavior

8

The Research Process

What do I want to know in this study? This is a critical beginning point. Regardless of point of view, and quite often because of our point of view, we construct and frame a question for inquiry. After this question is clear, we select the most appropriate methodology to proceed with the research project.

Valerie Janesick (1998, p. 37)

The sharp distinction between theory and method implied by many discussions is based on a vastly oversimplified picture of how research operates. . . . what we can know is determined by the available methods for knowing.

M. Scott Poole & Robert McPhee (1994, p. 43)

Chapter Outline

8.1. Relating Theory to Methodology
    8.1.1. Why We Need Methods
    8.1.2. Techniques of Measurement and Analysis
8.2. Basic Considerations in Research
    8.2.1. Stages of Research
    8.2.2. Induction and Deduction
    8.2.3. Validity and Reliability
    8.2.4. Purpose, Units, and Time
    8.2.5. Ethics in Research
8.3. Summary

8.1 ———

Relating Theory to Methodology

The previous chapter discussed some paradigms and various theories that have been, or could be, applied to information behavior. Both paradigms and theories are intertwined with one another and with the research methods chosen by the investigator. M. Scott Poole and Robert McPhee (1994) say that the "domains" of theory and methodology overlap in significant ways; what theories we use tend to indicate what methods are available to us. The overlap occurs because *both* theory and method must be concerned with our type of *explanation* (e.g., is our goal to demonstrate that one variable influences another?) and our approach to *inquiry* (e.g., whether we use a theory to guide observation, or whether we start making observations to build a theory, as discussed in the section on induction and deduction).

It is important to understand where theory and methodology do *not* overlap, too. Methodology is *not* concerned with *substantive assumptions* about what is being studied, which is a matter for theory (or, more specifically, for metatheory). Only theory addresses the basic assumptions that we make about the nature of reality — whether, for instance, we can ever be objective in our observations of other people. It is the theory that assumes, for example, that the *meaning* of a word is a matter of *agreement* between people (i.e., socially constructed), rather than an objective reality.

Likewise, our *techniques of observation* are *not* a part of theory but rather are of prime concern in methodology. These techniques and tools are what we call "methods" and will be an important focus in this chapter, which considers the process of designing and implementing research. Our choices of design and method have profound implications for what we can know about the phenomena we observe.

The purpose of this chapter is to highlight some basic considerations in *designing* investigations, and to point out different methods commonly used for studying information seeking, needs, and uses. Specific examples of methods will be provided in the chapter that follows this one. We must consider *how* information seeking has been studied to assess what we know about it. This is where methodology enters the picture.

8.1.1 Why We Need Methods

Methodology concerns how we can *find out*. What kind of principles, logic, and evidence would best advance our goal of learning (and most likely, recording) knowledge about an area or object of study? The specific ways, tools, and techniques of observation and measurement are what we call "methods." As Poole and McPhee emphasize (1994, p. 43), "method is one's point of contact with the world." We need to have methods to control for human error, which is always present when we are thinking and making observations about reality. Many methodologists (e.g., Babbie, 2000; Katzer, Cook, & Crouch, 1998; Schutt, 1999) have pointed out common sources of human error, including the following:

1. People are by nature poor observers. We make errors of both omission (not seeing what is there) and admission (seeing things that are not there) in the process. Unless we employ a conscious method, we tend to observe only a fraction of what we actually "see." The fact that you cannot recall much of what you passed the last time you drove to work is not merely a function of memory; you "saw" thousands of details but few were important to you at that time so you did not really "notice" them.

2. People tend to *overgeneralize* from small samples of evidence or opinion. If three friends claim that a local politician is corrupt, we tend to assume that they are right without investigating any further.

3. We tend to notice those things that support our beliefs and ignore evidence that does not. Akin to the "selective exposure" discussed in Chapter 4, this tendency is called *selective perception*.

4. We sometimes *make up information* to support our beliefs, no matter how illogical it might appear to another person. A common example is the so-called "gambler's fallacy": the belief that a run of bad luck (e.g., six tails in a row in coin-tossing) makes it even more likely that a good outcome will follow (i.e., "the next toss is sure to come up heads").

5. Our *ego* is often involved in what we "know" and profess to be true. We are prone to be defensive when several others challenge our point of view. We may go so far as to suspect that their disagreement is based on some personal bias against us, rather than a simple attempt to state their own opinions or evidence.

6. In the extreme case that we call "prejudice," we may simply *close our minds* to any new evidence about an issue. In such a case, no further observations or arguments will ever change our beliefs or opinions.

7. People are prone to *mystify* anything they don't understand. If an issue is too complex, the easy way out is to say that it is something that simply cannot be understood. (As former U.S. president Ronald Reagan sometimes said when faced with an intractable question, "It's a mystery.") Many observers would say the same thing regarding the use of information.

Research methods are intended to be a partial corrective for these human failings. By agreeing to guidelines for identifying research problems and gathering and interpreting evidence, scholars and scientists intend to establish communities of discourse regarding their topics of investigation. The point of epistemology and methodology is thus to provide a basis of agreement for debating and assessing knowledge claims in given areas. The resulting communities of discourse are loosely coupled and often disagree about the appropriateness of particular assumptions or techniques—but that is also the nature of science and scholarship.

Research methods are conscious attempts to (collectively) overcome some human failings, while promoting dialogue among researchers. To that end we employ techniques that guard us against the errors described previously. For instance, we might use instruments (notes, photographs, tape recordings, computer logs) to be more certain that we do not "miss" any information. We make lots of observations to have plenty of evidence on which to base our findings. To keep ourselves honest, we decide in advance which specific things we are going to observe. We state, again in advance, what we think our conclusions are likely to be. As scholars, we make a professional commitment to be methodical and rigorous in our studies and to be open to criticisms from our colleagues. We agree to a continuing dialogue about our research, and agree not to cling so strongly to our conclusions that no one can persuade us with compelling counterevidence. Finally, we agree that certain criteria must be met for findings to be widely accepted: they must make logical sense and agree with our observations.

In summary, methods (and the philosophical assumptions that underlie them) are about how best to explore reality through structured, personal experience (i.e., *inquiry*). Methods offer us a choice of plans for asking questions and finding answers to them.

8.1.2 Techniques of Measurement and Analysis

It is important to realize that the term "methods" often refers to two types of technique: *measurement* (i.e., observation and data collection) and *analysis*. Various authors (e.g., Poole & McPhee, 1994; Sonnenwald & Iivonen, 1999) have tried to tease apart the interactions of these two dimensions. A list of what I mean by techniques of measurement versus analysis is found in Table 8.1.

Obviously, one first *measures* something, and then one *analyzes* those measurements. So the choices of techniques are intertwined. It is because of this interdependence that we often refer to investigations as if they were solely the technique of measurement or analysis: experiments, surveys, case studies, and so forth. Some methods of measurement require certain kinds of analysis: experiments that gather quantitative data necessitate some kind of statistical analysis; collection of diaries probably dictates content analysis of the entries. In other cases, multiple types of analysis might be used with one type of evidence;

Table 8.1
Techniques of Measurement and Analysis

Techniques of Measurement
• Observation of experimental conditions
• Surveys (self-administered questionnaires, or interview schedules)
• Intensive interviews (e.g., ethnographic and focus group interviews)
• Participant observation
• Diaries (i.e., self-reports of experience, recorded electronically or on paper)
• Collection of other behavioral artifacts (e.g., paper or electronic documents)
Techniques of Analysis
• Statistical (e.g., analysis of variance, significance testing)
• Theory testing
• Model building
• Case study
• Content analysis
• Historical analysis
• Meta-analysis

for example, a study of book circulation records might use either statistical analysis or content analysis, or both.

Table 8.1 is a primer for the types of investigations that will be covered in the next chapter, with the exception of model building, which we discussed in the previous chapter. Chapter 9 includes explanations of each technique, along with examples how such methods have been used to study information behavior. Readers who are thoroughly familiar with general concepts like validity and with data gathering techniques such as surveys might wish to skip directly to the next chapter for descriptions and examples of specific types of methods.

This chapter will review the basic stages, concepts, and issues in social research; the terminology will be useful in critiquing the study examples that follow.

8.2
Basic Considerations in Research

8.2.1 Stages of Research

The classic view of the research process is often portrayed in five stages. These include: [1] imagining a research project, [2] designing a specific study,

[3] choosing and implementing research methods, [4] analyzing and interpreting observations, and [5] considering the overall results. Although in practice it is rarely as simple as all that, it is worth briefly considering these five stereotypical steps in the research process. Then we will consider some of the basic issues that lead researchers to choose one type of design or method over another.

The first stage is the one in which an investigation is conceptualized, and here theory may come into play, as well as personal motivation. It typically begins with an investigator who is drawn to a particular topic, issue, or problem for some reason. Sometimes researchers pursue topics simply because they are paid to do so. For instance, a market researcher or a chemist may work on an agenda strictly defined by their employer. In research involving people, more often the researcher has some personal connection to the object of investigation. Perhaps a scholar is drawn to research on primary education because he sees a need for improvement there, because he has been observing his own children as they learn, or because he feels some aspect of education offers a concrete place to study an abstract concept (e.g., self efficacy) — or because all three of these reasons apply.

In the second stage, a specific study is designed. Some kind of phenomena and/or venue is selected for observation, which can be as complex as a statistical sample of people or objects, or as simple as selecting a location from which to "watch life go by." A plan is derived for what goal is to be achieved in the study and how to go about it. Again, a theory (if employed) may dictate the goal of the research project and what kinds of designs and data are necessary to achieve it. Key considerations here are the resources available in terms of time and personnel.

The third step is to choose a method or methods of observation. Multiple sources of evidence contribute to more compelling conclusions and are thus to be preferred. (Much more will be said about methods later.)

Once evidence is gathered, it is analyzed and interpreted — in many cases, observations are being interpreted *while* they are made. Classification is the key to many analyses — how many instances of that type versus this type were observed? In survey and experimental research, for example, the measurement and analysis may be primarily quantitative, yet most data gathering involves some degree of interpretation and classification. Consider the common practice of allowing survey respondents to supply an "other" response not anticipated on the questionnaire — all of these responses must be categorized and coded in some way for convenient summary. Computer software packages have made it increasingly easy to record, interpret, and analyze data of types both qualitative (e.g., The Ethnograph, and QSR NUD*IST) and quantitative (e.g., SPSS, and SAS).

In a final and often underemphasized stage, researchers summarize and consider their findings. The investigators write and talk about what they have found, and in some cases they share their conclusions not merely with other researchers but also with the communities or individuals they have studied. Ideally this step leads to a reconceptualization of the research—whether it "worked," contributed to theory, was worth the effort, or could be improved upon.

8.2.2 Induction and Deduction

Most investigators have previously established assumptions and preferences that lead them to choose certain designs and techniques. A key consideration is whether they are to proceed inductively or deductively in their research. Taking an inductive approach means that the research will examine particular instances and reason toward generalization. That is, you are gathering, analyzing, and interpreting data in such a way that it may lead to general principles, such as theories. *Grounded theory* is a research goal that attempts to build theory from concrete observations and to keep any generalizations relatively close to the contexts in which they originated, rather than attempting to build an abstract theory that strives (and typically fails) to apply in all situations. Similarly, most "qualitative" methods tend to be inductive in nature, mainly because they assume that generalizations are difficult to make when one is studying people or their creations.

The deductive approach proceeds in the opposite fashion, reasoning from the general to the particular. This is typically the way science is portrayed, as applying a theory to a particular case in an attempt to test the theory. Presumably the theory is either supported or revised based on the results. However, the number of formal tests of theory are relatively sparse when it comes to studying information seeking. Rather, much of the research has been merely descriptive of a unique situation (i.e., a given information user or organization), or an inductive attempt to generalize about certain types of persons, sources, or effects.

Few investigators or studies stick solely to induction or deduction. Rather, they tend to move back and forth between those modes: collecting information that allows them to state a principle or tendency, then testing that generalization through further research, in an endless chain of logic. Even strong advocates of induction like Glaser and Strauss (1967) point out that the deductive approach can be useful in exploratory stages of research.

Particularly for those researchers who are testing theory, it is common to state a *research problem*. A research problem is a question that asks about the relationship between two or more variables. A problem might be stated as "What effect does an increase in the number of available information sources have upon the use of an individual source?" Problem statements typically express relations between *variables* and suggest ways in which they might be tested empirically. However, many interesting questions cannot be stated in such a manner because their phenomena are difficult to define and measure and are not amenable to formal testing. That is why we have a diversity of assumptions and methods in social research.

For research problems that test a preexisting theory, *hypotheses* are derived. A hypothesis is a conjectural statement about the relation between two or more variables. Most typically this formal approach to knowledge is used in experimental studies in which the researcher is able to manipulate (or at least anticipate) a change in the environment that might produce some kind of measurable effect among the people present. For example, a hypothesis such as "the introduction of a new information source into a previously stable set of sources will cause a decline in the use of the earlier sources" predicts that a new source will appear and that it will affect use of other information sources. Such concepts as "information use" must be defined so as to be measurable in some way. Once stated in a proper form, hypotheses can be tested through further research and shown to be "probably true" or "probably false." In this way, hypothetical statements can be used to build theory.

Early in the research process, the object(s) of observation must be identified and defined for measurement. This process is called *operationalization*. After explicating a concept of interest (for example, the explication of "information" in Chapter 3), we must lay out the procedures or operations we will use to measure that concept. We must specify the conditions under which an instance of the concept might be produced and observed. For example, where would we look to find an instance of "information"? How will we recognize it when we see it? What would indicate that "information" is present? How will we measure an instance of "information" once it is observed?

The resulting *operational definition* guides our *observation* of the phenomena. We discover ways to classify or quantify the things we observe: *attributes* (characteristics or qualities that describe something) of people (e.g., female versus male) or their behavior (e.g., asking a question versus not asking a question) are grouped together in logical sets called *variables* (e.g., gender = male or female). We develop a strategy for observing those variables in a particular context. Our method might involve watching or interviewing people, examining artifacts that people create (e.g., a log of their television watching or a record of what they have read), or any of a number of different observational possibilities.

8.2.3 Validity and Reliability

The twin concepts of validity and reliability determine how compelling the results of our study will be, and so are important considerations in the choice of methods and construction of measures. *Validity* is the extent that the measurement procedures accurately reflect the concept we are studying. Asking someone if she "knows a lot about world events" is not a particularly valid way of studying "news consumption." Asking the respondent if she subscribes to a newspaper would be more valid, as it gets closer to the heart of the matter. However, an answer to that question does not tell you whether she actually *reads* the newspaper; questions about her newspaper *reading habits* would have even more validity. Perhaps the most valid measures might be some questions—whether administered through an interview or on paper—that would tell us if she can identify the top news stories of the day or week, and so forth.

Reliability is demonstrated when measures are *repeated under the same conditions* and yield highly similar measurements each time. We expect a bathroom scale to give us the same weight from one minute to the next, because we have not had enough time to gain or lose significant weight in such a short period. We would not necessarily expect the scale to register the same weight 20 years later, because the conditions have changed, and we may have gained weight. In contrast, asking several observers to *guess* our weight (and then taking the average of their guesses) would likely be an unreliable measure, as human perceptions vary considerably across observers and even within the same person across time.

There can be a trade-off between validity and reliability. Measures that are highly reliable may not be high on validity, whereas highly valid measures sometimes have problems with reliability. Although it is easily possible to develop measures that are both invalid and unreliable (asking "is the sky blue today?" would not be a valid measure of color perception, and is likely to draw unreliable answers as well), it is difficult to come up with measures that are both highly valid and highly reliable.

Consider a situation in which we wish to study the use of materials in a library. One basic question would be how many people actually have an opportunity to use the library materials—by entering the building. To answer that simple question, we could station an observer at the door and have him or her count people. However, such a measurement will not be completely reliable; a second observer watching the crowd enter the library might come up with a slightly different count. A superior method would be to install a turnstile in the entrance; we could then assume that one "rotation" of the turnstile equals one "user" of the library. Now we have a reliable count of the persons entering the building.

But what does that simple count tell us about the actual use of the informational materials or services found in the library—the kinds of activities that people more commonly think of as constituting "use"? Virtually nothing: people might have entered merely to use the bathroom or the pay phone.

To capture a more valid measure of the use of materials and services we could distribute a questionnaire at the doorway with specific questions about such uses. Users would fill them out and we would have data about the use of materials by a large number of users. However, we would find that the more, and more detailed, questions we ask, the fewer the users who will complete the survey. The fewer the number of respondents, the less confident we are that we can generalize from our results to the entire population of users. In other words, we might encounter a trade-off between the depth and the breadth of the information we gather.

If we are searching for a really detailed picture of the information usage, we might consider close observations of a small number of users. Perhaps we could follow them around the library and they could talk to us in detail about their internal experience of searching and finding information. Obviously these methods (observation and interview) would require the consent of the participants and have various implications for our study, particularly in the obtrusive way they interfere in the activities of the library user.

Making these detailed observations, we would get closer to the phenomenon of concern: what people actually *do* when they use the library. So this data potentially has a great deal of validity. Pursuing this approach also has drawbacks, though. Some aspects of our methods may lower validity; gathering data from a smaller number of respondents than the earlier approaches will lead to a lack of generalizability. Also we are introducing an artificial element by having the respondent talk out loud, which also may lower the validity of our findings.

Other problems have serious implications for reliability. Reporting on our own thoughts and behaviors can be problematic, particularly due to the unreliability of memories. If we ask three witnesses to a crime what they saw and remember, do they say the same things? Because of both selective perception and variability of memory, typically the witnesses do not say *exactly* the same things, but multiple accounts are often close enough to draw some conclusions. Eyewitness testimony is not completely reliable, but it is often the best evidence we have. If eyewitnesses *always* gave radically different accounts of the same events, courts would have to abandon the use of such information, as it would be inherently unreliable. Likewise, reliability is absolutely basic to the conduct of research.

We can imagine many variations on the design and methods of the hypothetical study of library use, involving changes in the questions asked, the number of respondents studied, the type and manner of questions asked, the time frame for the investigation, and so forth. The point is that, as we move from crude but highly reliable measures toward measures that better reflect the concept under study, we encounter some trade-offs between validity and reliability.

Such trade-offs are partly behind the long-standing disputes over quantitative versus qualitative methods (an unhelpful argument, in most respects).

Research designs that intend to produce highly quantitative and reliable measures, such as laboratory experiments, suffer from validity problems because they invoke an artificial situation that may not reflect how people think and behave in the real world. A qualitative approach such as participant observation, however it may be grounded in the real world, raises issues about the reliability of what is observed and measured, because the specific contexts and measurements are difficult (and sometimes impossible) to replicate. By extension, then, we can talk about entire study designs as offering trade-offs in reliability and validity.

One way to conduct research that is both valid and reliable is to be found in the use of multiple methods and multiple sources of data. This will be brought out in the discussions of methods and the examples that follow in the next chapter.

8.2.4 Purpose, Units, and Time

Before selecting a particular method, there are several other considerations that come into play. Among these considerations are the *purpose* of our study, the type of things we intend to observe (typically called *units of analysis*), and the *time* dimension of the investigation.

Research may vary as regards its purpose. Particularly regarding topics that have not yet been widely studied, the goal is simply to *explore* the phenomenon to gain a basic understanding of it. For example, when new media appear, such as the World Wide Web (WWW), the first research questions that emerge may be: "What is this thing called the WWW?" "What does it do?" and "How do people use it?" When the object of study is novel, some aspects of it may not yet be defined well enough for precise measurement. Because new information sources and new variations on existing channels emerge with some frequency, exploratory studies are fairly common in information seeking research.

When a phenomenon is well established, the focus of investigation is likely to be on documenting its characteristics. *Descriptive* studies are intended to measure well-defined variables regarding the people or objects involved with the phenomenon. To use the World Wide Web as an example once more, descriptive research questions might be: "How many searches are being conducted on the WWW?" "How many Web sites are in existence?" "Which are the most popular sites?" "How many people are using the WWW, and with what frequency?" and "What are the demographic characteristics of WWW users?" Much of the information seeking literature, particularly the early studies that focused on channels, sources, and audiences for information, are chiefly descriptive in nature.

The ideal type of investigation is that which offers an *explanation* for the phenomenon observed. An explanatory study attempts to answer "why" questions about phenomena, particularly regarding the motives and actions of people. Where the WWW is concerned, such questions might include "Why do people use the WWW, rather than other sources of information?" "Why are companies spending so much money on Web site development and advertising?" and "Why is free speech such an issue for WWW content?" As studying and measuring human intentions is difficult, fewer investigations have attempted to offer explanations for information seeking behaviors. Constructing explanations for events brings into play the concept of causation: when does one thing cause another to happen? This in turn which requires rigorous evidence and logic to establish.

When designing a study we must be clear about what is our primary *unit of analysis*. Studies of information seeking, by definition, involve humans; therefore, individual *people* are most commonly observed and analyzed in such investigations. Yet there are also cases in which our main focus is on aggregates of individuals, as in a comparative study of organizations (e.g., companies or universities); in such cases our unit of analysis is actually a group, rather than the individual. In addition, any kind of human artifact—*objects*, such as books or TV programs, or social *events*, such as a conference or conversation—may also be a unit of observation and analysis. In other words, the design of a study is partly determined by what kind of thing we wish to discuss in our findings. Are we trying to reach a conclusion about the opinions of individuals, for example, or about the usage of a book? Deciding what we are observing and reasoning about will determine how our measures are developed and implemented.

The *time* dimension of the investigation is especially important, particularly when we wish to reason about causes and effects. Time is also important because people and their environments change constantly, so we are always faced with the issue of whether results from a decade ago are still applicable to the world of today. A typical distinction made in methodology is between studies that are conducted solely at *one point in time,* versus those in which multiple measures are taken over *several points in time*. These two approaches are called, respectively, *cross-sectional* versus *longitudinal* studies.

One could look at the time dimension as a question of sampling, just as we must do when we consider human populations: is it enough to sample one person/time, or should we sample many people/times? The considerable increase in effort required to study phenomenon over time has meant that relatively few studies in information seeking have incorporated a long time frame in their design. However, in the "quasi-experimental" design described in the next chapter, it is typical for some measurements to be repeated twice, at intervals of some weeks or months, to determine whether a change in the environment has had the expected effect. It is also not uncommon for some survey designs to ask the same questions several months or years apart to address the question of change over time.

8.2.5 Ethics in Research

Given human failings and motivations, it should come as no surprise that ethical considerations loom large in social research. Researchers are people, people have values and attitudes, and those predispositions inevitably creep into their investigations of other people. Investigators also have a strong desire to achieve interesting results. Competent researchers strive to keep their values from influencing the results of their studies — a difficult thing to do when one cares deeply about the topic — and to be candid with themselves and others regarding their own potential biases.

Ethics reflect our beliefs about what is just and right behavior versus what we judge to be unjust and wrong. Individuals often disagree about the ultimate bases for judgments of right and wrong, so ethics tend to be based on consensual group norms, sometimes called "standards of conduct." Social researchers have worked out a number of such standards through years of challenging experiences with investigations that have crossed into gray areas of behavior. Therese Baker (1999) reprints excerpts from the American Sociological Association's Code of Ethics, which are indicative of many common ethical problems faced in social research.

Four general ethical guidelines have evolved that are commonly followed in investigations involving humans: we must not harm participants, we must not deceive them, we must make participation voluntary, and we must make data confidential or anonymous. In many public agencies, entities sometimes called "human subject committees" serve as watchdogs to see that such principles are observed in research by their employees. Each of these four principles is discussed in turn, and the implications of each are identified, in what follows.

No Harm Should Come to Participants in a Study

Although it may seem obvious that causing *physical* harm to a study participant is forbidden, the more challenging issue is preventing potential *psychological* discomfort. Who can say for certain when and how mental discomfort might occur? Such harm could be something as subtle as embarrassment that might occur when certain information is revealed about an individual or even an identifiable group of persons — say, the fact that they read a particular magazine, enjoy a certain television series, or made a public comment on a controversial issue. This kind of concern makes it difficult to correlate, for example, individual reading habits as recorded in library circulation records with demographic data about those individuals. In fact, many libraries expressly forbid the release of borrowers' records as a matter of principle, to preserve the privacy of their clients.

Study Participants Should Not Be Deceived or Misled in Any Way

Respondents and informants should be fully informed about the purpose of the study and the nature of questions and observations that might be involved. In most investigations of information–related behavior, this is not an issue. Survey respondents might fully understand that they are going to be asked about what sources of information they turn to, and how they perceive the value of those sources.

However, imagine the potential difficulty in situations in which what the investigator is really interested in is something deeper and more psychological than the questions or observations that are made on the surface. For example, in Chapter 11 I discuss commentaries on journalists that suggest that they rely upon stereotypes, plot devices, or mental models of situations to understand news events and turn them into interesting stories. If one were to say bluntly to a participating journalist that "I'm going to ask you questions about how you report the news, so that I can see whether you perceive events according to stereotypical formulas," that could only lead to self-consciousness on the part of the respondent, and likely to diminished honesty in answering the questions as well. So the investigator may tread a fine line in disclosing fully what is of interest in the study. In many cases, they may not know in advance what themes and findings may emerge from the answers, and they cannot disclose their possible interpretations of what they have not yet heard from the participants.

Participation in Any Investigation Should Be Voluntary

In the early days of social research and even up to the mid-twentieth century, it was not unusual for institutions (e.g., schools, government agencies, the military) to require that certain individuals participate in studies and/or provide personal information to investigators. For several decades now, the norm in most developed countries has been that individuals have the right to refuse to be the subject of any social or psychological investigation, even if little harm could come from it. If the individual is under the legal age, a parent or guardian may be required to give permission as well. Even if participants are adults, investigators must take special care with any who are subordinate in status to the researchers, such as students who may imagine dire consequences if they refuse to cooperate.

The norm of voluntary participation presents a particular challenge to investigators in educational settings, who strive to obtain complete information about all of the students in a given class or age group, to give just one example.

In such situations the refusal of some people to participate will make the conclusions less valid, because it is difficult to know if there is not something systematically different about those people who declined to be studied.

Any Data Collected about Individuals Should Be Confidential

Ideally, information should be anonymous. If maintaining anonymity is impossible, it should remain at least confidential. A completed postal survey questionnaire that does not contain any name or identifying number is an example of anonymous data. In contrast, data collected in e-mail surveys or face-to-face interviews cannot be anonymous, but the investigator can agree to treat it confidentially; that is, the researcher would not reveal to others the connection between the data and any particular individual. Thus, in reporting the results of a study, care should be taken to see that individual responses are not identifiable in any way. Nevertheless, in some investigations of small organizations it is sometimes possible to make informed guesses about the origin of some quotations or opinions, if one knows the particular group studied. In such cases the investigator must exercise caution in reporting any expression that might be controversial or potentially embarrassing so that it cannot come back to haunt the participant. Imagine, for example, a report that quotes, without attribution, a controversial contribution to a mailing list discussion; it may not be difficult for a reader to search the archives of the forum in question and identify the e-mail address and its owner, making a mockery of confidentiality.

None of these four ethical principles has yet been a major problem in past research on information behaviors. At least according to what has been reported in the literature, past investigators have treated participants with sensitivity and care. Many investigators adhere to what Diener and Crandall (1978, p. 52), quoting Margaret Mead, hold up as an ideal way of treating research participants: "Anthropological research does not have subjects. We work with informants in an atmosphere of trust and mutual respect."

New Issues

New ethical issues continue to arise. The ubiquity of information exchange on the Internet, for example, has led to discussion among researchers regarding the ethics of collecting public submissions to mailing lists, discussion boards, and Web sites (e.g., Jones, 1999). Although chat rooms and individual e-mail exchanges are considered to be "private," some researchers maintain that postings to public channels like usenet and open mailing lists are fair game for analysis and reporting. Yet the increasingly common practice of collecting electronic discussions, particularly on controversial topics, raises the issue of whether the contributors are "fully informed" that they are subjects of study. Whatever individual investigators think about the ethicality of studying public discussions, institutional review boards typically ask for evidence that research subjects are informed of possible observation and its consequences. If the investigator is taking an active role in the discussion—posing questions to the list, for example—the issue becomes even more complex.

As computer and biomedical technology provide increased monitoring capability of overt behavior and physical responses, we can expect more challenges to the boundaries of acceptable research. Witness the increased awareness of privacy brought about by use of the Internet. Many users gradually became aware that commercial entities were not only tracking the most obvious data—their demographic background (such as they were willing to supply voluntarily) and electronic purchases—but were even recording their visits to Web sites in which transactions were *not* conducted. The pervasive use of tracking cookies and of online forms and questionnaires, coupled with the ability to aggregate and cross-reference data by individual computer user, has led to massive collections of data on electronic information seeking. That much of this has been collected without the full consent and understanding of Internet users is an example of how far things can go if ethical data-collection principles are not observed.

8.3

Summary

This chapter has described some basic aspects of methodology and the process of designing a research investigation. My comments about induction versus deduction, validity and reliability, and the design of studies may seem abstract to readers who are relatively new to social research methods. However, I think this brief background will be necessary as we move into the heart of this book: examining a few dozen studies that are representative of the bulk of research on information seeking.

I hope the reader will recognize that, although some investigations may be more compelling than others, there is no single way to approach this subject matter and therefore no "perfect" study design by which to judge the overall quality of all studies. The ultimate subject matter of information seeking studies is diverse, and therefore so are its methods. *All* investigations are forced to make trade-offs, and therefore have weaknesses. Yet it remains true that some studies have more than others.

For example, consider the issue of how choice of observational method interacts with the amount of data collected. A sample of 30 respondents may be entirely appropriate for a small population study that uses lengthy, face-to-face interviews as its primary method of collecting data. Gathering open-ended responses dictates a limited number of respondents. The focus of the investigation and the size of particular population studied (e.g., a case study of one organization) may do so as well.

But 30 respondents is not a convincing sample for an e-mail survey of a large population, such as "Canadians," "students," or even "IBM employees." Self-administered questionnaires lend themselves to collecting large numbers of relatively "shallow" responses to limited-choice questions; they should not be used to collect data from small samples if their intent is to reach conclusions worthy of broader notice.

Postal and e-mail surveys are so easy to throw together that they are often overused. This is particularly true of e-mail surveys, which have even more weaknesses than paper-based questionnaires. Unfortunately, the results of some of these electronic surveys still manage to get published, perhaps because of their relative novelty. In selecting examples for the next chapter I was tempted to include a few obviously "weak" investigations for the purpose of contrast. Ultimately, I decided against it, as there is little to be gained by pointing out that many weak studies are still conducted under the rubric of information behavior.

To serve as a template of what topics I include under the rubric of "methods," a distinction was made between techniques of measurement versus techniques of analysis. The listing of common ways that information behavior has been measured and analyzed will guide the choice of examples in Chapter 9.

I concluded by discussing ethical issues that arrive in studying information behaviors. Investigators of information behavior have avoided most of the problems that arise in studying humans, but increasing capabilities for electronic monitoring present new challenges for the ethical collection of data in that area.

The examples of investigations in the next chapter reflect a variety of designs. The purpose of most of them is to describe or explore, rather than to explain, the phenomena they investigate. In virtually all of the studies the unit of analysis is individuals — their characteristics (e.g., age or education), their orientations (e.g., attitudes or opinions), and most of all, their actions (e.g., the use of a particular information source). Some of the studies have taken multiple measures over time, while in other cases the time dimension is ignored. Together they represent a fair sampling of the types of research designs and methods common to information seeking research.

Recommended for Further Reading

Babbie, E. (2000). *The practice of social research* (9th ed). Belmont, CA: Wadsworth.
Babbie's work is perhaps the most popular introduction to social science methods ever written. It emphasizes quantitative approaches (especially surveys, experiments, and field experiments), but it also includes discussions of participant observation and case studies.

Barnbaum, D. R., & Byron, M. (2001). *Research ethics: text and readings.* Upper Saddle River, NJ: Prentice-Hall.

Although it is slanted toward medical research, this book contains a good summary of the philosophical principles underlying ethical theories, and of possible harms to participants.

Dillman, D. (1978). *Mail and telephone surveys—The total design method.* New York: Wiley.

The ultimate guide to conducting surveys, Dillman's book is still useful after all these years.

Glaser, B., & Strauss, A. (1967). *The discovery of grounded theory: Strategies for qualitative research.* Chicago: Aldine.

This classic work on the inductive approach to conducting investigations and building theory continues to be widely cited in investigations of information seeking. A more recent book by Strauss and Corbin (1990) provides a broader view of qualitative methods.

Katzer, J., Cook, K., & Crouch, W. (1998). *Evaluating information: A guide for users of social science research.* (4th ed.). Boston: McGraw-Hill.

A brief guide, in layman's language, to critical thinking and social scientific methods, this book intends to make its readers knowledgeable and competent consumers of research reports. It succeeds well beyond that, providing a basic background on quantitative methods, spiced with interesting examples, quotations, cartoons, and recommended readings.

Yin, R. (1981). The case study crisis: Some answers. *Administrative Science Quarterly, 26,* 58–65.

Yin provides basic a overview of the case study method, with some responses to critics of case studies.

9

Methods: Examples by Type

One can classify these studies in various ways . . . by research methodology (survey, observation, bibliometrics); by research purpose (system design improvement, evaluation, planning, hypothesis testing); by unit of analysis (individual, group, question or problem, information need, use made of information).

Jana Varlejs (1987, pp. 67–68)

Like Agatha Christie's fictional detective Hercule Poirot, the social detective must have an effective method because method is one's contact point of with the world. The types of constructs and propositions in our theories, as well as the degree of certainty attached to them, are all dependent on our methodological repertoire.

M. Scott Poole and Robert McPhee (1994, p. 43)

Chapter Outline

9.1. Types and Examples of Methods
    9.1.1. The Case Study: Analyzing an Analyst
    9.1.2. Experiments: Shopping for Cars and Cornflakes
    9.1.3. Surveys: CEOs and Scholars
    9.1.4. Brief Interviews: Studies of Everyday Folks
    9.1.5. Intensive Interviews: The Lives of Janitors and Brothers
    9.1.6. Focus Group Interviews: Doctors and Nurses Search for Information
    9.1.7. Diaries and Experience Sampling
    9.1.8. Unobtrusive Approaches: Historical Analysis
    9.1.9. Unobtrusive Approaches: Content Analysis
    9.1.10. Using Multiple Data Sources in a Single Investigation
    9.1.11. Meta-Analysis
9.2. Summary

Types and Examples of Methods

This chapter describes methodologies that have been used in studies of information needs, uses, seeking, and sense-making. The methods identified for discussion are not exhaustive of all possible methodologies, but rather reflect those that have been *used* with some regularity — in some cases frequently, in other cases rarely.

One particular approach is very common: a review by Järvelin and Vakkari (1993) found that 23% of research articles appearing in the information studies literature in 1985 used *survey* methodology; 20% to 22% of studies published in 1965 and 1975 also used some form of survey. None of the other methods examined accounted for such a high percentage of studies. Whether the data is collected through postal mail or by way of personal interview, survey methods have been a dominant means of investigation in this area as they have been in most of the human sciences.

Some mainstream social science methods are used rather sparingly in investigations of information seeking; experimentation is one of these. Other methods that were not so common 30 years ago, such as ethnographic interviews, have become increasingly popular for studying information seeking.

With a few exceptions, the following examples have been chosen for their overall quality and representativeness of both the methods and the topics pursued in information seeking studies. Beyond the overall assessments of quality and representativeness, the selection bias has been in the direction of investigations that, first, study larger samples of individuals, and second, are more recent. A few older and smaller investigations are mentioned to make particular points and comparisons. Table 9.1 includes most of the studies cited in this chapter.

9.1.1 The Case Study: Analyzing an Analyst

We begin by considering the *case study*, as it is regarded as a point of comparison for the more elaborate methods to follow. The notion of a case study evolves from the legal profession in which the main unit of analysis is the single instance: a complaint or dispute brought to a court for judgment. In trying a case, the court elicits all of the relevant facts of the situation and seeks precedent in earlier cases that share characteristics with the case under consideration. Because of its simplicity and groundedness in the real world, the analysis of cases has become a popular method of instruction in law schools and in other professions such as medicine and business. Sigmund Freud made great use of the case study method in his early studies of psychopathology.

Table 9.1
Works Reviewed, and Related Works Cited, for Methods

Method(s)	Works Reviewed to Illustrate Methods	Other Relevant Works Cited
Case studies	Kuhlthau 99	Campbell 63; Stake 98; Yin 81
Experiments		
Formal	Hauser 93	Cook 79
Quasi-/field	Cole 93	
Mail surveys	Chew 94	Babbie 00
E-mail / WWW	Zhang 00	Bruce 98
Interviews, brief		
Face-to-face	Atwood 82; Marcella 00	Palmour 79
Phone	Gantz 91	Dervin 82; Newhagen 94
Interviews, intensive		
Focus group	Mullaly-Quijas 94	Krueger 88; Lunt 96; Merton 56
Ethnographic	Chatman 90	O'Meara 89
Phenomenological	Mick 92	Csikszentmihalyi 90; Scott 94; Radway 85
Diaries	Reneker 93	Csikszentmihalyi 90; Kubey 96; Spencer 71
Unobtrusive		
Historical	Richmond 88	Darnton 00; Ziman 76
Content analysis	White 00	Julien 00; Krippendorff 80; Mokros 95
Multiple methods	Solomon 97	Fabritius 99
Meta-analysis	Haug 97	Covell 85

Note: Studies are listed by first author only, plus year. See the references.

Sometimes referred to as "case analysis" or "the case method," this research approach emphasizes *single* entities—a person, an organization, or a nation, for example. Only a single one of these entities may be sampled, or several individual cases may be examined with the intention of comparing their results. The case approach emphasizes the *context* of what is being studied—the individual in her social world, or the competitive environment in which an organization must make decisions, to give two examples—with as many of the key actors, connections, interactions, situations, processes, and information as can be identified.

The case study method is, then, a research *strategy* in which varied *types of evidence* may be collected (ranging from archival records to firsthand and secondhand accounts of thoughts and actions) by *various methods* (e.g., interviewing). The type of evidence gathered may be highly quantitative (e.g., sales records of a company, or circulation statistics of a library) but is more likely to be highly qualitative (notes or transcripts of an interview).

The noted methodologists Donald Campbell and Julian Stanley (1963) identify the case study as a reference point in assessing how much confidence we can have in our findings in contrast with what we would achieve using experimental methods. Campbell and Stanley compare the case method to various types of experiments, and conclude that case studies do not tell us very much in comparison. There are at least two reasons why findings from the case method can be difficult to establish, generalize, and rely upon.

First, case studies are typically limited in terms of the number of entities and variables that are investigated. Considering only one case is an obvious weakness, although more rigor can be achieved by including multiple cases. In addition, case analyses tend to focus on a single phenomenon (i.e., a change or event, such as the introduction of a new technology into an organization), and naturally tend to deemphasize other factors that might explain the resulting changes (e.g., external developments in the economy or culture).

A second weakness of the case method involves the *length* and *timing* of the investigation. Campbell and Stanley characterize the worst type of case study as a "one-shot" design in which measurements (e.g., observations, interviews) are conducted at only *one point in time*, sometimes after the occurrence of an event that is presumed to be important. In such a case we will know little about what the object of our study was like before we started investigating it; not knowing that, it is impossible to judge whether any real change has occurred at all. Even studying a person or organization both before and after a development can be inadequate if it is in the form of, for example, a single day of observations at two points in time. Such a before-and-after design, which resembles a simple experiment, may still ignore important events that might explain what is observed in the object of study. For example, a sharp raise in interest rates might have a greater effect on the activities of a for-profit organization than would some other factor (a new CEO) we are investigating at the time.

Yin (1981), Stake (1998), and others point out that case studies can be made more rigorous than Campbell and Stanley seem to imply. The case method is improved when it includes diverse sources of evidence (e.g., written records, field observations, verbal reports, etc.), multiple times of observation, and a holistic and process-oriented emphasis. In general, the same techniques that make for good case studies also make for good historical research (see Schutt, 1999, p. 329; Yin, 1981, p. 64).

A good example of a case study—and of a longitudinal investigation and intensive interviews as well—comes to us from Carol Kuhlthau (1999). Kuhlthau conducted a five-year study of a securities analyst as he progressed from a beginner to an experienced worker. Keeping in touch with respondents over a five-year period is, in itself, relatively uncommon in information seeking studies. One of the features that makes Kuhlthau's study remarkable is that she actually began following her subject in 1983 when he was a high school student, 15 years before the completion of her investigation. Earlier observations on this single case study were published by Kuhlthau in 1997, and this subject was included along with other case studies published in 1991 and 1988 (a and b).

Kuhlthau's case study was motivated by several basic questions regarding the development of expertise among people who work in information-intensive jobs. In this particular case, an analyst locates and absorbs a great deal of information regarding securities and the general economic environment, processes these, and then provides an analysis in the form of a report to his firm. In addition to understanding how this process happens, Kuhlthau was interested more specifically in *how such expertise develops over time*, hence the longitudinal element to her investigation.

Kuhlthau characterizes her research problem as one involving the concepts of uncertainty, decision making, and task complexity. Several earlier studies have noted that more complex tasks resulted in more variety of information sought and in more varied approaches to information seeking. Unlike some past studies, however, Kuhlthau is much more interested in *the process of identifying and interpreting* the information sources that are used by an analyst than in *the type and nature of the sources* themselves.

In a fashion typical of case studies, Kuhlthau identifies both a fruitful environment for such studies (the financial services industry) and a willing respondent (about whom she already had some background data). In case studies the purposeful selection of participants has the advantage of matching for characteristics useful to the study (e.g., a respondent who has the right kind of position and experience to be subject to the stimuli of interest to the study, and who is articulate); to that end, case studies can reinforce validity. Purposive sampling, however, can also introduce biases into a study, particularly a lack of variety in viewpoints and experience; for that reason, the reliability of the results can suffer. Quite appropriately, Kuhlthau places limits on her results by observing that "the findings from this study cannot be considered as describing information workers' process of information seeking in general, or even that of securities analysts in particular" (1999, p. 411).

Kuhlthau initially interviewed her respondent in 1983, when he participated in a study of searching for materials in a library. Since then, the investigator has conducted lengthy interviews with him every four to five-years. In 1990 and 1995 (the last five-year period of the study), Kuhlthau used eight questions to focus the respondent's comments on his search for, and use of, information on the job. Such questions concerned, for example, what uncertainties exist in various aspects of his job, the degree of complexity present in different tasks, how he goes about interpreting information, and the degree to which he uses certain kinds of information sources (e.g., trade journals or company reports).

Kuhlthau extracts and interprets the responses from transcripts of the two taped interviews. This allows her to contrast the respondent's perceptions as a "novice" (in 1990) versus his responses as an "expert" (in 1995). In doing so she focuses on the key issues she has raised—for example, the relationship of uncertainty to information seeking and the complexity of the analyst's task, and the relation of both of those concepts to the analyst's use of particular sources.

Kuhlthau draws a number of specific conclusions from her study, too many to discuss here in great depth. Among her more general findings are that feelings of uncertainty are closely associated with heightened anxiety; that the sense of uncertainty may be more affected by *perceptions* of complexity than by the *actual* complexity of a looming task; and that the analyst comes to see his job as the construction of a narrative, in which the chief objective is to "add value" to the information reported rather than merely to gather facts and deliver "true" conclusions.

Kuhlthau concludes that case studies of this type are a means of adding depth to wider-scale investigations (such as surveys) and that further research needs to go "beyond studying what categories of sources are used by information workers, to studying how and why these sources are used to accomplish a wide range of projects and tasks" (1999, p. 411).

Probably the most critical comment one can make in regards to a case study applies to this example as well: How much can we really learn from the details of one person's experience? This is the age-old question that divides the ideographic and monothetic modes of research, and, some would say, forms the boundary line between the humanities and social sciences.

A constant concern in case studies is whether the unit observed (in this case, a particular securities analyst) is representative of others in the population (i.e., all securities analysts). Whenever we have a sample of one, we have to ask, "Why that person?" It is possible that he might be unusual when compared to other securities analysts; for one thing, he is younger than most, and for another, he is aware of being a subject in an investigation, which might affect both his behavior and responses to questions.

Kuhlthau offers good reasons for the selection of the person she studies, but the more important point is that she is not trying to generalize her findings to the entire population of securities analysts. Bather, she is exploring a basic aspect of human information behavior. We do not have a strong reason to think that this particular person is radically different from all other human beings. In addition, case studies can have a cumulative effect; as further cases are investigated, we can compare findings and hope that they lead us in the direction of generalization.

Kuhlthau is certainly correct in implying that her findings can be applied in two ways. First, it makes an attempt at explaining *why* a person seeks information in particular forms and ways; other research strategies, such as experiments and surveys, usually do not address "why" questions very well. Second, the results of her study can lead to the implementation of further case studies, or to the design of complementary investigations that use entirely different research strategies.

9.1.2 Experiments: Shopping for Cars and Cornflakes

Experiments carry a great deal of baggage for both the researchers who use them and those who do not. Long considered to be the "queen of methodologies" by those social researchers studying a small set of well-defined variables, experiments offer the means of controlling for alternate influences and explanations in an investigation. However, laboratory experiments accomplish their control by eliminating so many real-world factors to such a degree that they are frequently criticized for being artificial and having results that may not apply to the world outside the laboratory.

The kind of controls that scientists use to investigate physical phenomena are not often applicable to studying human behavior, because people are aware. They know what experiments are, and may even intuit the possible motivations of experimenters. Humans are constantly learning, both from the world at large and from any experimental situation in which they might find themselves. In addition, experiments involving people have *ethical concerns*. Various laws, regulations, codes, and moral concerns prevent us from creating situations that might harm experimental subjects in any way, to any degree, physically or mentally. No matter how compelling might be the evidence generated by a certain experimental design, if it involves mental stress or severe deception, it cannot be implemented. I say *severe* deception because most experimentation concerning human mental or social phenomena can not be carried out without some degree of omission or deception regarding the purpose of the experiment, as merely being aware of the purpose may alter the responses of the experimental subjects.

Chiefly for these reasons, it is best not to picture human experiments as taking place in isolated "laboratory" settings (even though many do). For the purposes of investigating information seeking and other human cognitions and behaviors, experimental designs may fall on a continuum stretching from the ideal to the realistic. On the ideal end of the spectrum are found the classic experiment, conducted in a special setting in which many extraneous factors are controlled for, and in which the experiment is conducted as swiftly as possible so as to rule out the confusing events ("history effects") of the real world. The realistic position on the continuum is harder to define, but involves the study of cause and effect in uncontrolled social settings; in this case, the experimental "treatment" (i.e., a development thought to cause change in the human subjects) may be one that is not even introduced by the experimenter but rather by some external event: for example, the availability of a new source of information (e.g., a Web page), or the introduction of a new channel of communication (e.g., e-mail).

Two decades ago the methodologists Thomas Cook and Donald Campbell (1979) popularized the notion of "quasi-experiments" — investigations that took place in real-world ("field") settings to study intentional changes and their effects on people. Cook and Campbell addressed the needs of educators and policy analysts for research strategies to use in evaluating the effects of educational innovations and social programs. Their work taught a generation of researchers that aspects of the classic experiment could be used outside of the laboratory to help us understand, for example, whether programs like *Sesame Street* really made a lasting difference in the rate at which children learned language skills and other content. Moreover, the notion of quasi-experimental designs gave investigators a way of talking about trade-offs between the design of a study and the generalizability of the results, and served as a guide for assessing the reliability of specific measures and their outcomes. Hard line methodologists still exist who hold that "there is no such thing as a 'quasi-experiment'," one could also argue that, where people are concerned, there are *only* quasi-experiments; people are simply too clever, and the real world is simply too obtrusive, for "pure" experiments using human subjects.

In the remainder of this section, we will examine two contrasting examples of experimentation. Unless we define information seeking very broadly, we find relatively few laboratory experiments that shed meaningful light on such behavior. Of course there is basic research into the psychology of memory and cognition that might apply, but this is so far removed from the usual concern of information behaviors as to be unhelpful. Fortunately, research into *consumer behavior* includes a great number of attempts at using experiments to better understand how people search for, and use, information when they are faced with a purchase decision. What is purchased may be as trivial as laundry detergent or as major as a new car. As foreshadowed in a scenario from Chapter 2, we will consider a laboratory experiment concerned with how people search for information when they are shopping for a car.

Hauser, Urban, and Weinberg (1993), in an article entitled "How Consumers Allocate Their Time When Searching for Information," offer an example of an experiment in a highly controlled setting. Their eventual goal was to identify and predict the order in which consumers would choose types of information sources, and how much time they were likely to spend with each source. Hauser *et al.* chose new car purchases as a domain of interest, assuming that findings from such a study would prove useful to automobile makers (one of which funded the study), as well as provide insight into basic human information behavior in any domain.

In studying this topic, Hauser *et al.* assumed that consumers make relatively rational decisions based on the cost–benefit principle discussed in Chapter 5. One obvious assumption of cost–benefit approaches is that the value of any information must be weighed against the cost of obtaining it. In an ideal situation, we would spend as much time as we want to pursue as many sources of information as we desire. However, such a "hyperrational" search is not practical; our time is always limited and thus must be budgeted, based on our expectations of what we will gain from an allocation of time. Although a cost–benefit approach to time allocation does not apply very well to many of life's important tasks (e.g., raising a child), it certainly holds value for many economic transactions in our lives, such as purchases of necessary products and services.

Researchers studying purchase decisions can use a variety of strategies, including observations of shoppers, interviews with them, and/or analysis of the artifacts that shopping leaves behind such as sales records. As the phenomena of interest in this study were possible information sources and how people both think about them and use them, the choice of a laboratory simulation made a great deal of sense. It would be extremely difficult to identify and follow actual car buyers through their daily lives as they locate and read printed reviews of cars, talk to friends, visit automobile showrooms, examine cars, bargain with sales representatives, and so forth. Simulating a real-life search process is undoubtedly artificial, but it affords a way to restrict the information sources in such a way as to make them comparable and measurable across the experimental subjects who use them. It also means that a process that might take months in the real world is collapsed into perhaps an hour in the laboratory setting—another means of screening out stray events and influences that are not of interest in the investigation.

To make the information sources as uniform as possible, Hauser *et al.* tried to replicate all of them on a computer workstation in a laboratory setting, a refinement of an older practice of using physical media such as "story boards" on which information (e.g., photos and text) could be placed as needed. The computer monitor displayed information from a videodisc, which included magazine and television advertisements, videotapes of interviews with actual car buyers, simulations of articles from consumer reviews and car magazines, videos that depicted a car's interior and exterior, and simulated interactions with a salesperson in which the buyer chose questions from a menu and then viewed film clips of the salesperson answering each question. Users of the workstation could view any of these information sources, in any order, for a total search time of up to 13 minutes.

The experimental procedures were administered to 177 volunteer subjects, selected from a list of nearly a thousand recent car purchasers who were considering buying a new car. Before and after using the workstation to search for information, the subjects indicated on an 11-point scale how likely they were to purchase a particular model based on what they knew at that time. This "purchase intent" measurement was recorded by the computer, which also kept track of the sources used, the sequence of sources, and how much time a subject spent with each one.

Hauser *et al.* freely acknowledge the artificiality of these procedures, and discuss at some length the advantages and disadvantages of studying consumer behavior in this way. For instance, it is impossible to build into the experiment the actual costs involved for different sources: it may take me a half-hour to drive to a car dealer but merely a few minutes to call a dealer (or a friend) for information. Hauser *et al.* refer to other sources of data (interviews) that they used both to design the experiment and to supplement what they learned from conducting it. For example, they learned from their interviews that buyers typically consulted between two and three sources before an actual purchase. Therefore, the experimenters imposed time constraints on subjects using the workstation to insure that they did not view an unusually large number of sources.

What was learned from the experiment? Consumers showed a clear preference for visiting the virtual showroom to see the car and ask questions about it. Within the limited time they had to choose sources, 81% used the showroom visit and 48% made it their first choice. They spent the most time with this source and it was the most influential source by far. This is not surprising, given the nature of purchasing objects in general and cars in particular — we want to see them, and touch them if possible. We also want to get verbal answers to our questions, as high usage of the salesperson tapes demonstrated. The fact that the laboratory behavior mirrored what consumers tend to do in actual car purchases lends validity to the use of the experimental method to study such behavior.

The articles from magazines were the next most popular source, used by 65% of the subjects and the first choice for 24%, although subjects tended to spend less time reading than watching videos of various types. Close behind the articles were the taped interviews with car purchasers, used by 61% of the subjects, and a first choice for 19% of them. The subjects spent almost as much time watching consumer interviews as they did using the virtual showroom. Very few subjects (9%) chose to look at ads first, even though 38% examined them at some point. Most subjects went back to view the most popular sources a second time, particularly the showroom and the articles.

What can we learn from this example that might extend beyond its domain of car buying? Regarding research strategies, it should be obvious that such an approach to understanding information seeking has value outside of consumer research. For example (and assuming adequate resources), one could do some interesting experiments to examine differential usage of electronic sources of information. When, and under what conditions, might people choose to use Amazon.com rather than an online library catalog to find information on a current book? Given the access to both printed information and people through the Internet, how do seekers allocate their time between those two types of sources? That is, when (and why) might they search text files and when (and why) might they ask questions of correspondents via e-mail? Among the many pages of information found on the World Wide Web on a given topic, which are chosen most often and why? Answers to these broad questions can be approached in a number of ways, one of which would be to conduct experiments with a narrowed set of sources in a laboratory setting. Complementary approaches could include analysis of computer transaction logs (Rice & Borgman, 1983) and content analysis of e-mail messages exchanged by peers on an electronic discussion list (e.g., White, 2000).

Interestingly, the Hauser *et al.* study sidesteps the issue of "cognitive costs" (e.g., the effort it takes to read and understand a comparison of several car models). However, it may well be the case that the mental (and undoubtedly emotional) effort required to use different sources may prove to be the more compelling predictor of use — if we can measure it. The issue of "the cost of thinking" has been long discussed among consumer researchers (see Shugan, 1980), but it is usually considered in terms of formal decision rules and the potential cost of poor choices made by deviating from a rule, rather than as a factor in itself. Apprehension about the mental and emotional effort required to find and understand task-related information may be a key factor in how people go about information seeking, as Kuhlthau (1988a), Mellon (1986), Jiao and Onwuegbuzie (1997), and others have demonstrated.

Aside from a lesson regarding methodology, there is also a substantive finding from this, and other, consumer behavior studies that is worth contemplating: people with information needs often tend to prefer getting information from other people, even when that information might be less authoritative or reliable. Consider the motives of a car dealer in providing information, for example; aren't they naturally inclined to present information selectively and in a manner that presents the models they sell as superior? Although printed sources may be highly regarded, less time is spent in reading than in listening to others (or, in the Hauser study, to tapes of salespeople and consumers).

The point was made earlier that laboratory experiments, for all their advantages in terms of control, can suffer from artificiality. How can we trust the results when a situation is so staged? For this reason, and because some situations and variables cannot be adequately represented in the laboratory, many experiments take place in real-world settings. So-called "field experiments" trade off degrees of control in exchange for more realism (Cook & Campbell, 1979).

A good example of the use of field experimentation, and of how it contrasts with corresponding laboratory manipulations, is found in another study that examined shopping behavior. Cole and Balasubramanian (1993) investigated how consumers used information to select cereals in both the laboratory and the supermarket to compare results from the two different approaches. In this case, the experimenters' motives and funding source are quite different from those of Hauser *et al.*: Cole and Balasubramanian address the public policy issue of what information should be provided to consumers for them to make an informed choice regarding the nutritional content of the foods they buy. Specifically, they were interested in whether elderly consumers did more poorly than younger buyers when faced with such decisions. A variety of evidence from other studies shows that the degraded memory capacity of older adults influences them toward considering fewer factors when making decisions. Because it is more of a struggle to remember things, the elderly have less cognitive capacity available for processing information. Cole and Balasubramanian hypothesized that this would result in poorer decisions regarding the processed foods they purchase, based on what is known about the products' nutritional value.

Let's look at Cole and Balasubramanian's field experiment first and then consider the laboratory version. Their procedure began with the recruitment of 79 shoppers in three grocery stores. One at a time, each shopper was randomly given one of two tasks. Half of the consumers were asked to buy a box of cereal, using a $1 coupon they were given as an incentive to participate. The other consumers were asked to do the same, except they were required to use a *decision rule* in selecting the cereal: it must have less than 200 milligrams of sodium and at least 2 grams of fiber in a serving. The investigators showed the shoppers how to locate nutritional information on a box of cereal and confirmed that all subjects were able to locate and read it. All the experimental subjects were observed as they shopped; the numbers of boxes and nutritional panels they examined were noted. Afterward, each participant was interviewed to gather background information (e.g., age and education) and data relevant to the experiment (e.g., knowledge and use of cereal).

The results mostly conformed to the expectations of the researchers, as put forward in their hypotheses. That is, the elderly shoppers (who had an average age of 68) did less searching than the younger consumers (who averaged 36 years of age).

Younger shoppers were much less likely to be "satisficers" — choosing to buy the very first box of cereal they examined. The elderly examined fewer boxes and nutritional information; based on the criteria of the decision rule (low sodium and high fiber), the final choices they made were not as good as those of younger shoppers. Furse, Punj, and Stewart (1984) showed parallel results regarding the tendency of the elderly to satisfice when shopping for cars.

Cole and Balasubramanian's field experiment seems to correspond fairly closely to life in the real world. We can even imagine their experimental condition as having a parallel in everyday life: many elderly have been told by their physicians to "buy food that is high in fiber but low in salt." Yet field experiments have gaps in their results that leave them open to alternative explanations. In this case, Cole and Balasubramanian were not able to tell if the elderly shoppers were influenced by their *past shopping experience*. In particular, did they search less because they already knew (or thought they knew) the sodium and fiber content of some cereals? If they had been previously encouraged by doctors, friends, or the mass media to buy healthy cereals, then such a counterexplanation is highly plausible.

To strengthen their findings, Cole and Balasubramanian conducted a second experiment in a laboratory setting with the same task: select a cereal with low sodium and high fiber. This time they used five artificial brands of cereal (labeled A through E) rather than the actual brands found in stores; this eliminated the possibility that previous shopping experience influenced the results. They also introduced a condition aimed at testing whether degraded memory was the cause of less searching among the elderly. Half the experimental subjects were encouraged to write down information given to them about the five cereals; the others simply had to remember the data they read from a computer monitor regarding the nutritional content of the cereals.

The laboratory experiment included many careful design features and specific conclusions that we need not consider here. Suffice to say that the basic results of the field experiment were confirmed, while the rival explanation about prior knowledge was ruled out. The elderly participants continued to search less and make poorer choices than the younger consumers. Being able to write down the nutritional information encouraged some of the elderly to examine more information but it did not improve the quality of their choices in terms of the decision rule that they were asked to use.

By using two parallel types of experimental design—field and laboratory—Cole and Balasubramanian were able to improve upon the results that either one might have given if used on its own. The investigators were thus able to present compelling results of relevance to policy makers concerned about health and product regulation. At a time when recently introduced regulations required more nutritional information to appear on packaged foods, Cole and Balasubramanian were able to show that such data was not equally useful to all segments of the population, particularly for a vulnerable group like the elderly. On the basis of their results, the experimenters recommend that more consumer education is needed, or better yet that requirements stipulate the use of easily recognized symbols that require less capacity to process. Since the time of this research, figures indicating that a food is "heart-healthy" have begun to appear on menus and packages.

Of course, the strengths of experiments also translate into weaknesses of other kinds. The laboratory experiment is highly artificial, and the field procedures (e.g., the decision rule for selecting cereal) are somewhat unnatural as well. In both cases, the stimulus for the study — nutrition panels for breakfast cereal — is a very narrow domain. In the big picture of life, seeking information about breakfast cereals is merely a pixel.

9.1.3 Surveys: CEOs and Scholars

Simply put, the survey is a type of research in which a sample of individuals is asked to respond to questions. Many people associate surveys with the completion of a printed questionnaire, usually received and returned through the mail.

However, as a research strategy the survey approach encompasses a variety of methods of data collection, including individual interviews by phone or in person, the interviewing of people together in small groups, and the increasing use of electronic versions of questionnaires (i.e., by e-mail and Web page). Survey research can make use of a variety of question types and techniques, such as asking the respondent to relate a "critical incident" that illustrates an important type of event or change in the life of the respondent or an organization.

The printed questionnaire is an exemplar of the survey method, but interviews are harder to categorize. The strength of the survey method is gathering responses from large numbers of individuals — data that can easily be quantified. As interviews become longer and more intensive, we enter a different realm of data collection and research strategy. That is, interviews that require lengthy, unrestricted responses (such as critical incident questions) or that involve more than one respondent (e.g., focus group interviews) are considered to be "qualitative" approaches because responses are gathered verbatim and cannot be easily summarized.

This section will focus on quantifiable examples of survey research, such as large-scale studies using highly structured questionnaires or schedules (the latter being a survey instrument for use in interviews). We will leave the more qualitative uses of interviews for later in this chapter.

A complaint common to reviews of the information seeking literature is that surveys are overused in studying such phenomena. Hewins (1990) even goes so far as to exclude surveys from her otherwise comprehensive review of the 1986 to 1989 literature. Undoubtedly mail questionnaires have been abused because they require relatively little effort when compared to other methods. However, the popularity of surveys also springs from their other strengths, among which are their economy and standardization of data, and their potential for reaching reclusive audiences and encouraging candid responses (Babbie, 2000). Surveys are still an appropriate and valid approach to research problems that require the study of large populations.

The first example of the use of survey techniques in studying information seeking is one that makes use of mail questionnaires. Fiona Chew (1994) explored "The Relationship of Information Needs to Issue Relevance and Media Use" in a survey based on the work of Richard Carter (1978). Carter (who was a seminal influence on Brenda Dervin's sense-making research) had hypothesized that information needs are evidenced by three types of "questioning behaviors": Orientation ("What is happening?"; "What do the experts say about it?"), Reorientation ("Do I understand?"; "Am I following this correctly?"), and Construction ("What information can help me develop an opinion?"; "What do I need to reach a solution to the problem?"). Chew, in turn, hypothesized that these distinctions in questioning behavior may lead to differences in individuals' information needs, and subsequently in their use of media to find information, depending on the relevance of the issue.

Chew chose the survey method because she was interested in how members of the public thought about news events. Too much attention, she thought, had been directed at use of media for simple orientation — finding out what is happening, as opposed to finding information and reaching conclusions about events. Chew took advantage of a prominent news development — the 1991 Gulf War — and contrasted it with a more mundane public issue, the U.S. federal budget deficit. These issues had been identified during a nationwide public opinion poll conducted a week before Chew's survey as the two most important problems facing the nation at that time. The Gulf War, a new and shocking development, was regarded as much more important (and thus more relevant) than the budget deficit, which was a more technical and decade-old concern. Thus, the Gulf War became the "high relevance issue" and the deficit the "low relevance issue" for the purposes of the survey. A different survey instrument was devised for each issue, each containing questions about how much attention had been paid to reports about one issue (a great deal, some, little, not much), the degree to which they had certain question types in mind about the issue (e.g., "How does this situation affect me?"), accompanied by questions about type, frequency, and pattern of media use, along with the usual demographic questions.

Chew mailed about 1,000 surveys (500 of each type) to randomly selected households within one metropolitan area. It should be noted that Chew only obtained a response rate of 26%, which is considered by some methodologists (e.g., Babbie, 2000) to be dangerously weak for drawing conclusions. Chew could probably have boosted the response rate to between 30% and 40% by mailing more than one follow-up reminder. In another survey discussed in Chapter 11, Auster and Choo (1993) mailed up to four questionnaires to their target audience and followed it with a phone call if none of those instruments were returned; they brought their response rate up to 56%, an excellent result for their topic and audience (chief executive officers).

The responses to Chew's questionnaires show a distinct pattern: two-thirds of the respondents paid "a great deal of attention. To the Gulf War, with everyone paying at least some attention. In contrast, only a third paid a great deal of attention to the looming deficit, and nearly 11% paid little or no attention to it. Chew is able to relate these responses back to the three types of questioning behavior to show that they differed across the two issues. Regarding the Gulf War, respondents had a higher need to know how the situation would affect them, and what the experts had to say about it (Orientation questions). To a lesser degree they also had more Construction questions, related to identifying different viewpoints on the issue and forming their own opinion about it. The only question regarding the deficit was, again, "How does the situation affect me?" but this was weak compared to the Gulf War.

Chew was also able to demonstrate that the pattern of media usage differed across the two issues, depending on the questioning mode. Information seeking from television was high in all cases, but those respondents who asked only Orientation questions used other media (newspapers, magazines, radio) less. Those with Construction questions used those media more. Respondents who exhibited all three modes of questioning also reported using media more frequently than anyone else. Chew concludes that "information needs vary by issue relevance" (p. 684) and that "as information needs go beyond orientation, a variety of media are used in a complementary fashion" (p. 686).

A recent variation on the mail survey is the distribution of questionnaires via the Internet: electronic mail, discussion lists, newsgroups, and the Web. Zhang (2000) used multiple means of collecting survey data, chiefly through having respondents access the questionnaire on a Web page, but also allowing responses by postal mail and FAX. As well as introducing a novel twist to an older methodology, Zhang's article contains a good discussion of the strengths and weaknesses of using computers and networks to reach respondents.

Zhang's topic of study — the use of Internet-based scholarly sources by researchers — is not of prime interest here, but her methodological discussion and findings are of great relevance. Zhang points out that the Internet offers the potential of addressing two persistent problems that face postal surveys: low response rates and slow response times. Low response rates are a particularly intractable problem, which is usually an artifact of asking total strangers about topics that they may not care much about. Yet the ease of responding (at least to short lists of questions) offers to lower the effort barrier a bit for those willing to respond, thus potentially upping the response rate. And for those who *do* respond, the speed of the Internet can reduce response times by days, if not weeks (particularly so in international surveys).

Questionnaires can be distributed by e-mail to individuals or through discussion lists to preidentified groups of individuals with known interests. Responding to such surveys can be quite easy, particularly if they do not require much typing. However, inserting or even simply indicating a response is difficult if the e-mail software does not allow a received message to be altered and then forwarded or replied to (as many do not, for obvious reasons of maintaining authenticity of the original message). In such cases, the respondent may need to save the questionnaire as a file, then copy it again into an e-mail to return it the surveyor, an extra step that is bound to reduce response rates.

Another possibility, used by Zhang and her colleagues, is to direct the respondent (typically via an e-mail message) to visit a Web site and respond to a precoded questionnaire, which is then submitted for automatic processing. Such a method offers numerous advantages, including interactive checking for valid respondents and responses, and automatic tabulation of the responses.

Yet using any computer technology to conduct surveys also presents some difficult challenges to the validity of the research results. This is because of the danger of biasing the original sample (if they must be computer users to respond) and the usable survey returns (if respondents must be comfortable with computers to respond successfully). Respondents with fewer resources and less education, which may translate into less physical and intellectual access to computers, are likely to be left out. The resulting responses tend to suffer from bias by excluding some kinds of potential respondents and favoring the (self-) selection of others who have both access to and interest in computer-related resources.

Zhang in fact discovered that respondents who replied via the Web tended to have a higher perception of their own abilities to use the Internet, tended to use the Internet more, and tended to be younger. Gender and degree of Web access, however, were unrelated to how they chose to respond. Zhang found, as had several earlier studies that she reviews, that some respondents who had ample resources and education preferred not to respond to surveys electronically; about 20% in her study chose to respond by paper or FAX rather than via the Web.

There are other problems with electronically delivered surveys. Some respondents view them as even more impersonal than paper questionnaires, for example. The response rate—an important piece of data in determining the generalizability of the findings—may be inflated in electronic surveys (compared to postal surveys), because the researchers typically have better indications of whether the questionnaire was "undeliverable." And use of multiple electronic mailing lists may result in many respondents receiving multiple surveys, creating the potential for multiple responses from the same respondent (which can happen in any case) and exacerbating the problem of determining the sample size and thus the response rate. The additional complexity of an online questionnaire may also result in more failures to successfully complete and submit the instrument — 10% of Zhang's respondents gave up even after accessing and partially completing the form.

Unfortunately, many poorly-executed surveys are conducted now using an electronic means of distribution. Electronic mail may only encourage further use of an overused method. Given the increased ease and lowered costs of conducting surveys electronically, we would at least expect the survey populations to be larger (see Brown, 1999, for a recent example of an e-mail survey with severe weaknesses in sampling). This is not to conclude that e-mail surveys are necessarily weak, however, particularly when they are coupled with other methods of data gathering. Bruce (1998) is an example of an information seeking survey that succeeds nicely.

In conclusion, while self-administered survey methods have strengths, they also have weaknesses, especially superficiality. Questionnaires cannot easily capture the complexity of information seeking, nor can they observe the influence of context (e.g., place, time, and situation) in the actual use of information. In-depth interviews and participant observation (see the multiple data sources discussion) may be strong on capturing context, but have their own drawbacks as well.

9.1.4 Brief Interviews: Studies of Everyday Folks

The interview is a very flexible technique. An interview can last a short time or a long time. Interviews can be accomplished in person (i.e., face to face), or over the telephone or computer. Interview questions can be asked just once, or repeated over time with the same respondent. The interviewer can take the formal role of a neutral investigator, or the informal role of a participant in the same activities as the respondent. (The latter type will considered under the heading of "intensive interviews.") In this section, we consider three examples of "brief" interviews (i.e., typically one time, and much less than an hour in length) used to study information seeking.

Although they rather rare in the context of information seeking studies, door-to-door (or "doorstep") interviews are still conducted in other realms. The most familiar example in the United States is the visit from the census taker every 10 years. The main advantage of doorstep interviews is that they can survey hundreds of respondents and obtain answers of reasonable depth and reliability.

In a doorstep survey concerning information needs in the United Kingdom, Marcella and Baxter (2000) discussed the methodology of a random sample of almost 900 members of the public. The Citizenship Information research project was funded by the British Library from 1997 to 1999 to investigate the needs and acquisition of information by or about the government that "may be of value to the citizen either as a part of everyday life or in the participation by the citizen in government" (p. 2). The first stage of the project was a questionnaire survey of almost 1,300 citizens, conducted through public libraries and other agencies. The first stage of results was thought to be fairly representative of the British population, but it oversampled library users and thus was complemented with a large sample of doorstep interviews. The interview method could probe more deeply and reach individuals less likely to use the library, such as those lacking in literacy, education, or mobility, than could the distribution of questionnaires. But a key problem in door-to-door interviews is getting interviewers to choose a fair sample of residences to approach; if the choice of blocks or of residences within blocks is left to their own judgment, interviewers will be overly influenced by concerns about their safety and a desire to have "comfortable" interactions with others. This will lead them, consciously or unconsciously, to choose nicer blocks and houses—with corner houses tending to be particularly oversampled. However, the "random walk" method (often used in market research surveys) can be used to direct interviewers to a fair sample of households by using a detailed decision algorithm ("if the address is an apartment house, begin with the second apartment on each floor and..."). In this study, use of the random walk method was found to reach greater proportions of women, elderly, retired, homemakers, and lower social classes, in most cases forming a more representative sample than the questionnaire method (Marcella & Baxter, 2000).

Rita Atwood and Brenda Dervin (1982) report results from one of the largest studies of citizen information needs ever conducted (Palmour, Rathbun, Brown, Dervin, & Dowd, 1979). The two researchers were interested in the issue of whether race predicts information seeking behavior. The Palmour *et al.* study of information needs, in which Dervin was a key investigator, used a multistage probability sample of the 22 million residents of California at that time. One thousand individuals were selected, first by sampling geographic areas (to ensure ethnic diversity), then census blocks within the areas, then dwellings within the blocks. Face-to-face interviews were completed with 646 individuals among the thousand dwellings selected in the random sample.

Atwood and Dervin reanalyzed 205 of the original questionnaires (i.e., schedules) completed by the trained interviewers in the study. They selected matched samples of White, Black, and Hispanic respondents, then chose only those who were able to identify a single "most important question" among those information needs they reported.

The responses of these three similarly sized groups were analyzed to test the hypothesis that a "situated movement state" typology, representing the kinds of gaps that people reported, would be a better predictor than race of the kinds of questions respondents asked in bridging their gaps.

Three kinds of gaps were identified among those reported by the sample of respondents: (1) the need to make a *decision* (e.g., which house to buy); (2) the presence of a *barrier* (e.g., the car is broken and must be fixed); or (3) a *problematic* state over which the respondent has little or no control (e.g., the neighbors keep the respondent awake every night).

The responses to these gaps, as recorded on the interview schedules, were coded as comprising What, Why, How, or When questions that the respondents asked. Fourteen types of sources to which respondents turned to answer these questions were also coded and statistically reduced (using factor analysis) to five; these five factors represent, in effect, strategies used for answering the questions.

Atwood and Dervin's results show that the nature of a gap — as a decision, barrier, or problematic — is a better predictor of subsequent question-asking than is ethnicity. The use of two types of information sources, mass media/business sources and books/libraries, were predicted mainly by interactions (combinations) of the race and situation variables rather than by race or situation alone. In other words, an individual's situation is more influential than their race in determining information seeking, at least in terms of the kinds of behaviors (and their measures) examined in this study.

It is much more common to use brief, face-to-face interviews in settings other than the home. Many information seeking investigations have interviewed respondents, entirely or predominantly, in their place of employment (e.g., Cobbledick, 1996; Cole, 1993; Ellis, 1989; Florio & DeMartini, 1993; Gorman & Helfand, 1995; Wicks, 1999). Another common venue for interviews is the school, as used, for example, by Erdelez (1997), Ford (1986), Julien (1999), Kuhlthau (1988a, 1988b, 1993a), Mellon (1986), Seldén (2001).

An example of telephone survey comes to us from Gantz, Fitzmaurice, and Fink (1991). Gantz *et al.* were continuing several decades of research on how people learn of news, particularly dramatic events like assassinations, and how they react to such news. Past research had tended to emphasize the passive nature of audiences, and their tendency to wait for information to be presented to them by mass media channels. Gantz *et al.* wanted to answer three questions: (1) How frequently and for what topics do adults engage in information seeking? (2) What media do they use, and to what extent is their information seeking confined to their usual channels? (3) What is the relationship between interest in specific news topics and information seeking about those topics?

To answer these research questions Gantz *et al.* conducted a very large number of interviews by telephone. A random sample of 1,147 phone numbers was taken from Indianapolis phone directories (a technique that would be seriously flawed today, for reasons described later). Undergraduate students trained for the task made phone calls to each residence, reaching someone at 73% of the dwellings. Another 27% (about a third of the dwellings contacted) of the total sample refused to be interviewed or were otherwise unable to complete the survey. This left 46% of the original sample as respondents to the survey, a fair response rate for this type of survey, although leaving open a question of response bias.

The interviews took about 15 minutes to complete and consisted of structured questions regarding use of the news media, interest in 13 preselected topics (e.g., national politics, the economy, health), knowledge of a specific recent political event (a U.S.–Soviet summit conference), individual patterns of information seeking, and demographic attributes.

The investigators operationalized the concept of information seeking by asking respondents to state, for each of the topics, how many days of the week they "*actively* turn to the media looking for *more* information about something you've *already* heard about" (p. 633; italicized words were emphasized by the interviewers). Other data were collected by asking the respondent to choose among points on scales, or other predetermined categories.

The results tended to reinforce the stereotype of passivity, at least regarding these general categories. Respondents did *not* turn to the mass media on a daily basis to look for information on any of the 13 topics. The most actively researched topic — on average, about every other day — was the local weather, followed by catastrophic events like earthquakes. Between 24% and 38% of those who participated in the survey *never* looked for additional information on the other topics. And when individuals did attempt to learn more about a topic, it was unusual for them to go beyond the media channels (e.g., newspapers and TV) that they normally used.

Yet when individual information seeking was considered across all of the topics, "one could conclude that most respondents engage in some information-seeking behavior quite regularly" (p. 635) although not daily and not on just one specific topic. The more active viewers tended to be more educated, more wealthy, and more frequent consumers of the news media. More complex patterns were found when the data were examined by age and gender.

Gantz *et al.* concluded that their overall results showed more activity than earlier studies, possibly because their study included "weather" as a topic when other studies had not. Perhaps the inclusion of other topics would have uncovered more active information seeking among the respondents, they suggest. As for explaining the tendency for respondents to stick to their usual media when seeking information, the investigators invoke the cost–benefit model; that is, seeking involves a rational calculation of the potential reward (the personal, professional, and social value of the information) versus the expenditures (money, time, and effort) required to obtain and process the information (e.g., Atkin, 1972, 1973). Therefore, "it would not be worth the effort" for them to try new or rarely used channels of information. Finally, Gantz *et al.* acknowledge that their viewpoint may differ considerably from that of the respondent; where the investigators see an important distinction between "active" and "passive" seeking, the respondent may see merely slight differences in the way they monitor a distant environment. That is, for news that does not affect them directly (local weather being one exception), individuals have little incentive to go beyond the normal channels and usual degree of effort. Therefore, information seeking of news amounts to selective attention to specific news items offered by those media that one normally monitors.

In critiquing the Gantz *et al.* investigation we should first acknowledge that it was a very large-scale study for the topic. Very few surveys of information seeking behaviors (whether by mail, telephone, or in person) have involved samples of over 500 respondents. The research questions arose from a careful review of the literature and the resulting measures (i.e., the interview questions, their response categories and scales) were rigorously constructed. Those are the main strengths of this study.

On the downside, the topic is (necessarily) narrow and the measures artificial. Thirteen very general topics do not very well represent the actual interests that a reader/viewer of the news media would have, even though they may correspond to the formulaic nature of the news media. Although the investigators attempted to compensate by taking one actual news event, the international summit they chose as a focus turned out to be of only modest interest to the respondents despite their high level of reported awareness; 95% said they knew about the U.S.—Soviet summit, but fewer than half of those sought any further news about it. The response categories used in survey research (e.g., yes/no, days per week, five-point scales) automatically limit the "realness"(validity) of the data collected. Many of these limitations could be said to be the result of a focus on a narrow range of topics — those covered by the mass media. As the researchers point out, "the news" is almost by definition at some distance from the daily lives of the reader/viewer. Hence, instances of active information seeking are hard to document.

A further limitation that plagues survey research (as noted in other examples, above) is the issue of response bias. Are the people who responded like the people who did not? It is the surveyor's responsibility to make some attempt to answer this question. In the case of attempting a census of a strictly limited population about whom individual information is available (e.g., the faculty of one university) comparing respondents to nonrespondents is fairly easy. In surveying a sample of a very large population, it is not. At the least, however, the investigator can compare the demographics of the respondents with what is known about the entire population (typically using national or local census data). The Atwood and Dervin study made such comparisons (by age, race, and gender) whereas Gantz *et al.* did not. Could the latter study's nonrespondents have been different from the respondents in age, gender, education, and income level? Gantz *et al.* did not explore that important question.

There are other strategies that researches can use to assess nonresponse bias. Making additional calls to those households in which the phone was not answered would narrow that group of nonresponses. One can also ask those who answered, but declined to participate in the study, a critical question or two; for example, asking a single question about use of the newspaper would indicate whether those who refused are more likely to be nonreaders (to suggest one likely response bias). Even though many would refuse to answer even *that* single question, those who did would increase our knowledge about nonrespondents. As it is, Gantz *et al.* report nothing about the majority (54%) of their sample who did not participate; that is, the 27% who could not be reached, plus the 27% who were contacted but declined to participate. Might they have been rather different in their information seeking behaviors than the minority who were interviewed?

9.1.5 Intensive Interviews: The Lives of Janitors and Brothers

When interviews strive for in-depth information on the interviewee's feelings experiences and perceptions — data that are not very amenable to quantitative analysis — the investigator enters the realm of the *intensive* interview. Such qualitative interview techniques may or may not strive for generalization to individuals and settings beyond those that are observed. For example, intensive interviews are one of many data-gathering methods used by anthropologists to study human groups and their cultures, usually under the assumption that some degree of *objectivity* is possible (O'Meara, 1989). In the hands of other investigators, lengthy and deep interviews may be used to study phenomena that are entirely *subjective* in nature, and the explanations that result may be peculiar to the particular individuals, contexts, places, and times that the investigator observed. In this section we will consider one account of each type: the use of intensive interviews with a small sample of a large social group, in an attempt to understand an entire subculture, and a lengthy study of just three individuals to understand their personal viewpoints.

Elfreda Chatman (1990) used intensive interviews, along with observation, to "discover the social and information worlds of a poor population" (p. 357). This investigator studied a group of 52 janitors — a sample of "the working poor" — over a two-year period. Chatman's goal was to document the meanings, feelings, and language that reflect the social reality of this group, and examine this evidence in the light of theories of social alienation (see Chapter 5).

On repeated occasions over many months, Chatman followed these workers around during their jobs, talking with them and observing their actions. She asked open-ended questions about their lives and work, and asked more structured questions about their sources of information: the mass media, friends, neighbors, and relatives. Some of the evidence she gathered she summarized in six tables listing, for example, the differing types of information they received from radio, TV, newspapers, and magazines.

But most of Chatman's evidence is in the form of verbatim comments, recorded in her field notes, a type of data that are difficult to quantify. In her report of the research, representative samples of respondent comments are categorized by what theme they represent, such as "media channels to the outside world." The most compelling evidence is listed under the five headings — normlessness, powerlessness, meaninglessness, isolation, and self-estrangement — which are indicators of "alienation." For example, under the topic of "isolation" we find a respondent who says, "Workers are out for themselves. There be a lot of misunderstandings about things. Peoples talk about other people." According to Chatman's interpretation of this and related statements, views of this type explain why it is that the janitors typically do not share information with each other. As other respondents say, "I can't trust anybody around here," and "I don't talk to nobody around here." Thus, a number of individual comments and anecdotes support the theory that the janitor's world is one that lacks solidarity and trust, documenting the existence one of the sources of alienation. Chatman was able to find many instances supporting four of the indicators, but not the fifth, "normlessness."

In her conclusions, Chatman describes how mass media are used both for utilitarian purposes (e.g., learning about trends, such as the spread of AIDS, that might possibly affect them) and for escape (i.e., entertainment programming). The investigator concludes her report by building a case for the importance of studying the information needs and uses of the poor.

Although Chatman left open the possibility that her findings may apply to a larger group (i.e., janitors, or perhaps even "the working poor"), our next example does not attempt generalization. Mick and Buhl's (1992) study of three Danish brothers is an example of *phenomenological* interviewing, intended to uncover the meanings and intentions of the person studied — to see reality in the unique way that the respondent sees it. Mick and Buhl attempt to demonstrate why it is important to study the *meanings* that individual consumers attribute to print advertising. It is Mick and Buhl's contention that most advertising research focuses strictly on the *information* contained in ads, which is assumed to be absorbed by consumers in a relatively uniform way. Even when researchers *do* look beyond the simple content of ads, they tend to project their own interpretations onto the consumers they study. Mick and Buhl believe that a different approach is called for, one that takes into account the recurring themes and projects that characterize an individual's life and make his or her responses to a text different from those that other individuals might have.

Mick and Buhl based their research design on psychological theories regarding personal constructs (Kelly, 1963) and life themes (Csikszentmihalyi, 1990), among other sources. In their view, at an early age individuals begin to structure their goals and actions to create coherence in their lives; they establish one or more life themes (e.g., being for justice, not being taken advantage of). These themes help account for individual differences in the interpretations of objects and events. Therefore, the design of Mick and Buhl's study is intended to discover the individual interpretations and meanings attributed to examples of one type of object, advertisements that appear in magazines.

To achieve the depth they desired, Mick and Buhl chose three brothers already known to them, and "with a shared sociocultural and family heritage but who were now developing distinct lives." A close personal connection between Buhl and one of the brothers allowed both full cooperation and access to family background details that were useful in their interpretation.

Their study preceded in two phases. In the first phase, the brothers identified magazines of interest to them and were each interviewed about relevant advertising in those magazines. In the second phase, each brother was interviewed about his life, life themes, and life projects; three months later, each was interviewed about Danish society and its life-styles. Together the brothers generated hundreds of pages of transcripts from three interviews conducted over a four-month period. In addition, the investigators themselves kept diaries throughout the entire project, and recorded their reflections in more than 50 memoranda.

One might think that such narrowly directed and mundane objects as magazine ads would be of little interest to most individuals. But the photos and text in magazine advertising are often carefully crafted to elicit complex responses in the reader, to engage their thoughts and emotions.

In their lengthy journal article reporting the findings from this study, Mick and Buhl demonstrated that each of the three brothers *did* connect some closely held aspect of his life to elements within the ads. For example, their reactions to an ad for a fashionable suit varied widely, from one brother's indication of pride that he had achieved enough in life to be able to wear such a suit, to another's scornful judgment that people only wear such clothing to create a false image of themselves. Each brother's statement could, in turn, be tied to events, values, and choices revealed in their personal history. The significance of such conclusions for the study of information seeking is that seemingly utilitarian messages may have rather different effects, uses, and gratifications across individuals.

Other studies of consumer response are reviewed by Scott (1994), along with the *reader response* research from which some of those studies borrow.

Outside of the advertising realm, a notable example of the reader response approach is Janice Radway's *Reading the Romance* (1985).

The strengths of the intensive interview lie in the detail that is provided regarding the people studied. The study by Chatman, which samples a fairly large number of people over a long period of time, gives us a good idea of the trade-offs between this type of design and a large-scale survey conducted at one point in time. Chatman cannot interview the larger numbers of respondents that are typically sampled in survey research, but she samples a smaller number over more points in time. It is a group that would be difficult to study by other means, because of the very alienation she highlights in her investigation. The data she collects are rich in detail; some of her evidence can be summarized, but most cannot and must be sampled as it is reported.

Contrasting Chatman's investigation with that by Mick and Buhl (1992), we can see how far one can go to try to capture the viewpoint of the individual. Perhaps the ultimate extension of their method would be a biography of a single person, covering multiple years and focused on certain categories of experience (i.e., significant life events, decisions, and values). Given the limited resources available to most investigators, the desired level of detail for this kind of study is difficult to justify. Mick and Buhl draw on the perceptions of five different people (themselves and the three brothers) to reach their conclusions. They also employed a third investigator to check their translations and interpretations, and received comments on their reports from 10 additional reviewers.

Like other methods, the strength of Mick and Buhl's *ideographic* strategy is also its weakness. Granted, the accounts of each individual are vivid and rich but they tell us only about one individual's reality. Are the findings applicable beyond that of the individuals studied? Fortunately, in this case there are goals beyond that of the individual findings: first, they want to demonstrate the value of their "life story" method of collecting data; second, they wish to establish that the concepts of *life themes* and *life projects* are valuable in understanding reader responses to texts. It is fair to say that their evidence is compelling as regards the latter goals.

9.1.6 Focus Group Interviews: Doctors and Nurses Search for Information

The final example of interviews uses the focus group format (see Lunt & Livingstone, 1996, for a recent history and critique of the method). Like the intensive interview, focus group interviews are primarily a qualitative technique, because most (and possibly all) of the data they generate are not amenable to statistical analysis. Rather, the emphasis in a group interview is on capturing spontaneous, verbatim responses using observation, notes, tape recordings, and sometimes videotape. The focus group is particularly useful for uncovering the underlying reasons for opinions, and motivations for actions; emotions and feelings (sometimes captured by facial expressions and body movements as much as spoken words) can also be important data gathered in focus group observations. In addition to the interviewer(s), it is not uncommon to have one or more additional researchers observing the action; in market research, where focus groups are heavily used to evaluate product advertising, it is common to hide the observers behind a one-way mirror.

As the name implies, the interview is conducted with a group of respondents. The group size can vary widely, but most commonly it involves from 8 to 12 participants. Groups smaller than eight do not generate the diversity and critical mass typically needed by the investigators. Groups larger than 12 present difficulties in participation (individuals talk less in larger groups) and observation (it is difficult to observe many individuals at once).

Focus group interviews are typically conducted by a single facilitator, with the assistance of one or more helpers. The participants usually sit around a table or in a circle of chairs in a room that offers as little distraction as possible. Often specially prepared materials are used to provoke response: printed texts, photographs, or videotapes, for example. Flip charts or blackboards are sometimes used to record responses so that group members can remember and react to them.

Krueger (1988) says that focus groups offer several advantages as a research method. They have relatively high face validity, as they capture real-life data in a setting that is only slightly artificial (i.e., the group discussion); the method is flexible as to topics, number of participants, and specific techniques of questioning and data-gathering; and it offers quick results at relatively little cost. Krueger (1988) also points out that group interviews offer less control than individual interviews, can be difficult to put together, and require both a skilled moderator and a conducive atmosphere to be conducted properly. The resulting data, while gathered quickly, can be difficult to analyze and interpret.

Mullaly-Quijas, Ward, and Woefl (1994) offer a large-scale example of the use of focus groups to study information seeking. In their case the purpose of the group was to gather information from health care professionals about their information seeking in general and their use of particular library and information services available in their hospital and/or community. A total of 14 different groups were conducted, each with between 2 and 12 participants, with a typical group consisting of 10 members. The 121 participants included, in order of their numbers, nurses, pharmacists, doctors, allied health professionals, dentists, medical librarians, hospital administrators, and hospital residents. The interviews lasted about 90 minutes each and participants were paid for their time, a common practice in focus group research.

Information seeking was one of three topics addressed. Those behaviors were elicited by asking five general questions, several of which had multiple subquestions or "probes" for further information. For example, participants were asked:

- What sources do you use to obtain medical information?
- What factors play a role in your decision to use various sources?
- What are the biggest barriers to gaining access to this information?
- How do you use the information? How do you determine its quality?

Participants not only answered these questions individually, but they reacted to and discussed the responses of other participants. The recorded responses were typed up to form a transcript of more than 800 pages.

The final report on this study undoubtedly contained more information, but the results were summarized very succinctly in the journal article by Mullaly-Quijas *et al.* For each focus group, responses to some questions are distilled into a few words. For example, in response to the question about barriers to using information sources (many of which are electronic files), a common answer across nearly all groups was "lack of knowledge" about how to use the sources. In contrast, responses about how the information would be used varied widely across groups; physicians emphasized "patient care" but also had need of documentation for lawsuits, as did some hospital administrators; pharmacists and allied health professionals were more likely to need information for "patient education"; respondents in academic settings needed information for research and grant-writing; several other needs and uses were unique to specific locations.

The focus groups in this study were thought to be successful by the investigators, as their results could be used to design a "communication plan" to improve information services. The results indicated problems (e.g., lack of publicity or training) that could be addressed by agencies like the National Library of Medicine or by individual hospitals and librarians. The study also called attention to alternate sources of information, such as contacts with colleagues; pharmacists in particular were often called upon for information by other health professionals.

As acknowledged by the investigators, focus groups have weaknesses as a method when used in isolation, and are strengthened when used in combination with other methods. The sociologist Robert Merton (Merton, Fiske, & Kendall, 1956) was noted for his pioneering use of the focus group; Merton not only used group interviews to develop hypotheses and questions for survey research, he used them in the course of investigations to help interpret the results of his studies.

In this case as in other investigations, focus group results reflect only the opinions of particular participants in a given setting at a particular time. It is risky to generalize the results to a larger population, such as all health professionals. Like other methods that rely upon self-reports, answers to interview questions about specific behaviors can be far off the mark. For example, Covell, Uman, and Manning (1985) observed physicians making six times as many inquiries as they had previously estimated in completing a questionnaire about their information seeking. It always helps to use multiple methods to approach a given research topic.

9.1.7 Diaries and Experience Sampling

Another self-report method tries to use sampling of *time* in the lives of individuals to overcome part of the artificiality problems associated with survey data. The so-called *diary* method takes its name from the common type of daily journal in which we record our personal reflections. Such journals are still used in some investigations, such as the one by Mick and Buhl that was already described.

Diaries have a number of variations. A basic difference lies in whether the respondent chooses when to fill out the diary (as we do when we keep a personal journal), or if the investigator chooses the time (a far more common use of the technique). Another difference is in the form required for reporting, which could be completely "open" but more often involves the use of precoded forms of varying degree of complexity (Wheeler & Reis, 1991).

A recent example of the use of respondent-controlled diaries is found in Maxine Reneker's (1993) study of "information-seeking among members of an academic community." Renecker recruited 31 informants on the Stanford University campus, giving them microcassette recorders on which to record incidents of information seeking. The informants were directed to make a recording "whenever they had a question they could not answer 'out of their own heads'" over two, one-week time periods. Respondents recorded how they went about addressing their information need and whether or not they were satisfied with the answer they obtained (p. 491). In this way Reneker collected 2,050 information seeking incidents, which she transcribed and went over with the informants. She also interviewed the study respondents regarding the potential effect of the method on their behavior, as well as gathering other information from them.

Reneker is not able to convey much of the results that she obtained in the brief article she published on the study, given that the findings are "in the texts of the 2,050 incidents" (p. 494). She *does* summarize what she learned from her study by noting (among other things) that

- reasons for seeking information included physiological and affective needs as well as cognitive needs,

- the number of incidents varied widely by information (from 14 to 245) and in the length that was required to transcribe it (from a few lines to several pages of text),
- the recordings express needs accurately but do not reflect all the needs that informants may have experienced during that period, and
- she judges the method adequate to have described "the experiences of people in depth and what the experiences and interactions mean to them" (p. 495).

Time-sampling methods have gotten more sophisticated over the years. As a scientific tool, this version of the diary method originated in "work sampling" studies of employees and their tasks. Whereas early "time and motion" studies of factory workers relied upon observations by investigators, white collar tasks were more amenable to self-recording by the worker. In its earlier uses, investigators asked respondents to carry with them a notebook or precoded form and to record what they were doing during certain moments or periods of time. For instance, on a certain day they might be asked to record, at the top and bottom of each hour, what they were doing. Later, investigators, in order to make the method more reliable, sampled recording times randomly; a pager or some other kind of alarm mechanism was used to prompt the respondents, at random times, to record what they had been doing. The random selection of times got around the problem of respondents having to watch the clock, and their tendency to "anticipate" what they would be writing about in their diary entry. Such reports typically were used to calculate costs associated with certain tasks and generally to improve efficiency of operations in organizations, such as in libraries (Spencer, 1971).

Since the 1970s the random-alarm method has shifted to include what people are *thinking and feeling* (the internal dimension of experience) as well as what they are doing (the external dimension). Depending on the purpose and context of the study, respondents might be asked to record their thoughts and/or behaviors from 3 to 10 times per day, in periods ranging from a few days up to several months. Most of these studies continue to use simple pagers with both audio and vibrating signals, but some devices have been used that allow data entry by the respondent, or that simultaneously take physiological measures like respondent blood pressure.

Mihaly Csikszentmihalyi (1990) and his colleagues (Kubey & Csikszentmihalyi, 1990; Kubey, Larson, & Csikszentmihalyi 1996) use the phrase "Experience Sampling Method" (ESM) to describe the general technique of random alarm recordings of thoughts, feelings, and actions. Kubey, Larson, and Csikszentmihalyi (1996) report on 20 years of ESM studies of motivations, emotions, and cognitions associated with a variety of activities. The method has been used widely to study how individuals allocate their time within and across cultures. Csikszentmihalyi in particular has used it to study his notion of "flow" — experiences so involving and intrinsically motivating that the passage of time is not noticed.

In a study relevant to some of the modes of information gathering discussed in this book, Kubey and Csikszentmihalyi (1990) report studies of household activities that challenge the "uses and gratifications" view of the "active" television viewer. Their respondents consistently report low concentration and activity but high feelings of relaxation while watching TV programming. In contrast, the highest concentration levels were reported for reading.

9.1.8 Unobtrusive Approaches: Historical Analysis

"Unobtrusive" methods are those that do not intrude into the phenomenon being studied. Participant observation, interviews, questionnaires, and (especially) experiments are all intrusive, because to some degree they alter the way that subjects behave. The people being observed might have behaved differently had an investigation not been conducted.

The notion of unobtrusive social research methods was popularized by Eugene Webb and various colleagues in a 1966 book on "nonreactive measures" (an updated version was published in 1981). The theme of that book was that social researchers were making too much use of experiments, surveys, and other direct observations, and ought to supplement (but not replace) their other sources of evidence with an examination of "traces" of human behavior. What is it that people leave behind (or take away) in the course of their lives? Webb, Campbell, Schwartz, Sechrest, and Grove used the geological analogies of accretion and erosion to discuss possible sources of data about past human behavior. *Accretion* takes place when humans leave something in their wake, such as records of their birth and death, or more mundane indicators of their behavior like the "favorites" pages recorded on their Web browser. *Erosion* is the removal of something, such as the worn bindings on popular library books or the way that the most sought-after films are absent from the shelves of the video rental store. Social researchers are like detectives in finding and interpreting these traces of behavior.

Of course, the interpretation of evidence from the past is an old idea. It forms the basis for the "hermeneutic circle" that underlies the interpretation of religious texts and the writing of history. Examination of national statistics on causes of death formed the basis for the earliest sociological investigations of suicide, by Emile Durkheim (1897/1951). In the twentieth century, examination of one author's citations to the works of other authors became a major method of understanding what those authors had read (i.e., what information they used) and how that had influenced their thinking, as well as understanding larger issues of communication among scientists and scholars (e.g., Cronin, 1984; Leydesdorff, 1998; Zuckerman, 1987). Such studies of the past in no way *affect* the behavior of the persons of interest, and hence they are unobtrusive investigations.

There are two examples of unobtrusive research methods that will be explored here. The first is the traditional approach in history of examining a wide range of historical evidence and reasoning from that to build an explanation of past behavior. The second example will be the content analysis of e-mail.

An example of historical research comes to us from Colin Richmond (1988). Richmond's description of information gathering and use in England in the latter middle ages is an ambitious act of narrative and understanding, because relatively little evidence exists of the fifteenth century phenomenon he seeks to portray. However, one cannot help but be fascinated by what this historian *does* manage to piece together about a rather narrow aspect of information use in that distant time.

To establish his view, Richmond made use of primary documents kept in Oxford's Bodleian Library, and much more extensive use of secondary collections and discussions of fifteenth century court documents, chronicles, diaries, news bills, news letters, and personal letters — especially the letters of John and Agnes Paston. Such documents cannot tell us much about the "ninety percent of Englishmen" about whom "information. . . . was collected by their governors, in the main regarding their taxable capacity and their violent habits," but they do tell us *something* about both exchanges of information among "the governing class," and how that information trickled down to the commoner. Richmond proclaims

> what news of great events was gathered by the governed, what their perceptions of such events were, and how they informed one another of them is another story altogether. . . . All that remains of the story are tantalizing glimpses. . . . (p. 233)

The kind of news transmitted to "the governed" of England (beginning in the fourteenth century) were of wars, truces, and victories, royal claims and titles, laws, pardons, and significant deaths. An early example is the order of May, 13, 1431, for all sheriffs to proclaim penalties for the possession of seditious or defamatory bills. Sheriffs throughout England told the populace to destroy such bills on sight, and to report their writers or distributors (for which they would collect a reward); anyone found in possession of an outlawed bill would be presumed to be the author and faced serious punishment. Such royal proclamations were to be cried and posted in public places such as markets, fairs, or churches.

A particular limitation of these early methods of dissemination lay in their lack of detail and explanation; sometimes representatives of towns or businesses were required to report to London for a briefing to convey a greater depth of understanding to those they represented. Another general problem with governmental information was that those in power were much less likely to pass on bad news of the sort that might threaten their ability to govern.

For his own glimpse of information use, Richmond carefully limits his essay to the deteriorating state of English governance during the Hundred Years' War, and the ways in which a small circle of "soldiers, merchants, bureaucrats, and country gentlemen" exchanged political news to "act in their own and the national interest" (p. 245) to influence the King.

According to Richmond, King Henry V's network of allies and informants enabled him to thwart rebellions against him, and he was also skilled at manipulating public information. In contrast, the impending loss of English territory to the French later presented Henry VI with a political problem he could not overcome: news of compromise with the French led to political moves against the government. Richmond details how persons connected to the Pastons obtained political information and shared it through "news-letters," in some cases dispatching servants to distant places to serve as news correspondents. The Pastons collected and copied letters, both their own and those of others, expressing political news and opinions. This information was collected and disseminated to influence opinion and mobilize political action against a faltering government. Richmond's conclusion — unsurprising to anyone who has worked in any organization — is that "the intricate mesh of patronage which linked king, lords and gentlemen was also an information network, highly personal and highly charged" (p. 245).

Like other studies in history, Richmond's account suffers from both lack of evidence and selective use of what information exists, weaknesses to which the investigator freely admits. From such a distant time only modest amounts of evidence survive, and much of that in the form of biased personal accounts of human motives and actions. In any event, historians must select facts that fit their themes and narratives, especially when writing about more modern times from which a great mountain of evidence survives.

Richmond has carefully limited his research problem (how, where, and why did some citizens obtain government information?) to one he believes he can answer with a surviving body of letters and other documents. Still, he is faced with the task of piecing together a narrative with incomplete evidence, and this involves some guesswork and reasoned imagination. He must, for example, explain how the Duke of Suffolk's letter to his son came into the hands of Paston. He must also conjecture about the motives of the various personages involved in the "network," whether or not they tried to explain their motives in their own letters.

Richmond's study, while not entirely compelling, is nevertheless fascinating. Histories offer many examples of how individuals came into possession of certain facts; Richmond's is one of very few attempts to focus on information exchange among a social circle in a distant time. An essay by Robert Darnton (2000) achieves something similar for eighteenth century France. A history more in tune with the traditional concerns of information seeking (i.e., of elites) is of communication among scientists during the early years of the Royal Society of London during the seventeenth century, as related by Ziman (1976).

9.1.9 Unobtrusive Approaches: Content Analysis

A prominent text on content analysis (Krippendorff, 1980) explains how any artifact of communication — newspapers, journal articles, books, speeches, letters, songs, paintings — might be analyzed to understand themes and orientations. Either the *manifest* content (i.e., surface features, such as words), or the *latent* content (underlying themes and meanings) of such artifacts may be recorded and analyzed. Both types of content may be analyzed in the same investigation. The results are sometimes expressed in quantitative terms (e.g., counts of the occurrence of words and/or concepts), although qualitative judgments and interpretation are often involved as well. In fact, David Altheide (1987, 1996) advocates the use of content analysis as an ethnographic technique.

Brenda Dervin (1976b) reports an early use of content analysis to examine the kinds of needs reflected in letters to newspaper "problem-solver" columns. Marilyn White (2000) has used content analysis to study questions on colon cancer that were submitted to a consumer health electronic mailing list. She wanted to know what kinds of questions were being asked in an electronic environment, what aspects of disease that questioners were most concerned about, how the context of questions were portrayed, and what kind of patterns were manifest in the exchanges (e.g., if there were one or many questions per message).

White and her colleagues sampled 1,000 messages gathered from 3,000 submitted over nearly three months. Messages to the list came from 152 people (about half of the list) and 58% of these participants asked questions, an average of four per "questioner." The 365 questions that were asked were coded for type, subject, and context using coding schemes developed by other researchers. By far the most popular type (comprising 41% of all questions) were those asking for *verification* of information (e.g., "Do you have to make a special trip just to do gene testing?"), while the remaining 59% were scattered over 17 other categories of question type. Regarding the subject of the questions, about 45% of them were nonmedical (e.g., asking about the address of a new list). Among the medical questions, a third had to do with medication, 22% with diagnosis and 18% with treatment of cancer. The rest of the questions — a few percent each — concerned epidemiology, prognosis, diet, causes health, and prevention, in that order of frequency. In cross-tabulating type of question by subject, White notes that verification questions dominant each subject category: "The participants were usually verifying information from a variety of sources: a previous message, a physician, or something they had read or heard" (p. 320).

Perhaps the most interesting aspect of this study lies in its discussion of the way that a *context* was established for each question. In 84% of the questions, the participant made an effort to establish the context of the question, either by referring to an earlier message, by "carrying over" part of a previous message, by stating their purpose directly, by describing a journal article or other item, or (most commonly) by telling a story about illness. Given that it usually takes a lot more effort to type one's tale, this is more evidence of the compelling role of narrative in human information seeking.

In her conclusions, White points out that mailing lists serve as "empathetic communities" for their participants. Yet she finds that

> there is little evidence that [lists] figure significantly in the lives of many patients or their family members or caretakers. . . . the people to whom it may be most important are people who are isolated from others with the condition, who feel more comfortable asking sensitive question in the relatively anonymous environment of an electronic list rather than face-to-face, who simply like the convenience of communicating when the need arises, who prefer to hear many responses to a question (instead of just one), or who want to contact their peers, not necessarily medical professionals.

White's study raises interesting questions about the respective roles of both electronic lists and of question types in information seeking. Will such lists come to be a common vehicle for certain types of information seeking? Is it easier to raise questions about serious illness in an "anonymous environment"? How effective is each type of question in getting the type of response (not necessarily an "answer") that a participant desires? We can expect to see many more studies along these lines in the years to come.

Content analysis has also been used by Mokros, Mullins, and Saracevic (1995) to study transcripts of interactions between librarians and patrons, and by Julien (1996), and Julien and Duggan (2000) to study the content of the information behavior literature itself.

9.1.10 Using Multiple Data Sources in a Single Investigation

Most studies of human behavior rely strictly on one type of data and data-gathering technique. Investigations that employ multiple data sources are not uncommon, but usually rely on fairly predictable combinations of data types and methods. For example, surveys often combine self-administered questionnaires with some type of interview among a much smaller sample, as in a 10-participant focus group interview conducted before or after a mail survey of several hundred people. Another frequent combination is interviews combined with an examination of human artifacts such as personal documents or social statistics.

One investigation of information seeking that used a wide variety of evidence types is that of Paul Solomon (1997). Solomon conducted a three-year study of sense-making and information behavior in the annual work planning phase of a public agency. The agency provided technical assistance on natural resource conservation to external groups, and had been recently merged with a larger agency—a situation featuring a great deal of change and uncertainty. As the researcher himself describes it, "his interest was in discovering how the individuals separately and in consort made sense of their situation and in making sense how they defined, sought, and used information" (p. 1097).

Although the investigator describes his method generally as the *ethnography of communication*, this characterization does not do justice to the many sources of data and means of collecting them. Among the data collected and analyzed in this study were

- first-hand observation and participation in meetings,
- field notes and tape recordings of meetings,
- taped interviews with participants in the meetings,
- special logs kept by the participants regarding their related activities, and
- documents pertinent to the work-planning (e.g, memos and reports).

Thus, Solomon's research design combines aspects of several methods, mainly interviews, content analysis, and participant observation. The latter refers to Solomon's participation to some degree in the activities of the group, rather than merely observing. The results, which are reported in three journal articles (consisting of 42 pages of fine print) are difficult to summarize here. Here are a few of the more general findings.

- The participants did not see information, or information seeking or use, as something distinct from their work; rather, it was part and parcel of the tasks that needed doing. They tended to describe what they did as "making sense," rather than "using information."
- The Principle of Least Effort did not adequately explain many observed instances of information seeking. At times the participants went to great lengths to obtain, revisit, and process information to make sense of it before applying the information.

- Sense-making styles varied widely among participants and sometimes clashed.
- Information is embedded in human lives. By focusing on that, rather than the creation of meaning, researchers may be creating an artificial distinction that separates people from the systems and institutions intended to help them.

Solomon's research is to be praised for viewing information behavior from so many different angles. The portrait he paints is a rich one, full of great detail and many examples. Yet, like other ethnographic works, it leaves open to question how well the observations and interpretations may apply to other people and contexts.

A similar range of data sources is reflected in an investigation of journalists by Fabritius (1999), discussed in a later chapter. Fabritius's study also married participant observations and interviews with talk-aloud protocols, diaries, content analysis of documents, and other observation devices.

9.1.11 Meta-Analysis

As the prefix "meta" implies, meta-analysis takes us one level of abstractness above the methods we have been discussing. Meta-analysis is most commonly used in assessing multiple experiments or surveys, so it could have been discussed under those topics as well. However, given that meta-analysis relies on multiple sources of data, it makes sense to discuss it at this point.

Meta-analyses have been used for a number of years in epidemiology and to a lesser degree in the social sciences. In brief, meta-analysis is a procedure for synthesizing and interpreting the findings of several studies at once. Combining and reanalyzing comparable data from related investigations, meta-analyses extend what we can learn from the individual studies chosen. By combining results from different investigations, meta-analyses can expand the size and scope of the samples of human subjects and increase the generalizability of the findings (Cook & Leviton, 1980; Wolf, 1986).

Meta-analysis can also suggest when quantitative measurements are running out of steam. Morgan and Shanahan (1997), for example, analyzed 20 years of studies on "cultivation"—the way that cumulative exposure to television programming affects our view of reality (e.g., coming to believe that murder is commonplace in society because we see it so frequently on television). Morgan and Shanahan conclude that while some kind of effect is taking place, but most of the measured effects in the studies they examined could be attributable to statistical sampling error. Interestingly, they suggest that cultivation research should make more use of ethnography and studies of narrative to search for effects that escape large-scale surveys.

A more relevant example of meta-analysis for our purposes is that of Haug (1997). His analysis of 12 studies of physicians' preferences for information sources was published between 1978 and 1992. All 12 studies were quantitative observational investigations that resulted in data about the frequency of use and/or preferential ranking of various channels and sources of medical information.

As in many such analyses, comparisons among the investigations were limited by dissimilar research questions, instruments, and reports, and the typically small samples. Meta-analyses often combine results of tests of statistical significance, but such a procedure was not possible with these studies due to the differing nature of their data. However, Haug was able to identify nine comparable information sources and by reinterpreting some of the data, rank the first and second choices of sources of medical information among the many physicians surveyed in the 12 investigations.

Haug notes that doctors in seven of the studies indicated that they consult medical books first, then their medical colleagues. Yet another five studies showed medical journals as a first choice, then colleagues as a second preferred source. Two investigations showed colleagues as a first information source, then journals. Two others indicated meetings then workshops or courses. The five remaining studies consisted of mixes of colleagues, books, journals, "other sources," and then drug companies. Even though these data were collected over a 14-year period, Haug says there is no apparent trend or change over time.

So overall we might conclude that when physicians have an information need, they tend to consult formal sources first (i.e., medical literature — books and journals rank highly in a strong majority of the studies), and as a typical second choice they talk to nearby colleagues.

Haug's results do more to highlight the problems of validity that face survey research than they do to illustrate the advantages of meta-analysis. The problem is that these may be self-reports of idealized behavior, rather than accurate reportings of real actions. This is a problem that survey researchers call a "demand characteristic" of the survey situation: respondents tend to say what they should do, rather than what they actually do. Respondents tend to tell researchers what they think the investigators want to hear as well.

Other studies that use observational methods (e.g., Covell, Uman & Manning, 1985) found that, although doctors claimed to consult medical texts before colleagues, in practice they most often chose colleagues first, and then other sources, before consulting medical books and journals. This is, of course, in keeping with the Principle of Least Effort — asking a colleague tends to be easier and faster. Yet it also reflects something very human about information seeking: it is a social process, and typically it is more enjoyable when it involves interaction with people rather than things.

9.2
Summary

This chapter has offered up at least one example of each major type of research design and data-gathering technique commonly used in information seeking studies. The intention has been twofold. First, I sought to demonstrate the variety of ways in which information seeking may be investigated. Second, I wanted to show that each choice of method offers strengths and weaknesses that must be taken into account when reaching conclusions about the study results.

Most of the investigations described here are of the traditional type. They take an objective view of information, they assume that people are largely rational and that demographic characteristics predict information seeking actions, and they tend to downplay the role of context in the thoughts and actions of those looking for information. The major exceptions to these generalizations among the studies sampled here are the investigations by Kuhlthau (1999) and Mick and Buhl (1992). They reflect the influence of the new paradigm in information studies in their assumptions, as well as their reliance upon qualitative methods and longitudinal designs.

Advocates of the new paradigm point out that experiments and survey methods are often ineffective at uncovering basic aspects of human behavior that relate to information seeking and use, particularly the degree to which it is affected by context. In the worst case, results from such study designs may lead away from actual reality, as in the Covell *et al.* study demonstrating the unreliability of self-reports of information use by physicians.

The increasingly popular qualitative methods, of course, pose their own trade-offs. They offer a glimpse of more basic and meaningful aspects of information seeking and use. At the same time they resist easy summary and generalization (indeed, a frequent assumption is that generalization is both impossible and distasteful). From the investigator's standpoint they require a great deal of effort, particularly in the amount of time one must devote to the design of one's studies.

In the next chapter, we will review information seeking studies in a different framework: by the social *group* (e.g., occupation or demographic category) or social role (e.g., consumer, user) that each investigation addresses. By examining studies grouped in this way, we can obtain a better picture of the cumulative results of research: to what extent do the various studies agree, and what do they tell us about information seeking?

Recommended for Further Reading

Haug, J. D. (1997). Physicians' preferences for information sources: A meta analytic study. *Bulletin of the Medical Library Association, 85*(3), 223–232.

Haug provides a short introduction to the concept of meta-analysis, with an example taken from the information uses of medical doctors. The data used are based on simple rankings of preferred information sources, so the reader does not need to understand statistical significance tests to grasp the basic ideas behind meta-analysis.

Janesick, V. J. (1998). The dance of qualitative research design: Metaphor, methodolatry, and meaning. In N. Denzin & Y. Lincoln (Eds.), *Strategies of qualitative inquiry* (pp. 35–55). Thousand Oaks, CA: Sage.

A readable introduction to the varieties of qualitative designs, and their commonalities and distinctions. Of particular interest are Janesick's comments on the different ways that studies can be triangulated.

Krueger, R. (1988). *Focus groups: A practical guide for applied research.* Newbury Park, CA: Sage.

A basic text on how and why to conduct focused group interviews, and how to analyze and interpret the evidence collected while using them.

Lindlof, T. R. (1995). *Qualitative communication research methods.* Thousand Oaks, CA: Sage..

In his introduction to qualitative approaches, Lindlof addresses the theoretical sources of the interpretive paradigm, study design, and ethical considerations, as well as providing the usual "how to do it" advice.

Sandstrom, A., & Sandstrom, P. (1995). The use and misuse of anthropological methods in library and information science research. *Library Quarterly, 65,* 161–199.

This husband and wife team reviewed the assumptions behind traditions in anthropology to emphasize how associated methods have been, in some cases, misunderstood by researchers and epistemologists in information studies.

Stake, R. E. (1998). Case studies. In N. Denzin & Y. Lincoln (Eds.), *Strategies of qualitative inquiry* (pp. 86–109–). Thousand Oaks, CA: Sage.

Stake points to specific examples to illustrate the varieties of approaches that case studies have taken.

Five

Research Results and Reflections

10

Reviewing the Research: Its History, Size, and Topics

> Several thousand studies have appeared and, clearly, it is impossible to review *all* of this literature.
>
> Tom Wilson (1994, p. 15)

> The movement away from system-centred studies to person-centred studies did not begin until the 1980s. . . .
>
> Tom Wilson (1994, p. 30)

Chapter Outline

10.1. Overview of Part Five
    10.1.1. The History of Studying Information Behavior
    10.1.2. Estimating the Size of the Literature
    10.1.3. Contexts and Categories
    10.1.4. Choosing Examples of Studies
10.2. Summary

10.1
Overview of Part Five

The goals of Part Five of the book are, First, to frame the information behavior literature in terms of its size and development, and second, to familiarize the reader with it through examples of studies. Correspondingly, the focus on this chapter is on the history and development of that literature. The objective of the next two chapters will be to provide at least one recent example of each of the most-studied categories of information seekers. In contrast to the chapters concerning methodologies, the emphasis in this segment is on findings from genres of studies, rather than on the methods used in the studies. Also of concern in this part of the volume is the way that different divisions of human populations — by occupation, role, or demographic category — fit together.

As in the last two chapters, this segment of the book will describe highlighted publications in greater depth than found in past reviews of this corpus of literature (e.g., *ARIST*). Along with the studies reviewed in some detail, I cite a number of related investigations. Taking into account the distribution of such writings, and the usual groupings that have been employed, I have chosen to focus on the major occupations, social roles, and demographic segments found in the literature. The choices of particular studies under each category are reflected in tables in each of the next two chapters (you may wish to skip ahead to see what I mean). But first, a bit about the history and development of the information seeking literature.

10.1.1 The History of Studying Information Behavior

The history of research on information-related human behaviors demonstrates that the topic has remained salient for almost a century. According to Herbert Poole (1985), the first study of information uses dates back to 1902, when Charles Eliot wrote about the used and unused portions of a library's collection. Bouazza (1989, p. 144) says that "the history of user studies goes back to the 1920s," and Wilson (1994) credits a 1916 study by Ayres and McKinnie on Cleveland public libraries as the beginning of this genre. Whichever claim is correct, it is clear that the antecedents of information behavior research lie in these early investigations of what channels or sources people use to satisfy their information needs.

A trickle of studies in the first decades of the twentieth century became a flood by midcentury. Since 1902 many similar publications have appeared, most of them focusing on materials used rather than on users and their searches. Especially in the wake of World War II, with its great burst of energy into the endeavors of basic and applied sciences, attention (and funding) began to turn toward improving dissemination of information from research. Many investigations of "information needs and uses" were conducted during the 1950s and 1960s. Literature reviews of such studies followed soon after: Törnudd (1959), Menzel (1960), Davis and Bailey (1964), Auerba (1965), Paisley (1965), North American Aviation (1966; updating Auerbach), and DeWeese (1967; an update of Davis & Bailey). With few exceptions (such as William Paisley's 1965 review of studies in the behavioral sciences), most of the literature concentrated on investigations of science and engineering personnel and materials.

Stand-alone bibliographies of information needs and uses started to decline in number after 1966, when the new *Annual Review of Information Science and Technology (ARIST)* began to include comprehensive reviews of this body of publications. For the next quarter century, *ARIST* became the main vehicle by which interested scholars kept abreast of research on information behavior (as some have more recently preferred to call it — e.g., Wilson, 1999a; Wilson & Allen, 1999).

ARIST chapters on information needs and uses appeared in 1966 (Menzel, 1966b), 1967 (Herner & Herner), 1968 (Paisley), 1969 (Allen), 1970 (Lipetz), 1971 (Crane), 1972 (Lin and Garvey), 1974 (Martyn), and 1978 (Crawford). During this same period Tom and Enid Waldhart (1975) took a different slice at the literature in a bibliography of 1288 publications on "communication research in library and information science." The Waldhart's review covered the period of 1964 to 1973 and emphasized communication among workers in the sciences, technology, and social sciences; consequently, it covers most of the same literature as the *ARIST* reviews published up to 1975.

Perhaps because of the increasing availability of bibliographies on the topic, there was a pause in reviewing information needs and uses publications following Crawford's 1978 *ARIST* chapter. Later, comprehensive chapters reappeared in 1986 (Dervin & Nilan) and 1990 (Hewins). In the meantime, reviews by Hogeweg de Haart (1981), Hernon (1984), and Slater (1988) together reviewed several hundred studies on needs and uses in the social sciences, while Stone (1982) described 73 unique items in the humanities. Gradually, reviews of the information behavior literature grew more specialized and eventually lead to a virtual halt in attempts to review such publications in a general fashion.

It is interesting to look back on the patchwork nature of the *ARIST* reviews. The amount of time covered in the general *ARIST* chapters varied from as little as one year's worth of new writings to more than eight years of publications. Authors exercised some latitude in the scope of their reviews, apparently in consideration of their own interests, the amount of material to review, and what earlier *ARIST* chapters had covered. For example, the 1966 and 1967 chapters reviewed only science and technology literature, and the 1990 review purposefully excluded any studies that used survey methodology. Whatever the chosen time period, each *ARIST* chapter cited earlier reviews and studies in the midst of reviewing recent material from their assigned period. The general overlap among chapters coupled with the idiosyncratic choices of the chapter authors make it difficult to say exactly how many unique publications have been reviewed by *ARIST* alone, much less to come up with an estimate that includes other reviews of this literature.

10.1.2 Estimating the Size of the Literature

It may be helpful to first contemplate the size and rate of growth of the publications relevant to information needs, uses, and seeking. The sheer number of works illustrates the depth and duration of interest in these topics and suggests their importance. The wide range of emphases that these writings encompass have prompted both researchers and reviewers to define boundaries around their interests, however fuzzy those categories may be. I will build a parallel framework from a selective group of studies that best illustrate key concepts, emphases, and methodologies.

Since 1990, *ARIST* has not published any general "information needs and uses" chapters, although several overlapping reviews have appeared. A 1991 survey by Helen Tibbo of "information systems, services, and technology for the humanities" included only a few studies of "actual behavior" (p. 295). Three 1993 *ARIST* chapters, by Choo and Auster ("Environmental Scanning"), Chang and Rice ("Browsing"), and Metoyer-Duran ("Information Gatekeepers") covered some behaviors that have traditionally been considered in the information seeking literature. Late in 2001 several reviews appeared in volumes 34 and 35 on more peripheral topics: "the concept of situation in information science" (Cool, 2001); "using and reading scholarly literature" (King & Tenopir, 2001); "conceptual frameworks used in information behavior research" (Pettigrew, Fidel & Bruce, 2001); and "methodologies and methods for user behavioral research" (Wang, 2001). Again, the picture is of a research corpus that has grown so large that distinct subtopics are becoming more recognizable.

For the purpose of illustrating the size of the information-behavior–related corpus of writings, Table 10.1 lists the numbers of documents reviewed in the *ARIST* chapters, together with the two largest of the bibliographies that predated the *ARIST* series.

Together, the 11 general *ARIST* chapters published between 1966 and 1990 reviewed about a thousand documents—an average of 67 documents per year of coverage, although this table includes citations redundant with earlier volumes. The 1991 and 1993 thematic chapters, while highly redundant with pre-1993 general reviews, identified additional relevant literature.

The *ARIST* numbers are subject to some overlap, as each reviewer cited earlier "landmark" studies on particular topics. Yet the actual amount published is ultimately underestimated by these counts, because most *ARIST* authors said that there were many more studies potentially relevant to their chosen theme than they chose to review.

The chapter by Hewins (1990) amply illustrates both aspects: redundancy and underdetermination of relevant documents. To start, 20% (20 of 101) of her citations predate the four-year period she intends to review. These

Table 10.1

Early and *ARIST* Reviews of Information Needs, Uses, and Seeking

Author	Number of Documents Cited
Davis & Bailey (1964)	438
Auerbach (1965)	676
Menzel (1966b *ARIST*)	26
Herner & Herner (1967 *ARIST*)	38
Paisley (1968 *ARIST*)	68
Allen (1969 *ARIST*)	58
Lipetz (1970 *ARIST*)	114
Crane (1971 *ARIST*)	109
Lin & Garvey (1972 *ARIST*)	96
Martyn (1974 *ARIST*)	32
Crawford (1978 *ARIST*)	106
Dervin & Nilan (1986 *ARIST*)	136
Hewins (1990 *ARIST*)	101
	1,998

include several cited by earlier *ARIST* reviews. Second, Hewins relates in her introduction the necessity of, and criteria for, choosing among potentially relevant studies:

> A search of the literature on information needs and use studies during 1986–89 reveals several hundred citations. Past *ARIST* authors have also found this literature to be large. Some of these studies do not contribute to new knowledge, new methods or theory and model building; many others can be described as site-specific, system-specific, or service-specific.

So if Hewins identified, say, 400 relevant works over that four-year period, then the body of publications was growing by 100 items per year, of which she reviewed about a quarter. In contrast, Dervin and Nilan (1986, p. 3) chose to review 136 of the "more than 300 potentially useful citations since 1978" they uncovered, based on their desire "to focus on issues relating to the conceptualizations that drive the research." Using their criteria, the relevant literature was growing by perhaps 40 items per year and they reviewed about 40% of it. The most recent reviewer before Dervin and Nilan (Crawford, 1978) had estimated that over a thousand relevant papers had been published before 1978, and that the number was growing by at least 30 publications per year. The pattern suggested by these estimates is an escalating growth rate: 30 per year during the early 1970s, 40 per year during the early 1980s, and 50 to 100 per year by 1990.

A growth rate of 50 to 100 items per year is close to that estimated by some other scholars. For example, Reneker (1993, p. 487) suggested that "well over one thousand studies" had been published in the decade that preceded her article—or about 100 studies per year. This seems entirely possible if one takes a very broad view of what counts, and uses a very large sampling frame to find it. For instance, the database *Information Science Abstracts* indexed exactly 100 publications under the descriptor "information needs" during 1998.

Firmer empirical support for this rate of growth is found in a recent "longitudinal analysis of the information needs and uses literature"(Julien & Duggan, 2000) that counted only "full-length feature articles" indexed in the database *Library Literature* under either "information needs" and/or "use studies." The investigators identified 490 items published between 1984 and 1989, and 641 from 1995 through the middle of 1998, for a total of 1,131 articles over 9 1/2 years, or about 119 per year. Only 68% of these articles were classed as "research" (the rest being commentaries or reports about services), leaving us with about 81 studies per year—comfortably within the 50 to 100 estimate from other sources.

Whichever estimate we take, surely by 1990 the number of information needs, uses, and/or seeking studies must have passed the 3,000 mark. Considering those numbers, along with the selectivity applied by *ARIST* authors and the redundancy among chapters, it seems reasonable to conclude that since the late-1980s the relevant body of publications has been growing by at least 80 new documents per year, and possibly faster. As of 2002, studies of information seeking are certainly accruing more quickly than they were in the 1980s, due in part to the highly successful "Information Seeking in Context" conferences of 1996 to 2002.

Even assuming a conservative growth rate, there are probably 10,000 or more publications on information needs, uses, seeking and/or other aspects of information behavior, even in the stricter senses of those terms. Including documents that discuss information seeking in a less traditional way (e.g., as sense-making) could easily make the total much higher. This estimate is congruent with searches on bibliographic utilities like OCLC's FirstSearch, which generates thousands of hits on combinations of the term "information"with other keywords (need, use, seeking, etc.), among the literature of the most recent decade. If the search were to span *several* decades, only a tiny minority of the retrieved citations need to be relevant to achieve the 10,000 range.

Obviously it is impossible to be exhaustive in reviewing such a literature. First, it is simply difficult to decide where to draw the boundaries around the topic. And, second, there are issues of specificity and quality that lead one to determine that certain studies are not appropriate for inclusion in a review.

The authors of *ARIST* and other reviews of this literature have all faced these problems and made their corresponding choices, resulting in a series of incomplete pictures of the research area. This chapter adds another snapshot to this photo album of research results—one that is similarly selective, yet in greater detail than the others.

10.1.3 Contexts and Categories

An increasingly emphasized generalization is that information behavior takes place in a *context*. Brenda Dervin (1997, p. 14) says that there "is no term more often used, less often defined, and when defined defined so variously as context." She goes on to complain that

> virtually every possible attribute of a person, culture, situation, behavior, organization, or structure has been defined as context. . . . context has the potential to be virtually anything that is not defined as the phenomenon of interest.

Dervin provides a few examples that help, at least, to narrow the definition a bit. She quotes John Dewey (1960, p. 90) as saying that "context is . . . a selective interest or bias which conditions the subject matter of thinking." To Gregory Bateson (1978, p. 13) context is "the pattern that connects . . . without context there is no meaning." Talja, Keso, and Pietiläinen, in an article devoted to how information behavior researchers have dealt with the study of context (1999, p. 752), characterize context as "some kind of a background for something the researcher wishes to understand and explain":

> the site where a phenomenon is constituted as an object to us.... any factors or variables that are seen to affect individuals' information- seeking behavior: socioeconomic conditions, work roles, tasks, problem situations, communities and organizations with their structures and cultures, etc. (p. 754)

A term related to context, but which is sometimes given a narrower meaning, is *situation*. Investigators in information studies and in communication have had much to say about the importance and influence of situation in information behavior. Dervin (1997, p. 14) says that when research is "focused on relationships between people, then factors describing the situation can become context." Savolainen (1993, p. 17) holds that "the term situation refers to the time-space context in which sense is constructed." Vakkari (1997, p. 457) notes that information seeking is "seen as embedded in the actions, tasks and situations they are supporting" in his call for closer attention to the influences of group and society. Donohew and Tipton (1973, p. 248) see a person's "definition of situation as being composed of such things as immediate goals, priorities, and availability of information in the immediate situation."

Context and situation are important concepts for information behavior research, even if they are ill defined. Information needs do not arise in a vacuum, but rather owe their existence to some history, purpose, and influence. The seeker exists in an environment that partially determines, constrains, and supports the types of needs and inquiries that arise. The seeker also has his or her own memories, predispositions, and motivations — an internal environment of influence. Such is the importance of context that research on it has given rise to a series of conferences, the Information Seeking in Context (ISIC) meetings that have taken place in Tampere, Finland; Sheffield, England; and Göteborg, Sweden, since 1996. Many of the works cited in this volume were presented at, or inspired by, the study of context. How context has been defined is an important factor in establishing categories of investigations from which to sample.

As mentioned in earlier chapters, research attention has shifted over the years from a dominant interest in the *use of channels and sources* to an emphasis on the *encountering and seeking of information* and the *interpretation of meaning from that information*. In parallel fashion, this work is devoted to reviewing selected studies and findings that flesh out the aspects of information seeking of more recent interest, not all of them under the banner of "information needs and uses." Investigators have recognized that information seeking does not always boil down to the use of certain sources, an idea that is underscored in a commentary by Choo (1998):

> Our survey suggests that, over the years, information needs and uses studies have progressively broadened their research orientation and research focus.... studies have moved from an orientation that is primarily system-centered (in which information is objective, resides in a document or system, and where the main issue is how to get at this information) to an orientation that is also user-centered (in which information is subjective, resides in the users' minds, and is only useful when meaning has been created by the user). (p. 39)

However, many of the studies reviewed in this work still attempt to make generalizations about sources, groups of people, and the differences among them. Those research conclusions are related here, even though many researchers are skeptical that such generalization is possible. Talja (1997), for example, believes that

> generalizations about differences between individuals or groups are often problematic. Firstly, the diversity of the individual's social roles, tasks and identities is not taken into account.... Secondly, it is impossible to get unmediated knowledge about a person's cognitive skills or even information seeking behavior, because the ways in which they are accounted for are always mediated by culturally constructed interpretive repertoires. The explanations should not be taken as facts about the permanent attitudes or actual behavioural patterns of individuals or groups. (p. 74)

Despite Talja's reasonable skepticism, there is some value in striving for well-evidenced generalizations about individuals or groups; otherwise, there would be little point in investigating information seeking at all. Talja's comments serve to emphasize the importance of attending to elements of context, particularly those "social roles, tasks and identities," and are a reminder about sweeping claims regarding large, diverse populations of subjects.

Other reviewers of this body of publications have seen it in various ways. Most make the same distinction as Choo and Auster between studies that are really investigating information channels (e.g., journals) or systems (e.g., libraries) and those that are studying *people* (the emphasis in this book). Reviewers have used different terminology to reflect the latter type of investigations. For Choo and Auster they are studies of "work, organizational, and social settings of the users. . . . users' membership in professional or social groups, their demographic backgrounds" (1993, p. 284). Talja *et al.* (1999, p. 752) speak of "socioeconomic conditions, work roles, tasks, problem situations, communities and organizations" as contexts typically examined. Taylor (1991) talks about "information use environments" as consisting of four types: professions, entrepreneurs (including managers), special interest groups and socioeconomic groups. Dervin (1989) gives 10 examples of "demography" (e.g., age, gender, race, ethnicity, income, education) as one of the "traditional categories of users" that are studied, along with dozens of alternative ways of grouping people and behaviors.

To form the basis for my own review I have selected what is common among these various characterizations of the research literature: categories of occupation (profession, work role), demographic background (socioeconomic group, identity, community) and social role. Hence, occupations, social roles, and demography—as they relate to information needs and seeking behavior—form the highest-level categories that structure the sample of studies described here.

10.1.4 Choosing Examples of Studies

I hope to portray both the depth and breadth of the information behavior literature by presenting selected studies that illustrate key topics. Choosing which studies to highlight for this volume has been challenging, and I have employed three heuristics to guide my choices. The first mechanism is the use of the aforementioned framework (see Tables 11.1 and 12.1) to sample one or more studies representing certain *occupations*, *roles*, and/or *demographic groups* that people may fall into in life. The division between work-related roles and non–work-related roles is not a firm one, because an "occupation" is also a "role" we take in life. Unfortunately, "work" and "nonwork" have been treated rather separately by investigators until recently, as if activities outside the job did not matter. The subtle distinction between job and nonjob corresponds to the notion of the "way of life as 'order of things'," as articulated by Reijo Savolainen (1995):

> "things" stand for various activities taking place in the daily life world, including not only job but also necessary reproductive tasks such as household care and voluntary activities (hobbies) ... in most cases order of things is a relatively well-established constellation of work and nonwork activities.... (pp. 262–265)

Looking at information behavior more holistically, in terms of life projects and roles, represents a shift toward the perspective of the *person* (or, in language more dominant during the 1970s and 1980s, "the user"), and away from the views of the system (e.g., "use of the media," "use of library materials," or "use of the Internet").

The second rule of thumb has been to largely ignore investigations that focus on particular channels, sources, or systems. Most of these excluded studies concern the use of the Internet, online databases, or library catalogs, and together these constitute a huge literature. A few system-oriented studies *are* cited, however, as examples of how the mix of sources may influence everyday information seeking. For further reading, consider writings by Borgman (2000), Jacobson (1991), Marchionini (1995), Nicholas and Williams (1999), van de Wijngaert (1999), Rouse and Rouse (1984), and Savolainen (1998, 1999). These works, among many others, emphasize the importance of investigating contextual and individual differences in the choice and use of information systems and sources. Some of them are described in passing below.

The tables depicted in Chapters 11 and 12 do not sample all possible occupations, roles, or demographic categories, but rather those most commonly chosen as a focus of observation. I have exercised my own judgment in choosing studies that I think are well done, illustrative of a particular population or approach, unique, or, in a few cases, make use of especially large samples of respondents.

We have from Julien and Duggan (2000) some empirical evidence of the distribution of "groups studied" over the several hundred articles they examined in their investigation of the body of publications. Oddly, 17% of the publications were not specific about who they were studying. Eliminating those "unspecified" accounts from their estimates suggests that 24% of recent studies have concerned "students," 19% were about "scholars" (including "faculty or researchers" and scientists), 18% featured "professionals" (including physicians, nurses and engineers), 17% about the general public, and 14% about "specific groups"(such as medical patients or consumers); the remainder were studies of nonprofessional employees (1%) or multiple groups (6%).

The sample of studies discussed in the following chapters will loosely reflect this distribution, with one major exception: investigations of *students* will not be emphasized here, as the vast majority of published studies of students focus on their use of either libraries or electronic sources (online catalogs, databases, or the World Wide Web); both of these "information systems" are well covered by other literature reviews.

Finally the third heuristic I have employed is to favor more recent publications, especially those from the 1990s through 2001. In some cases older items are portrayed to highlight the shifts in assumptions, methods, and findings that have taken place over the last quarter century. By emphasizing works from the most recent decade I hope to provide an efficient means for reviewing developments in the literature, as well as to reduce it to a more manageable size.

10.2
Summary

This chapter has examined the size and nature of the information seeking literature. In it I have highlighted several characteristics:

• The literature is quite large, ranging somewhere in the thousands of studies, depending on how one defines the scope of the topic.

• Information behavior publications have grown more specialized over the years, leading to a virtual halt in general reviews of them.

• Recent reviews of the information behavior literature are now more likely to focus on occupations (e.g., physicians, managers), roles (e.g., gatekeepers, consumers), or demographic groups (e.g., the elderly, the poor).

This chapter has set the stage for an examination of recent publications using the latter divisions. In the two chapters that follow, selections of recent studies will consider how the literature has developed along three lines of inquiry: by occupation, by social role, and by demographic group. Decisions of what to review were based on three heuristics:

• Use of an empirically derived framework representing *occupations*, *roles*, and *demographic groups*.

• Elimination of most studies oriented toward general education (e.g., student outcomes), or information systems (e.g., computer, database, or Internet usage). Both of these literatures are massive on their own, and typically are concerned with issues other than "information behavior" per se.

• A preference for more recent investigations (i.e., post-1990).

Recommended for Further Reading

Dervin, B. (1989). Users as research inventions: How research categories perpetuate inequities. *Journal of Communication, 39*(3), 216–232.

The primary topic of Brenda Dervin's article is reification — the tendency for the labels we apply to groups to take on a life of their own. However, it can also serve as a comprehensive inventory of those labels. Dervin lists 12 general groupings under which "users" and their "uses" have traditionally been categorized, and within those provides 57 specific categories of individuals.

Dervin, B., & Nilan, M. (1986). Information needs and uses. In M. Williams (Ed.), Annual review of information science and technology (Vol. 21, pp. 3–33).

The most thoughtfully written of the more recent ARIST chapters on information needs and uses. With 136 citations, it was also the largest of its type.

Julien, H. & Duggan, L. (2000). A longitudinal analysis of the information needs and uses literature. Library and Information Science Research, 22, 291–309.

Julien and Duggan analyze the literature of information needs and uses to arrive at estimates of the proportions by type of group studied.

Talja, S., Keso, H., & Pietiläinen, T. (1999). The production of "context" in information seeking research: A metatheoretical view. Information Processing & Management, 35, 751–763.

Along with more specific tasks and situations, jobs, roles, and personal background have been used to characterize the "context" of individual information seeking. Talja et al. discuss the various ways that concept has been defined and studied.

11

Research by Occupation

In practice, context in INS [information needs and seeking] studies usually refers to... socioeconomic conditions, work roles, tasks, problem situations, communities and organizations...

S. Talja, H. Keso, and T. Pietiläinen, (1999, p. 752)

Reading the library surveys of the 1960s today, one is struck by how irrelevant they are for present conditions, and how even less relevant they are likely to seem within a very short space of time.

Tom Wilson (1994, p. 42)

Chapter Outline

11.1. By Occupational Category
    11.1.1. Scientists and Engineers
    11.1.2. Social Scientists
    11.1.3. Humanities Scholars
    11.1.4. Health Care Providers
    11.1.5. Managers
    11.1.6. Journalists
    11.1.7. Lawyers
    11.1.8. Other Occupations

11.2. Summary

11.1

By Occupational Category

Occupations have provided the most common structure for the investigation of information seeking. Based on Julien and Duggan's (2000) examination of this literature we can estimate that almost half of all *identifiable* respondents in such studies are occupational. The preponderance of work roles is also obvious from an examination of *ARIST* or other review documents: the majority of studies are of scientists and engineers (whether employed by universities or industry), scholars, professionals, and workers in general occupational categories like "manager."

The runner-up to occupational investigations are those by role, such as citizen, consumer, patient, or gatekeeper; these make up slightly less than a third of identifiable subjects. Another role, that of "student" accounts for about a quarter of the studies, although they are included sparingly under "roles." (Were I to include general studies of learning, the voluminous education literature would make the role of "student" the most numerous category of all. There are indeed thousands of studies of students, but few studies consider information seeking in more than a peripheral sense.) There are fewer still direct studies of demographic groups, even though demographic variables form a common schema for analyzing the results of these other investigations.

Most of the earliest *ARIST* chapters (1966 to 1974), along with other reviews of information needs and uses, were concerned primarily with scientists and engineers. Some time afterward, as researchers gained a firmer view of the pattern of behavior in science and engineering, attention turned first to the social sciences and later to the humanities (Bouazza, 1989, p. 159). As they did so, the academic world began to account for an even larger proportion of the studies than it did before, as the latter groups were less likely to be found outside of the university. Marcia Bates (1996) summarized that progression of attention by researchers in this way:

> In the 1950s and 1960s — in part because of the availability of U.S. Federal grant money — the emphasis was on the needs of scientists and engineers. . . . Needs in the social sciences were attended to in the 1970s, especially with some major research studies that were performed in Great Britain. . . . attention turned to the arts and humanities in the 1980s and 1990s. (p. 155)

Both the cumulation of studies on some individual disciplines, and the impracticality of studying *all* disciplines in any depth, led to a tendency to aggregate results along the lines of *metadisciplines*, such as science, social science, and the humanities. There are some gray areas (are historians chiefly humanists, or are some of them social scientists?); however, these three basic categories seem to appeal to those attempting to summarize information seeking results.

Therefore, in discussing these work-related roles, I will proceed in the same fashion in which the research has developed: starting with scientists and engineers, then going on to consider social scientists, then humanities scholars, and then other occupations (Table 11.1).

11.1.1 Scientists and Engineers

It is fitting to start this review with a description of the information seeking of scientists because this is where the research in this vein really got started. The "Big Science" (Price, 1963) sparked largely by World War II and

Table 11.1
Works Reviewed, and Related Works Cited, for Occupations

Occupation	Works reviewed to illustrate findings	Some other relevant works cited
Scientists	Bichteler 89; Palmer 91	Bouazza 89; Brown 99; Ellis 93
Engineers	Holland 95; Pinelli 91	Allen 69, 77; King 94; Leckie 96; Gralewska-Vickery 76; Gerstberger 68; Hertzum 00; Raitt 85; Shuchman 81
Social scientists	Ellis 89, 93	Hernon 84; Hogeweg de Haart 81; Paisley 65; Slater 88
Humanities scholars	Chu 99; Cole 98; Stam 95	Bates 96; Bouazza 89; Stone 82; Watson-Boone 94; Wiberley 89
Health care providers		Leckie 96; Marshall 93; Osheroff 91;
Physicians	Gorman 95, 99; Timpka 90	Urquhart 98, 99
Nurses and others	Blythe 93	Mullaly-Quijas 94; Strother 86; Wakeham 92
Managers	Auster 93	Baldwin 97: Choo 98; Culnan 83; Daft 86, 88; Kuhlthau 99; Swanson 87
Journalists	Fabritius, 99; Nicholas, 99	Katz 89; Ross 98
Lawyers	Sutton 94; Cole 00	Hainsworth 92 (judges); Leckie 96; Otike 99; Vale 88
Other occupations	Cobbledick 96 (artists) Wicks 99 (clergy)	Florio 93 (policymakers) Baldwin 97 (security analysts)

Note: Studies are listed by first only, plus year. See the references.

afterward by the Cold War resulted in an explosion of research material. There were simply too many findings being published for individual scientists and engineers to monitor effectively. The outcome was frustration and sometimes outright duplication of research efforts, because researchers did not always know that others were gathering or even publishing findings of interest to their work. As a result, money and attention became available to address problems in the dissemination of scientific information and to study communication among scientists and engineers.

A 1984 comment by Tom Wilson accurately characterizes the nature of the literature at that time: "the study of information-seeking behaviour can be said to be the study of *scientists*' information-seeking behaviour" (p. 199). From the 1940s through the 1970s, investigations of scientists (and to some extent, engineers) dominated all others. For better or worse, there seems to have been a relative decline in the number of information seeking studies of scientists since the mid-1980s. In part this may be because the phenomenon has been well-documented and "played out," and so researchers moved on to less-studied groups such as social scientists, humanists, physicians, and others; it may also reflect shifts in funding for such studies. Reviews of the literature on science and/or engineering (e.g., King, Casto, & Jones, 1994; Leckie, Pettigrew, & Sylvain, 1996; Palmer, 1991) continue to cite classic discussions that are now over 30 years old such as Nelson and Pollock (1970) or Gerstberger and Allen (1968).

That is not to say that the information behavior of scientists is no longer studied; indeed, there is more interest than ever in the behavior of scientists, especially in areas like scientometrics and bibliometrics (e.g., Borgman, 1990; Cronin, 1984; Leydesdorff, 1998) and the social construction of scientific problems and communities of discourse (e.g., Knorr-Cetina & Mulkay, 1983; Latour & Woolgar, 1979). It is simply that the once-common investigation of scientists' use of *sources* is much less common today than it was in past decades. A recent example of a typical source study is that of Noble and Coughlin (1997), who examined academic chemists.

One trend in recent investigations in science seems to be a move away from quantitative measures of large numbers of scientists and toward more naturalistic observations of information seeking behaviors. Judith Palmer (1991), for example, opted for in-depth interviews rather than large-scale survey techniques in her study of 67 agriculture researchers (a population studied by Majid, Anwar, & Eisenschitz, 2000, in a more conventional way). Palmer used a variety of structured (psychometric and personality) inventories and semistructured personal interviews to elicit patterns of communication, use, and importance of information sources, as well as strategies for locating and organizing information and respondent reflections on the organizational structure of their department.

After coding of her questionnaire data, Palmer used statistical cluster analysis to produce classifications of the researchers into five groups reflecting generic "information styles." These styles included the following: "nonseekers" who did little information gathering (predominantly statisticians among the researchers); "lone, wide rangers" who read/scanned a wide variety of literature and tended to work alone; a group of biochemists and entomologists who were shifting their research focus, referred to as "unsettled, self-conscious seekers"; "confident collectors," almost entirely entomologists, who felt on top of their field; and "hunters," composed strictly of biochemists, who paid very close attention to emerging research findings and patterns in their narrow area of investigation.

Interestingly, Palmer made a second categorization of information styles, based this time on her own judgments about the tendencies of the individual researchers as revealed in the interviews. The resulting six subjective stereotypes of information styles — overlords, entrepreneurs, hunters, pragmatists, plodders, and derelicts — grouped the scientists quite differently than the earlier cluster analysis, making clear a strong contrast between categorizations arrived at by personal assessments versus psychometric measures. Palmer discussed the implications of the cluster-derived styles for the management of research environments.

Ellis, Cox, and Hall (1993) conducted interviews with physicists and chemists to identify aspects of their information seeking. They described eight characteristics of seeking patterns (discussed below under "social scientists"), two of which were unique to the chemists in their sample. The other six characteristics were identified in an earlier investigation of social scientists; in other words, physicists and social scientists were highly similar in the ways they dealt with information in their work.

More traditionally oriented studies of scientists tend to focus on strictly on sources of information. An example is Bichteler and Ward's (1989) interviews with a sample of 56 geoscientists across the United States. They found that these scientists spent from 2 to 10 hours per week looking for information, averaging about four hours per week. Professional contacts, such as colleagues at work and elsewhere, were the most frequently used sources, followed by journal literature. Another investigation — an e-mail survey with a very limited sample — also focused on the use of sources within a community of astronomers, chemists, mathematicians, and physicists (Brown, 1999).

One final comment on studying the information seeking of scientists (as well as anyone else): we cannot necessarily rely on their self-reports. Barry (1995) questioned the reliability of accounts she collected from theoretical physicists regarding their use of electronic sources of information. She suggested that even scientists may exaggerate their use of, and success with, sources of information if that is what they think the researcher wants to hear.

Let us turn now to engineers. In their review of a broad variety of information seeking literatures, Leckie, Pettigrew, and Sylvain (1996) described engineering as a highly specialized profession (mechanical, chemical, electrical, etc.) working in a broad range of environments. Engineers are not only engaged in the design, development, testing, and manufacturing of items, but also in research, management, consulting, and sales roles. Their work emphasizes the solving of particular technical problems rather than the production of general conclusions, a fact that separates them from the scientists with whom they are so often conflated in studies. As Derek Price (1965, p. 562) once generalized, "the scientist wants to write but not read, and the technologist wants to read but not write."

A consistent finding in examinations of the information seeking of engineers (e.g., Allen, 1977; Case, Borgman, & Meadow, 1986; Holland and Powell, 1995; King, Casto, & Jones, 1994; Pinelli, 1991; Raitt, 1985; Shuchman, 1981) has been that they make more use of their own knowledge, colleagues, and other within-organization sources of information than they do of the technical literature. What literature they *do* use tends to be from their trade — reports, catalogs, handbooks, and trade journals — more than research publications. This is perfectly in keeping with the context in which most engineers work: in private firms, with specific objectives that are not intended to contribute to the engineering knowledge base but rather to produce a particular thing or service. In such situations, the journal literature may be neither specific nor timely enough for the practical matters at hand, but can be useful at early stages for monitoring the environment that is shared with competitors. The most pertinent information is to be found out from clients and colleagues concerned with the objectives, and they are typically perceived as the most accessible and familiar sources, which tends to reinforce their usage (Allen, 1977; Gerstberger & Allen, 1968; Hertzum & Pejtersen, 2000).

One series of investigations of aerospace engineers — one of the first populations to be targeted in information studies of the 1950s and 1960s — was reported by Pinelli, Barclay, Glassman, Kennedy, and Demerath (1991). A survey jointly sponsored by the United States Department of Defense (DoD) and National Aeronautics and Space Administration (NASA) attempted to ascertain how aerospace knowledge diffuses among engineers and scientists. The first phase of the project sent questionnaires to random sample of 3,298 members of an aeronautics organization; 70% responded. Although the focus of the study was the use of technical reports among other information sources, "the broader purpose of the study is to provide insight regarding the information-seeking habits and practices of... engineers and scientists" (Pinelli *et al.*, 1991, p. 315).

In a series of questions asking about why they used certain information sources, responding engineers and scientists indicated that the relevance of sources was the most compelling reason for their use, followed by accessibility and "technical quality or reliability." Although at first glance the importance of such factors may seem obvious, they represent a subtle shift away from some earlier findings regarding use of information sources by engineers. Earlier studies (e.g., Gerstberger & Allen, 1968; Rosenberg, 1967), and hence federal information policies, had emphasized *accessibility* as the major determinant of whether a source would be used; however, the more recent investigators concluded that "accessibility is simply not the issue that it apparently was 25 years ago" (p. 320) due to efforts made by the U.S. federal government during the 1970s and 1980s to improve technical information flow. An increase in electronic channels of distribution, along with improved indexing, organization, and dissemination have apparently made aeronautical information easier to access. Another difference with Pinelli's respondents was that they were *least* sensitive to the *expense* of sources.

Interestingly Pinelli *et al.* refer to measures of "accessibility, ease of use, expense, familiarity, and reliability" as "sociometric" variables. More typically, sociometric data are those indicating "who talks to whom" in a work and/or social environment, thus mapping out a social *network*. The classic sociometric study among engineers was that of Allen and Cohen (1969), whose results pointed to a strong overlap between social and work reasons for communicating with colleagues. Allen and Cohen noted a chicken-and-egg problem in understanding why people in laboratories talk to one person more than another: did an engineer come to prefer communicating with a certain colleague because she works with him frequently, or dose she talk with that colleague more simply because she like him in the first place? Whatever "causes" such behavior patterns, Allen and Cohen documented the way in which the organization charts differ from the actual network of communication in two laboratories, and the important role that informal communication plays in work environments. Their closer examination of "sociometric stars" in the laboratories is a classic example of the role of gatekeepers in organizations (Metoyer-Duran, 1993).

One final study worth mentioning, for its documentation of the importance of interpersonal information seeking among engineers, is that of Holland and Powell (1995). They asked very detailed questions of 60 engineers regarding their information sources at work, and the relative importance of those sources. The single most highly rated source was "word of mouth," just edging out their own collections of documents and far exceeding any use of libraries or databases. The most highly ranked interpersonal sources were people within the engineer's own work group, followed by others in the company. People outside the company were also well thought of as sources. Interestingly, these engineers reported that the most highly ranked "people" source of information was *intra*personal, that is, their own "personal knowledge" of engineering; to a much lesser degree, they also favored "personal experimentation" as a source of information.

11.1.2 Social Scientists

The aforementioned tendency to generalize about metadisciplines—science, social science, and the humanities—has typically placed social scientists "between" scientists and humanists in terms of their habits and preferences (e.g., Bebout, Davis, & Oehlerts, 1975; Case, 1986). There are some gray areas in this typology. For example, are psychologists who are concerned with physiological influences on behavior chiefly scientists or do they belong with the social scientists? Are historians chiefly humanists, or are some of *them* social scientists, too? And where do professions like education or interdisciplinary fields like communication belong?

Nevertheless, the three basic categories of science, social science, and humanities have appealed strongly to many of those who have attempted to review information seeking results (e.g., the series edited by Constance Gould, 1988, 1989, 1991). For instance, many reviewers have concluded that the primary literature of science is in journals, where as that of the humanist is more likely to be found in books and archives. Brittain (1970) noted that journal literature is highly important to social scientists just as it is to scientists; however, the former also rely on institutional data (e.g., governmental records of births, deaths, education, and taxation) generated for reasons other than social research. Perhaps humanists can be said to have even broader sources of information, once we consider how much they draw upon artifacts of popular culture across the ages. Although different studies have reached varying conclusions about the role of informal channels of communication (with scientists frequently singled out as heaviest users of an "invisible college"), recent consensus seems to be that all kinds of scientists and scholars satisfy much of their information needs through contact with their colleagues in the workplace and at conferences.

Such generalizations about metadisciplines may be true as far as they go, but they do not further our understanding of the important mechanisms of information seeking, nor are they particularly useful in application, as in designing a university information system to serve particular disciplines. The conclusions are far too general for specific application, however interesting they may be. To make matters somewhat more complicated, anyone conducting research *between* disciplines is faced with a more "scattered" array of information sources, and consequently with a higher level of information seeking, as confirmed in a variety of empirical studies (Bates, 1996; Case, 1991; Meho & Haas, 2001). Hogeweg de Haart (1981) and Paisley (1986, 1990) each proposed matrixes that sorted out relationships among individual social sciences and related interdisciplines, such as among academic scholars of management or communication.

There is also the issue of "applied" fields, which proceed from fairly straightforward correspondences in information generation and application among science and engineering disciplines, to the messier relationships between such pairings as social workers and the social sciences, or between practicing artists and the humanities disciplines. Practitioners make highly variable use of knowledge generated by academic disciplines, with some (e.g., clinical psychologists) more tightly linked to formal channels and others (school teachers and lower level managers, as examples) making little use of research findings.

Although generalizations about disciplines and metadisciplines are suspect, the work of Bouazza (1989) is among the best and most recent of such attempts. In reviewing studies about use of information sources by scientists, social scientists and humanists, Bouazza concluded that

> although physical scientists, social scientists, and humanists tend to rely more on formal sources of information than on informal ones, they do not behave in the same way as far as information use is concerned. . . . The factors that affect the information use [include]. . . (a) The availability, accessibility, quality, cost, and ease of use of information. (b) Seniority, experience, specialty, educational level, professional orientation, and the subjective impressions of the users. (c) The stage of a research project; and the physical, social, political, and economic environments surrounding the user (p. 159)

The differences that Bouazza cites are taken partly from a review by Bebout, Davis, and Oehlerts (1975). Bouazza's own research, on a sample of 240 scientists, social scientists, and humanists from Carnegie-Mellon University, found that these three groups differed in the way that they used informal sources of information, especially in the data collection stage of research and in course preparation.

The most comprehensive review of social science information needs and uses (with ample comparisons to those in science) is that by the Dutch writer Hogeweg de Haart (1983). Emphasizing documentary sources of information, it does an excellent job of summarizing virtually all of the studies conducted up to 1980. A larger but narrower review of social scientists, featuring historians and government publications, appeared in the United States a few years later (Hernon, 1984). A commentary by Cronin (1984) emphasized research on social networks and gatekeepers among social scientists. Finally, Gould and Handler (1989) provided highlights from findings of social science studies, suggesting practical implications for libraries and communication systems.

One example of research about social scientists is the study by David Ellis (1989) focusing on the stages and process in their information seeking. He conducted interviews with 47 social scientists: 20 psychologists and the rest from eight other departments. His analysis of the resulting 250 pages of interview transcripts revealed six characteristics of information seeking patterns in these disciplines, which Ellis called starting, chaining, browsing, differentiating, monitoring, and extracting. Informal contacts were particularly important in the starting phases of projects and were also employed in monitoring developments in a field; the other activities mostly involved published literature. As the labels imply, browsing has to do with semidirected searches of publications or collections; chaining is the following of references from one document to another; differentiating concerns judgments made about the status, orientation, or quality of sources; and extracting is pulling out from sources specific information of interest.

To improve their understanding of these characteristics, Ellis, Cox, and Hall (1993) compared their earlier findings with new observations of academic physicists and chemists. They found no major differences between the research behaviors of physicists and social scientists. However, in the activities of the chemists they identified two novel kinds of behaviors, which they labeled "verifying" and "ending." Verifying reflected the efforts of chemists to find errors in their own work, particularly in numerical data but also in equations and citations. Ending referred to the tendency of some chemists to search the literature again following the completion of a project to check on relevant developments that might have taken place since they began their work.

11.1.3 Humanities Scholars

Although Ellis and his colleagues took pains to say that the behaviors they saw among social scientists did not occur in a strict sequence, the existence of "stages" in research projects has long been suggested by studies of various occupations. For example, Clara Chu (1999) surveyed the research habits of literary scholars, an underinvestigated community of scholarship. Using in-depth interviews and a lengthy questionnaire, Chu uncovered the phases through which scholars move when analyzing, criticizing, and interpreting literature. Her emphasis on stages of information seeking among a particular group of scholars was motivated by the tendency for past studies (and reviews) to generalize across all humanities disciplines.

Chu started by interviewing 31 literary critics in Ontario universities, collecting individual accounts of research projects and scholars' activities in their own language; these were used to create a descriptive model of the process of literary criticism. The second stage of her own research was to test the model by surveying a sample of 800 scholars, using an 11-page questionnaire of mostly closed items. Chu confirmed a series of six stages typical of literary scholarship: idea generation, preparation, elaboration, analysis and writing, dissemination, and then "further writing and dissemination." Each of these stages was accompanied by specific activities such as searching for, reading, and annotating materials in the preparation stage, and outlining and discussing ideas for a written work in the elaboration phase. In turn, each stage was seen as having "information functions," such as relating primary materials to different perspectives and themes in the preparation phase, or determining central and peripheral focuses in the elaboration phase. The preparation stage features the highest use of information, according to Chu, where as the dissemination phase has the least. She was careful to point out that these hypothesized stages do not necessarily occur in a strict sequential order; rather, their sequence is highly susceptible to the newness of the project, competing projects, and personal working style. Chu also found that informal communication among colleagues and other human sources is just as important in literary scholarship as it is in other kinds of work roles.

In comparing her findings with studies of the work stages of other disciplines, Chu noted that her stages are fewer in number than the 11 identified among scientists (Garvey, 1979), more than the three broad phases said to exist among economists (White, 1975), and most like the six stages portrayed in Stone (1980). She makes an argument for more investigations on, among other things, the motivation for scholarly work, the nature of collaborative projects, and informal communication among specific humanities disciplines.

An investigation of "information acquisition in history Ph.D. students" was conducted by Charles Cole (1998). In interviews with 45 doctoral students from six English universities using the grounded theory approach (see Chapter 5), Cole tried to understand how it is that historians learn to make inferences from what they read. His discussion is one that is less concerned with seeking than with *thinking*, and is informed by cognitive models of reading comprehension (particularly van Dijk & Kintsch, 1983). Using the analogies of pictures (i.e., background data) and jigsaw puzzles (i.e., the thesis), Cole concluded that these historians created knowledge structures through a four-stage "information process" that distinguishes "experts" from "novices" in a given knowledge domain. The doctoral student's need to demonstrate their expertise to their thesis committee — the reason why they seek information — determines "how they become informed — that is, the cognition involved in information acquisition" (p. 49).

The ultimate, in-depth investigation might be a study focused on a single scholar. In this category we have Stephen Nissenbaum's (1989) first-person account of his research on the poem "The Night Before Christmas." Nissenbaum described the 15-year evolution of his thoughts on the origins and purpose of the poem, his questions about it, the search for evidence, the development of findings, and the resulting shift in his own views regarding the nature of cultural change — the ultimate "result" of his scholarship. Although self-reports may present problems of reliability, they are the only avenue for knowing about such unique searches for information as Nissenbaum's.

A study of a more heterogeneous population is that of Wiberley and Jones (1989), studying 11 "humanities" scholars, including two anthropologists and a political scientist who were exploring the humanistic roots of their disciplines. Wiberley and Jones's results, like Sievert and Sievert's (1989) interviews with 27 philosophers, emphasize the solitary nature of such scholarship, with most information acquired through reading. Brown's (2000) investigation of the communication patterns of music scholars is also relevant to humanities scholarship.

Reviews by Gould (1988), Bouazza (1989), and Watson-Boone (1994) are the best entry points into the pre-1990 humanities information seeking literature.

11.1.4 Health Care Providers

There are a number of reasons why health-related information seeking attracts so much attention these days. For one thing, many parts of the world, including many developing countries, have enjoyed prosperity in recent years; this is even more true of developed economies like those in North America and Europe. With affluence comes longer life and better health care, but also other medical problems (obesity, drug abuse) and higher expectations of health care systems (no one wants to suffer or die before their time). Medical research continues to develop expensive drugs and procedures to address health problems and extend life. However, these advances exacerbate the problem of the affordability of health care. The debate over support of, and standards for, health care in the United States, for example, has become a prominent issue in presidential elections. In addition, there has been a social movement to promote the active involvement of patients in their own health care (see the next chapter for examples of patient information seeking).

All of these factors regarding medicine and health have an important consequence: there is ever more health-related information in existence and an increasing need to stay informed about it. This need applies most strongly to health care providers (physicians, nurses, dentists, and administrators) but also to the public at large. As a result, there has been both interest and funding for research related to health information, both for improving dissemination and for usage of information (from the "producer" side). A greater degree of attention is being devoted to how people actually use (or do not use) medical information.

I begin by reviewing studies of physicians, as they constitute the most high profile community the health care system, along with nurses. Even though nurses are more numerous — and, along with other physician assistants, are increasingly important — fewer studies have been done of them.

What is it that health care providers need to know, and how do they find it out? Nearly every study addresses these questions in terms of formal information sources, and that emphasis is too important to ignore here. Practitioners need to know, on the one hand, about the world of medical practice and research findings, and on the other, about their patients' conditions. Both aspects receive treatment in the information seeking literature but the overwhelming emphasis has been on how providers learn about things like treatment modalities, procedures, equipment, and medication.

There have been several good, comprehensive reviews of the medical information seeking literature (see, for example, Marshall, 1993), and some of the empirical studies also describe previous investigations fairly thoroughly. The best organized entry points into the literature on physicians are found in selective reviewed by Paul Gorman (1995, 1999). Gorman (1995) reviewed in depth 11 investigations, conducted between 1979 and 1995, of the "information needs of physicians." The 11 studies consist of a mix of mail survey, interview, ethnographic, and "stimulated recall" methodologies, and are used to establish a taxonomy of types of information needed by medical doctors—the lack of which, Gorman says, has hindered comparisons of studies.

The taxonomy that Gorman created is useful in considering the other medical information studies reviewed in this chapter. He divides "information used" into five general types: patient data (on an individual, taken from the patient's medical records, family, friends, and self-reports); population statistics (aggregated data on many patients, recalled from memory or taken from public health reports); medical knowledge (generalizable research and practice, taken from journals and textbooks); logistical information (policies, procedures, and forms used "to get the job done"); and social influences (the patterns of local practice, as learned from talking with colleagues). Gorman emphasizes, though, that a typical clinical question (e.g., "Does Norpace cause fatigue?") contains multiple categories of information.

The "information need" side of the equation is matched to these categories through the 11 studies reviewed. Gorman classified types of needs into four types: *recognized* (obvious needs, articulated by the respondent); *pursued* (needs actually followed up on by the doctor interviewed); *satisfied* (by referring to sources of established medical knowledge or patient data); and *unrecognized* (possibilities not initially recognized by the physician). In each case, the nature of the need is either reported by the respondent in the interview, or observed directly by the researcher in the office setting. Much of Gorman's analysis is of "needs," but obviously these also imply actions—seeking and use of information.

Doctors who face patients generate a stream of information needs; what is unclear is how large that stream really is. Osheroff, Forsythe, Buchanan, Bankowitz, Blumenfeld, and Miller (1991) found that each patient generated five questions, while Covell, Uman, and Manning's (1985) study indicated two questions for every three patients, and Ely, Burch, and Vinson's (1992) found that it is more like one for every 15 patients. One might well ask how estimates can vary so much. The answer is found in the study designs: each of these are based on very different physician samples and varying criteria for what constitutes a "question." The highest estimate (Osheroff *et al.*) comes from medical rounds by teams of doctors, residents, and students in an academic setting, and included all types of questions; the lowest estimate (Ely *et al.*) excluded from observation several types of common questions, and included a sample of rural physicians, who ask markedly fewer questions than their urban colleagues.

However many questions there are, more than two-thirds of them are probably *not pursued*, according to Covell *et al.* and to Gorman and Helfand (1995), although Gorman (1999) says that answers are sought to almost half of questions that arise if we adopt a broader definition of "information need." Most of the information needs that are pursued are satisfied by textbooks, drug texts, and people (colleagues, consultants, and nonphysicians), with a strong preference for colleagues; and other highly familiar sources; relatively little use is made of library or Internet resources. As described in Chapter 6, Haug's (1997) meta-analysis of 12 physician studies also concluded that the most common patterns of sources consulted were local textbooks and colleagues. Given that drug-prescribing questions are the most common type that arise, it is logical that texts featuring pharmaceutical information such as the *Physicians' Desk Reference*, are the only published sources commonly used on a daily (or at least weekly) basis (Connelly, Rich, Curley, & Kelly, 1990; Covell, Uman, & Manning, 1985; Ely *et al.*, 1992).

According to Osheroff *et al.* (1991) about half of the information that a physician needs to treat a patient can be answered from the medical record; answers to the remaining needs are evenly split between published sources and a synthesis of the physician's existing knowledge and information from the patient. For the physician's practice to actually *improve* (i.e., for doctors to go beyond their education and be innovative), personal reading of journals and textbooks is typically not enough; interaction with up-to-date colleagues is a more likely avenue for continuing education in medicine (Davis, Thomson, Oxman, & Haynes, 1995; Urquhart, 1998).

Gorman concluded that the clinical questions that doctors have "tend to be highly complex, embedded in the context of a unique patient's story" (p. 729). There are two related aspects of this conclusion that bear emphasis. The first is a familiar refrain: the primary information comes from humans rather than recorded sources; stories need to be sifted and interpreted before the information they contain is written down.

The second implication of Gorman's review is that much of the knowledge physicians use in treating patients is a narrative: the story of the patient's history of symptoms and treatments (Tannenbaum, 1994). As Gorman says,

"The reliance on stories to communicate information need, because of the complexity and patient specificity, may be one reason for the consistent finding that physicians rely heavily on human sources of information" (p. 734). This kind of knowledge is not merely a list of facts about conditions and implied treatment options that could be pulled from a handbook or database.

One of the studies contained in Gorman's review can serve as a useful example of the investigation of physician information needs and seeking. Timpka and Arborelius (1990) offer an original research approach to physician information seeking. Rather than examining the usual "well-formed questions" and corresponding source preferences, as do most studies in this genre, they investigate "dilemmas" — perplexing situations in which physicians struggle to understand a case that does not make sense. Although the goal of this investigation was to inform the development of decision-support systems for doctors, their findings hold more general interest for students of information seeking.

Timpka (a physician) and Arborelius (a psychologist) conducted an in-depth study of 12 general practitioners (GPs), videotaping and analyzing 46 of their consultations with patients. These video recordings were reviewed twice with the GP who was taped. The first time, the physician was asked to stop the tape any time she or he had comments to make (which were recorded for analysis). During the second review, the GP stopped the tape any time he or she had felt uncertain about how to go on.

Timpka and Arborelius sorted the comments made during these sessions into a series of dichotomous categories, such as "spontaneous comments" versus "interviewer initiated comments," and "stimulated recall" versus "new aspects" of the situation. Those spontaneous comments that identified problems in the consultation session, based on stimulated recall, were dubbed "dilemma situations." Dilemma situations were further broken down into three categories in which knowledge was needed of a medical (32%), personal (19%), or social (49%) type.

Among the 46 consultations, 262 dilemmas were identified. These were cases in which "the GP found it difficult to understand the situation as a whole" (p. 23). An example of a medical dilemma is the case of patient who presents multiple symptoms for which there is no clear and immediate diagnosis; the diagnosis was the source of 55% of the medical knowledge dilemmas, and the puzzle with most of these was with what kind of treatment to recommend.

The least frequent type of dilemma was of a personal nature, primarily having to do with the competence of the physician in controlling the consultation. These were often cases in which the physician found himself wondering, "What is the right thing to do just now?" An example that Timpka and Arborelius related is of a physician who inadvertently reminds a patient of the death of that person's father, and wonders what he can then say to comfort the patient or address the faux pas.

The situations in which the "knowledge needed" was of the third kind, social, highlighted breakdowns in organizational structure or interpersonal communication. An example of organizational interruption is the misplacing of portions of the patient's medical record. Of particular interest were 99 breakdowns in interpersonal communication, which were analyzed using the universal pragmatics approach of Jürgen Habermas (1979). These were classified into

> situations where the GP did not understand the patient (11%), perceived that the patient violated a social norm (25%), did not trust the patient (42%), did not agree with the patient on the truth of the facts (11%), or was disturbed (11%). (Timpka & Arborelius, 1990, p. 26)

Examples of each type of communication breakdown include: not understanding why a patient needed medical attention; perceiving the client as being uncooperative, or as trying to control the diagnostic interview; not trusting a patient's statements or understanding of medical terminology; not agreeing with the client's self-diagnosis; and being interrupted by noises or phone calls.

Timpka and Arborelius concluded with an enlightened discussion of "problems in the doctor-patient communication" that suggest difficulties in sense-making on both sides. For instance, they suggest that mistrust is an underexamined issue in medical consultations. Only rarely did Timpka and Arborelius witness confirming kinds of communication strategies, such as the physician asking the patient, "Did you understand what I just explained?"

In the view of Timpka and Arborelius, the GP is faced with the interpretation of narratives, and so is similar to the historian in how he or she reconstructs the truth of a situation. It is only when physicians do not have insights (i.e., "don't get the joke") that they turn to reference sources. Descriptions of disease in the literature are described by Timpka and Arborelius as "iconic" compilations of clinical narratives, which help the doctor to form meaning despite being at times vague and incomplete. They conclude that decision support systems in medicine may have something to learn from multimedia sources in the humanities in the way that those sources support learning and interpretation. Timpka and Arborelius also make a case for their "phenomenological approach with stimulated recall reports" as a superior method to "standard data collection techniques (study of written material, observation, participation, questionnaires, interviewing, and group brainstorming)" in understanding task-based information needs and uses (p. 29).

Another innovative approach to studying physician information seeking has entailed the use of clinical case histories, or "vignettes"(Urquhart, 1998, 1999). In such studies, physicians were presented with several vignettes and asked "a series of questions aimed a eliciting how confident they were in implementing therapy without recourse to additional information. . . . and which sources would be used if they did seek further information" (Urquhart, 1998, p. 424).

Results from such studies indicate a strong preference to consult with a specialist in those cases in which physicians had doubts about proceeding with treatment. A related finding has been that doctors often develop confidence in their knowledge after treating as few as two cases, suggesting that feelings of uncertainty may be extinguished rather quickly by a little practical experience. However, Urquhart (1999) questions whether vignettes are as valid a diagnostic tool in studies of physicians as they have been in studies of other kinds of professionals.

Nurses are much more numerous than physicians but have received much less attention from researchers. Even more so than doctors, nurses are focused on patient care and so, correspondingly, are their information needs and seeking. Studies by Corcoran-Perry and Graves (1990), Wakeham (1992), Blythe and Royle (1993), and Pettigrew (2000), among others, emphasize that nurses consult primarily local sources of information in the context of caring for clients. This includes patient records and laboratory results, coupled with interpersonal sources such as physicians, pharmacists, and other nurses. To this list, Haig (1993) adds nursing journals, if their content is relevant to patient care; Wakeham (1992) notes that these are more often personal subscriptions than publications found in the library.

Urquhart (1998) related several studies of British nurses that used vignettes in their research design. A typical vignette used in the nursing study began by proposing a situation requiring some action from the respondent, such as "Your colleague needs to know about all the ways in which alternative/complementary medicine might be used in your ward. . . ." (Urquhart, 1998, p. 281). These studies found a wide range of responses to each vignette, with most interviewees suggesting at least one or two sources that could be used to respond to the situation proposed. About 25% of the respondents were characterized as "expert" and "confident" information seekers, who could identify more than two sources of relevant information and had a strategy in mind for approaching the problem. However, 45% of the interviewees were seen as having relatively limited knowledge and skills in information seeking, suggesting the need for further continuing education of nurses.

Other health care providers who have been studied include dentists (e.g., Strother, Lancaster, & Gardiner, 1986; Mullaly-Quijas, Ward, & Woefl, 1994 — the latter is discussed in Chapter 6 as an example of focus group research) and mental health care workers (Salasin & Cedar, 1985 — also mentioned in Chapter 12 under the topic of "rural dwellers"). According to a review of this literature by Leckie, Pettigrew, & Sylvain (1996), dentists are most like physicians in their need for information on patient care and changes in the environment regarding techniques, treatments, equipment, and the administration and regulation of their practice. It is apparent from these studies that health care professionals have a great deal in common in regards to their preferences for information sources.

11.1.5 Managers

The heterogeneity of this group must be acknowledged right off the bat: "managers" *could* be almost anybody. A person who directs the operations of a convenience store with four full-time employees is a manager, as is the chairman of General Motors. However, as studied in the information seeking literature, managers are typically higher-level employees of large organizations, often described as "executives" or "CEOs." Most literature reviews also assume that "managers" are educated (having at least a bachelor's degree and perhaps a master's in business administration, or a comparable degree in another field), even though higher education was not as prevalent in early studies of managers. For our purposes, "managers" will be assumed to be individuals who have at least some university education and who work in a sizable organization.

A review by Choo and Auster (1993) of "acquisition and use of information by managers" is a good place to start for this group. Choo and Auster focused on "environmental scanning" — a subset of the literature on managers' needs, uses, and seeking — but they offer a useful framework for summarizing findings in this area. Given their focus on scanning, Choo and Auster discuss primarily information that is *external* to the organization (such as what competitors are doing), rather than internal. They highlight findings similar to those among scientists and scholars: informal sources and ease of accessibility of information is even more important to managers than to the other groups. To this they add that people and conversations are the primary way that managers acquire information, and that a defining context of managerial work is the solving of immediate problems. It is the latter characteristic that makes managers most different from scholars and scientists, who may identify research problems and work on them for long periods of time before reaching conclusions; managers, in contrast, rarely have the luxury of extended contemplation, and for that reason are much less likely to spend time reading.

Auster and Choo (1993) were interested in how managers acquire and use information about the external business environment. As described in Chapter 3, this monitoring of the environment is sometimes referred to as "scanning" in the management literature. Auster and Choo studied how managers regarded uncertainty in the environment and specifically how perceived uncertainty affected their use and evaluation of sources. In framing their research problem, the investigators built on early work by Aguilar (1967), Rosenberg (1967), Gerstberger and Allen (1968), and on more recent studies of these concepts by Culnan (1983) and Daft et al. (1986, 1988), among many others. Their questionnaire was thus able to replicate measures found to be predictive in earlier studies.

To study their research problem, Auster and Choo first picked two information-intensive and fast-moving industries: publishing and telecommunications. They focused their inquiry on Canadian firms with revenues of greater than $5 million and identified the CEOs of the resulting 207 firms.

Following the widely used survey techniques of Dillman (1978), the investigators mailed as many as four questionnaires to their target population, followed by a phone call if none of those instruments were returned. It took that degree of effort to obtain a response rate of 56% (115 respondents of 207 initially contacted); given the nature of the respondents and their lack of direct connection to the investigators, it was remarkable to have attained such a level of response.

Auster and Choo found that CEOs see customers and technological trends as the most strategic portions of the environment to pay attention to; those sectors are also the most uncertain for CEOs. Higher perceptions of uncertainty in the environment were associated with more scanning of the environment. To keep track of environmental change, CEOs relied on multiple sources, both internal and external, both personal and impersonal. Examples of internal sources included the company managers and staff (who were also "personal" sources), while external sources included printed and broadcast media (obviously "impersonal"). A finding that contradicted some earlier studies was that the perceived quality of the source was a better predictor of use than either the accessibility of the source or even the perceived degree of uncertainty in the environment. The two sources that can most be relied upon are subordinate managers and company customers; internal memos, although they were close at hand and used with some frequency, were ranked only in the mid-range in terms of "quality" of information.

Auster and Choo suggest that an increasingly complex and fast-changing business environment prompts CEOs to stress the quality of information over ease of accessibility. Likewise, a study of 186 management report users by Swanson (1987) found that "information value" was more important than accessibility. Thus, both of these studies differ in that respect from the still often cited findings of Allen (1977), which emphasized accessibility as the most influential variable. Along with Auster and Choo, the studies by Culnan (1983) and Pinelli et al. (1991) argued that a more complex and turbulent environment places a premium on the reliability of information.

Kuhlthau's (1999) and Baldwin and Rice's (1997) reports also contain good reviews of managerial information usage, as background to their respective investigations of security analysts.

11.1.6 Journalists

The communications scholar Elihu Katz once wrote a fascinating essay in the journal *American Behavioral Scientist* (1989) on the topic of "journalists as scientists." Katz's theme was that journalists do not so much resemble professions like doctors and lawyers (who serve individual clients rather than a larger constituency) as much as they are like applied scientists. Journalists, like scientists, have theories and methods, and sometimes make predictions about future events. In the case of journalism, the theories are about people, society, events, and news itself; the methods of inquiry are very rudimentary, however.

The accompanying articles in this issue on journalism are equally interesting. Dominique Wolton (1989), for example, mostly agreed with Katz's statements about theory but stressed the different reality of journalists, who "must produce information on a daily basis... structuring the world as events continue to unfold... giving form to a world that is rarely rational," unlike scientists, who have "the luxury of standing back from events" (p. 249). In contrast Dina Goren (1989) flatly disagreed with Katz: journalists do not have explicit theories or methods and are rarely held accountable for the veracity of their pronouncements, as are scientists and professionals. And Itzhak Roeh (1989) eschewed the comparison with scientists entirely, arguing that no matter how much journalists may deny it, what they actually do is "tell stories" rather than "report facts."

Whatever is the appropriate way to view the job of news reporting, it is a fascinating profession to study in the context of information seeking. In a very concrete way, journalism is *largely* information seeking, along with the prime job of transferring what is found through writing, speaking, and/or filming. Despite the large number of investigations of the audience for news (reader, viewer, or listener studies), there are relatively few focused, empirical studies of what journalists actually do. Instead, much of what we know about them tends to come from essays and observations about the press as an institution (e.g., Epstein, 1973).

One investigation stands out: Hannele Fabritius (1999, 2000) conducted a qualitative study of journalists using a variety of methods and sources of data. Indeed, a subtheme of her research was how one may triangulate theory, methods, and data to gain a fuller picture of a phenomenon—in this case, the work practices of reporters and their use of electronic sources in that work. Fabritius observed and interviewed a number of journalists in four departments of a Finnish newspaper, including attending editorial meetings and employing talk-aloud protocols to better understand some aspects of journalistic work. In addition, she used a number of other methods and observations. Fabritus had 18 journalists complete "diary" forms after writing a news item, indicating the sources used and their importance; she coupled the resulting 250 diary entries to the actual published items in which they resulted, and so linking process to outcome. She collected documents (such as editorial meeting agendas and press releases) from the newspaper, and kept a diary of her fieldwork experience. Fabritius also experimented with yet other observation devices, such as videotape and photographs, as well as critical incident interviews, which turned out to be less productive methods than the others.

Fabritus's findings (which are not easily summarized) establish the influence of the various "cultures" to which journalists belong. The concentric cultures of the profession, a particular medium (such as a newspaper), and the particular news beat within a medium (e.g., foreign news) are manifested in the values, norms, activities, and routines that make up work practice in that context. Together, these determine the criteria by which news is selected and produced, and the patterns of information seeking that accompany the processing of stories. Fabritus said that "continuous, proceeding stages" can be discerned in the production of news, "logical steps" that "do not follow each other in a strict chronological order" (p. 411). Searching for and evaluating information (facts and opinions) takes place in interaction with a wide variety of sources (e.g., people, documents, firsthand observation). Fabritus concluded that the way journalists learn to process news items, along with "situational factors such as lack of time" are the strongest constraints on the ways that information is sought in journalism (p. 411).

Scholars who make more informal observations of journalistic work practice (e.g., Goren, 1989; Katz, 1989) would agree with Fabritus' emphasis on the culture of journalism and the constraints of time and institutions; indeed, some of them (e.g., Stocking & Gross, 1989) see journalistic work as dominated strongly by predetermined frames of perception and labeling that tend to bias news.

Other studies of actual information seeking and use among journalists are relatively rare, and tend to be source oriented. Nicholas and Williams (1999), for example, raised the question of whether the Internet is widely used as a source. In a study of 150 journalists and news librarians in the United Kingdom, they concluded that fewer than 20% were making much use of the Internet for finding information relevant to their reporting. Surprisingly, the heaviest users tended to be midcareer reporters rather than the very youngest (and supposedly most computer literate). Unsurprisingly, the most-used sites to be those of online newspapers. Nicholas and Williams categorized the relationships that these news workers have with the Internet as ranging from worship to complete disdain for it as an information source. Their study contrasts rather sharply with online surveys of journalists conducted in the United States (e.g., Garrison, 2000; Ross & Middleberg, 1998), which have painted a much more enthusiastic picture of the use of online sources.

11.1.7 Lawyers

Attorneys share with many scientists an absolute need to stay current with published literature relevant to their current work; they cannot afford to miss any new ruling, decision, or regulation that concerns their practice. It may be the case that some areas of the law (e.g., taxation, health and safety regulation) require more research than others, but all lawyers face a rapidly expanding universe of knowledge to which they must attend.

Sutton (1994, p. 199) noted that "there is little known empirically of the information seeking behavior of attorneys"and that we have relied upon anecdotes and legal research primers for what we know about them. The analysis of attorney information seeking by Leckie, Pettigrew, and Sylvain (1996), for example, rests mainly on texts about the nature and practice of legal research. Those authors said that the primary activities of attorneys — advocacy (with its accompanying legal research), drafting of legal documents, counseling of clients, negotiating outcomes, and managing their practice — all imply a great deal of information seeking of various types.

Sutton's own analysis (1994) theorized about the "mental model" of legal reasoning held by attorneys. The focus of his article is improving information retrieval systems for the law, but it contains a fascinating discussion of the way lawyers think about legal cases, and what this predicts about their search for court decisions that bear on a case. According to Sutton, lawyers rely on their legal education to first identify key cases that define an areas of law, then work from those to find cases that apply the relevant legal principal to facts that are similar to the case at hand — a process that Sutton calls "context-sensitive exploration." Ultimately the search for relevant cases may come down to "tracking" citations from one legal decision to another, which can be a massive and frustrating task. Not only are there many potentially relevant cases, but some of them will have been overruled, criticized, or ignored by more recent decisions, the status of which may not be fully reflected in the indexing systems for case law. Thus, it is a difficult task to identify and analyze all of the cases that might be cited by the other side in a legal battle.

Cole and Kuhlthau (2000) studied 15 attorneys, some at the start of their career and the rest at more advanced stages. Drawing on psychological studies of problem solving, Cole and Kuhlthau argued that part of what makes one "expert" in the law is an ability to link the recognition of a problem to potential solutions. Through interviews, they obtained examples of how this comes about, which they expressed in terms of a four-point "value added arc."

The first of Cole and Kuhlthau's four points is that experts are more efficient at identifying what information is most relevant to a case, for example, knowing what previous cases are most likely to be cited. Second, expert lawyers are able to see the case in terms of how certain information will affect the client; they are able to question witnesses and outline cases in ways "that will benefit the client or jury and judge" (p. 6). The third point in the arc of value is the way that seasoned attorneys are able to package what they know in such a way "so that it is effectively communicated to the client or jury and judge"(p. 6); they have learned to cover all the necessary points in a case, to present facts to the court in a concrete way, and to prepare effective opening and closing statements. Finally, the fourth "further refinement" occurs when lawyers package their knowledge in a such way that the judge, jury, or client will act on it; this may be accomplished, for example, by working backward from the charges given to the jury in terms of what facts need to be established to decide the case.

Cole and Kuhlthau described their four points as mechanisms for constructing and packaging information, and then using it to persuade others. Legal expertise can be improved, they say, by "simple almost formulaic devices" that stimulate lawyers to think in terms of how the information will be used" (p. 8). Their future research promises to examine the sources that feed into the four phases of the value-added arc.

Several other investigations of lawyers have been conducted in the United States and England, mostly as theses for master's or doctoral degrees. These include studies by Cheatle (1992), Gelder (1981), Hainsworth (1992), Otike (1999), Vale (1988), and Walsh (1994). Hainsworth has conducted an investigation of the information seeking behavior of judges. Some of these are difficult to obtain, but fortunately they are all reviewed briefly in the article by Otike (1999).

11.1.8 Other Occupations

The occupations discussed above have been the subject of several, or in some cases dozens, of investigations; the occupations mentioned under this heading have been the focus of few, if any, empirical studies. Observations here include the work of artists and members of the clergy.

Susie Cobbledick (1996) conducted interviews with four artists of different media: a sculptor, painter, fiber artist, and a metalsmith. She makes a startling point in her introduction when she discusses how little artists have been studied compared to other occupations. Based on 1995 estimates, there must be almost a million "professional" (i.e., not including part-time or periodic) artists in the United States alone. This is more than the number of lawyers in the United States and also more than the combined number of scientists and social scientists in a country known for an abundance of all three types of professionals. Artists have certainly not enjoyed the kind of attention to information needs and uses that scientists and social scientists have had. Cobbledick argues that this is partly because of a stereotype of the artist as "self-contained individuals who create via inspiration" (p. 344). People like that, we might presume, have information needs that are entirely fulfilled through divine inspiration!

Cobbledick found that artists do indeed have a need for inspiration — it is one of five types of information needs they have, in fact. The inspiration need is fulfilled in a variety of ways. The sculptor visits the site where the work will be exhibited, the fiber artist surveys nature for interesting patterns, the metalsmith visits churches for inspiration from their structure and content. All of them examine images from published work, although not necessarily works related to their art. Fiber artist, for example, may find the kind of patterns that inspire her in pictures of clouds or cell structures.

Artists also have needs for "specific visual information." These are visual elements that appear in their works of art, and are more likely to come from printed pictures, or from their own experimental drawings. A third kind of information that artists need is technical: "the characteristics and properties of the various techniques and media used to create art" (p. 352). This kind of knowledge is most often found out from other artists and sometimes from books or experimentation. "Current developments in the visual arts," the fourth need, is mainly the province of fine arts journals but also can be gleaned from popular magazines, art exhibits, and colleagues. A fifth type of information about "shows, commissions, and sales" is used for finding work, and exhibiting and selling work product; these are learned about through art journals and personal contacts.

Cobbledick found that the practices of these four artists were diverse yet included a common reliance on printed material and reading; they do not rely entirely on images to foster creativity, and some of the information they need has nothing to do with "art" per se. In contrast to the observations of other writers on information seeking in the arts (e.g., Downey, 1993; Layne, 1994; Stam, 1984, 1995), *browsing* of materials was not especially important; Cobbledick's respondents browsed only

> within limited subject areas. . . . None of the artists describes happy accidents of serendipitous discovery in the library. . . . For these artists, happy accidents occur in the studio while working with their various media.

Cobbledick also found that people, especially other artists, were very important sources in many contexts. She concludes that the information needs of artists are as broad as human experience itself—needs that are hard to place into the usual categories.

Donald Wicks (1999) has studied the "information-seeking behavior of pastoral clergy"making use of social network theory and role theory. Wicks hypothesized that the behavior of clergy was "influenced by the interaction of their work worlds and the work roles" (p. 208). A pastor's worlds are of three types: theological (religious beliefs and positions), denominational (affiliation with an established church), and congregational (the local church in which he or she works). Likewise, there are three roles that clergy undertake: preacher, caregiver, and administrator. Wicks further hypothesized that information seeking among clergy could be characterized as following on a continuum from "open" to "closed," depending on "the particular world in which the pastor is operating and the specific role he or she is performing at the time" (p. 209).

Based on a postal survey of 378 Canadian pastors from six religions, coupled with interviews with 20 clergy members, Wicks was able to demonstrate an interaction between roles that shaped the sources of information to which pastors turned and the degree to which they looked outside their own "small world." A "closed" pattern of information seeking was found in regards to all theological world roles, and (unsurprisingly) in the denominational and congregational worlds when acting as an administrator. The clergy were more open to information from outside their social group when providing care to others. The pastor's denomination influenced how open he or she was to outside information in the preaching role, with three affiliations (Anglican, Roman Catholic, and United Church) being more closed than the other three (Baptist, Pentecostal, and Presbyterian). Wicks suggests that this difference is due to size of the denomination, with the larger ones having more internal sources of information (e.g., offices and publications). Wicks compared his findings with other investigations of work roles in other fields, and a dozen earlier investigations of the work of clergy. He argues that the fairly large numbers of working clergy, along with their influence over many members of society, make them an important group to study.

Many other types of occupations have been studied. Some examples are professors (e.g., Case, 1986, 1991; Chu, 1999; Ocholla, 1996, 1999), farmers (Case & Rogers, 1987; Leckie, 1996), janitors (Chatman, 1990), policymakers (Florio & DeMartini, 1993), teachers (Savolainen, 1995), and securities analysts (Baldwin & Rice, 1997; Kuhlthau, 1999).

11.2
Summary

This chapter has examined the size and nature of the information seeking literature. Through a selection of recent studies we have considered how the literature has developed along three lines of inquiry: by occupation, by social role, and by demographic group.

It can be seen that there is great variety in the kinds of populations and activities that have been examined. In recent years more attention has been paid to contextual, situational, or role variables than the usual demographic variables. Relatively small populations (e.g., Canadian literary critics, homeless parents, experts on stateless nations) have been sampled for investigation. Yet despite this diversity in the types of social groups studied, investigations concerned with health information seeking have become the dominant genre in terms of numbers, rivaled mainly by the ever-constant attention to students of all types and ages.

One thing that these studies have in common, however, it is a concern with sources and channels — typically interpersonal channels versus mass and/or specialized media. A frequent finding is that people still turn to other people for information. Despite an effort to examine the process of information seeking, much of it still comes down to "who or what do people consult for information?" This is an old question within the information needs, uses, and seeking literature and continues to dominate the discussion of findings.

Recommended for Further Reading

Fabritius, H. (1999). Triangulation as a multiperspective strategy in a qualitative study of information seeking behaviour of journalists. In T. D. Wilson & D. K. Allen (Eds.), *Information behaviour: Proceedings of the second international conference on research in information needs, seeking and use in different contexts, 13/15 August 1998*, Sheffield, UK (pp. 406–419). London: Taylor Graham.

Fabritius's study is a fine example of the use of multiple methods and sources of data in studying a single population: participant observation, interviews, diaries kept by participants and the investigator, talk-aloud protocols, videotaping, and photography.

Gorman, P. (1995). Information needs of physicians. *Journal of the American Society for Information Science, 46,* 737–742.

Paul Gorman, a leading figure in the investigation of physician information needs, offers a concise summary of what we know about doctors' information seeking.

Nissenbaum, S. (1989). The month before "The Night before Christmas." In: B. P. Lynch (Ed.), *Humanists at work: disciplinary perspectives and personal reflections* (pp. 43–78). Chicago: University of Illinois at Chicago, Institute for the Humanities and the University Library.

Historian Stephen Nissenbaum describes the evolution of his thoughts over a 15-year period regarding the origins and purpose of a famous poem, and how he went about his search for evidence to establish his interpretation. The result is perhaps the most detailed first-person account of the research process ever recorded.

Pinelli, T. E. (1991). The information-seeking habits and practices of engineers. *Science & Technology Libraries, 11*(3), 5–25.

A very readable discussion of the difference between science and technology, and how scientists differ from engineers. Pinelli, a scientist with the National Aeronautics and Space Administration (NASA), summarizes six major studies of engineers and their information needs.

12

Research by Social Role and Demographic Group

Being a member of a group, such as abused spouses, cancer patients, senior citizens, or janitors, is seen as sufficient to influence individual information-seeking behaviors and patterns.

Bryce Allen (1996, p. 74)

Information needs and uses need to be examined within the work, organizational, and social settings of the users. Information needs vary according to users' membership in professional or social groups, their demographic backgrounds, and the specific requirements of the task they are performing.

Chun Choo and Ethel Auster (1993, p. 284)

Chapter Outline

12.1. Two Other Ways of Studying People

12.2. By Role
    12.2.1. Citizen or Voter
    12.2.2. Consumer
    12.2.3. Patient
    12.2.4. Gatekeeper
    12.2.5. Other Roles

12.3. By Demographic Group
    12.3.1. Age
    12.3.2. Racial and Ethnolinguistic Minorities
    12.3.3. Socioeconomic Status
    12.3.4. Other Demographic Groups

12.4. Summary

12.1
Two Other Ways of Studying People

The most common approach to studying information seeking has been occupational—sampling a group of people working in a type of job or profession. Yet sometimes information seeking investigations are not based on occupations, but rather on nonwork characteristics of people.

In some investigations (particularly of a psychological nature) what is desired is basic knowledge regarding human capacities, behaviors, and habits, in which case the demographic backgrounds of the people sampled are not so important, and their occupation is virtually irrelevant. At other times, a demographic variable must be considered to ensure that the people studied are comparable; for example, an investigation might select only adults or only children.

Usually, though, some more restrictive element of the population's background or behavior is introduced to focus the investigation. For example, one might be studying only those people who are eligible to vote in a certain election ("voters"), or only those who buy products ("consumers"), or only those enrolled in formal classes of study ("students"). It is this type of focus that is referred to by the label "role."

Table 12.1
Works Reviewed, and Related Works Cited, for Role and Group

Social role	Works reviewed to illustrate findings	Some other relevant works cited
Citizen/voter	Savolainen 98	Chen 82; Dervin 84; Newhagen 94; Popkin 93
Consumer	Belk 88	Bloch 89; Mick 92; Sherry 90
Patient	Sligo 00	Johnson 97; Pifalo 97; Rees 00
Gatekeeper	Agada 99	Metoyer-Duran 91, 93; Shoemaker 91
Other roles	(Students, etc.)	Gundry 94; Jiao 97; Kuhlthau 88b; Mellon 86; Morrison 93; Sligo 00; Williamson 00
Demographic group		
Age	Julien 99; van der Rijt 96; Walter 94; Williamson 97	Biesecker 88, 90; Chatman 92; Clarke 73; Gourash 78; Tinker 93; Todd 84
Racial or ethnic	Newhagen 94; Spink 99, 01	Agada 99; Atwood 82; Chatman 87, 96; Freimuth 93; Gourash 78; Hsia 87
Socioeconomic status	Hersberger 01	Chatman 85, 91, 95; Childers 75; Dervin 72; Freimuth 90; Savolainen 95
Other groups	(Gender, urban/rural, etc.)	Anwar 98; Baker 96; Case 87; Creelman 90; Freimuth 89, 93; Harris 88, 94; Whitt 93

Note: Studies are listed by first author only, plus year. See the references.

Also in this chapter we consider demographic categorizations of people. The *analysis* of populations by their background characteristics (e.g., age, gender, race, socioeconomic status, education) is very common in many investigations of humans. However, it is typically not the main *focus* of the study, which is more likely some occupation or role that is practiced by the population under study. Here we consider a few studies in which demographic background has played a key role in the selection of respondents (Table 12.1).

12.2
By Role

Under the heading of "roles" I review those commonly investigated classifications that we tend to impose upon the general population: citizen (or voter or person-in-the-street), consumer (or shopper), patient, gatekeeper, student, teacher, parent, and so on.

Brenda Dervin makes the point in a 1989 article on "users as research inventions" that such categorizations (along with demographic groupings) are usually a function of marketing segmentation and the consumer/user mentality that goes with it. Whether the goal is to sell someone something or to study their use of some "system" so that it may be improved, the result is not always positive for those studied. When people are "clustered" into groups and labeled, the resulting categories come to be *reified* — researchers, policymakers, and the general public begin to believe that such categories are *real*, rather than just convenient fictions for the purpose of analysis and planning. The diverse individuals who make up these groups, and their perspectives, tend to be lost in the results. There is also the common situation in which an individual is simultaneously a member of several categories, an issue of "overlap" discussed here further under "Other Demographic Groups."

Unfortunately, it is not the case that such analyses of user categories lead automatically to improvements in services or systems. Indeed, Dervin claims that sometimes they reinforce inequities, finding, for example, that "the poor use computers less than the rich" does not suggest a solution to that inequity, but rather may lead to feelings of resignation and blame.

Nevertheless, a common approach in information behavior literature has been to examine large populations in terms of particular, nonwork roles that they play.

12.2.1 Citizen or Voter

Obviously some investigations can be classified in several different ways. Investigations of "citizens" or "voters" often aspire to improve community and democracy, but can also cover many other areas of interest to the average citizen. Thus, there is some degree of overlap between this category and some of the others that follow, particularly the demographic emphases that flavor many of these general studies. The emphasis in this particular subsection will be on general investigations of human communities, including their media use. Readers interested specifically in information behavior related to voting and politics are advised to consult Popkin's (1993) review of voter reasoning and "information shortcuts,"and a study of the "friends and neighbors effect" by Bowler, Donovan, and Snipp (1993).

The classic, large-scale investigations of the information needs and uses of citizens are quite old now: Warner, Murray, and Palmour (1973); Williams, Dordick, and Horstmann (1977); Palmour, Rathbun, Brown, Dervin, & Dowd (1979); Chen and Hernon (1982); and Dervin, Ellyson, Hawkes, Guagnano, and White (1984). Of these, the most widely cited is Chen and Hernon's (1982) study of 2,400 New England residents. Among the more important findings of the Chen and Hernon study was the individual (and context-driven nature) of information seeking.

Fifty-two percent of the 3,548 "information-seeking situations" recounted by Chen and Hernon's informants were needs for information to solve day-to-day problems; the rest were scattered across 18 different problem situations, with none accounting for more than 6% of the total. Typical "problems" fell into the following categories (roughly in order of importance): having to do with work or jobs in general, or performing specific tasks; consumer issues, such as finding product information; home and housing issues, such as finding, renting, or buying a dwelling, or repairing cars or items around the home; and issues related to education, such as identifying schools and courses, financing a degree, or parenting children.

In each case, interpersonal providers of information were ranked as much more important than institutions or the mass media. In relating who or what they considered consulting to address their problems, 74% of respondents cited their "own experience" as a source of information; this was also rated the "most helpful" source. The other popular sources were "friend, neighbor or relative" (57%), "newspaper, magazine or book" and "store, company or business" (both 45%), "coworker" (43%), and "professional (e.g., doctor or lawyer)" at 41%. Other sources (government, TV/radio, library, telephone book, social service agency, religious leader) were all cited much less frequently (10–27%).

Chen and Hernon's research, along with that by Durrance (1984) and Dervin, Ellyson, Hawkes, Guagnano, and White (1984), highlight a methodological shift in surveys of the general citizenry. These surveys asked more questions about basic human problems and situations, and less about the usual institutions that were supposed to address them. Dervin et al., especially, probed deeper into the origins of, and solutions to, personal "gaps" in life. That investigation interviewed 1,040 Californians, who reported an average of 8.5 problem situations within the last month. These situations most commonly concerned (in order): family/friends, managing money, shopping/buying, or learning—all of which were reported by over two-thirds of the respondents. Other common gaps involved current events, recreation, health, jobs, children, transportation, or housing, each of which was mentioned by 40% or more of those questioned. As in the Chen and Hernon study, the most common strategy was to turn to one's "own experience" (89% said this), followed by "authorities/professionals" (58%), "family members" (52%), and "friends/neighbors" (48%). Other popular sources of help, ranging in order from 40% down to 30%, were coworkers, media, schools/colleges, business persons, and libraries. By allowing for more specific responses to some questions—such as by breaking down the category of "day to day problems," and separating "family members" from "friends/neighbors" as sources—the California study learned more about the nature of information needs. Other results from Dervin *et al.* (1984) are mentioned when we discuss demography.

An emphasis on the problems of everyday life is apparent in a study by Savolainen (1995). He equated "citizen information seeking" with any "nonwork" consumption of media, noting how the degree to which the study of "everyday life" has been "overshadowed by surveys of job-related information needs, seeking and use" (p. 259). Savolainen urges that greater attention be paid to how people encounter information in the course of activities like leisure and hobbies. His investigation of 22 Finnish citizens—half middle-class and half working class—involved 90-minute interviews on their jobs, consumption habits, leisure time, media use, and the values they attached to information and information seeking. Savolainen also had respondents choose a recent "problematic situation" and relate how they dealt with it (p. 270).

Savolainen describes a pattern of "passive monitoring" of everyday events that takes place when life moves along as we expect, versus "active seeking of practically effective information" that happens when the unexpected arises. A person may watch television absentmindedly to "keep an eye on life," and read the daily paper as an aspect of "belonging in the community" (p. 273). Thus, some aspects of media use (and "information seeking" in a broader sense of the term) are not purposeful but rather are simply a part of everyday life practices.

Savolainen found relatively few class differences in most aspects of lifestyle. Where they existed, differences involved priorities for the use of free time, including the greater consumption of literature and "facts" by the middle-class teachers when compared to the workers he interviewed, who emphasized entertainment (p. 274). After collecting data on both preferences for media content, and how much time was spent with individual media, Savolainen classified each respondent as being primarily oriented to media in a manner that was either *Cognitive* (preferring cultural, social, political, and science content, more inclined to reading and to "serious" broadcasting programs), *Affective* (inclined to entertainment, crime, and accident reports, more inclined to watch television than read), or *Balanced* (making use of both types of elements). These three classifications were mapped across three other categories: light, medium, or heavy use of media. In this way, each respondent was located on two nine-cell matrices, one for print media and a second for electronic media. Reflecting on the distribution of the 22 respondents on these two charts, Savolainen noted that

> social class will not solely determine the type of media orientation. Although all teachers were not cognitively oriented and all workers not affectively oriented, way of life based on social class seems to play its own role in the direction of media use.... Teachers tend to prefer more markedly "serious" programs, devoting less time to entertainment and to electronic media in general.... In contrast, watching television, chiefly entertainment, all evening long with minor interruptions is not very unusual among workers.... affective elements tend to be emphasized in industrial worker's [sic] media orientation. (p. 279)

Where problem-oriented information seeking is concerned, Savolainen had similar findings to earlier, large-scale studies like Chen and Hernon (1982): types of everyday problems were diverse, with employment (7 cases), health (3), and financial worries (3) being mentioned most frequently. Which sources were pursued for problem-solving depended largely on availability and accessibility, with informal sources (e.g., acquaintances) being used much more commonly than formal sources; the middle-class respondents were noted as having more access to experts than the workers.

12.2.2 Consumer

Information seeking has been heavily studied from the marketing perspective. This has led to a number of studies of "consumers, "buyers," "shoppers," and the like, mostly published in journals of advertising or marketing. Many scholars may assume that consumer research is exclusively product oriented, that it says little about basic human behaviors, and that it is of no use to anyone other than profit-oriented companies.

At this point it is worth recalling that the third most common "gap" in the Dervin *et al.* (1984) study was a "shopping/buying" situation, and that the third most common source in Chen and Hernon's (1982) survey was "store, company or business." Although it is true that the majority of consumer studies are experiments, surveys, and descriptive focus groups aimed at marketing, the breadth of consumer research has widened greatly over the past two decades. More business studies have embraced qualitative methods and pursued more basic questions about human behavior. A growing minority of investigations have less to do with sales and more to do with sense-making.

Recent consumer research has embraced ethnomethodology and phenomenology (e.g., Mick & Buhl, 1992; Sherry, 1990). Some market researchers have turned to unlikely literatures, such as theories of play and classification (Holt, 1995), reader response (Scott, 1994), and poetic explication (Stern, 1989) in attempting to understand individual differences in reaction to objects and advertising. Of particular interest is how consumer research has awakened to the importance of *context* in the understanding of human reactions to things and messages (Foxall, 1983; Mick & DeMoss, 1990). Consumer research relevant to information seeking ranges from experiments on formal information search in making purchases (Hauser, Urban, & Weinberg, 1993), to browsing in stores (Bloch, Ridgway, & Sherrell, 1989), to making sense of advertising (McCracken, 1987).

In the introduction to a special issue of the *Journal of Marketing* entitled "How do Customers and Consumers Really Behave?," Donald Lehmann (1999) declares "for the past 20 years, the dominant paradigm in [consumer behavior] has been information processing. . . . borrowed from psychology [and] economics. . . . In terms of method, the typical approach has used a lab study with controlled manipulation of a few factors" (p. 16). Lehmann predicts that more progress can be made using different approaches. In particular he advocates less emphasis on psychological and economic theory and more research using biological and historical analogies. The focus must shift, Lehmann says, away from viewing the consumer as a conscious, rational "decision maker" and toward the customer as an emotional, unfocused, learning human. Allegedly "irrational" behavior should not be merely identified as an aberration but should be modeled and explained as much as possible. The microlevel focus on specific product attributes as judged by individuals must give way to the study of how people set goals, make *important* decisions (e.g., where to live, how to allocate their time), and are influenced by other people in their choices. Moving in these directions will require a change in methods, including increased use of qualitative and ethnographic methods, and less use of statistical significance for proving what are often, Lehmann says, trivial hypotheses.

Thus, a chief problem of the old style of consumer research was that it fails to consider the *context* of information seeking. Consumer researchers have not been blind to this deficit. Gordon Foxall (1983), for instance, devotes much of his book *Consumer Choice* to what he calls "situation" and the accompanying problem of intervening variables. Foxall decries the "piecemeal" application of mainstream behavioral methodologies to consumer research, and the tendency to treat the consumer as a "black box" about which the main thing to be studied are "attitudes" (beliefs, emotions, and action tendencies). Instead, Foxall argues for an emphasis on the way that situations influence the actions and choices of consumers (1983, pp. 90–93). He identifies the following as "situational characteristics": physical surroundings, social surroundings (other persons present, their characteristics, roles, and interpersonal interactions), temporal perspective (time of day, season of the year, time since/until other relevant action, deadlines, etc.), task definition (e.g., to obtain information about a purchase), and antecedent states and behavior (such as momentary moods and conditions, as distinct from chronic individual traits).

The notion of "situational variables" was first advanced by Belk (1975), who has since built upon them an agenda of naturalistic research. Belk, Sherry, and Wallendorf (1988), for example, have documented the "research process" of consumers browsing flea markets and swap meets.

Some old marketing topics have been extended. "Consumer search behavior," for example, used to be viewed almost exclusively in the context of learning about products to prepare for a purchase. However, Bloch, Sherrell and Ridgway (1986, p. 119) argue that "such activities as browsing in an antique shop or subscribing to an automotive magazine by persons not in the market for these products are not addressed by traditional search theories." They have expanded the notion of search behavior to include the everyday, ongoing acquisition of information. In their investigation, which used data from a conventional mail survey but without the usual emphasis on demographic variables as predictors, Bloch *et al.* found that a significant portion of search behavior was hedonic as well as utilitarian. That is, respondents said that they enjoyed learning about products, even when they did not have an immediate intention to buy; their acquisition of product information was described as a source of fun and pleasure.

The findings of consumer behavior now range far afield and are increasingly hard to generalize. The phenomenological study of three Danish brothers (Mick & Buhl, 1992), described in a previous chapter, is another example of how diverse this literature has become.

12.2.3 Patient

A number of factors have contributed to a greater interest, in recent years, in the seeking of medical information by *patients* (or "health care consumers"): an increased concern with health in general and with preventive medicine in particular; a growing number of "self-help" and homeopathic medicine texts; and the proliferation of consumer health information sites on the Internet.

On this last point, consider recent results of the Pew Internet Project (Rainie & Packel, 2001), which found that 56% of all U.S. adults were using the Internet, and that 57% of those said they had "gone online to get medical information." This rate of usage is much lower than the top-ranked purposes ("look for hobby information," 79%; "browse for fun," 68%; or "get news," 63%) yet higher than most other common uses, including "buy a product"(52%), "do research for job" (52%), or "get financial information" (45%). So although only 32% (i.e., 57% of 56%) of the adult population may be using the Internet, that still represents almost 60 million users in the United States alone, among whom health-related information is the fourth most popular use of the Internet. The trend, according to the Pew study, is for most uses of the Internet to grow in popularity by a few percentage points per year, suggesting that it will eventually become an almost universal venue for health-related information seeking.

Although the dissemination of health advice to the general public has always been important, where the layperson is concerned the more critical question is increasingly "why don't people *act* on the information they have?" Making useful (and potentially life-saving) information available to patients is the easier part of the equation; getting them to apply it is much harder. At the core of this problem are the issues raised in Chapter 4 of this book under the headings of "avoidance" and "overload." An excellent review of the problem of nonuse of health information — dubbed the "knowledge-behavior gap" — is found in the background to a study by Sligo and Jameson (2000), which is the featured example here of health information seeking and use among the general public. I draw extensively upon their discussion in the paragraphs that follow.

The issue of how behaviors may be purposefully changed has long been of central concern among scholars of attitude, persuasion, compliance, propaganda, diffusion, and like topics. Hyman and Sheatsley's (1947) discussion of "why information campaigns fail" is usually cited as the earliest explanation of why information does not always change behavior, although the roots of this line of thinking go back to at least to Gabriel Tarde's (1903) treatise on "imitation" and the diffusion of ideas and behaviors.

Sligo and Jameson (2000) examined the issue of information seeking and use from the perspective of populations at risk from disease. One aspect of what they call "the knowledge-behavior gap in use of health information" is whether individuals receive relevant information in the first place — the "information poverty" problem discussed in Chapter 4. The related "knowledge gap hypothesis," that segments of the population may acquire information at differential rates, originated over 30 years ago with Tichenor, Donohue, and Olien (1970) and continues to attract scholarly attention (e.g., Gaziano, 1997; Viswanath & Finnegan, 1996).

Yet even when knowledge gaps are overcome, we cannot be sure it will make a difference for the individual. Gaziano (1997) noted that "barriers" to the gain (and subsequent application) of information have both internal and external origins. The internal barriers are both social and psychological, having to do with personality, motivation, interest, and involvement with others. Barriers considered external are social and situational, including socialization and identity issues, membership in socioeconomic and ethnic groups, and access to information sources. Sligo and Jameson point out that internal and external barriers overlap in various ways; they review, for example, literature emphasizing that learning from others is highly sensitized to local social norms (external) and the internal perception that another is similar to oneself (an "insider").

Sligo and Jameson's empirical study concerned information about cervical cancer, screening, and related topics among Pacific Island immigrants living in a small New Zealand city. They conducted lengthy interviews with a snowball sample of 20 women from Fiji, Samoa, Tonga, and other islands — a group that could be considered comparable to the urban, lower socioeconomic level groups in North American studies of knowledge gaps. However, Sligo and Jameson found less isolation and more learning than did investigations by Chatman (1996) and Greenberg, Bowes, and Dervin (1970). Perhaps the most interesting aspect of their findings is the way in which cultural norms (e.g., taboos about discussing sexual matters) differentially influenced getting information versus acting on that information: participants preferred learning about cervical health through their own cultural networks, yet preferred (for reasons of privacy) to have health care provided by practitioners outside of their ethnic group.

Sligo and Jameson suggest (along with Hornik, 1989) that attention is shifting away from the internal and psychological reasons that people fail to acquire and act on information, and toward "structural" explanations for lack of behavior change: do factors in the environment (e.g., the economic and social consequences of change) *support* the actions implied by the acquired information? To put this in terms of some of Sligo and Jameson's findings: information is hard to absorb when a local vocabulary is lacking for it (some Pacific languages have no word for "cervix," for example); culture is a filter for health information (e.g., "not all cultures believe that disease can exist in the absence of adverse symptoms," p. 866); however, information from "outsiders" will be accepted as long as it is sanctioned by passage through local channels (e.g., ethnic community organizations).

The investigation by Sligo and Jameson was strictly limited in the size, uniqueness, and sample of its sample (i.e., small numbers of diverse women from various islands, living in one New Zealand city), but it raises fascinating questions about the role of both culture and interpersonal networks in the diffusion of health information, while offering practical advice for health care providers in that context. Best of all, it asks us to question the generalizations of past research regarding urban minorities and their "gaps" in knowledge regarding medicine.

Many other investigations exist of "patients" or "consumers of health care" and attendant information needs. Johnson (1997) and a review by Rees and Bath (2000) cover the literature that has to do with cancer information, reflecting the largest proportion of serious health problems that can precipitate information seeking. Women seeking advice on breast cancer treatment is a topic that has received special emphasis by investigations, given the serious threat that the disease poses to both the physical and psychological well-being of sufferers. Baker (1996) has considered the information needs of women suffering from multiple sclerosis, and Pettigrew (1999) has conducted an ethnographic study of visitors to a chiropody clinic. Freimuth, Stein, and Kean (1989), Marshall (1993), Muha, Smith, Baum, Ter Maat, and Ward (1998), and Pifalo, Hollander, Henderson, DeSalvo, and Gill (1997) describe the extent of use of patient libraries and other health information services by several hundred consumers, most of whom used the telephone to contact the services. These studies emphasize the role of information in helping patients to "cope" with health problems as much as in aiding them to talk with care providers and make decisions about treatment.

Only the most recent reviews and studies (e.g., Berland *et al.*, 2001) examine the increased availability of health information through computer networks, which promises to be a widely used source of medical advice. White (2000), discussed in Chapter 9 as an example of content analysis, is one such investigation.

12.2.4 Gatekeeper

The noted sociologist Robert Merton (1973, p. 521) credits psychologist Kurt Lewin (1943) for introducing "the notion of the gatekeeper role . . . into social science." Although Lewin used the term in a very specific context — to discuss how housewives influence the eating habits of their household — it has since been applied widely to many types of organizations and institutions. "Gatekeeping" has been invoked particularly in the study of scientists (e.g., Crane, 1967), with a defining aspect being the "two-step flow" of information: that a single person receives the information first, then passes it on to other members of his or her group. Rogers (1994) suggests that the concept (although not the term) goes much further back in time to Robert Parks' (1922) discussion of the power exercised by newspaper editors. It was subsequently used to characterize the behavior of community "opinion leaders" who mold the knowledge and attitudes of their neighbors.

A gatekeeper is one who controls the flow of information over a channel: shaping, emphasizing, or withholding it (Rifkin, 2000; Shoemaker, 1991). Gatekeepers provide a key link between their organization, audience, or community and the outside environment. Merton and Crane believed that the gatekeeping role was critical in the development and evaluation of junior scientists. Baldwin and Rice (1997) characterized gatekeepers in research organizations in this way:

> Gatekeepers read more journals, have more external contacts, generate more ideas, and engage in more problem solving than non-gatekeepers. Gatekeepers not only provide information, but they also give practical and political advice. (p. 675)

A comprehensive review by Metoyer–Duran (1993) found 803 publications on gatekeepers appearing between 1977 and the end of 1992. Her review focuses on their role in the health sciences, education, science and technology, communication studies, journalism, and information studies. A complete explication of "gatekeeping" is found in Shoemaker (1991); as she notes, it has proved to be a robust concept, despite its age.

Gatekeeping continues to be the focus of investigation in information seeking. A 1999 study by John Agada featured in-depth interviews with 20 gatekeepers in an African American neighborhood of inner-city Milwaukee, Wisconsin. In this study of "information use environments," gatekeepers were described as individuals able to move between cultures and link their communities with resources. Agada identified his 20 informants through community organizations and interviewed them about their information needs regarding race relations, crime, and family. As he found, "interpersonal sources were preferred over all other sources because of concerns about trustworthiness and credibility" (p. 74).

The most frequently cited needs had to do with discrimination and race relations, followed by crime and safety, and family planning and birth control. After those three categories of need, there was a sharp drop in frequency; the most common among the remaining 16 categories were child care and family relationships, recreation and culture, health, housekeeping and household maintenance, and employment. Some categories that were ranked highly in earlier studies ranked much lower in this one: finance and housing (Dervin, 1976b) and public affairs and education (Metoyer–Duran, 1993). Agada concludes that this is due to the short-term orientation of the urban poor, which leads them to "seek coping information rather than information and activities that would transform their socioeconomic conditions" (p. 79). By far the top strategies were to ask a neighbor/friend/acquaintance and or the relevant agency. Thirteen other sources for information, including other gatekeeper/opinion leader, telephone directory, newspapers, family member, libraries, acquaintances working at agencies, and politicians, in that order. Agada provides some interesting examples of how people describe their needs, and the ways that they might be resolved, based on Robert Taylor's (1991) categories of information use.

Baldwin and Rice (1997) also invoked the concept of gatekeeper in their telephone survey of 100 randomly selected, securities analysts, who they note "think of themselves as gatekeepers in their organizations" (p. 688). A sophisticated statistical analysis of data on individual characteristics (e.g., years of experience, gender, age), use of different information sources (e.g., magazines, communication with management and other analysts), and their institutional resources (e.g., having an assistant, having a budget for travel) led to their conclusion that "individual characteristics have little influence on the information sources and communication channels used by analysts, and thereby do not have a significant influence on the outcomes of analysts' information activities" (p. 674). Rather, the degree of *institutional resources* available were found to have a strong influence on both the analysts' use of source and channels, and the outcomes of their work (e.g., income, ranking in polls of analysts, and number of research reports published). Baldwin and Rice discuss the implications of their study for improving the gatekeeping role within organizations.

12.2.5 Other Roles

Humans take on many roles in society, not all of which can be examined here. One of the most widely studied roles of all (given the voluminous research literature on education) is that of "student" — a category that virtually everyone inhabits at some point during their lives. Because being a student coincides with other categories discussed here (particularly age-based findings) research on that role will be noted here only briefly.

Students of all types have received some attention in this literature. As described in an earlier chapter, Constance Mellon (1986) studied a large sample of university students to explore the role of anxiety in the search for information in libraries, a theme also explored in other studies of college (e.g., Jiao & Onwuegbuzie, 1997) and high school (Kuhlthau, 1988a, 1991) students. The information seeking of doctoral students was studied by Cole (1998) and Seldén (2001). University students were investigated by Ford (1986), Green (1990), and Thórsteinsdóttir (2000), among many others. As featured under "age," Julien (1999) and Clarke (1973) examined different aspects of the information seeking of high-school age students. For younger students, Sever (1990, 1994) has explored the relationship between play and reading.

As a group distinct from "students," children have received only modest attention. Walter (1994) has investigated the information needs of children in general (see a description of her work under "age"). Kleiber, Montgomery, and Craft-Rosenberg (1995) have written about "information needs of the siblings of critically ill children," describing the ways that information can help them cope with emotionally difficult situations.

Other roles reported in the information behavior literature include newcomer (e.g., Gundry & Rousseau, 1994; Louis, 1980; Morrison, 1993; Ostroff & Kozlowski, 1992), parent (e.g., Hersberger, 2001; Walter, 1994), victim of discrimination (e.g., Agada, 1999; Whitt, 1993; Williamson, Schauder, & Bow, 2000), opinion leader (e.g., Agada, 1999; Sligo & Jameson, 2000), prisoner (Chatman, 1999), and of course, the ubiquitous "user," the abstract object of thousands of studies.

12.3

By Demographic Group

As already mentioned, demographic breakdowns figure prominently in studies of roles that people take on in their lives. As in most social research, the factors most commonly examined have been age, gender, and racial or ethnic (or, in the language of Metoyer-Duran, 1993, "ethnolinguistic") membership. Gender has been less likely to be the central focus of information seeking investigations, and gender differences are treated sparingly at the end of this section. Geographic categories, such as "rural" and "urban," likewise tend to be secondary considerations, although they have been implicitly examined in some studies of "citizen information needs."

12.3.1 Age

Age has been the focus of several investigations, particularly the ends of the continuum: children and the elderly. I begin by reviewing recent studies of children and teenagers, then move on to the elderly.

Virginia Walter (1994, p. 111) declared that "very little is known" about the information needs of children. Her investigation interviewed 25 adults — school nurses, social workers, probation workers, child care providers/administrators, police officers, recreation center directors, and others — who worked with children in two California counties. Walter asked these informants what they thought were the primary information needs of children, where and how children found that information, and what the information gaps were and how they occurred. Her findings are summarized in terms of Abraham Maslow's (1970) "hierarchy of needs": self-actualization, esteem, love/belonging, safety, and physiological, with the latter being the most basic.

Walter found that physiological and safety needs — knowing how to avoid risky behaviors, understanding basic health and nutrition, and knowing what to do in an emergency — were the categories mentioned most often, considered the most important, and also as most often cited as unmet. The need for sex education was found in all but the top category of the hierarchy, while the need to instill children with ethics and values to guide them emerged in all but the bottom two categories. Informants saw children as having many potential information sources, such as parents and teachers, but they were prone to receiving misinformation from peers and the media. They saw children's barriers to information as stemming from their low status in society, ineffective parental communication, and competition from the media.

Children's use of information electronic sources will not be reviewed here, but nevertheless it has been the subject of a number of recent reports and commentaries, including Dresang (1999), Enochsson (2000), Hirsh (1997), Kafai and Bates (1997), Large, Beheshti, and Breuleux (1998), and Tapscott (1997). A conclusion of some of these is that children will increasingly turn to the World Wide Web for answers to their questions.

Information seeking behaviors of teenagers have been studied by some researchers. Julien (1998, 1999) studied their decisions about future careers through a two-part study. First, she surveyed 399 male and female teenagers in one Canadian city, and then followed up with interviews of 30 of them, evenly divided by gender. Julien found that a majority of the adolescents had questions about careers. Some had very general questions ("What should I do?") while others wanted more specific facts (what school to attend to pursue their goal). Their information needs are described as "wondering . . . what jobs are like . . . what they would enjoy . . . what they would be good at" (1998, p. 377). There was a narrow difference in the frequency of the top information sources, which in order were self (own thinking), books/pamphlets, guidance counselor, friends, worker, mother, and father — each used by 35% or more of the teenagers. The least-used sources were public libraries and work experiences, even though 88% had work experience. Books and counselors were seen as less helpful than friends, workers, or family members. According to Julien, 40% of those surveyed did "not know where to go for help in making decisions, and a similar proportion feel that there are too many places to go for help in their information seeking." Most career information was found incidentally, rather than purposefully, and teenagers' decision making "does not follow the logical pattern suggested in the career development literature" (1998, p. 379). She concludes that emotional support may be more important than instrumental help (e.g., with understanding choices) in making decisions about careers at such ages.

An interesting, older study seemingly neglected in the information seeking literature is that of Peter Clarke (1973), who examined the ways that teenagers communicate with one another about popular music. Clarke makes a distinction between information *seeking* (involving sources outside of one's social system) and information *sharing*, in which verbal and nonverbal information is exchanged within a social group, rather than deliberately sought out. In the latter type (sharing) of behavior, one important goal may be to learn about other people, making judgments about them that may or may not lead to a closer relationship, while in information seeking mode "the individual usually recognizes that the source he approaches has more to tell him than he has to tell the source" (p. 552). Clarke found that measuring how frequently respondents listened to music was not as good a predictor of music information seeking as the number of peers with whom they shared music. Use of the mass media was found to correlate "equally with *finding out* from others about music and *telling* others about music" (p. 559). Clarke concludes that sharing and seeking are more appropriate labels for human behavior in this context than the more typical discussions (at the time) of media "flows" and "power relationships." The theme of "sharing information" has been revived recently in a study by Erdelez and Rioux (2000).

On the other end of the age distribution, Williamson (1997) and her colleagues interviewed 202 elderly (aged 60 and older) Australian residents to understand how their physical, social, and cultural environments shaped their information seeking. In three focused interviews respondents related episodes in which they "had needed to 'find out, understand or clarify' something for their everyday lives" (p. 340). Participants were later prompted with a series of topics commonly found to come up at community information centers, and with potential sources of information found to be relevant in the Chen and Hernon (1982) and Warner, Murray, and Palmour (1973) community studies. In addition, each respondent completed telephone diaries over a two-week period. The diaries asked the participants to record why they made each telephone call and what it was about, in their own words.

Williamson found that health and financial topics came up in every interview, reflecting not only the typical ailments of the aged but also the fact that over 60% were on a fixed, retirement income. Recreation or leisure activities, along with volunteering, were also frequent areas of interest. The telephone conversations reflected in the diaries were much more likely to be about personal events than information of a more common type. The most frequent sources of information were, in order, family, newspapers, friends, television, other printed information (e.g., pension newsletters and "junk mail"), and radio. Information was obtained both purposefully and incidentally from all sources; however, there were definite patterns in regard to these. Incidental information gathering was more likely to take place from mass media, such as newspapers, radio, and television.

Less frequently used sources of information included professionals, organizations such as stores and self-help groups, magazines, government departments, and information agencies such as libraries; these were used to seek information purposefully. No information was sought from digital sources even though a few respondents had both computers and modems at home. Professionals were the top choice for information as far as health, drugs, and the law were concerned.

Williamson (1997) offers a good discussion of the importance of unconscious information needs and incidental information seeking, as opposed to information purposefully sought in reaction to a well-defined, conscious need. However, distinguishing between purposeful and incidental information seeking turned out to be difficult in many cases. Williamson gives the example of happening across a listing for a television program on cancer and then deciding to watch it; such incidents were coded as incidental if they were not part of a regular pattern of viewing. Williamson acknowledges the arbitrariness of deciding when watching, reading, or listening passes from incidental to purposeful. She concludes her study by proposing an "ecological model of use" for everyday information.

A rather different investigation, but with some parallel results, is reported by van der Rijt (1996), who conducted a secondary analysis of a survey of 319 elderly (aged 65 and older) Dutch citizens. This time there was more of an emphasis on health information and the measures were exclusively quantitative. Van der Rijt found that by far the highest interest item on a list of 27 topics was "provision for elderly living independently" (52% indicated interest in this), followed by information about a healthy diet (43%), physical symptoms of aging (38%), and social benefits/compensation (35%). About half of the remaining 23 items (e.g., housing, crime, safety, leisure) were of interest to between 20% and 31% of respondents, while the bottom four topics (e.g., information about drinking problems, employment, and handicaps) were of interest to only 5% or fewer.

Van der Rijt's main focus was the factor analysis of these data and a multiple regression of the resulting factors. He concludes that having experienced a health problem (e.g., "I become tired quickly") was the most powerful influence in seeking information. He expected to find associations by gender (e.g., that women would be more interested in health and safety while men would be more concerned about finances) but these did not emerge, except in a great interest in leisure information by younger men. Four general "orientations" to health emerged, including Preventative (avoiding harm), Fatalism (seeing health as a matter of luck), Internal Control (believing one was in complete control over health), and Unconcern (simply not worrying about it). The Preventative orientation was found to be particularly influential in information seeking; if an individual was intent upon staying healthy through positive diet and exercises habits while avoiding unhealthy practices, they were more likely to seek information than individuals of other orientations.

Other studies of the elderly include those by Tinker, McCreadie, and Salvage (1993), and Todd (1984).

In between teenagers and the elderly, age-focused studies of the information seeking of general populations do not appear to be common. However, "adult" populations—which include the elderly but not children and teenagers—have been widely studied. Age-based differences are noted in the statistical analyses of the studies of "citizens."

The health information seeking literature includes a number of observations about age, which are summarized by Johnson (1997). For example, Gourash (1978) documented the tendency for "help-seeking" to decline with age. Biesecker (1988, 1990) find that the elderly are less likely to question physicians themselves and more likely to bring someone along to do so on their behalf. Turk-Charles, Meyerowitz, and Gatz (1997) found no difference among age cohorts of cancer patients in terms of learning from friends and mass media.

12.3.2 Racial and Ethnolinguistic Minorities

The assumption that membership in an ethnic or racial minority predicts attitudes, beliefs, and behaviors seems to underlie many studies. Along with age and gender (the two most commonly measured variables), racial and/or ethnic background are usually recorded even when it is not particularly important to the investigation, as it is commonly regarded as "potentially useful" information for analysis.

Likewise, in studies of information needs and uses, such demographic information tends to be collected when it is available, either through self-report (on questionnaires) or through observation by an investigator. It is not certain that racial or ethnic minority status predicts information seeking in most cases. Since at least the publication of "Challenges to Sociocultural Predictors of Information Seeking"(Atwood & Dervin, 1982), Brenda Dervin has argued that the *situation* (or context) in which information seeking takes place is a much more powerful predictor of thoughts and behavior in that regard than is personal background. In other words, Dervin's research, as well as her sense-making paradigm, says that people have much in common in the way that they react to the kinds of problematic situations that prompt a search for information or other "help."

Dervin's research *does* demonstrate associations between racial/ethnic groups and certain types of problems. For example, Dervin *et al.* (1984) shows African Americans more likely to experience "gap situations" and problems related to transportation, housing, and safety or crime, while Hispanics were more likely to face issues of caring for children. Underlying factors—having more time, money, opportunities, and other resources—are the source of these situations.

When information consumption is habitual, rather than situational, a better argument can be made for racial (as well as ethnic and class) differences. Among the investigations that have featured race in regard to information consumption is John Newhagen's (1994) study of "media use and political efficacy." A journalism professor, Newhagen conducted a telephone survey of 356, randomly selected residents of Maryland in 1992. The study tested racial and class differences in perceived *self-efficacy* (Bandura, 1977) in regard to politics. Newhagen wanted to know if amount and type of media use predicted how politically involved and effective respondents felt they were, and if they believed that the political system included them. For example, someone who agreed strongly with statements like "I consider myself well-qualified to participate in politics" would be said to feel effective on a personal level, where as agreeing with items like "the people have the final say in how the country is run" indicates a judgment that the political *system* is effective.

The knowledge gap hypothesis (see Chapters 4 and 5), along with previous research on social class membership, would predict that African Americans would have a different belief structure than their white counterparts, including feeling less powerful and less involved in politics. What was the role of media use and social class (middle-class versus poor neighborhood) in political efficacy? Newhagen's results suggest several interesting conclusions. Paying attention to news and opinion (whether newspaper, radio, or TV) results in higher feelings of self-efficacy, regardless of race, economic status, or even education; listening to talk radio was even more highly correlated with feelings of political effectiveness. However, racial differences became apparent in watching of primetime TV: the more entertainment programming that African Americans watched, the more they felt that the political system was ineffective, and that they were powerless to change it. Newhagen concluded that political efficacy is neither race nor class driven, yet he is unable to explain the correlation of low efficacy with entertainment. Is it the case that people who feel powerless watch entertainment programs, or that a heavy diet of entertainment programming makes one feel ineffective? Whichever the direction of causation, it seems that one's choice of source for information about political realities shapes one's belief system, and hence a person's degree of participation in the world — including whether one seeks further information about a particular issue.

Spink, Bray, Jaeckel, and Sidberry (1999; also reported in Spink & Cole, 2001) investigated "everyday life information-seeking by low-income African American households" in Dallas, Texas, describing it as the largest such study ever conducted. They interviewed 300 heads of households in a low-income housing development, asking questions about their needs for services and information, as well as their activities (including use of media) and demographic background data. In-depth follow-up interviews have since been conducted with a subsample of residents. What these residents most wanted to know about were local news (e.g., about local activities and family events), followed by information relevant to personal security and health. Education and employment information was judged less important, while state, national, and international events were "of little direct interest" (p. 380). Respondents ranked family and school as the most important sources of news events, followed by television, newspapers, radio. Friends and neighbors were the least important source for general news; they were the second- and third-ranked sources (preceded by newspapers — by far the best source) for information on employment. Spink *et al.* discuss these findings in the context of the "information environment" for these families, and how they relate to theories regarding *habitus*—ways of seeing and thinking that guide choices in life (Bourdieu, 1984).

Other studies including racial or ethnic groups include Agada (1999, discussed under "gatekeepers"), Chatman (1991, 1996), and Metoyer-Duran (1991). A review by David Johnson (1997) pointed out studies indicating that health information seeking practices may be influenced by membership in racial and ethnic groups. Freimuth, Edgar, and Fitzpatrick (1993), for example, found that African Americans are more likely to be fatalistic about health problems and therefore less likely to do something about them, including learning more about prevention. Gourash (1978) found African Americans less likely than European Americans to seek help of any kind. According to Hsia (1987), Mexican Americans rely almost exclusively on friends and relatives for health information; the less-educated and less affluent among this group have much lower levels of information seeking.

12.3.3 Socioeconomic Status

I use the term "socioeconomic status" to characterize any comparisons of information seekers by income group (e.g., "the poor"), or social or economic "class."

Childers and Post (1975) were among the earliest to associate demographic factors with a "culture of information poverty," associating it primarily with low income groups, such as public housing tenants. An earlier review by Dervin and Greenberg (1972) claimed that about 200 studies relevant to the "communication environment of the poor" existed at that time; they examined 30 of the most relevant, mostly from 1967 to 1972. Their summary suggested that the poor in America did not lack in access to information channels, and depended heavily on television as a source. Greenberg, Bowes, and Dervin's (1970) research in Cleveland showed that low income African American adults used TV for both escape and learning (e.g., about what life is like, and how others solve problems). Many investigations since that time have explored the degree to which TV viewing can lead to misconceptions about the "real" world (Morgan & Shanahan, 1997). Among all poor populations, newspaper readership was low, with most attention being paid to headlines and advertising. In the Cleveland study, Greenberg, Bowes, and Dervin found that professionals, lawyers, relatives, neighbors, and health care providers had been common sources of "help or information" in the past.

More recently, Dervin et al. (1984) found that higher income respondents were more likely to report problematic situations overall, and more gaps that involved recreation, learning something new, and concerns about jobs, government, and current events. These same situations were of concern to those respondents with more years of education than the others. However, their data also demonstrated that demographic factors are less effective for predicting the questions that people have, the barriers they face, and the kind of help they need, than are situational factors (e.g., whether they feel "stopped" because they need to make a decision, or because they feel lost, out of control, or in need of a guide).

Several studies by Chatman (1985, 1987, 1991), described in previous chapters, along with Chatman and Pendleton (1995) are also relevant to this theme. These ethnographic studies of the working poor, like earlier studies, found a preference for interpersonal sources and a heavy use of television for escape and for surveillance.

For an example of a study of this demographic segment, consider Julie Hersberger's (2001) "everyday information needs and information sources of homeless parents." While "parent" could also be considered a social role, the homeless are by definition also "poor"; in fact, they are, at least temporarily, the very poorest in our society. Hersberger spent a year as participant observer in six homeless shelters in Indianapolis, Indiana. In addition to her other observations, she conducted interviews with 28 informants, generating over 800 pages of transcripts. Obviously, financial needs were the most pressing issue among this sample, followed by child care, then housing, health, employment, education, transportation, public assistance, and problems associated with living in the shelter. Altogether Hersberger identified 16 major problem categories and 145 specific needs within them. Social service staff were the most frequently mentioned information sources in nearly all major categories of need, with friends and family, personal experience, and other shelter residents also common sources of help. For some problems, additional sources were prominent: newspapers and signs (in the case of housing and employment), television talk shows (child behavior problems), and health care professionals (health problems).

In her conclusions, Hersberger discussed the "complex and messy" nature of everyday life for the homeless, relating it to Chatman's characterizations of the poor and "insiders." Some informants, experienced at being homeless, knew how to find out what they needed to know. Others "often failed to seek information when required or recommended to by others" — reinforcing the insider pattern of ignoring sources of information from "outside." Hersberger found that it was rare for homeless parents to consider public libraries or the electronic sources they offered, preferring instead interpersonal sources.

Poverty is also a major factor in health information seeking. Freimuth (1990) says that the poor not only know less about cancer than the affluent, but also have a greater need for information due to risk factors. She noted that they are more likely to rely on television and folk tales for medical information, and are less likely to read about it.

12.3.4 Other Demographic Groups

The demographic classification most obviously missing among the above sections is gender. Gender does not seem to have been a primary focus of many information seeking studies, although it appears frequently in analyses of results. More commonly it emerges in combination with some other variable or situation. Roma Harris (1988) and Harris and Dewdney (1994), for example, write about "the information needs of battered women," and Baker (1996) studies "the nature of information needed by women with Multiple Sclerosis," while Creelman and Harris (1990), and Whitt (1993), investigate the information needs of lesbians as they relate to library collections and services. Freimuth *et al.* (1989, 1993) note that women are more likely to be information seekers than are men in the context of health matters in general and cancer in particular.

Another category that has received some attention is that of the urban/rural divide. Some aspects of this were mentioned in the context of surveys of "citizen" information needs. Most studies have been implicitly urban, or at least suburban — after all, that is where most people live. A few studies have explicitly sampled rural populations. Anwar and Supaat (1998) examined the "information needs of rural Malaysians" in a survey of 108 people living in three villages. Vavrek (1995), in a discussion of rural public libraries, provided some data on the information needs and seeking of rural residents. Case and Rogers (1987) described the information environment of small farm operators. Dee (1993) examined how rural physicians may differ in their use of sources from their urban counterparts; this was also a concern of Ely, Burch, and Vinson (1992). Salasin and Cedar (1985) surveyed a large sample of rural mental health care workers about their communication patterns.

Some demographic groups studied are relatively small, and may be the subject of only a single investigation. Williamson, Schauder and, Bow (2000), for example, say that theirs is the only study of "information seeking by blind and sight impaired citizens." Based on their figures, this group (in which membership is a matter of degree) may constitute only about 1.5% of a nation's population. Undoubtedly, many other differently-abled groups and other population segments have never been examined from the perspective of information needs. Partly this may be a question of resources (do we have the time and money to study every group?) and partly a factor of utility (would the study result in useful knowledge?).

The uneven pattern of studies is also an issue of overlap. It is important to remember that people are members of several groups at once. A French-Canadian lawyer who is a member of the Green Party, practices Catholicism, and is an environmental activist and an urban dweller could be studied from a number of perspectives. She could be a respondent in a study of the information needs of Canadian citizens, urban residents, attorneys, or political, religious, or ethnic minorities, to name just a few possibilities. Who is sampled, and from what perspective, is up to the motivations of the investigators and their sponsors.

Dervin (1989) raised challenging questions about the value and validity of demographic-based investigations. However, when a background characteristic such as having a disability results in *persistent* situational differences, a study of that small segment of the population makes more sense.

12.4
Summary

It can be seen that there is great variety in the kinds of populations and activities that have been examined. In recent years more attention has been paid to contextual, situational, or role variables, rather than the usual demographic variables. Relatively small populations (e.g., the sight-impaired, Canadian literary critics, or homeless parents) have been sampled for investigation. Investigations concerned with health information seeking have become a prominent genre, rivaled mainly by the ever-constant attention to students of all types and ages.

One thing that these studies have in common, however, it is a concern with sources and channels, typically interpersonal channels versus mass and/or specialized media. A frequent finding is that people still turn to other people for information. Despite an effort to examine the process of information seeking, much of it still comes down to "who or what do people consult for information?" This is an old question within the information needs, uses, and seeking literature and it continues to dominate the discussion of findings.

In the final chapter I will summarize a few of the things we have learned from nearly a century of studying information seeking by occupation, role, and demographic category. I point out some trends and gaps in this vast literature and suggest some directions for the future.

Recommended for Further Reading

Baldwin, N. S., & Rice, R. E. (1997). Information-seeking behavior of securities analysts: Individual and institutional influences, information sources and channels, and outcomes. *Journal of the American Society for Information Science, 48,* 674–693.

This is an example of a quantitative, source- and channel-oriented study. Baldwin and Rice offer a model depicting individual characteristics, institutional resources, channels used, and the effect of these on "outcomes," such as the incomes and satisfactions of the 100 securities analysts they study. Baldwin and Rice demonstrate that the resources available to an analyst — such as the size of firm, staff, and budget — both directly and indirectly affect information seeking. More importantly for this chapter, they also discuss the way in which these analysts were gatekeepers in their organizations.

Kuhlthau, C. C. (1991). Inside the search process: Information seeking from the user's perspective. *Journal of the American Society for Information Science, 42*, 361–371.

A seminal discussion of how information seeking looks (and feels!) to high school and college students. This piece nicely brings together theory and empirical observations to chart the psychological stages of information seeking.

Newhagen, J. (1994). Media use and political efficacy: The suburbanization of race and class. *Journal of the American Society for Information Science, 45*, 386–394.

An investigation that considers both race and social class in regard to patterns of information consumption. Based on a telephone survey of 356 people, Newhagen's investigation explored perceived self-efficacy regarding politics, finding that neither race nor class predicted feelings of low efficacy as much as did watching television entertainment programming. Newhagen's results suggest that one's main source of information about politics largely determines whether one seeks further information from other sources, and whether one becomes more involved (e.g., by voting).

Savolainen, R. (1995). Everyday life information seeking: Approaching information seeking in the context of "way of life." *Library and Information Science Research, 17*, 259–294.

Savolainen's study of the lifestyles and media habits of 22 ordinary people makes fascinating reading. A highly original piece of research, it describes theories and methods not previously used in studies of this type. It also sheds some light on class differences in media usage.

13

Reviewing, Critiquing, Concluding

> Studies have moved from an orientation that is primarily system-centered . . .
> to an orientation that is also user-centered.
>
> Choo and Auster (1998, p. 39)

> There is a need for an integrative model of information need, information-
> seeking behaviour and information use. That integrative model is already
> almost complete: it is a person-centred model, based largely on Dervin's
> "sense-making" approach. . . .
>
> Tom Wilson (1994, p. 42)

Chapter Outline

13.1. Reviewing

13.2. Critiquing
    13.2.1. A History of Complaint
    13.2.2. Current Criticisms

13.3. Concluding
    13.3.1. Eight Lessons of Information Behavior Research

13.1
Reviewing

This book has described the ways in which people look for information
and how that phenomenon has been studied. Let us first consider what we have
read, and then I will make eight conclusions about the changing emphasis of
information behavior research.

Chapter 1 briefly considered the history and scope of information seeking, emphasizing the changing nature of the research conducted over about eight decades of scholarly interest in the topic. I introduced 10 myths about information that Brenda Dervin highlighted in 1976, and suggested that these were useful for understanding why research on information behavior has taken the path that it has. We will take a fresh look at those myths in a few pages.

In Chapter 2 we considered five "scenarios" of information seeking to look at the process from the individual's point of view. We cannot learn any "facts" from such hypothetical examples, but they serve to sensitize us to the wide range of thoughts and actions that might be included under the label of *information seeking*. It also shows the effects of such variables as time pressure, types of motivations and sources, and the scope of relevant information. Taken as a whole, the five scenarios may illustrate why it is that some investigators are now more focused on the phenomenology of sense-making than on the ways that a particular source (or channel) of information is used by its intended audience.

In Chapter 3 we explored the central concept of *information*. We learned that attempting to define information in a rigorous way runs headlong into difficult problems of scope. For starters, is information distinct from its associated terms, such as data, fact, and knowledge, or does it subsume them? For the purposes of this book, I have chosen a broad — and also vague — definition of information as "any difference that makes a difference" to a human being, an inclusive concept that allows us to go beyond the narrow limits of source-oriented and system-oriented information research.

In contrast, other writers have made difficult choices regarding other issues surrounding the definition of information. Some have argued that information must be defined as something factually *true*, while I consider "misinformation" to be a subset of a more general concept of information. Must information be communicated to us intentionally to be information? I do not believe so. I hold that it could also be a mere difference that we perceive in our environment. Does information always reduce uncertainty? No, sometimes it increases uncertainty, as when learning a fact raises further questions and concerns about it. Must information be "useful" for some practical purpose, such as for solving a problem or making a decision? No, sometimes information, while noticed, has no immediate application. Can entertainment itself be considered to be information? Yes. I made the case that the artificial distinction between cognitive input that is "useful" and input that is "hedonistic" is unnecessarily judgmental and restrictive.

In Chapter 4 we examined definitions of two derivative concepts (e.g., information need and information seeking) that are central to this book. "Information needs" are not directly observable, but are inferred from actions or cognitions. I described various characterizations of how information needs are thought to arise. The concept of "information seeking" was explored as it has been discussed by various authors. I made a case that the term "information behavior" is better suited for characterizing the many types of human behaviors that concern information.

Chapter 5 considered many other concepts relevant to information seeking literature—including relevance itself—along with decision making, problem solving, browsing, foraging, encountering, selective exposure, avoidance, overload, information anxiety, knowledge gaps, information poverty, pertinence, relevance, salience, entertainment, situation, and context. In that chapter I pointed out that most writers assume that information seeking arises out of a sense of uncertainty—an anomaly, gap, or problem. Attempts to define and address the feeling of uncertainty give rise to a "need" that might later be expressed as a question or action. Issues of relevance and pertinence arise when information is considered as a potential response to the need. Several conditions may be invoked in this process, including at times anxiety, creativity, play, and entertainment. Context determines much of a person's perceptions throughout this process, and it affects one's choice of sources and meanings.

It is difficult to summarize Chapters 6 through 12 in just a few words, so I will merely remind the reader of their sequence and content. For readers who are new to research in general, these were undoubtedly complex. Chapters 6 and 7 examined first some of the more prominent models used to study information behavior, and then the various paradigms and theories that have been applied to do so. In particular I focused on the models of David Johnson, James Krikelas, Gloria Leckie, and Tom Wilson, and the paradigms of Least Effort, Sense-Making, Decision making, Uses and Gratifications, Media Use as Social Action, and Play Theory. Chapter 8 discussed methods in a general way, and Chapter 9 offered examples of investigations of information seeking that used each method.

In Chapter 10 I reviewed the origins and growth of the information needs, seeking, and uses literature, highlighting its character and topics, and offering evidence that the corpus of studies could easily stretch into the five-digit range, even if narrowly construed. Chapter 10 also built a justification for the sampling scheme I used in Chapters 11 and 12. The latter two chapters described roughly 30 studies and cited another 80 or so that were related to them in topic, findings, or methods—an admittedly modest sample of the many thousands of investigations of information seeking. Chapter 11 reviewed individual studies of information seeking to illustrate the research findings by *occupation*, and Chapter 12 considered the *social roles* and *demographic* segmentations that are sometimes the focus of such investigations. I pointed out trends toward more study of contexts and roles, and of smaller populations. However, it is still apparent that many studies continue to be concerned with long-standing questions of which sources and channels are used in which situations. "Other people" remain a chief source of answers to many common questions.

Now that I have, in the traditional fashion, "told you what I told you," I will move on to a critique of information behavior research. I will start with the complaints of three decades ago, and then move on to some criticisms that are more current.

13.2
Critiquing

13.2.1 A History of Complaint

In 1966, Herbert Menzel of New York University published what was to become the first among the series of the *Annual Review of Information Science and Technology (ARIST)* chapters on "information needs and uses." Menzel, whose concern was strictly limited to reviewing the burgeoning number of studies on scientists and engineers, opined that "all is not well with the quality of work performed in the field during the past few years" in which "sometimes excellent ideas lead to results that are either of dubious reliability and validity, or else of a barren superficiality" (1966b, p. 42). Menzel alluded to "poorly designed opinion polls," "primitive data-gathering instruments," and "categories too much tied to specific situations to make generalizations and extrapolations plausible" in his list of the faults of studies of "communication gathering behavior" (1966b, pp. 42–44). Menzel's suggested corrective was that researchers should draw upon "methods and techniques . . . in communication behavior research and other branches of sociology and psychology," among other disciplines (p. 42).

Thus began a steady stream of complaints and remedies directed at the study of information needs and seeking. Just a year after Menzel's review, another one by Herner and Herner (1967) lambasted studies of information users for seven alleged faults: using a narrow range of research techniques, studying too many disparate groups of users, failing to use consistent language, failing to innovate, failing to build on past findings, failing to learn from mistakes, and not using experimental designs.

In 1968 William Paisley pointed out the "defective methodology" and "shallow conceptualization" apparent in this research, expressing his

> concern over the field's failure to adopt the sound methods of its own best work. Mistakes of the 1950s are repeated in the 1960s. Inconclusive studies are conducted to fill gaps left by previous inconclusive studies. (p. 2)

Paisley also regretted that "the field has almost no theory" (p. 26), yet was able to conclude that it was "growing in size and maturing in quality. . . . More adequate theories of information-processing behavior will follow" (p. 23).

Two years later, Tom Allen griped about "the sort of trivia that many authors submit as research reports," particularly those "so involved with local circumstances that any generalization is questionable"; still, Allen thought there was "a strong corpus of good research in the field" (1969, p. 3).

This pattern of criticism represented by Paisley and Allen — disparaging remarks about the state of findings and methodology, coupled with optimistic comments about recent and future improvements — has persisted for more than three decades. In 1970, Lipetz's *ARIST* chapter observed that "the study of information needs and uses is still in its infancy, yet it exhibits considerable vigor"(p. 25). Diana Crane (1971) of Johns Hopkins University praised advances in methodology while acknowledging weaknesses in theory. Lin and Garvey (1972) declared that the literature lacked a conceptual framework.

The 1974 *ARIST* chapter by John Martyn spoke of a literature "cluttered with the results of an enormous number of surveys of indifferent quality . . . what this reviewer classes as 'Gee Whiz' research" (p. 4). Martyn suggested that progress could be made by focusing more on "communication" and less on "information" (p. 21), a point that Brenda Dervin reinforced in 1976 and that Tom Wilson later argued had yet to be fully realized even by 1994.

The fault-finding intensified in the 1980s. The problem was not so much with a general definition for information, wrote Tom Wilson in 1981, "as with a failure to use a definition appropriate to the . . . investigation" (p. 3). Four years later, Wersig and Windel (1985) objected to a lack of "empirically supported theoretical basis," particularly that which would explain "the subjective and nonrational aspects of information behavior" (p. 12). The *ARIST* review by Dervin and Nilan in 1986 cited several of the complaints mentioned above, characterizing them as a "concern for conceptual impoverishment" that had impeded the development of definitions and theories. And yet they still concluded that "a quantum and revolutionary conceptual leap in this area has been made since 1978" (p. 24).

The most recent broad literature review, a 50-year perspective by Tom Wilson (1994), agreed with Dervin and Nilan about those "leaps" forward. Wilson believed that there *has* been discernible progress accomplished in five decades of research on information needs and uses, although "much time has been wasted." In particular, Wilson concluded that "a firmer theoretical base now exists than was the case fifty (or even twenty) years ago" (p. 43).

What is there about this topic of study that leads to both pessimism and optimism? Has any other literature generated so many complaints of low quality, or exhibited so many signs of being overstudied? Katzer, Cook, and Crouch (1991) suggest that several social science and professional literatures also contain more chaff than wheat. Katzer *et al.* single out research on education for particular criticism, citing one finding that about half of it should not have been published at all. Yet even some epistemologists of the natural sciences (e.g.,

Rescher, 1978) consider a preponderance of "weak" research to be a necessary evil to the progress of a field. So investigations of information behaviors are at least not alone in exhibiting an uneven quality.

13.2.2 Current Criticisms

At this point the reader might well ask, Are we making progress toward better understanding of information behaviors? Or is "progress" in research simply an illusion, as some epistemologists would have it? The received view among many information seeking researchers, as represented by the most heavily cited scholars (e.g., Dervin and Wilson), is that more meaningful research — if not actual progress — can be attained through shifts in theoretical orientation (toward the more phenomenological, contextual, and hermeneutic) and by a more qualitative emphasis (which typically involves studying fewer people but in greater depth). It is as though repeated criticisms of traditional survey methodologies during the 1960s and 1970s lead inevitably to the embrace of the phenomenological and hermeneutic in the 1990s. Despite that trend, many investigations (particularly in the very active area of health information) still use the same kinds of questionnaires, interviews, and firsthand observations that have been used for decades.

Diversity of method is undoubtedly a good thing. It leads to more varied perspectives on the same phenomena. As I emphasize in Chapters 11 and 12, there is certainly a great deal of diversity in the kind of people and behaviors that are being studied, and in the methods that are being used to study them. However, that also means that there is more *fragmentation* than ever before among the thousands of diverse examples of human information seeking.

After decades of "de-contextualized" studies that tried to make generalizations about large groups (e.g., "engineers"), are we now facing the other extreme: tinier and tinier samples of smaller and smaller groups? In information seeking studies it is not unusual to encounter samples of fewer than 10, or even of a single individual. Even the anthropological studies that are so often emulated these days often typically tried to capture the cultural world of some hundreds or thousands of individuals through interaction with at least a few dozen members. The populations that are studied are sometimes rather small in themselves ("social science faculty studying the Kurds" is one recent example; see Meho & Haas, 2001), although we hope that the basic processes uncovered in such investigations might be generalizable.

The historical trend toward studies of smaller and smaller groups recalls Ward Just's (1968) reference to the "left-handed battalion commander syndrome" in Vietnam War reportage. Just quotes a journalist who explained that, desperate for something reportable, they would focus on an unusual "first," such as the first time a left-handed battalion commander had led troops into battle in this or that province. Just's account is cited by Fischer (1970) as an example of the "prodigious fallacy": the mistaken idea that uniqueness makes for significance, that an unusual event is, by definition, important. The objects of information seeking research have become, likewise, increasingly "unusual."

And what of the *utility* of information behavior studies? The origins of today's investigations lie in earlier "information needs and uses" research aimed at improving the performance of an institution's operations. Those studies were conducted by librarians to know what books to buy; by journalism instructors to understand which news had the most impact; and by social workers to learn how to better serve their clients. Yet to read some of today's information seeking research it would seem that we have now reached the point where the scholarliness of the studies correlates with their degree of *uselessness* for institutional purposes. Certainly we could say that information behavior research has become more "scholarly," but perhaps also more pointless as well.

It is also hard to resist the conclusion that the information behavior literature is somewhat faddish. Certain themes and sources are cited by one study that are picked up in later studies, but without necessarily leading either to an advancement of theory or to an accumulation of comparable findings. As Pettigrew and McKechnie (2001) have recently noted, theories are often cited with little explanation and sometimes without reference to any supporting publications. And the results appear to be less cumulative than ever: it is increasingly difficult to summarize a genre of studies, or even a single study, if its main result is merely a "thick description" of what the investigator observed rather then a clearly stated conclusion or theme. Types of occupations, roles, and other variables are repeatedly studied in ways that make the various results difficult to relate to one another.

13.3

Concluding

More research on information behavior is being conducted than ever before. Whatever has led to this renewed interest in an old topic, information seeking research has at last come into its own. The seeker has come into focus, resulting in more attention to the search process, more attempts to "get inside the head" of the seeker, more time spent with individual informants, and greater depth of description overall.

There is an important conclusion regarding information seeking that even yet may not be apparent to the reader, even though it has been emphasized in several places in this text: the way that we conceptualize and study information seeking has changed profoundly over the last quarter century. As this book emphasizes the more recent literature among nearly a century of publications, the changes in theory and methods may not be so apparent to the reader. Yet the shift in thinking has been major, although slow to emerge.

Probably the single most obvious way that our view of information seeking has changed is the rise of the "sense-making" paradigm — and, before that, the constructivist models of thought on which sense-making research, is built. Within traditional information seeking research, the shift began nearly 30 years ago, with the appearance of various writings by Brenda Dervin questioning the static ways in which information seeking had been characterized in past studies.

Dervin's 1972 book chapter with Bradley Greenberg raised important questions about the information seeking habits of the urban poor. Four years later, Dervin published an article that clearly stated her rethinking of the then-current tendency to characterize use of informal sources of information as "least effort" and "irrational" behavior. Her 1976 *Journal of Broadcasting* article described a case of "disciplinary schizophrenia" among communication researchers studying information needs and uses. According to Dervin,

> our research data and our practitioner experiences say "relativism" loud and clear. Meanings are in people. People construct their own reality. No knowledge is absolute. Messages sent do not equal those received. The same person is different across time and space. On the other hand, we commit ourselves to research and action efforts which seek deterministic answers. We continue to look for normative, nonvariant rules. We seek enduring personality variables that persist across time and space. (1976a, p. 324)

Dervin's counter assumptions took some time to have an effect — Wilson (1994) believes that it took at least a decade. Some of her arguments are still widely ignored even today, in investigations that try to discover general rules about what kind of people use what kinds of information. But the movement to pay more attention to context and meaning has had a lasting effect; many more investigators are trying to study the aspects of time, space, and situation that make a difference in the ways that people create, perceive, ignore, seek, and use information.

13.3.1 Eight Lessons of Information Behavior Research

I will conclude this book by reinterpreting Dervin's 10 myths in light of what has happened since they were introduced. In the list below I have merged several of Dervin's related assumptions together into six main points, and restated them in terms of the lessons I think we can take away from them. I have also added two conclusions of my own, in consideration of what has been said in this book.

1. *Formal sources and rationalized searches reflect only one side of human information behavior.* Empirical research tells us that many people use formal sources rarely, relying instead on informal sources such as friends and family, or knowledgeable colleagues at work, along with what they learn from mass media and other elements of their environment. Some investigators have been disturbed that *least effort seeking* is so common. Yet there are inherent efficiencies in least effort behavior — for instance, searching takes no longer than is necessary to produce, on average, a satisfactory result. Thus, it is wrong to interpret least effort information seeking as "irrational." Such behavior can be both satisfying and successful.

2. *More information is not always better.* We have seen that a major preoccupation of humans is filtering, interpreting, and understanding the overload of information with which they are faced. There is justification for consciously ignoring or filtering relevant information in situations in which there is not enough time or energy to consider all of it. Ignoring or avoiding information is at times a rational strategy for living and working.

3. *Context is central to the transfer of information.* Information seeking research demonstrates that people strive toward a holistic view of their world. Sometimes they do not connect external information to their internal reality because of anxiety, or because they do not see the relevance of it. Partly for this reason, humans are prone to ignoring isolated bits of information — sometimes at great cost to their goals and lives.

The individual's definition of the situation will shape his or her needs as much as does the "real" situation itself. Much of what we bring to bear on information in creating meaning from it is not only "outside" of the package (as has been frequently pointed out) but also outside of the information itself: our accumulated personal experiences and secondhand experiences, including our understanding of the world and of language.

4. *Sometimes information — particularly generalized packages of information — doesn't help.* "Information" on its own does not satisfy many human needs. Humans want to "understand," but they more often need information to pursue more basic needs such as food, shelter, and clothing. It is not clear that there is a basic "need for information," although some scholars believe this to be true. Often people facing problems are looking for a customized solution, rather than the standardized response of an information system or agency. Even when individuals really do need information, the "chunks" of it encompassed by books, articles, and television programs may not provide the instructions or answers that they need.

5. *Sometimes it is not possible to make information available or accessible.* Institutions and their formal information systems often are not able to keep up with the unique and unpredictable demands they face. Formal systems will never be able to satisfy most information needs. Yet we often act as if we expect

them to do so. The current debate over the "digital divide"(Compaine, 2001; Goslee, 1998) illustrates some aspects of this expectation.

6. *Information seeking is a dynamic process.* Information needs may quickly arise and either be satisfied or fade away. The nature of one's "question" may change at various points in a search. Satisfying one information need may simply give rise to yet another question or problem. But the difficulty of studying such a shifting scenario leads to a tendency to look at an information seeking episode as something rather simple, linear, and complete. The usual script assumes that a need arises, a person conducts a search of a single source in a particular channel, and finds an answer — end of search! But human information seeking simply is not so simple. It is neither straightforward nor typically complete; it is more like a series of interruptions, punctuated by other interruptions. In keeping with this realization, more recent models of information seeking (e.g., ASK) have emphasized the dynamic, iterative nature of needs and searches.

7. *Information seeking is not always about a "problem" or "problematic situation."* Some information-related behavior is truly *creative* in its origins — it is not driven by the need to provide a response to a situation. The creative urge bears on the study of information seeking in this way: traditional information seeking research, even the more recent versions of it, implicitly assumes that people react to a problem state. In most cases, this is true enough: people often *do* seek information to solve problems or even to find explicit answers to specific questions. However the oft-stated inadequacies of information seeking research (e.g., its inability to explain why people act as they do) indicate that information seeking is much more than solving problems, finding facts, or making decisions. This is where creativity enters the picture.

8. *Information behavior is not always about "sense-making" either.* Despite the recent emphasis on sense-making rather than "usage," the study of information seeking is still largely the study of *sources.* Perhaps in part this is due to the popularity of the World Wide Web, the latest "source" to be widely studied and one that is potentially profitable. It has encouraged both investigation and speculation on the inner desires of the public for information, entertainment, and transactions. It is certainly true that the steady stream of health-related research still emphasizes formal information; "making sense of one's situation" can only be of limited usefulness or comfort when faced with a potentially fatal illness, for example.

Many information behavior researchers have rallied around the sense-making paradigm, which has done the invaluable service of revitalizing research on information seeking. But life is not all about uncertainty, gaps, or discontinuities. And early questions raised about the notion of sense-making (e.g., Heap, 1975) have still not been resolved. The sense-making approach, while still valuable, does not capture all aspects of information behavior. For certain problems it remains useful to think in "old" terms like source preference and audience segmentation.

Information behavior research finds itself at a crossroads. It still retains themes, theories, and methodologies from half a century past, and some of these older approaches remain useful. At the same time it has embraced new perspectives, theories, and methods that would have been considered heretical even a quarter century ago. The new vigor it has shown over the last decade — with many productive researchers still in the early stages of their careers — bodes well for the future.

Appendix:
Questions for Discussion and Application

Chapter 1 ————————————————————————————
(Introduction)

1. How much information do you encounter in a day? Leaving aside the difficult issue of how to assess images (i.e., what you see around you or on television screens), let's just think about amounts simply in terms of *words*. If you could count up all the words that you hear or read in a typical day, about how many thousands would there be?

Assume that most half-hour television or radio broadcasts contain about 3,000 words, that newspaper articles are about 1,000 words long, that there are about 500 words on a typical book page, and that people speak (conversationally) at roughly 100 words per minute. Consider what you hear, see, or read in the course of a typical work day, starting with any news you may read or listen to in the morning and continuing through to the last things you hear or read before falling asleep. Don't forget to consider the following: conversations you have with others, announcements or conversations that you overhear, signs and billboards that you pass along the way, and of course, conscious watching, listening, or reading of news and entertainment.

2. Have you ever read a research study that aimed to understand how people are affected by information? Relate what you remember from it. Did the original description reach any conclusions? If so, did the conclusions make sense? Did the topic of the study itself seem important enough to be worthy of investigation? If not, what kind of topic *would* be worthy of a study?

3. Some people believe that information can never be "objective" — that is, that the "truth" and meaning of the information is always open to interpretation. Among other implications, this stance suggests that any advice from "experts" is always open to doubt.

Consider the common (and difficult) case in which a medical doctor recommends a surgical procedure based on a diagnosis of cancer. If you were the patient, which of the following choices would seem most comfortable to you? [1] Agree to the treatment without question. [2] Agree only after some thought and discussion with loved ones. [3] Agree only after much reading of medical literature on the topic. [4] Agree only if a second doctor renders the same opinion. [5] Agree only if you think there is a "fair" balance between the degree of risk and pain involved (on one hand), and the goodness of the possible outcome of the procedure (e.g., What are my chances of a permanent "cure"?). For each of these choices of action, how much weight is being given to the expert's opinion versus your own thoughts and feelings?

Chapter 2 _____
(Scenarios)

1. Which of the scenarios described in this chapter seemed most familiar to you? Are they familiar because you have done the kind of seeking depicted, because you are interested in the topic of the search, because you identified with the character, or for another reason?

2. Invent your own scenario and describe it in 100 to 300 words. Base your story on a situation with which you are familiar enough to describe the kinds of results that might be found by a person actively seeking information. If are not sure where to begin, modify the following scenario according to your knowledge, interests, and circumstances: You have just received news that a close friend or relative has been reported to be missing on a hiking trip in a remote location in Chile. What would you do to find out more? Who would you call or e-mail and what would you ask? Would you search the Internet or a library for a map and/or travel information? In what order would you proceed and what would you do in response to each "answer" you receive to your queries?

3. Do you vary your level of attention and selectiveness depending on the *context* in which you seek information? For instance, does the setting, your purpose, and the type of people involved affect how you acquire information? Consider these three scenarios:

a. You are in a large bookstore looking for several books to take on vacation with you.

b. You are sitting at a computer in a public place while you search the Internet to find some information on a topic for a report you are writing.

c. You are at a conference interviewing several people to find out their reactions to the meeting content, hotel services, and choice of conference location.

In each case, consider how easy (or hard) it is to obtain the result you are seeking; what the nature of your motivation is; how thorough you think you would need to be; what the time or social pressures you may feel are (e.g., are other persons waiting to look at what you are browsing?); and how specific reliable, and believable the information you are likely to encounter will be.

Chapter 3
(The Concept of Information)

1. Information can be a commodity but it does not always "behave" in the same way as other commodities. For one thing, if I give (or sell) information to you, I still retain it myself rather than giving it up (as would be the case with a normal commodity). Another difference is the way that giving away valuable information may actually increase its value. Here are two examples. [1] Broadcast television programs provide their programs for "free" (actually, in exchange for audience attention to advertising); the more people who take advantage of this free programming, the more valuable it becomes as both a topic of conversation among audience members and as a source of revenue for broadcasters and advertisers. [2] Although music producers clearly deserve their royalties, it appears that peer-to-peer trading of music on the Internet (e.g., using Napster) has actually increased sales of music recordings. So while copyright holders complain about loss of revenue from songs being downloaded without charge, in some cases their revenues have increased as a larger audience is exposed to their music and is more willing to buy the CDs from which the songs came now that they have had an opportunity to preview what they will be getting when they buy the album.

Can you think of other examples in which information differs from other potential commodities—and changes human behavior as a result? How about ways in which information is treated as *similar* to other commodities like carrots, cars, clothing, or condos?

2. Advertisers are often willing to pay a lot to place their message on a billboard along a busy highway. But how much information can actually be conveyed in a glimpse that lasts only a few seconds? And how likely is it to result in the viewer purchasing or using the advertised product or concept? For each of the following signs, answer these three questions: [1] How much information—in terms of distinct concepts—would you say is actually conveyed by the sign? [2] How likely are people to take in the information—can it be easily (and perhaps, amusingly) absorbed and understood in a few seconds? [3] How likely are people to respond in the way the advertiser wants—how soon can they respond, and how costly will it be to do so?

The content of the highway billboards:

a. "Radio WXYZ, 109.9 FM. It's all you need to have on." (Background: Picture of several naked men and women, taken from the back.)
b. "Vista Del Basura Estates — if you lived here, you would already be home!" (Background: Outline of a palatial home.)
c. "Wouldn't you like to see your grandchildren grow up? Quit smoking. You'll live to see that, and more." (Background: No picture, but a second message below it, in smaller type: "The National Council of Health Maintenance Organizations urges you to stop smoking—for your children's sake, and yours.")
d. "Drink Vishnu Cola." (Background: Image of a smiling young man, holding a bottle near his face.)

3. Is a picture *typically* "worth a thousand words"? Or is it closer to either 100 or 10,000 words? Imagine a few of the photographs you've taken in the last year; about how many words would it take to describe their content? If, instead of photographs, each had been one minute of video, how many more words would be needed to describe them?

Chapter 4 ——————————————————————
(Needs and Seeking)

1. Do people really "need" information, or is it just a by-product of other things we need? Consider the type of subjects and outcomes that are typical of primary education (i.e., what school systems try to teach children from ages 5 through 12). Are all of them directly related to another, more basic need such as making a living? Are all of them really necessary, in your view? What is the role and relative importance of each of the following in an elementary curriculum: story time, art class, play time, and sports?

2. Recollect and describe two episodes in your life in which learning some information led to more uncertainty in your life. This could be, for example, a doctor's comment that you needed a certain medical test, the realization that you could not locate your keys, or incomplete news about an event.

3. Have you ever been aware that you *should* know something, but don't? How did you recognize that state of mind? Did you have a feeling of "anxiety" or a sense of "nagging doubt"? Or was it that somebody reminded you that you were "ignorant of the facts"? What were the circumstances that led to your realization that you lacked useful knowledge, and how did you resolve the situation?

Chapter 5 ———————————————————————
(Related Concepts)

1. Consider how the spoken phrase "that's the thing that is causing the problem" might be interpreted in these different cases:

a. a discussion of how Palestinians have expressed their grievances in Israel
b. a mechanic pointing under the hood of a car
c. one of two friends, referring to a continuing misunderstanding between them

What could the statement possibly *mean* in each case? That is, how does the *context* of the statement change the potential range of *meanings* that an observer might attribute to it?

2. Look at one of Richard Saul Wurman's *Access* guides—bookstores and public libraries often have several in the series (e.g., *New York/Access* or *Hawaii/Access*). Ask yourself whether you would find it easier (or harder) to locate what you want within an unfamiliar city using an *Access* guide versus a more typical guidebook. What information do you most value in a tourist guide, and in what formats do you find it most useful?

3. Do you believe that "knowledge gaps" exist between different segments of society? For instance, is there a "digital divide" that separates people who have access to Internet resources from those who do not have access? If you believe that some groups have considerably less *information* than others, then which of these factors are most responsible for (or at least correlated with) such gaps: wealth, class, gender, age, race, ethnicity, or geography?

For examples, consider the following questions: Do "the rich get richer" mainly because of who they know? Do men tend to know more than women in such a way that consistently maintains their power differential? Are the elderly usually wiser than the rest of us? Does being a minority (in any sense—racial, ethnic, religious, or simply being left-handed) mean that some doors are often closed? Are rural people always "the last to know" about trends in society? If you find some kernel of truth in these questions, then how would you go about gathering evidence to demonstrate the truth of each statement?

Chapter 6 ———————————————————————
(Models)

1. Models are often said to precede theories, which is why this chapter appears before the chapter describing theories. Other than Wilson's second model, which explicitly mentions several possible theories, would you say that any of the other models embody any theories or assumptions about that way

that people perceive, seek, and/or use information? For instance, one possible assumption is that information resides in people (i.e., in terms of meanings) rather than in things ("containers" like books or films). For each model, then, would you say that the information seeking it describes is more of a search for meaning, or more about finding and examining the contents of information containers? Can you identify other basic assumptions behind these models?

2. Which of the models depicted in this chapter makes the most sense to you? Which factors are most influential in your choice: The level of detail? The particular words chosen to describe the process? The emphasis (e.g., written information, or everyday life information)?

3. The models described in this chapter appear to vary the most in regard to the "outcomes" — the explicit actions or other behaviors that come about as a result of the factors highlighted in the earlier stages of the model. Outcomes are variously characterized in terms of words like demands, success, satisfaction, attention, search, seeking, gathering, giving, interpersonal contact, and various kinds of "information use." Why do models differ so much in the way that they describe human behavior that results from information seeking situations? Why isn't there more agreement on a standard vocabulary for describing these things? Consider the main factors identified by each model and how that limits or proscribes what kinds of outcomes are likely in the case of each model.

Chapter 7 —————————————————————————————————————

(Paradigms and Theories)

1. Which of the theories presented in this chapter makes the most sense to you? Why? Is it due to the level of detail? The words chosen to describe the process? The emphasis (e.g., formal written information versus everyday life information)? The ease with which you can think of human behavior that seems to fit the theory? Make a case for why the particular theory you chose is the most useful of those described in this chapter.

2. Information seeking researchers are divided regarding the importance and suitability of Zipf's Principle of Least Effort for investigating information seeking. Some critics say it is purely descriptive of overall tendencies, rather than an adequate explanation of specific behaviors. Others complain that it tends to be used to blame people for not searching rigorously enough, when it should focus on the barriers that discourage us from being systematic in our searches for information.

Does the Principle of Least Effort seem valid to you? What evidence (examples of your behavior or that of others) can you offer that either support or contradict this principle?

3. Thirty years ago it was fair to say that most theories applied in information seeking studies tended to come from the disciplines of psychology, sociology, or communication. In your view, is that still chiefly true? In recent years we have had a few examples of theory coming from anthropology and ecology (foraging theory), and from the study of literature (reader response theory). Based on your own familiarity with academic disciplines, are there other sources of theory that might be useful in studying information behavior? For instance, do the humanities disciplines offer alternative views of information seeking?

Chapter 8 _____

(Methods)

1. If you were to begin a study of information seeking today, which methodological approach would you be most comfortable with, and why? Consider a group with which you are familiar — students in a particular discipline, members of an organization you belong to, or people who share your interest in a particular sport or hobby. How would you go about investigating their information needs and behaviors?

2. Qualitative approaches to studying information behavior such as participant observation and ethnographic interviews have been on the increase over the last three decades. Why might they be? In your view do such approaches to studying people hold more promise than methods more commonly used in decades past — especially surveys and experiments?

3. If you were studying the workings of an organization and you overheard the following statements from an employee, what could you assume about the meaning and implications of the word "murp," given the context in which it is used?

a. "Bill has been murping the development committee meetings again. It's so hard to reach consensus in a group that size, and his behavior doesn't help matters."

b. "The murp in the computer room needs to be replaced again. It seems to be randomly deleting e-mail messages."

c. "If we could just agree on how to evaluate the murp, we could move ahead with the study. Some of the staff think that there's no way to measure it directly."

In each case, imagine yourself to be a *participant observer* who needs to understand if the statement has any implications for information flows within the organization. Other than the obvious question ("Excuse me, but what is a 'murp'?"), *what would you ask* to understand the problem implied in each case?

How else would you observe (through watching, interviewing, or reading relevant documents) so that you could understand whether "murp" has an important (or trivial) effect on information transfer within the organization?

Chapter 9 _____

(Methodological Examples)

1. Choose one of the empirical studies cited in this chapter and locate the original article or chapter in which it was reported. Read it carefully and develop responses to the following questions:

a. What kind of phenomenon or problem is being studied? In your view, does the researcher make good arguments as to *why* it is being studied? Does it seem important to *you*?
b. Are definitions offered for the key terms and concepts used in the study? Is there any indication of how those words relate to one another? Does it explain how we know that the concepts really exist, and how to recognize and/or measure them?
c. What has been left out of any literature review that precedes the study? What other literature might have been reviewed that you are aware of as being somewhat relevant to the subject of the study?
d. Consider the choice of words used by the author to report the study. Is the language biased in any way? Is it slanted toward a particular view of people or the phenomenon being studied? An example would be words that suggest that the persons studied are "lazy" in seeking information, or that assume that the only valid information is that from an institutional source.

2. Choose one of the empirical studies cited in this chapter and locate the original article or chapter in which it was reported. Read it carefully and develop responses to the following questions:

a. Do you see any weaknesses in the design of the study? Are you convinced by the researcher's reasons for designing the investigation in the way it is designed?
b. When and where were the observations made? Who made them? What might have been left out of the observations? Consider other evidence that might have been gathered in this investigation. For example, what other kinds of behaviors might have been examined, and what other kinds of people might have been sampled, that would provide examples of the phenomenon of interest?

c. Do you agree with the interpretations and conclusions suggested in the article? Do you see any weaknesses in the arguments that accompany it? Can you suggest another interpretation of the results than the author conveyed?

3. The next time that you are in a bookstore or library watch for any outward signs of uncertainty, frustration, and similar cognitive and emotional states. Is anyone moving quickly from place to place? Do you hear expressions of uncertainty like "It should be around here somewhere" or direct questions to others such as "Do you know where X is?" Are there any overt signs of frustration, such as shaking of head or throwing up of hands? How do people respond to a failure to find something to satisfy a cognitive need? How would you study uncertainty or frustration?

Chapter 10 ———————————————————————
(Reviewing Research: Size and History)

1. Are you surprised by what is said about the history and size of the information behavior literature? Would you agree that the study of this topic actually began in the early twentieth century, or would you choose a later date for when serious investigation really began? Do you agree with the way that I have defined the scope of "information behavior" by relying on published reviews of "information needs and uses" studies? What other means could we use to define and measure this literature? If you think that the scope of the topic could be defined differently (i.e., including or excluding certain topics), would you revise my estimate of the size of the relevant literature upward or downward?

2. This chapter suggests that there seems to have been a marked slow-down in the number of information behavior studies conducted during the 1980s when compared to the 1970s and 1990s. Can you think of reasons why this would have been so?

3. Which of the following research methods seems most fruitful to you for the goal of understanding basic aspects of information behavior? Try ranking the usefulness of each approach, considering its relative reliability and validity.

a. Case studies
b. Ethnographic interviews
c. Questionnaires (paper)
d. Questionnaires (via e-mail)
e. Laboratory experiments
f. Field experiments

Chapter 11 ———————————————————————————————
(Reviewing Research by Occupation)

1. A great many investigations have been conducted of a relatively small number of occupations—especially scientists, engineers, medical doctors, and managers. Is this degree of research attention deserved, compared to other possible occupations (e.g., lawyers, historians, or journalists)? Why or why not? Which occupation(s) do you believe have not received enough research attention, and why?

2. In your view is it still worthwhile to conduct investigations of the information behavior of "metadisciplines" such as the humanities, sciences, or social sciences? Why or why not? If you believe that studies of "scientists" or "humanists" are too broad to be of much use, then how narrow should information behavior investigations be? That is, should they attempt to generalize about entire disciplines (e.g., psychologists) or focus on much smaller occupational groups (e.g., cognitive psychologists studying "the role of mental models in learning" at Cambridge University)?

3. Is it a problem that medical doctors so often choose not to pursue questions they have regarding diseases and treatments? Or is this just an unavoidable circumstance of being a busy professional whose time is highly valuable? How might a hospital or clinic make it easier for doctors to find the answers to questions that come up in the course of examining patients?

Chapter 12 ———————————————————————————————
(Reviewing Research by Role and Demographic Group)

1. Why do you think it is that few studies have focused on differences between men and women in their information seeking? Is it because there are no systematic differences between them? Or is it that such differences are overshadowed by (i.e., better predicted by) other variables such as education, age, interests, and situations?

2. One common role is not comprehensively reviewed in this chapter: that of "student." What might we be able to learn from investigations of student use of print and electronic materials? In what ways might the role of student differ from the others reviewed in this chapter? For example, can we assume that most students are fairly competent at seeking and using information, given their frequent exposure to instruction and assignments?

3. A common finding of studies of general populations (e.g., "citizens") has been that they rely first on their own experience and second on family and friends before ever turning to formal sources (e.g., professionals or books).

Are there situations (e.g., health problems) or topics (e.g., financial security) for which this pattern is possibly dysfunctional or cause for public concern?

Chapter 13 ――――――――――――――――――――

(Reviewing, Critiquing, Concluding)

1. Do you judge information behavior research to be less rigorous, less conclusive, or in any other way "weaker" than most other social research?

2. Do you disagree with any of the "eight lessons of information behavior research"? For example, do you accept the conclusion that "sometimes information doesn't help," or "information seeking is not always about "sense-making"? Why or why not?

3. Now that you have read this book, how would you rate the importance of information behavior research? How important is this line of research, compared to other topics with which you are familiar? Make some explicit comparisons to research in other fields.

References

Abelson, R., & Levi, A. (1985). Decision making and decision theory. In G. Lindsay & E. Aronson (Eds.), *The handbook of social psychology* (3rd ed., pp. 231–309). New York: Knopf.

Adler, R. (1999). *Information literacy: Advancing opportunities for learning in the digital age*. Washington, DC: Aspen Institute.

Agada, J. (1999). Inner-city gatekeepers: An exploratory survey of their information use environment. *Journal of the American Society for Information Science, 50,* 74–85.

Aguilar, F. (1967). *Scanning the business environment*. New York: Macmillan.

Ainslie, T. (1986). *Ainslie's complete guide to thoroughbred racing* (3rd ed.). New York: Simon & Schuster.

Allen, B. L. (1996). *Information tasks: Toward a user-centered approach to information systems*. San Diego, CA: Academic Press.

Allen, T. J (1977). *Managing the flow of information*. Cambridge, MA: MIT Press.

Allen, T. J. (1969). Information needs and uses. In C. Cuadra (Ed.), *Annual review of information science and technology* (Vol. 4, pp. 3–29). Chicago: Encyclopaedia Britannica.

Allen, T. J., & Cohen, S. I. (1969). Information flow in research and development laboratories. *Administrative Science Quarterly, 14,* 12–19.

Allport, G. W., & Postman, L. (1947). *The psychology of rumor*. New York: Holt.

Altheide, D. (1987). Ethnographic content analysis. *Qualitative Sociology, 10,* 65–77.

Altheide, D. (1996). *Qualitative media analysis* (Vol. 38). Thousand Oaks, CA: Sage.

Anderson, D. R., Collins, P. A., Schmitt, K. L., & Jacobvitz, R. S. (1996). Stressful life events and television viewing. *Communication Research, 23,* 243–260.

Anwar, M., & Supaat, H. (1998). Information needs of rural Malaysians: An exploratory study of a cluster of three villages with no library service. *International Information & Library Review, 30,* 23–37.

Apted, S. (1971). General purposive browsing. *Library Association Record, 73,* 66–78.

Artandi, S. (1973).Information concepts and their utility. *Journal of the American Society for Information Science, 24*(4), 42–245.

Atkin, C. (1972). Anticipated communication and mass media information-seeking. *Public Opinion Quarterly, 36,* 188–199.

Atkin, C. (1973). Instrumental utilities and information-seeking. In P. Clarke (Ed.), *New models for mass communication research* (pp. 205–242). Beverly Hills, CA: Sage.

Atkin, C. (1985). Informational utility and selective exposure to entertainment media. In D. Zillmann & J. Bryant (Eds.), *Selective exposure to communication* (pp. 63–91). Hillsdale, NJ: Erlbaum.

Atwood, R., & Dervin, B. (1982). Challenges to sociocultural predictors of information seeking: a test of race vs situation movement state. In M. Burgoon (Ed.), *Communication yearbook* (Vol. 5, pp. 549–569). New Brunswick, NJ: Transaction Books.

305

Auerbach. (1965). DOD user needs study, Phase I; Final technical report 1151-TR3. Philadelphia, PA: Auerbach Corporation.

Auster, E., & Choo, C. (1993). Environmental scanning by CEOs in two Canadian industries. *Journal of the American Society for Information Science, 44,* 194–203.

Ayris, P. (1986). *The stimulation of creativity: A review of the literature concerning the concept of browsing,* 1970–1985 (CRUS Working Paper No. 5). Sheffield, England: Centre for Research on User Studies (CRUS), University of Sheffield.

Babbie, E. (2000). *The practice of social research* (9th ed.). Belmont, CA: Wadsworth.

Baker, L. (1996). The nature of the information needed by women with multiple sclerosis. *Library & Information Science Research, 18,* 67–81.

Baker, S. (1986). Overload, browsers, and selections. *Library & Information Science Research, 8,* 315–329.

Baker, T. L. (1999). *Doing social research* (3rd ed.). New York: McGraw-Hill.

Baldwin, N. S., & Rice, R. E. (1997). Information-seeking behavior of securities analysts: Individual and institutional influences, information sources and channels, and outcomes. *Journal of the American Society for Information Science, 48,* 674–693.

Bandura, A. (1977). *Social learning theory.* Englewood Cliffs, NJ: Prentice-Hall.

Barnbaum, D., & Byron, M. (2001). *Research ethics: text and readings.* Upper Saddle River, NJ: Prentice-Hall.

Barry, C. (1994). User-defined relevance criteria: An exploratory study. *Journal of the American Society for Information Science, 45,* 149–159.

Barry, C. (1995). Critical issues in evaluating the impact of IT on information activity in academic research: developing a qualitative research solution. *Library and Information Science Research, 17,* 107–134.

Bates, M. J. (1989). The design of browsing and berrypicking techniques for the online search interface. *Online Review, 13*(5), 407–424.

Bates, M. J. (1996). Learning about the information seeking of interdisciplinary scholars and students. *Library Trends, 45*(2), 155–164.

Bateson, G. (1972). Steps to an ecology of mind. New York: Ballantine.

Batson, C., Coke, J., Chard, F., Smith, D., & Taliaferro, A. (1979). Generality of the "glow of goodwill": Effects of mood on helping and information acquisition. *Social Psychology Quarterly, 42,* 176–179.

Bebout, L., Davis, J., & Oehlerts, D. (1975). User studies in the humanities: A survey and a proposal. *RQ, 15*(1), 40–44.

Becker, H. S. (1970). *Sociological work: method and substance.* Chicago: Aldine.

Becker, H. S. (1982). *Art worlds.* Berkeley, CA: University of California Press.

Belk, R. W. (1975). Situational variables and consumer behavior. *Journal of Consumer Research, 2,* 157–167.

Belk, R. W., Sherry, J., Jr., & Wallendorf, M. (1988). Naturalistic inquiry into buyer–seller behavior at a swap meet. *Journal of Consumer Research, 14,* 449–469.

Belkin, N. J. (1978). Information concepts for information science. *Journal of Documentation, 34,* 55–85.

Belkin, N. J., Oddy, R., & Brooks, H. (1982). ASK for information retrieval. *Journal of Documentation, 38*(2), 61–71.

Belkin, N. J., & Robertson, S. (1976). Information science and the phenomenon of information. *Journal of the American Society for Information Science, 27*(4), 197–204.

Belkin, N. J., & Vickery, A. (1985). *Interaction in information systems: A review of research from document retrieval to knowledge-based systems.* Boston Spa, England: British Library.

Benoit, G. (2000). Critical theory as a foundation for pragmatic information systems design. *Information Research, 6*(2). Retrieved March 15, 2001, from the University of Sheffield Web site at http://www.she.ac.uk/~ is publications/infres/6-2/paper98a.html.

Berger, C. R. (1997). Message production under uncertainty. In G. Philipsen & T. Albrecht (Eds.), *Developing communication theories* (pp. 29–56). Albany, NY: State University of New York Press.

Berger, P. L., & Luckmann T. (1966). *The social construction of reality*. New York: Doubleday.

Berland, G. K., Eilliott, M. N., Morales, L. S., Algazy, J. I., Kravitz, R. L., Broder, M. S., Kanouse, D. E., Muñoz, J. A., Puyol, J. -A., Lara, M., Watkins, K. E., Yang, H., & McGlynn, E. A. (2001). Health information on the Internet: Accessibility, quality, and readability in English and Spanish. *Journal of the American Medical Association, 285*(20), 2612–2621.

Berlo, D. (1960). *The process of communication: An introduction to theory and practice*. New York: Holt, Rinehart and Winston.

Berlo, D. (1977). Communication as process: Review and commentary. In B. Ruben (Ed.), *Communication yearbook* (Vol. 1, pp. 11–28). New Brunswick, NJ: Transaction Books.

Berlyne, D. E. (1960). *Conflict, arousal, and curiosity*. New York: McGraw-Hill.

Bichteler, J., & Ward, D. (1989). Information-seeking behavior of geoscientists. *Special Libraries, 79*(3), 169–178.

Bierbaum, E. (1990). A paradigm for the '90s. *American Libraries, 21,* 18–19.

Biesecker, A. E. (1988). Aging and the desire for information and input in medical decisions: Patient consumerism in medical encounters. *The Gerontologist, 28,* 330–335.

Biesecker, A. E., & Biesecker, T. D. (1990). Patient information-seeking behaviors when communicating with doctors. *Medical Care, 28,* 19–28.

Bloch, P., & Richins, M. (1983). Shopping without purchase: An investigation of consumer browsing behavior. *Advances in Consumer Research, 10,* 543–548.

Bloch, P., Ridgway, N., & Sherrell, D. (1989). Extending the concept of shopping: An investigation of browsing activity. *Journal of the Academy of Marketing Science, 17,* 13–21.

Bloch, P. H., Sherrell, D. L., & Ridgway, N. M. (1986). Consumer search: An extended framework. *Journal of Consumer Research, 13,* 119–126.

Blythe, J., & Royle, J. (1993). Assessing nurses' information needs in the work environment. *Bulletin of the Medical Library Association, 81*(4), 189–196.

Blumer, H. (1986). *Symbolic interactionism: Perspective and method*. Englewood Cliffs, NJ: Prentice-Hall.

Bogart, L. (1983). Mass media: Knowledge as entertainment. In K. Boulding & L. Senesh (Eds.), *The optimum utilization of knowledge: Making knowledge serve human betterment* (pp. 216–231). Boulder, CO: Westview Press.

Borgman, C. L. (Ed.). (1990). *Scholarly communication and bibliometrics*. Newbury Park, CA: Sage.

Borgman, C. L. (1996). Why are online catalogs still hard to use? *Journal of the American Society for Information Science, 47,* 493–503.

Borgman, C. L. (2000). *From Gutenberg to the global information infrastructure: Access to information in the networked world*. Cambridge, MA: MIT Press.

Bosman, J., & Renckstorf, K. (1996). Information needs: Problems, interests and consumption. In K. Renckstorf (Ed.), *Media use as social action* (pp. 43–52). London: John Libbey.

Bouazza, A. (1989). Information user studies. *In Encyclopedia of library and information science* (Vol. 44, Suppl. 9, pp. 144–164). New York: Dekker.

Boulding, K. (1956). *The image: Knowledge in life and society*. Ann Arbor, MI: University of Michigan Press.

Bourdieu, P. (1984). *Distinction: A social critique of the judgement of taste* (R. Nice, Trans.). London: Routledge.

Bourdieu, P. (1990). *The logic of practice* (R. Nice, Trans.). Cambridge: Polity Press.

Bowers, J. W., & Bradac, J. J. (1982). Issues in communication theory: A metatheoretical analysis. In M. Burgoon (Ed.), *Communication yearbook* (Vol. 5). New Brunswick, NJ: Transaction Books.

References

Bowler, S., Donovan, T., & Snipp, J. (1993). Local sources of information and voter choice in state elections: Microlevel foundations of the "friends and neighbors" effect. *American Politics Quarterly, 21*, 473–489.

Boyce, B., Meadow, C., & Kraft, D. (1994). *Measurement in information science*. San Diego, CA: Academic Press.

Breivik, P. (1998). *Student learning in an information age*. Phoenix, A2: Oryx.

Brier, S. (1992). Information and consciousness: A critique of the mechanistic concept of information. *Cybernetics and Human Knowing, 1*(2–3), 71–94.

Brittain, J. M. (1970). *Information and its users: A review with special reference to the social sciences*. New York: Wiley-Interscience.

Broder, A., Kumar, R., Maghoul, F., Raghavan, P., Rajagopalan, S., & Stata, R., Tomkins A., & Wiener J. (1999). Graph structure in the web. Retrieved December 15, 2001, from IBM Almaden Research Center, Computer Science Principles and Methodologies Department Web site: http://www.almaden.ibm.com/cs/k53/www9.final/.

Brown, C. (1999). Information seeking behavior of scientists in the electronic information age: Astronomers, chemists, mathematicians, and physicists. *Journal of the American Society for Information Science, 50*, 929–943.

Brown, C. (2000, August 16–18). *The role of computer-mediated communication in the research process of music scholars: an exploratory investigation*. Paper presented at the Information Seeking in Context, Göteborg, Sweden.

Brown, J., & Duguid, P. (2000). *The social life of information*. Boston: Harvard Business School Press.

Brown, J. S., & Walsh-Childers, K. (1994). Effects of media on personal and public health. In J. Bryant & D. Zillmann (Eds.), *Media effects: Advances in theory and research* (pp. 389–415). Hillsdale, NJ: Erlbaum.

Bruce, H. (1994). A cognitive view of the situational dynamism of user-centered relevance estimation. *Journal of the American Society for Information Science, 45*, 142–149.

Bruce, H. (1998). User satisfaction with information seeking on the Internet. *Journal of the American Society for Information Science, 49*(6), 541–556.

Brucks, M. (1985). The effects of product class knowledge on information search behavior. *Journal of Consumer Research, 12*, 1–16.

Bruner, J. S. (1973). *Beyond the information given: Studies in the psychology of knowing*. New York: Norton.

Bruner, J. S. (1990). *Acts of meaning*. Cambridge, MA: Harvard University Press.

Bryant, J., & Zillman, D. (1984). Using television to alleviate boredom and stress: Selective exposure as a function of induced excitational states. *Journal of Broadcasting, 28*, 1–20.

Buckland, M. K. (1991a). Information as thing. *Journal of the American Society for Information Science, 42*, 351–360.

Buckland, M. K. (1991b). *Information and information systems*. New York: Greenwood Press.

Buckland, M. K. (1998). What is a "document"? In T. Hahn & M. Buckland (Eds.), *Historical studies in information science* (pp. 215–220). Medford, NJ: Information Today.

Buckland, M. K., & Hindle, A. (1969). Library Zipf. *Journal of Documentation, 25*, 54–57.

Budd, J. (1995). An epistemological foundation for library and information science. *Library Quarterly, 65*(3), 295–318.

Burrell, G., & Morgan, G. (1988). *Sociological paradigms and organizational analysis*. Portsmouth, NH: Heinemann.

Cacioppo, J. T., & Petty, R. E. (1982). The need for cognition. *Journal of Personality and Social Psychology, 42*, 116–131.

Cacioppo, J. T., Petty, R. E., Feinstein, J. A., & Jarvis, W. B. (1996). Dispositional differences in cognitive motivation: the life and times of individuals varying in need for cognition. *Psychological Bulletin, 119*, 197–253.

Campbell, D., & Stanley, S. (1963). *Experimental and quasi-experimental designs for research.* Chicago: Rand McNally.

Campbell, J. (1982). *Grammatical man: Information, entropy, language, and life.* New York: Touchstone.

Canter, D., Rivers, R., & Storrs, G. (1985). Characterizing user navigation through complex data structures. *Behaviour and Information Technology, 9,* 93–102.

Cappella, J. (1977). Research methodology in communication: Review and methodology. In B. Ruben (Ed.), *Communication yearbook* (Vol. 1, pp. 37–53). New Brunswick, NJ: Transaction Press.

Carlson, D. K. (1999, October 4). *Poll shows continuing strong American reading habits.* Retrieved December 15, 2001, from Gallup Organization Web sites: http://www.gallup.com/poll/releases/pr991004b.asp.

Carter, R. (1965). Communication and affective relations. *Journalism Quarterly, 42,* 203–212.

Carter, R. (1973). *Communication as behavior.* Paper presented at the Annual Meeting of the Association for Education in Journalism, Fort Collins, CO.

Carter, R. (1978). A very peculiar horse race. In G. Bishop, R. Meadow, & M. Jackson-Beeck (Eds.), *The presidential debates.* New York: Praeger.

Case, D. O. (1986). Collection and organization of written information by social scientists and humanists: A review and exploratory study. *Journal of Information Science, 11*(3), 97–104.

Case, D. O. (1991). The collection and use of information by some American historians: A study of motives and methods. *The Library Quarterly, 61*(1), 61–82.

Case, D. O., Borgman, C. B., & Meadow, C. T. (1986). End-user information-seeking in the energy field: Implications for end-user access to DOE RECON databases. *Information Processing & Management, 22,* 299–308.

Case, D. O., & Rogers, E. M. (1987). The adoption and social impacts of information technology in U.S. agriculture. *The Information Society, 5*(2), 57–66.

Chaffee, S. (1991). *Communication concepts 1: Explication.* Newbury Park, CA: Sage.

Chang, S., & Rice, R. (1993). Browsing: A multidimensional framework. In M. Williams (Ed.), *Annual review of information science and technology* (Vol. 28, pp. 231–276). Medford, NJ: Learned Information.

Chatman, E. A. (1985). Information, mass media use, and the working poor. *Library and Information Science Research, 7,* 97–113.

Chatman, E. A. (1986). Diffusion theory: A review and test of a conceptual models in information diffusion. *Journal of the American Society for Information Science, 37,* 377–386.

Chatman, E. A. (1987). The information world of low-skilled workers. *Library and Information Science Research, 9,* 265–283.

Chatman, E. A. (1990). Alienation theory: Application of a conceptual framework to a study of information among janitors. *RQ, 29,* 355–368.

Chatman, E. A. (1991). Life in a small world: Applicability of gratification theory to information-seeking behavior. *Journal of the American Society for Information Science, 42,* 438–449.

Chatman, E. A. (1992). *The information world of retired women.* Westport, CT: Greenwood Press.

Chatman, E. A. (1996). The impoverished life-world of outsiders. *Journal of the American Society for Information Science, 47,* 193–206.

Chatman, E. A. (1999). A theory of life in the round. *Journal of the American Society for Information Science, 50,* 207–217.

Chatman, E. A., & Pendleton, V. (1995). Knowledge gap, information seeking and the poor. *The Reference Librarian, 49/50,* 135–145.

Cheatle, E. (1992). *Information needs of solicitors.* Unpublished Masters of Science, City University, London.

Chelton, M. K. (2001). Young adults as problems: How the social construction of a marginalized user category occurs. *Journal of Education for Library and Information Science, 42*(1), 4–11.

Chen, C., & Hernon, P. (1982). *Information-seeking: Assessing and anticipating user needs*. New York: Neal-Schuman.

Cherwitz, R., & Hikins, J. (1986). *Communication and knowledge: An investigation in rhetorical epistemology*. Columbia, SC: University of South Carolina Press.

Chew, F. (1994). The relationship of information needs to issue relevance and media use. *Journalism Quarterly, 71*, 676–688.

Chew, F., & Palmer, S. (1994). Interest, the knowledge gap, and television programming. *Journal of Broadcasting and Electronic Media, 38*, 271–287.

Childers, T., & Post, J. (1975). *The information-poor in America*. Metuchen, NJ: Scarecrow.

Choo, C. (1998). *The knowing organization: How organizations use information to construct meaning, create knowledge, and make decisions*. New York: Oxford University Press.

Choo, C., & Auster, E. (1993). Environmental scanning: Acquisition and use of information by managers. In M. Williams (Ed.), *Annual review of information science and technology* (Vol. 28, pp. 279–314). Medford, NJ: Learned Information.

Chu, C. (1999). Literary critics at work and their information needs: A research phases model. *Library and Information Science Research, 21*(2), 247–273.

Cicourel, A. V. (1964). *Method and measurement in sociology*. New York: Free Press.

Clarke, P. (1973). Teenagers' coorientation and information seeking about pop music. *American Behavioral Scientist, 16*, 551–566.

Clements, J. (1999, June 29). Investors' game: "The price is right." *Wall Street Journal*, p. C1.

Cobbledick, S. (1996). The information-seeking behavior of artists: Exploratory interviews. *Library Quarterly, 66*, 343–372.

Cohen, A. R., Stotland, E., & Wolfe, D. M. (1955). An experimental investigation of need for cognition. *Journal of Abnormal and Social Psychology, 51*, 291–294.

Cole, C. (1993). Shannon revisited: Information in terms of uncertainty. *Journal of the American Society for Information Science, 44*, 204–211.

Cole, C. (1994). Operationalizing the notion of information as a subjective construct. *Journal of the American Society for Information Science, 45*, 465–476.

Cole, C. (1998). Information acquisition in history Ph.D. students: Inferencing and the formation of knowledge structures. *The Library Quarterly, 68*(1), 33–54.

Cole, C., & Kuhlthau, C. (2000). *Information and information seeking of novice versus expert lawyers: how experts add value. The New Review of Information Behaviour Research, 1*, 103–116.

Cole, C. A., & Balasubramanian, S. (1993). Age differences in consumers' search for information: Public policy implications. *Journal of Consumer Research, 20*, 157–169.

Compaine, B. M. (Ed.). (2001). *Digital divide: Facing a crisis or creating a myth?* Cambridge, MA: MIT Press.

Connelly, D., Rich, E., Curley, S., & Kelly, J. (1990). Knowledge resource preference of family physicians. *The Journal of Family Practice, 30*(3), 353–359.

Cook, T., & Campbell, D. (1979). *Experimental and quasi-experimental designs for research*. Chicago: Rand McNally.

Cook, T., & Leviton, L. (1980). Reviewing the literature: A comparison of traditional methods with meta-analysis. *Journal of Personality, 48*, 449–472.

Cool, C. (2001). The concept of situation in information science. In M. Williams (Ed.), *Annual Review of Information Science and Technology*, (Vol. 35, pp. 5–42). Medford, NJ: Information Today, Inc.

Corcoran-Perry, S., & Graves, J. (1990). Supplemental-information-seeking behavior of cardiovascular nurses. *Research in Nursing & Health, 13*, 119–127.

Cornelius, I. V. (1996). *Meaning and method in information studies*. Norwood, NJ: Ablex.

Cove, J., & Walsh, B. (1988). Online text retrieval via browsing. *Information Processing and Management, 24*, 31–37.

Covell, D., Uman, G., & Manning, P. (1985). Information needs in office practice: Are they being met? *Annals of Internal Medicine, 103*, 596–599.

Crane, D. (1967). The gatekeepers of science: some factors affecting the selection of articles for scientific journals. *American Sociologist, 2*(4), 195–201.

Crane, D. (1971). Information needs and uses. In C. A. Cuadra & A. W. Luke (Eds.), *Annual review of information science and technology* (Vol. 6, pp. 3–39). Chicago: Encyclopaedia Britannica.

Crane, D. (1972). *Invisible colleges: diffusion of knowledge in scientific communities.* Chicago: University of Chicago Press.

Crawford, S. (1978). Information needs and uses. In M. E. Williams (Ed.), *Annual review of information science and technology* (Vol. 13, pp. 61–81). White Plains, NY: Knowledge Industry.

Creelman, J., & Harris, R. M. (1990). Coming out: The information needs of lesbians. *Collection Building, 10*(3/4), 37–41.

Cronin, B. (1984). *The citation process.* London: Taylor Graham.

Cronin, B., & Hert, C. A. (1995). Scholarly foraging and network discovery tools. *Journal of Documentation, 51*(4) 388–403.

Csikszentmihalyi, M. (1990). *Flow: The psychology of optimal experience.* New York: Harper & Row.

Cuadra, C., & Katter, R. (1967). Opening the black box of "relevance" *Journal of Documentation, 23*, 291–303.

Culnan, M. J. (1983). Environmental scanning: The effects of task complexity and sources accessibility on information gathering behavior. *Decision Sciences, 14*(2), 194–206.

Curry, A. (1994). *American Psycho:* a collection management survey in Canadian public libraries. *Library & Information Science Research, 16*, 201–217.

Cutler, N. E., & Danowski, J. A. (1980). Process gratification in aging cohorts. *Journalism Quarterly, 57*, 269–276.

Cyert, R., Simon, H., & Trow, D. (1956). Observation of a business decision. *Journal of Business, 29*, 237–248.

Daft, R., Sormunen, J., & Parks, D. (1988). Chief executive scanning, environmental characteristics, and company performance: An empirical study. *Strategic Management Journal, 9*, 123–139.

Daft, R. D., & Lengel, R. H. (1986). Organizational information requirements, media richness and structural design. *Management Science, 32*, 207–224.

Daniels, P. (1986). Cognitive models in information retrieval—An evaluative review. *Journal of Documentation, 42*(4), 272–304.

Darnton, R. (2000). Paris: The early Internet. *The New York Review of Books, 97*(12), 42–49.

Davis, D. A., Thomson, M. A., Oxman, A. D., & Haynes, R. B. (1995). Changing physician performance: A systematic review of the effect of continuing medical education strategies. *Journal of the American Medical Association, 274*(9), 700–705.

Davis, M. (1986). "That's classic!" The phenomenology and rhetoric of successful social theories. *Philosophy of the Social Sciences, 16*, 285–301.

Davis, R., & Bailey, C. (1964). *Bibliography of use studies* (Project No. 195). Philadelphia, PA: Drexel Institute of Technology.

Dee, C. (1993). Information needs of the rural physician: A descriptive study. *Bulletin of the American Medical Association, 81*(3), 259–264.

DeMey, M. (1982). *The cognitive paradigm: Cognitive science, a newly explored approach to the study of cognition applied in an analysis of science and scientific knowledge.* Dordrecht, The Netherlands/Boston: Reidel.

Derr, R. L. (1983). A conceptual analysis of information need. *Information Processing & Management, 19*, 273–278.

Derr, R. L. (1985). The concept of information in ordinary discourse. *Information Processing & Management, 21*(6), 489–499.

Dervin, B. (1976a). Strategies for dealing with human information needs: Information or communication? *Journal of Broadcasting, 20*(3), 324–351.

Dervin, B. (1976b). The everyday information needs of the average citizen: A taxonomy for analysis. In M. Kochen & J. Donahue (Eds.), *Information for the community* (pp. 23–35). Chicago: American Library Association.

Dervin, B. (1977). Useful theory for librarianship: Communication not information. *Drexel Library Quarterly, 13*, 16–32.

Dervin, B. (1983a). More will be less unless: The scientific humanization of information systems. *National Forum, 63*(3), 25–27.

Dervin, B. (1983b). Information as a user construct: The relevance of perceived information needs to synthesis and interpretation. In S. A. Ward & L. J. Reed (Eds.), *Knowledge structure and use: Implications for synthesis and interpretation* (pp. 153–184). Philadelphia: Temple University Press.

Dervin, B. (1989). Users as research inventions: How research categories perpetuate inequities. *Journal of Communication, 39*(3), 216–232.

Dervin, B. (1991). Comparative theory reconceptualized: From entities and states to processes and dynamics. Communication Theory, *1*, 59–69.

Dervin, B. (1992). From the mind's eye of the user: The sense-making qualitative-quantitative methodology. In J. Glazier & R. Powell (Eds.), *Qualitative research in information management* (pp. 61–84). Englewood, CO: Libraries Unlimited.

Dervin, B. (1997). Given a context by any other name: Methodological tools for taming the unruly beast. In P. Vakkari, R. Savolainen, & B. Dervin (Eds.), *Information seeking in context: Proceedings of a meeting in Finland 14–16 August 1996* (pp. 13–38). London: Taylor Graham.

Dervin, B. (1999). On studying information seeking methodologically: The implications of connecting metatheory to method. *Information Processing & Management, 35*, 727–750.

Dervin, B., & Dewdney, P. (1986). Neutral questioning: a new approach to the reference interview. *RQ, 25*, 506–513.

Dervin, B., Ellyson, S., Hawkes, G., Guagnano, G., & White, N. (1984). *Information needs of California— 1984.* Davis, CA: Institute of Governmental Affairs, University of California, Davis.

Dervin, B., & Greenberg, B. S. (1972). The communication environment of the urban poor. In F. Kline & P. Titchenor (Eds.), *Current perspectives in mass communication research* (pp. 195–235). Beverly Hills, CA: Sage.

Dervin, B., Jacobson, T., & Nilan, M. (1982). Measuring aspects of information seeking: A test of a quantitative/qualitative methodology. In M. Burgoon (Ed.), *Communication yearbook* (Vol. 6, pp. 419–445). Beverly Hills, CA: Sage.

Dervin, B., & Nilan, M. (1986). Information needs and uses. In M. Williams (Ed.), *Annual review of information science and technology* (Vol. 21, pp. 1–25). White Plains, NY: Knowledge Industry.

Dervin, B., Nilan, M., & Jacobson, T. (1982). Improving predictions of information use: A comparison of predictor types in a health communication setting. In M. Burgoon (Ed.), *Communication yearbook* (Vol. 5, pp. 807–830). Beverly Hills, CA: Sage.

Deutsch, K. W. (1963). *The nerves of government: Models of political communication and control.* New York: Free Press.

DeWeese, L. (1967). *A bibliography of use studies: A supplement to Davis, R. A. and Bailey, C. A. "Bibliography of use studies," Drexel Institute of Technology, 1964.* Layfayette, IN: Purdue University.

Dewey, J. (1933). *How we think.* Boston: D.C. Heath. (Originally published in 1910.)

Dewey, J. (1960). *On experience, nature, and freedom.* New York: Liberal Arts Press.

Diener, E., & Crandall, R. (1978). *Ethics in social and behavioral research.* Chicago: University of Chicago Press.

Dillman, D. (1978). *Mail and telephone surveys — The total design method.* New York: Wiley.

Donnelly, W. (1986). *The confetti generation: How the new communications technology is fragmenting America.* New York: Henry Holt.

Donohew, L., Nair, M., & Finn, S. (1984). Automaticity, arousal, and information exposure. In R. Bostrom & B. Westley (Eds.), *Communication yearbook* (Vol. 8, pp. 267–284). Beverly Hills, CA: Sage.

Donohew, L., & Tipton, L. (1973). A conceptual model of information seeking, avoiding and processing. In P. Clarke (Ed.), *New models for mass communication research* (pp. 243–269). Beverly Hills, CA: Sage.

Donohew, L., Tipton, L., & Haney, R. (1978). Analysis of information-seeking strategies. *Journalism Quarterly, 55,* 25–31.

Dorsch, J. L., & Pifalo, V. (1997). Information needs of rural health professionals: A retrospective study. *Bulletin of the Medical Library Association, 85,* 341–347.

Downey, M. (1993). *Information-seeking practices of artists in the academic community.* Unpublished M.L.S., Kent State University, Kent, OH.

Doyal, L., & Gough, I. (1984). A theory of human needs. *Critical Social Policy, 11,* 147–150.

Dozier, D., & Rice, R. (1984). Rival theories of electronic newsreading. In R. Rice (Ed.), *The new media* (pp. 103–128). Beverly Hills, CA: Sage.

Dresang, E. (1999). More research needed: Informal information-seeking behavior of youth on the Internet. *Journal of the American Society for Information Science, 50,* 1123–1124.

Dretske, F. I. (1981). *Knowledge and the flow of information.* Cambridge: MIT Press.

Dretske, F. I. (1983). Précis of "Knowledge & the flow of information." *Behavioral and Brain Sciences, 6,* 55–90.

Driscoll, J. M., & Lanzetta, J. T. (1965). Effects of two sources of uncertainty in decision making. *Psychological Reports, 17,* 635–648.

Duncan, R. (1972). Characteristics of organizational environments and perceived environmental uncertainty. *Administrative Science Quarterly, 17,* 313–327.

Dunn, W. (1983). Social network theory. *Knowledge: Creation, Diffusion, Utilization, 4*(3), 453–461.

Durkheim, E. (1951). *Suicide.* Glencoe, IL: Free Press. (Originally published in 1897).

Durlak, J. (1987). A typology of interactive media. In M. McLaughlin (Ed.), *Communication yearbook* (Vol. 10, pp. 743–757). Beverly Hills, CA: Sage.

Durrance, J. C. (1984). *Armed for action — Library response to citizen information needs.* New York: Neal-Schuman.

Durrance, J. C. (1988). Information needs: Old song, new tune, In: *Rethinking the library in the information age: A summary of issues in library research* (pp. 159–178). Washington, DC: Office of Library Programs, Office of Educational Research and Improvement, U.S. Department of Education, 1988.

Eisenberg, M. (1988). Measuring relevance judgments. *Information Processing & Management, 24,* 373–389.

Eisenberg, M., & Carol, B. (1988). Order effects: A study of the possible influence of presentation order on user judgments of document relevance. *Journal of the American Society for Information Science, 39,* 293–300.

Eliot, C. W. (1902). The divisions of a library into books in use, and books not in use. *Library Journal, 27*(July), 51–56.

Ellis, B. E. (1985). *Less than zero.* New York: Simon & Schuster.

Ellis, B. E. (1991). *American psycho.* New York: Vintage Books.

Ellis, D. (1989). A behavioural approach to information retrieval design. *Journal of Documentation, 45,* 171–212.

Ellis, D., Cox, D., & Hall, K. (1993). A comparison of the information seeking patterns of researchers in the physical and social sciences. *Journal of Documentation, 49,* 356–369.

Ely, J., Burch, R., & Vinson, D. (1992). The information needs of family physicians: Case-specific clinical questions. *The Journal of Family Practice, 35*(3), 265–269.

Enochsson, A. (2000, August 16–18). *Children choosing web pages.* Paper presented at the Information Seeking in Context, Göteborg, Sweden.

Epstein, B. (1973). *News from nowhere.* New York: Random House.

Erdelez, S. (1997). Information encountering: a conceptual framework for accidental information discovery. In P. Vakkari, R. Savolainen, & B. Dervin (Eds.), *Information seeking in context: Proceedings of a meeting in Finland 14–16 August 1996* (pp. 412–421). London: Taylor Graham.

Erdelez, S. (1999). Information encountering: it's more than bumping into information. *Bulletin of the American Society for Information Science, 25*(3), 25–29.

Erdelez, S., & Rioux, K. (2000). Sharing information encountered for others on the web. *The New Review of Information Behaviour Research, 1,* 219–234.

Fabritius, H. (1999). Triangulation as a multiperspective strategy in a qualitative study of information seeking behaviour of journalists. In T. D. Wilson & D. K. Allen (Eds.), *Information behaviour: Proceedings of the second international conference on research in information needs, seeking and use in different contexts, 13/15 August 1998,* Sheffield, UK (pp. 406–419). London: Taylor Graham.

Fabritius, H. (2000). *Materialised uses of information in journalistic item processing.* Paper presented at the Information Seeking in Context, Göteborg, Sweden.

Fairthorne, R. (1975). Information: One label, several bottles. In A. Debons & W. Cameron (Eds.), *Perspectives in information science* (pp. 65–73). Leyden, The Netherlands: Noordhof.

Farace, R. V., Monge, P. R., & Russell, H. M. (1977). *Communicating and organizing.* Reading, MA: Addison-Wesley.

Finn, S. (1985). Information-theoretic measures of reader enjoyment. *Written Communication, 2*(4), 358–376.

Finn, S. (1986). Unpredictability as a correlate of reader enjoyment of news articles. *Journalism Quarterly, 62,* 334–339.

Fischer, D. H. (1970). *Historians' fallacies.* New York: Harper & Row.

Fish, S. (1987). *Is there a text in this class? The authority of interpretive communities.* (2nd ed.). Cambridge, MA: Harvard University Press.

Fishbein, M., & Ajzen, I. (1975). *Belief, attitude, intention and behavior: An introduction to theory and research.* Reading, MA: Addison-Wesley.

Florio, E., & DeMartini, J. (1993). The use of information by policymakers at the local community level. *Knowledge: Creation, Diffusion, Utilization, 15,* 106–123.

Folkman, S. (1984). Personal control and stress and coping processes: A theoretical analysis. *Journal of Personality and Social Psychology, 46,* 839–852.

Ford, N. (1986). Psychological determinants of information needs: A small-scale study of higher education students. *Journal of Librarianship, 18,* 47–62.

Forsythe, D., Buchanan, B., Osheroff, J., & Miller, R. (1992). Expanding the concept of medical information: An observational study of physicians' information needs. *Computers and Biomedical Research, 25,* 181–200.

Foucault, M. (1972). *The order of things: An archaeology of the human sciences.* London: Tavistock.

Foucault, M. (1980). *Power/knowledge: Selected interviews and writings, 1972–1977.* London: Harvester Press.

Fox, C. J. (1983). *Information and misinformation.* Westport, CT: Greenwood Press.

Foxall, G. R. (1983). *Consumer choice.* New York: St. Martin's Press.

Freimuth, V. (1990). The chronically uninformed: Closing the knowledge gap in health. In E. Ray & L. Donohew (Eds.), *Communication and health: Systems and applications* (pp. 171–186). Hillsdale, NJ: Erlbaum.

Freimuth, V., Edgar, T., & Fitzpatrick, M. (1993). Introduction: the role of communication in health promotion. *Communication Research, 20,* 509–516.

Freimuth, V., Stein, J., & Kean, T. (1989). *Searching for health information: The Cancer Information Service model.* Philadelphia, PA: University of Pennsylvania Press.

Freud, S. (1922). *Beyond the pleasure principle* (C. Hubback, Trans.). London: International Psycho-Analytical Press.

Freud, S. (1960). *Jokes and their relation to the unconscious.* New York: Norton. (Originally published in 1905.)

Frey, D. (1982). Different levels of cognitive dissonance, information seeking, and information avoidance. *Journal of Personality and Social Psychology, 43,* 1175–1183.

Frey, D., & Rosch, M. (1984). Information seeking after decisions: the roles of novelty of information and decision reversibility. *Personality and Social Psychology Bulletin, 10,* 91–98.

Frické, M. (1997). Information using likeness measures. *Journal of the American Society for Information Science, 48,* 882–892.

Friestad, M., & Wright, P. (1994). The persuasion knowledge model: How people cope with persuasion attempts. *Journal of Consumer Research, 21,* 1–27.

Fritz, R. (1989). *The path of least resistance: learning to become the creative force in your own life.* (Rev. ed.). New York: Random House.

Froehlich, T. J. (1991). *Towards a better conceptual framework for understanding relevance for information science research.* Paper presented at the ASIS '91: Proceedings of the 54th Annual Meeting of the American Society for Information Science, Medford, NJ.

Froehlich, T. J. (1994). Relevance reconsidered—Towards an agenda for the 21st century: Introduction to special topic issue on relevance research. *Journal of the American Society for Information Science, 45,* 124–134.

Furse, D., Punj, G., & Stewart, D. (1984). A typology of individual search strategies among purchasers of new automobiles. *Journal of Consumer Research, 10,* 417–431.

Gadamer, H. G. (1976). *Philosophical hermeneutics* (D. Linge, Trans.). Berkeley, CA: University of California Press.

Gandy, O., Jr. (1993). *The panoptic sort: A political economy of personal information.* Boulder, CO: Westview Press.

Gantz, W., Fitzmaurice, M., & Fink, E. (1991). Assessing the active component of information-seeking. *Journalism Quarterly, 68,* 630–637.

Gardner, H. (1985). *The mind's new science: A history of the cognitive revolution.* New York: Basic Books.

Garfinkel, H. (1967). *Studies in ethnomethodology.* Englewood Cliffs, NJ: Prentice Hall.

Garner, W. R. (1962). *Uncertainty and structure as psychological concepts.* New York: Wiley.

Garrison, B. (2000). Online information use in newsrooms. *Convergence: The Journal of Research in New Media Technologies, 6,* 84–105.

Garvey, W. D. (1979). *Communication: The essence of science.* Oxford: Pergamon.

Gaziano, C. (1997). Forecast 2000: Widening knowledge gaps. *Journalism and Mass Communication Quarterly, 74*(2), 237–264.

Geertz, C. (1973). *The interpretation of culture.* New York: Basic Books.

Gelder, A. (1981). *A study of information needs and habits of different groups of users of employment law.* Unpublished Master's of Science, City University, London.

Gerstberger, P., & Allen, T. (1968). Criteria used by research and development engineers in the selection of an information source. *Journal of Applied Psychology, 52,* 272–279.

Gettier, E., Jr. (1963). Is justified true belief knowledge? *Analysis,* vol23, 121–123.

Getzels, J., & Csikszentmihalyi, M. (1976). *The creative vision: A longitudinal study of problem finding in art.* New York: Wiley.

Ghiselin, B. (Ed.). (1952). *The creative process: A symposium.* New York: New American Library.

316

Giddens, A. (1984). *The constitution of society: Outline of the theory of structuration.* Cambridge, England: Polity Press.

Giddens, A. (1989). The orthodox consensus and the emerging synthesis. In B. Dervin, L. Grossberg, B. O'Keefe, & E. Wartella (Eds.), *Rethinking communication: Paradigm Issues* (Vol. 1, pp. 53–65). Newbury Park, CA: Sage.

Glaser, B., & Strauss, A. (1967). *The discovery of grounded theory: Strategies for qualitative research.* Chicago: Aldine.

Glass, A., Holyoak, K., & Santa, J. (1979). *Cognition.* Reading, MA: Addison-Wesley.

Goffman, E. (1956). *The presentation of self in everyday life.* Harmondsworth: Pelican Books.

Goffman, E. (1975). *Frame analysis.* Harmondsworth: Pelican Books.

Goffman, E. (1983). Interaction order. *American Sociological Review, 48,* 1–17.

Goldman, A. I. (1970). *A theory of human action.* Princeton, NJ: Princeton University Press.

Goldstein, W. M., & Hogarth, R. M. (1997). *Research on judgment and decision-making: Currents, connections and controversies.* New York: Cambridge University Press.

Goren, D. (1989). Journalists as scientists or prophets? Comments on Katz. *American Behavioral Scientist, 33,* 251–254.

Gorman, P. (1995). Information needs of physicians. *Journal of the American Society for Information Science, 46,* 737–742.

Gorman, P. (1999). Information seeking of primary care physicians: Conceptual models and empirical studies. In T. D. Wilson & D. K. Allen (Eds.), *Information behaviour: Proceedings of the second international conference on research in information needs, seeking and use in different contexts, 13/15 August 1998,* Sheffield, UK (pp. 226–240). London: Taylor Graham.

Gorman, P., & Helfand, M. (1995). Information seeking in primary care: How physicians choose which clinical questions to pursue and which to leave unanswered. *Medical Decision Making, 15,* 113–119.

Goslee, S. (1998). *Losing ground bit by bit. Low-income communities in the information age.* Washington, DC: Benton Foundation.

Gould, C. (1988). *Information needs in the humanities: An assessment.* Stanford, CA: Research Libraries Group.

Gould, C., & Handler, G. (1989). *Information needs in the social sciences: An assessment.* Stanford, CA: Research Libraries Group.

Gould, C., & Pearce, K. (1991). *Information needs in the sciences: An assessment.* Mountain View, CA: Research Libraries Group.

Gourash, N. (1978). Help seeking: A review of the literature. *American Journal of Community Psychology, 6,* 413–423.

Graber, D. (1984). *Processing the news: How people tame the information tide.* New York: Longman.

Graber, D. (1989). Content and meaning: What's it all about? *American Behavioral Scientist, 33,* 144–151.

Gralewska-Vickery, A. (1976). Communication and information needs of earth science engineers. *Information Processing and Management, 12*(4), 251–282.

Granovetter, M. S. (1973). The strength of weak ties. *American Journal of Sociology, 78,* 1360–1380.

Granovetter, M. S. (1982). The strength of weak ties: A network theory revisited. In P. Marsden & N. Lin (Eds.), *Social structure and network analysis* (pp. 105–130). Beverly Hills, CA: Sage.

Gratch, B. (1990). Exploring the principle of least effort and its value to research. *C&RL News, 51,* 727–728.

Green, A. (1990). What do we mean by user needs? *British Journal of Academic Librarianship, 5,* 65–78.

Greenberg, B., Bowes, J., & Dervin, B. (1970). Communication and related behaviors of a sample of Cleveland Black adults. Project CUP, Report No. 13, *Communication among the urban poor. East Lansing, MI: Michigan State University.*

Grunig, J. (1989). Publics, audience and market segments: Segmentation principles for campaigns. In C. Salmon (Ed.), *Information campaigns: Balancing social values and social change* (pp. 199–228). Beverly Hills, CA: Sage.

Gundry, L. K., & Rousseau, D. M. (1994). Critical incidents in communicating culture to newcomers. *Human Relations, 47,* 1063–1087.

Habermas, J. (1979). *Communication and the evolution of society* (T. McCarthy, Trans.). Boston: Beacon Press.

Habermas, J. (1984). *Theory of communicative action. Reason and rationalization of society* (T. McCarthy, Trans.). (Vol. 1). Boston: Beacon Press.

Habermas, J. (1987). *Theory of communicative action. Lifeworld and system: A critique of functionalist reason.* (Vol. 2). New York: Polity Press.

Hagen, I. (1997). Communicating to an ideal audience: News and the notion of the "informed citizen." *Political Communication, 14,* 405–419.

Haig, P. (1993). Nursing journals: Are nurses using them? *Nursing Standard, 8*(1), 22–25.

Hainsworth, M. M. (1992). *Information seeking behavior of judges.* Unpublished doctoral dissertation, Florida State University, Tallahassee.

Hampshire, S. (1982). *Thought and action.* Notre Dame, IN: University of Notre Dame Press.

Hancock-Beaulieu, M. (1990). Evaluating the impact of an online library catalogue in subject searching behavior at the catalogue and at the shelves. *Journal of Documentation, 46,* 318–338.

Hardy, A. (1982). The selection of channels when seeking information: cost/benefit vs. least effort. *Information Processing & Management, 18,* 289–293.

Harris, R. M. (1988). The information needs of battered women. *RQ, 27,* 62–70.

Harris, R. M., & Dewdney, P. (1994). *Barriers to information: how formal help systems fail battered women.* Westport, CT: Greenwood Press.

Harter, S. P. (1992). Psychological relevance and information science. *Journal of the American Society for Information Science, 43,* 602–615.

Haug, J. D. (1997). Physicians' preferences for information sources: A meta analytic study. *Bulletin of the Medical Library Association, 85*(3), 223–232.

Hauser, J., Urban, G., & Weinberg, B. (1993). How consumers allocate their time when searching for information. *Journal of Marketing Research, 30,* 452–466.

Hayes, R. (1993). Measurement of information. *Information Processing & Management, 29,* 1–11.

Heap, J. (1975). What are sense making practices? *Sociological Inquiry, 46,* 107–115.

Heeter, C., & Greenberg, B. (1985). Profiling the zappers. *Journal of Advertising Research, 25*(2), 15–19.

Hempel, C. (1952). *Fundamentals of concept formation in empirical science. International Encyclopedia of United Science,* II, No. 7. Chicago: University of Chicago Press.

Henning, B., & Vorderer, P. (2001). Psychological escapism: Predicting the amount of television viewing by need for cognition. *Journal of Communication, 51*(1), 100–120.

Herner, S. (1954). The information-gathering habits of workers in pure and applied science. *Industrial and Engineering Chemistry, 46,* 228–236.

Herner, S. (1970). Browsing. In A. Kent & H. Lancour (Eds.), *Encyclopedia of library and information science* (Vol. 3, pp. 408–415). New York: Dekker.

Herner, S., & Herner, M. (1967). Information needs and uses in science and technology. In C. A. Cuadra (Ed.), *Annual review of information science and technology* (Vol. 2, pp. 1–34). Chicago: Encyclopaedia Britannica.

Hernon, P. (1984). Information needs and gathering patterns of academic social scientists, with special emphasis given to historians and their use of U.S. government publications. *Government Information Quarterly, 1,* 401–429.

Hersberger, J. (2001). *Everyday information needs and information sources of homeless parents. The New Review of Information Behaviour Research, 2,* 119–134.

318

References

Hertzum, M., & Pejtersen, A. M. (2000). The information-seeking practices of engineers: searching for documents as well as people. *Information Processing & Management, 36*, 761–778.

Hewins, E. T. (1990). Information need and use studies. In M. E. Williams (Ed.), *Annual review of information science and technology* (Vol. 25, pp. 145–172). New York: Elsevier.

Higgins, M. (1999). Meta-information, and time: factors in human decision making. *Journal of the American Society for Information Science, 50*, 132–139.

Hirschman, E. C., & Holbrook, M. B. (1986). Expanding the ontology and methodology of research on the consumption experience. In D. Brinberg & R. Lutz (Eds.), *Perspectives on methodology in consumer research* (pp. 213–252). New York: Springer-Verlag.

Hirsh, S. (1997). How do children find information on different types of tasks? Children's use of the science library catalog. *Library Trends, 45*, 725–746.

Hogeweg de Haart, H. P. (1981). *Characteristics of social science information.* Budapest, Hungary: Hungarian Academy of Sciences/International Federation for Documentation.

Holland, M. P., & Powell, C. K. (1995). A longitudinal survey of the information seeking and use habits of some engineers. *College and Research Libraries, 55*(1, 7–15.

Holmöv, P. (1982). Motivation for reading different context domains. *Communication Research, 9*, 314–320.

Holt, D. (1995). How consumers consume: A typology of consumption practices. *Journal of Consumer Research, 22*, 1–16.

Horkheimer, M. (1972). *Critical theory: Selected essays.* Translated by M.J. O'Connell. New York: Herder & Herder.

Hornik, R. (1989). The knowledge-behavior gap in public information campaigns:. development communication view. In C. Salmon (Ed.), *Information campaigns: Balancing social values and social change* (pp. 113–138). Beverly Hills: Sage.

Howard, D. L. (1994). Pertinence as reflected in personal constructs. *Journal of the American Society for Information Science, 45*, 172–185.

Hsia, H. (1968). Output, error, equivocation, and recalled information in auditory, visual, and audiovisual information processing with constraint and noise. *Journal of Communication, 18*, 325–353.

Hsia, H. J. (1987). The health-information seeking behavior of the Mexican-Americans in West Texas. *Health Marketing Quarterly, 4*, 107–117.

Huberman, B., Pirollis, P., Pitkow, J., & Lukose, R. (1998). Strong regularities in World Wide Web surfing. *Science, 280*, 95–97.

Hyman, H. H., & Sheatsley, P. B. (1947). Some reasons why information campaigns fail. *Public Opinion Quarterly, 11*, 412–423.

Ignatieff, M. (1984). *The needs of strangers.* London: Chatto and Windus.

Ingwersen, P. (1996). Cognitive perspectives of information retrieval interaction: Elements of a cognitive IR theory. *Journal of Documentation, 52*, 3–50.

Iser, W. (1978). *The act of reading.* Baltimore: Johns Hopkins University.

Jacobson, T. L. (1991). Sense-making in a database environment. *Information Processing & Management, 27*(6), 647–657.

Jacoby, J. (1984). Perspectives on information overload. *Journal of Consumer Research, 10*, 432–435.

Jacoby, J., Speller, D. D., & Berning, C. A. (1974). Brand choice behavior as a function of information load: Replication and extension. *Journal of Consumer Research, 1*, 33–42.

Janes, J., & McKinney, R. (1992). Relevance judgments of actual users and secondary judges: A comparative study. *Library Quarterly, 62*(2), 150–168.

Janesick, V. J. (1998). The dance of qualitative research design: Metaphor, methodolatry, and meaning. In N. Denzin & Y. Lincoln (Eds.), *Strategies of qualitative inquiry* (pp. 35–55). Thousand Oaks, CA: Sage.

Järvelin, K., & Vakkari, P. (1993). The evolution of library and information science 1965–1985: A content analysis of journal articles. *Information Processing & Management, 29*, 129–144.

Jiao, Q., & Onwuegbuzie, A. (1997). Antecedents of library anxiety. *The Library Quarterly, 67*, 372–389.

Johnson, J. D. (1996). *Information seeking: An organizational dilemma.* Westport, CT: Quorum Books.

Johnson, J. D. (1997). *Cancer-related information seeking.* Cresskill, NJ: Hampton Press.

Johnson, M. (1987). *The body in the mind: The bodily basis of meaning, imagination, and reason.* Chicago: University of Chicago Press.

Jones, S. G. (Ed.). (1999). *Doing Internet research. Critical issues and methods for examining the net.* Thousand Oaks, CA: Sage.

Julien, H. (1996). A content analysis of the recent information needs and uses literature. *Library and Information Science Research, 18*, 53–65.

Julien, H. (1998). Adolescent career decision making and the potential role of the public library. *Public Libraries, 37*(6), 376–381.

Julien, H. (1999). Barriers to adolescent information seeking for career decision making. *Journal of the American Society for Information Science, 50*, 38–48.

Julien, H., & Duggan, L. (2000). A longitudinal analysis of the information needs and uses literature. *Library and Information Science Research, 22*, 291–309.

Just, W. S. (1968). *To what end? Report from Vietnam.* Boston: Houghton Mifflin.

Kafai, Y. B., & Bates, M. (1997). Internet web-searching in the elementary classroom: Building a foundation for information literacy. *School Library Media Quarterly, 25*, 103–111.

Katz, D., & Kahn, R. (1978). *The social psychology of organizations* (2nd ed.). New York: Wiley.

Katz, E. (1989). Journalists as scientists. *American Behavioral Scientist, 33*, 238–246.

Katz, E., Blumler, J., & Gurevitch, M. (1974). Utilization of mass communication by the individual. In J. Blumler & E. Katz (Eds.), *The uses of mass communication: Current perspectives on uses and gratifications research.* Beverly Hills, CA: Sage.

Katz, E., & Foulkes, D. (1962). On the use of the mass media as escape: Clarification of a concept. *Public Opinion Quarterly, 26*, 377–388.

Katzer, J., Cook, K., & Crouch, W. (1998). *Evaluating information: A guide for users of social science research* (4th ed.). Boston: McGraw-Hill.

Kay, H. (1955). Toward an understanding of news-reading behavior. *Journalism Quarterly, 32*, 15–32, 94.

Keegan, W. (1974). Multinational scanning: A study of the information sources utilized by headquarters executives in multinational companies. *Administrative Science Quarterly, 19*, 411–421.

Kefalas, A., & Schoderbek, P. (1973). Scanning the business environment — Some empirical results. *Decision Sciences, 4*(1), 63–74.

Kellermann, K., & Reynolds, R. (1990). When ignorance is bliss: The role of motivation to reduce uncertainty in uncertainty reduction theory. *Human Communication Research, 17*, 5–75.

Kelly, G. (1963). *A theory of personality: The psychology of personal constructs.* New York: Norton.

Kemp, D. (1974). Relevance, pertinence and information system development. *Information Storage and Retrieval, 10*, 37–47.

Kenner, H. (1986). Neatness doesn't count after all. *Discover, 7*(4), 86–93.

Kerlinger, F. (1973). *Foundations of behavioral research.* New York: Holt, Rinehart and Winston.

Kiesler, S., & Sproull, L. (1982). Managerial response to changing environments: Perspectives on problem sensing from social cognition. *Administrative Science Quarterly, 27*, 548–570.

King, D., Casto, J., & Jones, H. (1994). *Communication by engineers: A literature review of engineer's information needs, seeking processes, and use.* Washington, DC: Council on Library Resources.

King, D. W., & Tenopir, C. (2001). Using and reading scholarly literature. In M. Williams (Ed.), *Annual Review of Information Science and Technology,* (Vol. 34, pp. 423–478). Medford, NJ: Information Today, Inc.

Klapp, O. (1982). Meaning lag in the information society. *Journal of Communication, 32*(2), 56–66.

Klapper, J. (1960). *The effects of mass communication.* Glencoe, IL: Free Press.

Kleiber, C., Montgomery, L. A., & Craft-Rosenberg, M. (1995). Information needs of the siblings of critically ill children. *Childrens Health Care, 24,* 47−60.

Knorr-Cetina, K. D., & Mulkay, M. J. (Eds.). (1983). *Science observed: Perspectives on the social study of science.* London: Sage.

Krikelas, J. (1983). Information-seeking behavior: patterns and concepts. *Drexel Library Quarterly, 19,* 5−20.

Krippendorff, K. (1980). *Content analysis: An introduction to its methodology.* Beverly Hills, CA: Sage.

Krippendorff, K. (1984). Paradox and information. In B. Dervin & M. Voigt (Eds.), *Progress in communication sciences* (Vol. 5, pp. 45−72). Norwood, NJ: Ablex.

Krueger, R. (1988). *Focus groups: A practical guide for applied research.* Newbury Park, CA: Sage.

Kubey, R., & Csikszentmihalyi, M. (1990). *Television and the quality of life: How viewing shapes everyday experience.* Hillsdale, NJ: Erlbaum.

Kubey, R., Larson, R., & Csikszentmihalyi, M. (1996). Experience sampling method applications to communication research questions. *Journal of Communication, 46*(2, 99−120.

Kuhlthau, C. (1988a). Developing a model of the library search process: Cognitive and affective aspects. *Reference Quarterly, 28,* 232−242.

Kuhlthau, C. (1988b). Longitudinal case studies of the information search process of users in libraries. *Library and Information Science Research, 10,* 251−304.

Kuhlthau, C. C. (1991). Inside the search process: Information seeking from the user's perspective. *Journal of the American Society for Information Science, 42,* 361−371.

Kuhlthau, C. C. (1993a). *Seeking meaning: A process approach to library and Information services.* Norwood, NJ: Ablex.

Kuhlthau, C. C. (1993b). A principle of uncertainty for information seeking. *Journal of Documentation, 49,* 339−355.

Kuhlthau, C. C. (1997). The influence of uncertainty on the information seeking behavior of a securities analyst. In P. Vakkari, R. Savolainen, & B. Dervin (Eds.), *Information seeking in context: Proceedings of a meeting in Finland 14−16 August 1996.* London: Taylor Graham.

Kuhlthau, C. C. (1999). The role of experience in the information search process of an early career information worker: Perceptions of uncertainty, complexity, construction, and sources. *Journal of the American Society for Information Science, 50,* 399−412.

Kuhn, T. (1962). *The structure of scientific revolutions.* Chicago: University of Chicago Press.

Lachman, R., Lachman, J. L., & Butterfield, E. C. (1979). *Cognitive psychology and information processing: An introduction.* Hillsdale, NJ: Erlbaum.

Langer, E. J. (1978). Rethinking the role of thought in social interaction. In J. Harvey, W. Ickes, & R. Kidd (Eds.), *New directions in attribution research* (Vol. 2). Hillsdale, NJ: Erlbaum.

Large, A., Beheshti, J., & Breuleux, A. (1998). Information seeking in a multimedia environment by primary school students. *Library & Information Science Research, 20,* 343−376.

Lasch, C. (1995). *The revolt of the elites and the betrayal of democracy.* New York: Norton.

Latour, B., & Woolgar, S. (1979). *Laboratory life: The social construction of scientific facts.* Beverly Hills, CA: Sage.

Layne, S. S. (1994). Artists, art historians, and visual art information. *Reference Librarian, 47,* 23−36.

Lazersfeld, P. F. (1941). Remarks on administrative and critical communications research. *Studies in Philosophy and Social Science, 9*(1), 2−16.

Leckie, G. J. (1996). Female farmers and the social construction of access to agricultural information. *Library & Information Science Research, 18,* 297−321.

Leckie, G. J., Pettigrew, K. E., & Sylvain, C. (1996). Modeling the information seeking of professionals: A general model derived from research on engineers, health care professionals and lawyers. *Library Quarterly, 66,* 161−193.

Lederer, K., Galtung, J., & Antal, D. (Eds.). (1980). *Human needs, a contribution to the current debate.* Cambridge, MA: Oelgeschlagen, Gunn & Hain.

Lehmann, D. (1999). Introduction: Consumer behavior and Y2K. *Journal of Marketing, 63,* 14−18.

Leung, L., & Wei, R. (1999a). The gratifications of pager use: Sociability, information-seeking, entertainment, utility, and fashion and status. *Telematics and Informatics, 15*(4, 253−264.

Leung, L., & Wei, R. (1999b). Seeking news via the pager: An expectancy-value study. *Journal of Broadcasting and Electronic Media, 43*, 299−315.

Levine, M. (1969). An essay on browsing. *RQ, 9*(1, 35−36, *93*.

Levitan, K. B. (1980). Applying a holistic framework to synthesize information science research. In B. Dervin & M. Voigt (Eds.), *Progress in communication science* (Vol. 2, pp. 241−273). Norwwod, NJ: Ablex.

Levy, M., & Windahl, S. (1984). Audience activity and gratifications: A conceptual clarification and exploration. *Communication Research, 11*, 51−78.

Lewin, K. (1943). Forces behind food habits and methods of change. *Bulletin of the National Research Council, 108*, 65.

Leydesdorff, L. (1998). Theories of citation? *Scientometrics, 43*, 5−25.

Liebnau, J., & Backhouse, J. (1990). *Understanding information.* London: Macmillan.

Lin, C. (1993). Modeling the gratification-seeking process of television viewing. *Human Communication Research, 20*, 224−244.

Lin, N., & Garvey, W. D. (1972). Information needs and uses. In C. Cuadra & A. W. Luke (Eds.), *Annual review of information science and technology* (Vol. 7, pp. 5−37). Washington, DC: American Society for Information Science.

Lincoln, Y. S., & Guba, E. G. (1985). *Naturalistic inquiry.* Newbury Park, CA: Sage.

Lindlof, T. (1995). *Qualitative communication research methods.*Thousand Oaks, CA: Sage.

Line, M. B. (1974). Draft definitions: Information and library needs, wants, demands and uses. *Aslib Proceedings, 27*(7, 87−97.

Linz, C. (1992). Setting the stage: Facts and figures. In J. A. Krentz (Ed.), *Dangerous men and adventurous women: Romantic writers on the appeal of the romance* (pp. 11−14). Philadelphia: University of Pennsylvania Press.

Lipetz, B. -A. (1970). Information needs and uses. In C. A. Cuadra & A. W. Luke (Eds.), *Annual review of information science and technology* (Vol. 5, pp. 3−32). Chicago: Encyclopaedia Brittanica.

Littlejohn, S. W. (1983). *Theories of human communication.* Belmont, CA: Wadsworth.

Losee, R. (1997). A discipline independent definition of information. *Journal of the American Society for Information Science, 48*, 254−269.

Louis, M. (1980). Surprise and sensemaking: What newcomers experience in entering unfamiliar organizational settings. *Administrative Science Quarterly, 25*, 226−251.

Lunt, P., & Livingstone, S. (1996). Rethinking the focus group in media and communications research. *Journal of Communication, 46*(2), 79−98.

Machlup, F. (1983). Semantic quirks in studies of information. In F. Machlup & U. Mansfield (Eds.), *The study of information: Interdisciplinary messages* (pp. 641−672). New York: Wiley.

Machlup, F., & Mansfield, U. (1983). Cultural diversity in studies of information. In F. Machlup & U. Mansfield (Eds.), *The study of information: Interdisciplinary messages.* New York: Wiley.

MacKay, D. (1969). *Information, mechanism and meaning.* Cambridge, MA: MIT Press.

Majid, S., Anwar, M., & Eisenschitz, T. (2000). Information needs and information seeking behavior of agricultural scientists in Malaysia. *Library and Information Science Research, 22*, 145−163.

Mann, T. (1993). The principle of least effort, *Library research models: A guide to classification, cataloging and computers* (pp. 91−101). New York: Oxford University Press.

Mansfield, R. S., & Busse, T. V. (1981). *The psychology of creativity and discovery.* Chicago: Nelson-Hall.

Marcella, R., & Baxter, G. (2000). Information need, information seeking behaviour and participation, with special reference to needs related to citizenship: Results of a national survey. *Journal of Documentation, 56*, 136−160.

322

March, J. (1994). *A primer on decision making: How decisions happen.* New York: Free Press.

March, J., & Shapira, Z. (1992). Behavioral decision theory and organizational decision theory. In M. Zey (Ed.), *Decision making: Alternatives to rational choice models* (pp. 273–303). Newbury Park, CA:Sage.

Marchionini, G. (1995). *Information seeking in electronic environments.* New York: Cambridge University Press.

Marcuse, H. (1964). *One-dimensional man.* Boston: Beacon Press.

Marshall, J. (1993). Issues in clinical information delivery. *Library Trends, 42*(1), 83–107.

Martyn, J. (1974). Information needs and uses. In M. Williams (Ed.), *Annual review of information science and technology* (Vol. 9, pp. 3–23). Washington, DC: American Society for Information Science.

Maslow, A. H. (1963). The need to know and the fear of knowing. *The Journal of General Psychology, 68*, 111–125.

Maslow, A. H. (1970). *Motivation and personality* (2nd ed.). New York: Harper & Row.

Masterman, M. (1970). The nature of a paradigm. In I. Lakatos & A. Musgrave (Eds.), *Criticism and the growth of knowledge: Proceedings of the International Colloquium in the Philosophy of Science, London, 1965* (Vol. 4). Cambridge, England: Cambridge University Press.

McCombs, M. (1972). Mass communication in political campaigns: Information, gratification, and persuasion. In F. Kline & P. Tichenor (Eds.), *Current perspectives in mass communication research.* Beverly Hills, CA: Sage.

McCracken, G. (1987). Advertising: meaning or information? In M. Wallendorf & P. Anderson (Eds.), *Advances in consumer research* (Vol. 14, pp. 121–124). Provo, UT: Association for Consumer Research.

McCreadie, M., & Rice, R. (1999). Trends in analyzing access to information. Part I: Cross-disciplinary conceptualizations of access. *Information Processing and Management, 35*, 45–76.

McQuail, D., & Gurevitch, M. (1974). Explaining audience behavior: Three approaches considered. In J. Blumler & E. Katz (Eds.), *The uses of mass communication: Current perspectives on uses and gratifications research* (pp. 287–302). Beverly Hills, CA: Sage.

McQuail, D., & Windahl, S. (1993). *Communication models for the study of mass communication* (2nd ed.). New York: Longman Publishing.

Meho, L. I., & Haas, S. W. (2001). Information-seeking behavior and use of social science faculty studying stateless nations: A case study. *Library & Information Science Research, 23*, 5–25.

Meier, R. (1963). Communication overload: Proposals from the study of a university library. *Administrative Science Quarterly, 7*, 521–544.

Mellon, C. (1986). Library anxiety: A grounded theory and its development. *College and Research Libraries, 47*, 160–165.

Mendelsohn, H. (1966). *Mass entertainment.* New Haven, CT: College and University Press.

Mendelsohn, H. (1973). Some reasons why information campaigns can succeed. *Public Opinion Quarterly, 37*, 50–61.

Menzel, H. (1960). *Review of studies in the flow of information among scientists.* New York: Columbia University Bureau of Applied Social Research.

Menzel, H. (1964). The information needs of current scientific research. *Library Quarterly, 34*, 4–19.

Menzel, H. (1966a). Can science information needs be ascertained empirically? In L. Thayer (Ed.), *Communications: Concepts and perspectives* (pp. 279–295). Washington, DC: Spartan Books.

Menzel, H. (1966b). Information needs and uses in science and technology. In C. A. Cuadra & A. W. Luke (Eds.), *Annual review of information science and technology* (Vol. 1, pp. 41–69). Chicago: Encyclopaedia Britannica.

Merton, R. (1968). *Social theory and social structure.* (2nd ed.). New York: Free Press.

Merton, R. (1973). *The sociology of science: Theoretical and empirical investigations.* Chicago: University of Chicago Press.

Merton, R., Fiske, M., & Kendall, P. (1956). *The focused interview*. New York: The Free Press.

Metoyer-Duran, C. (1991). Information seeking behavior of gatekeepers in ethnolinguistic communities: Overview of a taxonomy. *Library & Information Science Research, 13,* 319–346.

Metoyer-Duran, C. (1993). Information gatekeepers. In M. Williams (Ed.), *Annual review of information science and technology* (Vol. 28, pp. 111–150). Medford, NJ: Learned Information.

Mick, D., & Buhl, C. (1992). A meaning-based model of advertising experiences. *Journal of Consumer Research, 19,* 317–338.

Mick, D., & DeMoss, M. (1990). Self-gifts: Phenomenological insights from four contexts. *Journal of Consumer Research, 17,* 322–332.

Miller, G. A. (1968). Psychology and information. *American Documentation, 19,* 286–289.

Miller, G. A. (1983a). Information theory in psychology. In M. Machlup & U. Mansfield (Eds.), *The study of information: Interdisciplinary messages* (pp. 493–496). New York: Wiley.

Miller, G. A. (1983b). Informavores. In F. Machlup & U. Mansfield (Eds.), *The study of information: Interdisciplinary messages* (pp. 111–113). New York: Wiley.

Miller, G. A., Galanter, E., & Pribram, K. H. (1960). *Plans and the structure of behavior.* New York: Holt.

Miller, J. G. (1960). Information input overload and psychopathology. *American Journal of Psychiatry, 116,* 695–704.

Miller, J. G. (1978). *Living systems.* New York: McGraw-Hill.

Mintzberg, H. (1975). *Impediments to the use of management information.* New York: National Association of Accountants.

Mizzaro, S. (1998). Relevance: The whole history. In T. Hahn & M. Buckland (Eds.), *Historical studies in information science* (pp. 221–243). Medford, NJ: Information Today.

Mokros, H., Mullins, L., & Saracevic, T. (1995). Practice and personhood in professional interaction: Social identities and information needs. *Library and Information Science Research, 17,* 237–257.

Mooers, C. N. (1960). Mooers' law, or why some information systems are used and others are not. *American Documentation, 11*(3), (unpaged editorial).

Morgan, M., & Shanahan, J. (1997). Two decades of cultivation research: an appraisal and meta-analysis. In B. Burleson (Ed.), *Communication yearbook* (Vol. 20, pp. 1–45). Thousand Oaks, CA: Sage.

Morowitz, H. (1991). *The thermodynamics of pizza.* New Brunswick, NJ: Rutgers University Press.

Morris, R. C. T. (1994). Toward a user-centered information service. *Journal of the American Society for Information Science, 45,* 20–30.

Morrison, E. W. (1993). Newcomer information seeking: Exploring types, modes, sources, and outcomes. *Academy of Management Journal, 36,* 557–589.

Muha, C., Smith, K., Baum, S., Ter Maat, J., & Ward, J. (1998). The use and selection of sources in information seeking: The Cancer Information Service experience. Part 8. *Journal of Health Communication, 3*(Suppl.), 109–120.

Mullaly-Quijas, P., Ward, D., & Woefl, N. (1994). Using focus groups to discover health professionals' information needs: A regional marketing study. *Bulletin of the Medical Library Association, 82*(3), 305–311.

Mullins, N. (1973). *Theories and theory groups in contemporary American sociology.* New York: Harper Row.

Murdock, G., & Golding, P. (1989). Information poverty and political inequality: Citizenship in the age of privatized communications. *Journal of Communication, 39*(3), 180–195.

Nauta, D. (1972). *The meaning of information.* The Hague: Mouton.

Nelson, C. E., & Pollock, D. K. (1970). *Communication among scientists and engineers.* Lexington, MA: Heath Lexington Books.

Newhagen, J. (1994). Media use and political efficacy: The suburbanization of race and class. *Journal of the American Society for Information Science, 45,* 386–394.

Newhagen, J. (1997). The role of feedback in the assessment of news. *Information Processing & Management, 33*, 583–594.

Nicholas, D., & Williams, P. (1999). The changing information environment: The impact of the Internet on information seeking behavior in the media. In T. D. Wilson & D. K. Allen (Eds.), *Information behaviour: Proceedings of the second international conference on research in information needs, seeking and use in different contexts, 13/15 August 1998*, Sheffield, UK (pp. 451–462). London: Taylor Graham.

Nissenbaum, S. (1989). The month before "The Night before Christmas." In B. P. Lynch (Ed.), *Humanists at work: Disciplinary perspectives and personal reflections* (pp. 43–78). Chicago: University of Illinois at Chicago, Institute for the Humanities and the University Library.

Noble, R., & Coughlin, C. (1997). Information-seeking practices of Canadian academic chemists: A study of information needs and use of resources in chemistry. *Canadian Journal of Communication, 20*(3/4), 49–60.

Nørretranders, T. (1998). *The user illusion: Cutting consciousness down to size.* (J. Sydenham, Trans.). New York: Viking (Originally published in 1991).

North American Aviation. (1966). *Final report DOD user-needs study, Phase II; Flow of scientific and technical information within the defense industry. Volumes I–III.* Anaheim, CA: North American Aviation, Autonetics Division.

O'Connor, B. (1993). Productive browsing: A framework for seeking functional information. *Knowledge: Creation, Diffusion and Utilization, 15*, 211–232.

O'Connor, J. (1968). Some questions concerning "information need." *American Documentation, 19*(2), 200–203.

O'Meara, J. (1989). Anthropology as empirical science. *American Anthropologist, 91*, 354–369.

O'Reilly, C., III. (1980). Individuals and information overload: Is more necessarily better? *Academy of Management Journal, 23*(4), 684–696.

Ocholla, D. (1996). Information-seeking behaviour by academics: A preliminary study. *International Information & Library Review, 28*, 345–358.

Ocholla, D. (1999). Insights into information-seeking and communicating behaviour of academics. *International Information & Library Review, 31*, 119–143.

Orr, R. (1970). The scientist as information processor: A conceptual model illustrated with data on variables related to library utilization. In C. Nelson & D. Pollock (Eds.), *Communication among scientists and engineers* (pp. 143–189). Lexington, MA: D.C. Heath.

Osheroff, J., Forsythe, D., Buchanan, B., Bankowitz, R., Blumenfeld, B., & Miller, R. (1991). Physicians' information needs: an analysis of questions posed during clinical teaching. *Annals of Internal Medicine, 114*, 576–581.

Ostroff, C., & Kozlowski, S. W. (1992). Organizational socialization as a learning process: The role of information acquisition. *Personnel Psychology, 45*, 849–874.

Otike, J. (1999). The information needs and seeking habits of lawyers in England: A pilot study. *International Information & Library Review, 31*, 19–39.

Overhage, C. F., & Harman, R. J. (1965). *Intrex: Report of a planning conference on information transfer experiments.* Cambridge, MA: MIT Press.

Ozanne, J. L., Brucks, M., & Grewal, D. (1992). A study of information search behavior during the categorization of new products. *Journal of Consumer Research, 18*, 452–463.

Paisley, W. J. (1965). *The flow of (behavioral) science information—A review of the research literature.* Stanford, CA: Institute for Communication Research, Stanford University.

Paisley, W. J. (1968). Information needs and uses. In C. Cuadra (Ed.), *Annual review of information science and technology* (Vol. 3, pp. 1–30). Chicago: Encyclopaedia Britannica.

Paisley, W. J. (1986). The convergence of communication and information science. In H. Edelman (Ed.), *Libraries and information science in the electronic age* (pp. 122–153). Philadelphia, PA: ISI Press.

Paisley, W. J. (1990). Information science as a multidiscipline. In J. Pemberton & A. Prentice (Eds.), *Information science: The interdisciplinary context* (pp. 3–24). New York: Neal-Schuman.

Paisley, W. J. (1993). Knowledge utilization: The role of new communication technologies. *Journal of the American Society for Information Science, 44,* 222–234.

Palmer, J. (1991). Scientists and information: I. Using cluster analysis to identify information style. *Journal of Documentation, 47,* 105–129.

Palmgreen, P. (1984). Uses and gratifications: A theoretical perspective. In R. Bostrom (Ed.), *Communication yearbook* (Vol. 8, pp. 20–55). Beverly Hills, CA: Sage.

Palmour, V., Rathbun, P., Brown, W., Dervin, B., & Dowd, P. (1979). *Information needs of Californians.* Rockville, MD: King Research.

Papa, M., Singhal, A., Law, S., Pant, S., Sood, S., Rogers, E., & Shefner-Rogers, C. (2000). Entertainment-education and social change: An analysis of parasocial interaction, social learning, collective efficacy, and paradoxical communication. *Journal of Communication, 50*(4), 31–55.

Park, T. (1994). Toward a theory of user-based relevance: A call for a new paradigm of inquiry. *Journal of the American Society for Information Science, 45,* 135–141.

Parks, R. E. (1922). *The immigrant press and its control.* New York: Harper.

Pascal, B. (1940). *Pensées* (W. Trotter, Trans.). New York: Modern Library. (Original published in 1670.

Pavitt, C. (1999). The third way: Scientific realism and communication theory. *Communication Theory, 9,* 162–188.

Pearlin, L. I. (1959). Social and personal stress and escape television viewing. *Public Opinion Quarterly, 23,* 255–259.

Perrow, C. (1989). On not using libraries. In B. P. Lynch (Ed.), *Humanists at work: Disciplinary perspectives and personal reflections* (pp. 29–42). Chicago: University of Illinois at Chicago, Institute for the Humanities and the University Library.

Perse, E. (1990). Audience selectivity and involvement in the newer media environment. *Communication Research, 17,* 675–697.

Pettigrew, K. E. (1999). Waiting for chiropody: Contextual results from an ethnographic study of information behaviour among attendees at community clinics. *Information Processing and Management, 35,* 801–817.

Pettigrew, K. E. (2000). Lay information provision in community settings: How community health nurses disseminate human services information to the elderly. *Library Quarterly, 70,* 47–85.

Pettigrew, K. E., Fidel, R., & Bruce, H. (2001). Conceptual frameworks in information behavior. In M. Williams (Ed.), *Annual Review of Information Science and Technology* (Vol. 35, pp. 43–78). Medford, NJ: Information Today Inc.

Pettigrew, K. E., & McKechnie, L. (2001). The use of theory in information science research. *Journal of the American Society for Information Science and Technology, 52,* 62–73.

Petty, R. E., & Cacioppo, J. T. (1986). The elaboration likelihood model of persuasion. *Advances in Experimental Social Psychology, 19,* 123–205.

Piaget, J. (1952). *The language and thought of the child.* London: Routledge & Kegan Paul.

Pifalo, V., Hollander, S., Henderson, C., DeSalvo, P., & Gill, G. (1997). The impact of consumer health information provided by libraries: The Delaware experience. *Bulletin of the Medical Library Association, 85*(1), 16–22.

Pinelli, T. E. (1991). The information-seeking habits and practices of engineers. *Science & Technology Libraries, 11*(3), 5–25.

Pinelli, T. E., Barclay, R., Glassman, N., Kennedy, J., & Demerath, L. (1991). The relationship between seven variables and the use of U.S. government technical reports by U.S. aerospace engineers and scientists. In J. Griffiths (Ed.), *ASIS '91: Proceedings of the 54th ASIS Annual Meeting,* Washington, DC, October 27–31, 1991 (Vol. 28, pp. 313–321). Medford, NJ: Learned Information.

Poole, H. (1985). *Theories of the middle range.* Norwood, NJ: Ablex.

Poole, M. S., & McPhee, R. D. (1994). Methodology in interpersonal communication research. In M. L. Knapp & G. R. Miller (Eds.) *Handbook of inter personal communication* (2nd ed., pp. 42–99). Thousand Oaks, CA: Sage.

Popkin, S. L. (1993). Information shortcuts and the reasoning voter. In B. Grofman (Ed.), *Information, participation and choice: An economic theory of democracy in perspective* (pp. 17–35). Ann Arbor, MI: University of Michigan Press.

Popper, K. (1972). *Objective knowledge: An evolutionary approach.* London: Oxford University Press.

Potts, R., & Sanchez, D. (1994). Television viewing and depression: No news is good news. *Journal of Broadcasting & Electronic Media, 38,* 79–90.

Pratt, A. D. (1977). The information of the image. *Libri, 27*(3), 204–220.

Price, D. (1965). Is technology historically independent of science? *Technology and Culture, 6,* 553–568.

Price, D. (1963). *Little science, big science.* New York: Columbia University Press.

Proper, H., & Bruza, P. (1999). What is information discovery about? *Journal of the American Society for Information Science, 50,* 737–750.

Radford, M. L. (2001). Encountering users, encountering images. *Journal of Education for Library and Information Science, 42*(1), 27–41.

Radway, J. (1985). *Reading the romance: Women, patriarchy, and popular literature.* Chapel Hill: University of North Carolina Press.

Rainie, L., & Packel, D. (2001). *Pew Internet Project: Internet tracking report.* Washington, DC: The Pew Internet & American Life Project.

Raitt, D. L. (1985). The information-seeking and communication habits of scientists and engineers. In C. A. Parkhurst (Ed.), *ASIS '85: Proceedings of the 48th Annual Meeting of the American Society for Information Science* (Vol. 22, pp. 319–323). Medford, NJ: Learned Information.

Rayburn, J. D., II, & Palmgreen, P. (1984). Merging uses and gratifications and expectancy-value theory. *Communication Research, 11,* 537–562.

Reagan, J. (1996). The "repertoire" of information sources. *Journal of Broadcasting & Electronic Media, 40,* 112–121.

Rees, A., & Saracevic, T. (1966). The measurability of relevance. *Proceedings of the American Documentation Institute, 3,* 225–234.

Rees, C. E., & Bath, P. A. (2000). Mass media sources for breast cancer information: Their advantages and disadvantages for women with the disease. *Journal of Documentation, 56*(3), 235–249.

Reeves, B. (1989). Theories about news and theories about cognition. *American Behavioral Scientist, 33*(2), 191–198.

Renckstorf, K., & McQuail, D. (1996). Social action perspectives in mass communication research: An introduction. In K. Renckstorf (Ed.), *Media use as social action: European approach to audience studies* (pp. 1–17). London: John Libbey.

Reneker, M. (1993). A qualitative study of information seeking among members of an academic community: Methodological issues and problems. *Library Quarterly, 63,* 487–507.

Rescher, N. (1978). *Scientific progress: A philosophical essay on the economics of research in natural sciences.* Pittsburgh: University of Pittsburgh Press.

Reynolds, P. D. (1971). *A primer in theory construction.* New York: Bobbs-Merrill.

Rice, R., & Atkin, C. (Eds.). (1989). *Public communication campaigns.* Newbury Park, CA: Sage.

Rice, R., & Atkin, C. (1994). Principles of successful public communication campaigns. In J. Bryant & D. Zillmann (Eds.), *Media effects: Advances in theory and research* (pp. 365–387). Hillsdale, NJ: Erlbaum.

Rice, R., & Borgman, C. (1983). The use of computer-monitored data in information science and communication research. *Journal of the American Society for Information Science, 34,* 247–256.

Rice, R., & Paisley, W. (1981). *Public communication campaigns.* Beverly Hills, CA: Sage.

Richmond, C. (1988). Hand and mouth: Information gathering and use in England in the later middle ages. *Journal of Historical Sociology, 1*, 233–252.

Rifkin, J. (2000). *The age of access: the new culture of hypercapitalism, where all of life is a paid-for experience.* New York: Jeremy P. Tarcher/Putnam.

Ritchie, L. D. (1986). Shannon and Weaver: Unraveling the paradox of information *Communication Research, 13*, 278–298.

Ritchie, L. D. (1991). *Information.* (Vol. 2). Newbury Park, CA: Sage.

Roberts, R. M. (1989). *Serendipity: Accidental discoveries in science.* New York: Wiley.

Robertson, R. D. (1980). Small group decision making: The uncertain role of information in reducing uncertainty. *Political Behavior, 2*, 163–188.

Roeh, I. (1989). Journalism as storytelling, coverage as narrative. *American Behavioral Scientist, 33*(2), 162–168.

Rogers, E. M. (1982). The empirical and the critical schools of communication research. In M. Burgoon (Ed.), *Communication yearbook* (Vol. 5, pp. 125–144). New Brunswick, NJ: Transaction Books.

Rogers, E. M. (1983). *Diffusion of innovations.* New York: Free Press.

Rogers, E. M. (1986). *Communication technology: The new media in society.* New York: Free Press.

Rogers, E. M. (1994). *A history of communication study: A biographical approach.* New York: Free Press.

Rokeach, M. (1960). *The open and closed mind.* New York: Basic Books.

Rosch, E., & Lloyd, B. (Eds.). (1978). *Cognition and categorization.* Hillsdale, NJ: Erlbaum.

Rosenberg, V. (1967). Factors affecting the preferences of industrial personnel for information gathering methods. *Information Storage and Retrieval, 3*, 119–127.

Rosengren, K. (1974). Uses and gratifications: A paradigm outlined. In J. Blumler & E. Katz (Eds.), *The uses of mass communication: Current perspectives on uses and gratifications research.* (pp. 269–286) Beverly Hills, CA: Sage.

Rosengren, K. (1989). Paradigms lost and regained. In B. Dervin, L. Grossberg, B. O'Keefe, & E. Wartella (Eds.), *Rethinking communication: Paradigm issues* (Vol. 1, pp. 21–39). Newbury Park, CA: Sage.

Ross, C. S. (1999). Finding without seeking: the information encounter in the context of reading for pleasure. *Information Processing and Management, 35*, 783–799.

Ross, S. S., & Middleberg, D. (1998). The Middleberg/Ross media in cyberspace study, fourth annual national survey 1997. Retrieved December 15, 2001, from Middleberg + Associates Web site at: http://www.middleberg.com/toolsforsuccess/cyberstudy97.pdf.

Rouse, W. B., & Rouse, S. H. (1984). Human information seeking and design of information systems. *Information Processing & Management, 20*, 129–138.

Ruben, B. D. (1992). The communication-information relationship in system-theoretic perspective. *Journal of the American Society for Information Science, 43*, 15–27.

Rubin, A. M. (1983). Television uses and gratifications: The interactions of viewing patterns and motivations. *Journal of Broadcasting, 27*, 37–51.

Rubin, A. M. (1994). Media uses and effects: A uses-and-gratifications perspective. In J. Bryant & D. Zillmann (Eds.), *Media effects: Advances in theory and research* (pp. 417–436). Hillsdale, NJ: Erlbaum.

Rubin, R. (1998). *Foundations of library and information science.* New York: Neal-Schuman.

Russell, B. (1959). *The problems of philosophy.* London: Oxford University Press.

Salasin, J., & Cedar, T. (1985). Information-seeking behavior in an applied research/special delivery setting. *Journal of the American Society for Information Science, 36*, 94–102.

Salomon, L., & Koppelman, F. (1992). Teleshopping or going shopping? An information acquisition perspective. *Behaviour and Information Technology, 11*, 189–198.

Salton, G., & McGill, M. (1983). *Introduction to modern information retrieval.* New York: McGraw-Hill.

Sandstrom, A., & Sandstrom, P. (1995). The use and misuse of anthropological methods in library and information science research. *Library Quarterly, 65,* 161–199.

Sandstrom, P. (1994). An optimal foraging approach to information seeking and use. *Library Quarterly, 64,* 414–449.

Saracevic, T., Shaw, J. W. M., & Kantor, P. B. (1977). Causes and dynamics of user frustration in an academic library. *College & Research Libraries, 38,* 7–18.

Saunders, C., & Jones, J. (1990). Temporal sequences in information acquisition for decision making. *Academy of Management Review, 15,* 29–46.

Savolainen, R. (1993). The sense-making theory: Reviewing the interests of a user-centered approach to information seeking and use. *Information Processing & Management, 29,* 13–28.

Savolainen, R. (1995). Everyday life information seeking: Approaching information seeking in the context of "way of life". *Library and Information Science Research, 17,* 259–294.

Savolainen, R. (1998). User studies of electronic networks: A review of empirical research and challenges for their development. *Journal of Documentation, 54*(3), 332–351.

Savolainen, R. (1999). Seeking and using information for the Internet: the context of nonwork use. In T. D. Wilson & D. K. Allen (Eds.), *Information behaviour: Proceedings of the second international conference on research in information needs, seeking and use in different contexts,* 13/15 August 1998, Sheffield, UK (pp. 356–370). London: Taylor Graham.

Savolainen, R. (2001). "Living encyclopedia" or idle talk? Seeking and providing consumer information in an Internet newsgroup. *Library & Information Science Research, 23,* 67–90.

Schamber, L., Eisenberg, M., & Nilan, M. (1990). A reexamination of relevance: Toward a dynamic, situational definition. *Information Processing & Management, 26,* 755–776.

Schement, J. R. (1993a). An etymological exploration of the links between information and communication. In J. R. Schement & B. Ruben (Eds.), *Information and behavior* (Vol. 4, pp. 173–187). New Brunswick, NJ: Transaction Books.

Schement, J. R. (1993b). Communication and information. In J. R. Schement & B. Ruben (Eds.), *Information and behavior* (Vol. 4, pp. 3–33). New Brunswick, NJ: Transaction Books.

Schiller, H. (1996). *Information inequality: The deepening social crisis in America.* New York: Routledge.

Schmidt, J., & Spreng, R. (1996). A proposed model of external consumer information search. *Journal of the Academy of Marketing Science, 24*(3), 246–256.

Schutt, R. (1999). *Investigating the social world: The process and practice of research.* Thousand Oaks, CA: Pine Forge Press.

Schutz, A. (1962). *Collected papers, I: The problem of social reality.* The Hague: Martinus Nijhoff.

Schutz, A. (1964). *Collected papers, II: Studies in social theory.* The Hague: Martinus Nijhoff.

Schutz, A. (1967). *The phenomenology of the social world.* Evanston, IL: Northwestern University.

Scott, L. (1994). The bridge from text to mind: Adapting reader-response theory to consumer research. *Journal of Consumer Research, 21,* 461–480.

Searle, J. (1983). *Intentionality. Essays in the philosophy of mind.* Cambridge, UK: Cambridge University Press.

Sears, D., & Freedman, J. (1967). Selective exposure to information: A critical review. *Public Opinion Quarterly, 31,* 194–213.

Seldén, L. (2001, Academic information seeking—careers and capital types. The New Review of Information Behaviour Research, 2, 195–216.

Sever, I. (1990). Reading and playing: The laboratory of children's librarianship revisited. *Libri, 40,* 327–335.

Sever, I. (1994). *Beginning readers, mass media and libraries.* Metuchen, NJ: Scarecrow Press.

Shannon, C. (1949). The mathematical theory of communication. In C. Shannon & W. Weaver (Eds.), *The mathematical theory of communication* (pp. 31–125). Urbana: University of Illinois Press.

Shapiro, G. (1986). *A skeleton in the darkroom: Stories of serendipity in science.* San Francisco: Harper & Row.

Shepherd, M., Duffy, J., Watters, C., & Gugle, N. (2001). The role of user profiles for news filtering. *Journal of the American Society for Information Science and Technology, 52*, 149–160.

Shera, J. H., & Cleveland, D. B. (1977). History and foundations of information science. In M. E. Williams (Ed.), *Annual review of information science and technology* (Vol. 12, pp. 249–275). White Plains, NY: Knowledge Industry.

Sherry, J., Jr. (1990). A sociocultural analysis of a midwestern American flea market. *Journal of Consumer Research, 17*, 13–30.

Sheth, J. N., Newman, B. I., & Gross, B. L. (1991). Why we buy what we buy: A theory of consumption values. *Journal of Business Research, 22*, 159–170.

Shoemaker, P. J. (1991). *Gatekeeping* (Vol. 3). Newbury Park, CA: Sage.

Shuchman, H. L. (1981). *Information transfer in engineering*. Glastonbury, CT: Futures Group.

Shugan, S. (1980). The cost of thinking. *Journal of Consumer Research, 7*, 99–111.

Sievert, D., & Sievert, M. (1989). Philosophical research: report from the field. In B. P. Lynch (Ed.), *Humanists at work: Disciplinary perspectives and personal reflections* (pp. 95–99). Chicago: University of Illinois at Chicago, Institute for the Humanities and the University Library.

Simon, H. (1992). Decision making and problem solving. In M. Zey (Ed.), *Decision making: Alternatives to rational choice models* (pp. 32–53). Newbury Park, CA: Sage.

Simon, J., & Burstein, P. (1985). *Basic research methods in social science* (3rd ed.). New York: Random House.

Skinner, Q. (Ed.). (1985). *The return of grand theory in the human sciences*. Cambridge, UK: Cambridge University Press.

Slater, M. (1988). Social scientists' information needs in the 1980's. *Journal of Documentation, 44*, 226–237.

Slife, B., & Williams, R. N. (1995). *What's behind the research? Discovering hidden assumptions in the behavioral sciences*. Thousand Oaks, CA: Sage. Inc.

Sligo, F. X., & Jameson, A. M. (2000). The knowledge-behavior gap in use of health information. *Journal of the American Society for Information Science, 51*(9), 858–869.

Smith, E. A., & Winterhalder, B. (Eds.). (1992). *Evolutionary ecology and human behavior*. New York: Aldine.

Solomon, P. (1997). Discovering information behavior in sense making: I. Time and timing; II. The social; III. The person. *Journal of the American Society for Information Science., 48*(12), 1097–1138.

Sonnenwald, D. H., & Iivonen, M. (1999). An integrated human information behavior research framework for information studies. *Library & Information Science Research, 21*, 429–457.

Spacks, P. (1985). *Gossip*. New York: Knopf.

Spencer, C. C. (1971). Random time sampling with self-observation for library cost studies: Unit costs of interlibrary loans and photocopies at a regional medical library. *Journal of the American Society for Information Science, 22*, 153–160.

Sperber, D., & Wilson, D. (1995). *Relevance: Communication and cognition*. (2nd ed.). Cambridge, MA: Harvard University Press.

Spink, A. (1997). Information science: A third feedback framework. *Journal of the American Society for Information Science, 48*, 728–740.

Spink, A., Bray, K. E., Jaeckel, M., & Sidberry, G. (1999). Everyday life information-seeking by low-income African American households: Wynnewood healthy neighborhood project. In T. D. Wilson & D. K. Allen (Eds.), *Information behaviour: Proceedings of the second international conference on research in information needs, seeking and use in different contexts*, 13/15 August 1998, Sheffield, UK (pp. 371–383). London: Taylor Graham.

Spink, A., & Cole, C. (2001). Information and poverty: Information-seeking channels used by African American low-income households. *Library and Information Science Research, 23*, 1–22.

Spradley, J. (1979). *The ethnographic interview*. New York: Holt, Rinehart and Winston.

Stake, R. E. (1998). Case studies. In N. Denzin & Y. Lincoln (Eds.), *Strategies of qualitative inquiry* (pp. 86–109). Thousand Oaks, CA: Sage.

Stam, D. C. (1984). How art historians look for information. *Art Documentation, 3*(1), 117–119.

Stam, D. C. (1995). Artists and art libraries. *Art Libraries Journal, 20*(2), 21–24.

Steinbruner, J. D. (1974). *The cybernetic theory of decision.* Princeton: Princeton University Press.

Stephenson, W. (1967). *The play theory of mass communication.* Chicago: University of Chicago Press.

Stern, B. B. (1989). Literary explication: A methodology for consumer research. In E. C. Hirschman (Ed.), *Interpretive Consumer Research* (pp. 48–59). Provo, UT Association for Consumer Research.

Stern, B. B. (1992). Crafty advertisers: Literary versus literal deceptiveness. *Journal of Public Policy and Marketing, 11*, 72–81.

Stewart, J. (1997). Developing communication theories. In G. Philipsen & T. Albrecht (Eds.), *Developing communication theories* (pp. 157–192). Albany, NY: State University of New York Press.

Stocking, S. H., & Gross, P. H. (1989). *How do journalists think? A proposal for the study of cognitive bias in newsmaking.* Bloomington, IN: ERIC Clearinghouse on Reading and Communication Skills.

Stone, A., & Shiffman, S. (1992). Reflections on the intensive measurement of stress, coping, and mood, with an emphasis on daily measures. *Psychology and Health, 7*, 115–129.

Stone, S. (1980). CRUS Humanities Research Programme. In S. Stone (Ed.), *Humanities information research: proceedings of a seminar; Sheffield, 1980.* BLR & DD Report No. 5588 (pp. 15–26). Sheffield, UK: University of Sheffield.

Stone, S. (1982). Humanities scholars: information needs and uses. *Journal of Documentation, 38*(4), 292–313.

Strauss, A., & Corbin, J. (1990). *Basics of qualitative research. Grounded theory procedures and techniques.* Newbury Park, CA: Sage.

Strother, E., Lancaster, D., & Gardiner, J. (1986). Information needs of practising dentists. *Bulletin of the Medical Library Association, 74*(3), 227–230.

Suleiman, S., & Crosman, I. (Eds.). (1980). *The reader in the text.* Princeton, NJ: Princeton University Press.

Sutton, S. (1994). The role of attorney mental models of law in case relevance determinations: An exploratory analysis. *Journal of the American Society for Information Science, 45*, 186–200.

Swanson, E. (1987). Information channel disposition and use. *Decision Sciences, 18*, 131–145.

Talja, S. (1997). Constituting "information" and "user" as research objects: A theory of knowledge formations as an alternative to the information man–theory. In P. Vakkari, R. Savolainen, & B. Dervin (Eds.), *Information seeking in context: Proceedings of a meeting in Finland* 14-16 August 1996 (pp. 67–80). London: Taylor Graham.

Talja, S., Keso, H., & Pietiläinen, T. (1999). The production of "context" in information seeking research: A metatheoretical view. *Information Processing & Management, 35*, 751–763.

Tannenbaum, S. J. (1994). Knowing and acting in medical practice: The epistemological politics of outcomes practice. *Journal of Health Politics, 19*(1), 27–44.

Tapscott, D. (1997). *Growing up digital — The rise of the Net generation.* New York: McGraw-Hill.

Tarde, G. (1903). *The laws of imitation* (E.C. Parsons, Trans.). New York: Holt.

Taylor, R. (1962). The process of asking questions. *Journal of the American Society for Information Science, 13*, 391–396.

Taylor, R. S. (1968). Question-negotiation and information seeking in libraries. *College and Research Libraries, 29*, 178–194.

Taylor, R. S. (1991). Information use environments. In B. Dervin & M. Voigt (Eds.), *Progress in communication sciences* (Vol. 10). Norwood, NJ: Ablex.

Thayer, L. (1987). How does information "inform"? In B. D. Ruben (Ed.), *Information and behavior* (Vol. 2, pp. 13–26). New Brunswick, NJ: Transaction Books.

Thompson, F. (1968). The organization is the information. *American Documentation, 19*, 305–308.

Thompson, R., & Croft, B. (1989). Support for browsing in an intelligent text retrieval system. *International Journal of Man-Machine Studies, 30*, 639–668.

Thórsteinsdóttir, G. (2000). Information seeking behaviour of distance-learning students. *Information Research, 6*(2). Retrieved March 15, 2001, from the University of Sheffield Web site at http://www.she.ac.uk/~is/publications/infres/infres/6-2/ws7.html.

Tibbo, H. (1991). Information systems, services, and technnology for the humanities. In M. Williams (Ed.), *Annual review of information science and technology* (Vol. 26, pp. 287–346). Medford, NJ: Learned Information.

Tichenor, P. J., Donohue, G. A., & Olien, C. N. (1970). Mass media flow and differential growth of knowledge. *Public Opinion Quarterly, 34*, 159–170.

Timpka, T., & Arborlelius, E. (1990). The GP's dilemmas: a study of knowledge need and use during health care consultations. *Methods of Information in Medicine, 29*, 23–29.

Tinker, A., McCreadie, C., & Salvage, A. (1993). *The information needs of elderly people — An exploratory study.* London: Age Concern Institute of Gerontology.

Todd, H. (1984). The information needs of newly retired people. *Health Libraries Review, 1*, 22–35.

Toms, E. G. (1999). What motivates the browser? In T. D. Wilson & D. K. Allen (Eds.), *Information behaviour: Proceedings of the second international conference on research in information needs, seeking and use in different contexts,* 13/15 August 1998, Sheffield, UK (pp. 191–208). London: Taylor Graham.

Törnudd, E. (1959, November 16–21). *Study on the use of scientific literature and references services by scandinavian scientists and engineers engaged in research and development.* Proceedings of the International Conference on Scientific Information, Washington, DC: November 16–21, 1958, Volume I. Washington, DC: Mathonal Academy of Science-National.

Tuominen, K., & Savolainen, R. (1997). A social constructionist approach to the study of information use as discursive action. In P. Vakkari, R. Savolainen, & B. Dervin (Eds.), *Information seeking in context: Proceedings of a meeting in Finland* 14–16 August 1996 (pp. 81–96). London: Taylor Graham.

Tufte, E. (1983). *The visual display of quantitative information.* Cheshire, CT: Graphics Press.

Turk-Charles, S., Meyerowitz, B., & Gatz, M. (1997). Age differences in information seeking among cancer patients. *International Journal of Aging and Human Development, 45*(2), 85–98.

Urbany, J., Dickson, P., & Wilkie, W. (1989). Buyer uncertainty and information search. *Journal of Consumer Research, 16*, 208–215.

Urquhart, C. (1998). Personal knowledge: A clinical perspective from the Value and EVINCE projects in health library and information services. *Journal of Documentation, 54*(4), 420–442.

Urquhart, C. (1999). Using vignettes to diagnose information seeking strategies: Opportunities and possible problems for information use studies of health professionals. In T. D. Wilson & D. K. Allen (Eds.), *Information behaviour: Proceedings of the second international conference on research in information needs, seeking and use in different contexts,* 13/15 August 1998, Sheffield, UK (pp. 277–289). London: Taylor Graham.

Vakkari, P. (1997). Information seeking in context: A challenging metatheory. In P. Vakkari, R. Savolainen, & B. Dervin (Eds.), *Information seeking in context: Proceedings of a meeting in Finland* 14–16 August 1996 (pp. 451–463). London: Taylor Graham.

Vakkari, P. (1999). Task complexity, problem structure and information actions. Integrating studies on information seeking and retrieval. *Information Processing and Management, 35*, 819–837.

Vale, M. (1988). *Information structure and information seeking behavior of lawyers.* Unpublished doctoral dissertation, Stanford University, Stanford, CA.

van de Wijngaert, L. (1999). A policy capturing study of media choice: The effect information [sic] of needs and user characteristics on media choice. In T. D. Wilson & D. K. Allen (Eds.), *Information behaviour: Proceedings of the second international conference on research in information needs, seeking and use in different contexts*, 13/15 August 1998, Sheffield, UK (pp. 463–478). London: Taylor Graham.

van der Rijt, G. (1996). Information needs of the elderly. In K. Renckstorf (Ed.), *Media use as social action: European approach to audience studies* (pp. 163–178). London: John Libbey.

van Dijk, T. A., & Kintsch, W. (1983). *Strategies of discourse comprehension*. Orlando, FL: Academic Press.

Van Snippenburg, L. (1996). Viewership of information-oriented TV programmes. In K. Renckstorf (Ed.), *Media use as social action: European approach to audience studies* (pp. 113–125). London: John Libbey.

Varlejs, J. (1987). Information seeking: Changing perspectives. In J. Varlejs (Ed.), *Information seeking: Basing services on users' behaviors. Proceedings of the twenty-fourth annual symposium of the graduate alumni and faculty of the Rutgers School of Communication, Information, and Library Studies*, 10 April 1986 (pp. 67–82). Jefferson, NC: McFarland.

Vavrek, B. (1995). Rural information needs and the role of the public library. *Library Trends, 44*(3), 21–48.

Viswanath, K., & Finnegan, J. (1996). The knowledge gap hypothesis: 25 years later. In B. Burleson (Ed.), *Communication yearbook* (Vol. 19, pp. 187–227). Thousand Oaks, CA: Sage.

Voigt, M. (1961). *Scientists' approaches to information*. Chicago: American Library Association.

Wakeham, M. (1992). The information seeking behavior of nurses in the UK. *Information Service and Use, 12*, 131–140.

Waldhart, T. J., & Waldhart, E. S. (1975). *Communication research in library and information science: A bibliography on communication in the sciences, social sciences, and technology*. Littleton, CO: Libraries Unlimited.

Walsh, R. L. (1994). *Lawyers' attitude toward information*. Unpublished Masters of Science, City University, London.

Walter, V. A. (1994). The information needs of children. In I. Godden (Ed.), *Advances in librarianship* (Vol. 18, pp. 111–129). San Diego, CA: Academic Press.

Walters, C. (1974). *Consumer behavior: Theory and practice*. London: Irwin.

Wang, P. (2001). Methodologies and methods for user behavioral research. In M. Williams (Ed.), *Annual Review Information Science and Technology* (Vol. 34, pp. 53–99). Medford, NJ: Information Today, Inc.

Warner, E., Murray, A. D., & Palmour, V. E. (1973). *Information needs of urban citizens, final report*. Washington, DC: U.S. Department of Health, Education and Welfare, Office of Education, Bureau of Libraries and Learning Resources.

Watson-Boone, R. (1994). The information needs and habits of humanities scholars. *RQ, 34*, 203–216.

Watt, J., Jr., & Krull, R. (1974). An information theory measure for television programming. *Communication Research, 1*, 44–68.

Weaver, W. (1949). Recent contributions to the mathematical theory of communication. In C. Shannon & W. Weaver, *The mathematical theory of communication* (pp. 1–28). Urbana" University of Illinois Press.

Webb, E., Campbell, D., Schwartz, R., Sechrest, L., & Grove, J. (1981). *Nonreactive measures in the social sciences*. Boston: Houghton Mifflin.

Weick, K. (1970). The twigging of overload. In H. Pepinsky (Ed.), *People and information* (pp. 67–129). New York: Pergamon.

Weick, K. (1995). *Sensemaking in organizations*. Thousand Oaks, CA: Sage.

Weisberg, R. W. (1986). *Creativity: Genius and other myths*. New York: W.H. Freeman.

Wellisch, H. (1972). From information science to informatics: A terminological investigation. *Journal of Librarianship, 4*, 157–187.

Wersig, G., & Neveling, U. (1975). The phenomena of interest to information science. *Information Scientist, 9*, 127–140.

Wersig, G., & Windel, G. (1985). Information science needs a theory of "information actions." *Social Science Information Studies, 5,* 11−23.

Westley, B. H., & Barrow, L. C. (1959). An investigation of news-seeking behavior. *Journalism Quarterly, 36,* 431−438.

Westley, B. H., & Maclean, M., Jr. (1957). A conceptual model for communications research. *Journalism Quarterly, 34*(1), 31−38.

Wheeler, L., & Reis, H. (1991). Self-recording of everyday life events: Origins, types and uses. *Journal of Personality, 59*(3), 339−354.

White, H. D. (2001). Authors as citers over time. *Journal of the American Society for Information Science and Technology, 52,* 87−108.

White, M. D. (1975). The communications behavior of academic economists in research phases. *Library Quarterly, 45,* 337−354.

White, M. D. (2000). Questioning behavior on a consumer health electronic list. *Library Quarterly, 70,* 302−334.

Whitt, A. J. (1993). The information needs of lesbians. *Library and Information Science Research, 15,* 275−288.

Wiberley, S., & Jones, W. (1989). Patterns of information seeking in the humanities. *College & Research Libraries, 50,* 638−645.

Wicks, D. A. (1999). The information-seeking behavior of pastoral clergy: A study of the interaction of their work worlds and work roles. *Library & Information Science Research, 21,* 202−226.

Williams, F. (Ed.). (1987). *Technology and communication behavior.* Belmont, CA: Wadsworth.

Williams, F., Dordick, H., & Horstmann, F. (1977). Where citizens go for information. *Journal of Communication, 27,* 95−100.

Williamson, K. (1997). The information needs and information-seeking behaviour of older adults: An Australian study. In P. Vakkari, R. Savolainen, & B. Dervin (Eds.), *Information seeking in context: Proceedings of a meeting in Finland* 14-16 August 1996 (pp. 337−350). London: Taylor Graham.

Williamson, K. (1998). Discovered by chance: The role of incidental information acquisition in an ecological model of information use. *Library & Information Science Research, 20,* 23−40.

Williamson, K., Schauder, D., & Bow, A. (2000). Information seeking by blind and sight impaired citizens: an ecological study. *Information Research, 5*(4), Retrieved March 15, 2001, from the University of Sheffield Web site at http://www.she.ac.uk/~is/publications/infres/infres/paper79.html.

Wilson, P. (1973). Situational relevance. *Information Storage and Retrieval, 9,* 457−471.

Wilson, P. (1983). *Second-hand knowledge: An inquiry into cognitive authority.* Westport, CT: Greenwood Press.

Wilson, P. (1995). Unused relevant information in research and development. *Journal of the American Society for Information Science, 46,* 45−51.

Wilson, P. (1996). Research and information overload. *Library Trends, 45,* 194−203.

Wilson, T. (1981). On user studies and information needs. *Journal of Documentation, 37,* 3−15.

Wilson, T. (1984). The cognitive approach to information seeking behavior and information use. *Social Science Information Studies, 4,* 197−204.

Wilson, T. (1994). Information needs and uses: Fifty years of progress? In B. C. Vickery (Ed.), *Fifty years of information progress: A Journal of Documentation review* (pp. 15−52). London: Aslib.

Wilson, T. (1997). Information behaviour: An interdisciplinary perspective. In P. Vakkari, R. Savolainen, & B. Dervin (Eds.), *Information seeking in context: Proceedings of a meeting in Finland* 14-16 August 1996 (pp. 39−49). London: Taylor Graham.

Wilson, T. D. (1999a). Models in information behaviour research. *Journal of Documentation, 55*(3), 249−270.

Wilson, T. D. (1999b, December 14). Re: information behaviour [message 003358, 133 lines]. Retrieved December 15, 2001, from open Lib/Info Sci Education Forum (JESSE) Listserv

archive (http://listserv.utk.edu/archives/jesse.html):
http://listserv.utk.edu/cgi-bin/wa?A2=ind9912&L=jesse&F=&S=&P=5004.

Wilson, T. D., & Allen, D. K. (Eds.). (1999). *Information behaviour: Proceedings of the second international conference on research in information needs, seeking and use in different contexts*, 13/15 August 1998, Sheffield, UK. London: Taylor Graham.

Wolf, F. M. (1986). *Meta-analysis: Quantitative methods for research scientists*. Newbury Park, CA: Sage.

Wolton, D. (1989). Rationality and subjectivity in applied science, social science, and journalism: Comments on Katz. *American Behavioral Scientist, 33*(2), 247–250.

Wurman, R. S. (1989). *Information anxiety*. New York: Doubleday.

Yin, R. (1981). The case study crisis: Some answers. *Administrative Science Quarterly, 26*, 58–65.

Yoon, K., & Nilan, M. S. (1999). Toward a reconceptualization of information seeking research: Focus on the exchange of meaning. *Information Processing & Management, 35*, 871–890.

Yovits, M., & Foulk, C. (1985). Experiments and analysis of information use and value in a decision making context. *Journal of the American Society for Information Science, 36*, 63–81.

Zerbinos, E. (1990). Information seeking and information processing: Newspapers versus videotext. *Journalism Quarterly, 67*, 920–929.

Zey, M. (Ed.). (1992). *Decision making: Alternatives to rational choice models*. Newbury Park, CA: Sage.

Zhang, Y. (2000). Using the Internet for survey research: A case study. *Journal of the American Society for Information Science, 51*, 57–68.

Zillman, D., & Bryant, J. (Eds.). (1985). *Selective exposure to communication*. Hillsdale, NJ: Erlbaum.

Zillman, D., & Bryant, J. (1986). Exploring the entertainment experience. In J. Bryant & D. Zillman (Eds.), *Perspectives on media effects* (pp. 303–324). Hillsdale, NJ: Erlbaum.

Zillman, D., & Bryant, J. (1994). Entertainment as media effect. In J. Bryant & D. Zillman (Eds.), *Media effects: Advances in theory and research* (pp. 437–461). Hillsdale, NJ: Erlbaum.

Ziman, J. (1976). *The force of knowledge: The scientific dimension of society*. Cambridge, England: Cambridge University Press.

Zipf, G. (1949). *Human behavior and the principle of least effort: An introduction to human ecology*. New York: Addison-Wesley.

Zuckerman, H. (1987). Citation analysis and the complex problem of intellectual influence. *Scientometrics, 12*, 329–338.

Zunde, P. (1984). Selected bibliography on information theory applications to information science and related subject areas. *Information Processing and Management, 20*, 417–497.

Zweizig, D. (1977). Measuring library use. *Drexel Library Quarterly, 13*, 2–15.

Index

A

Abelson, R., 80, 91, 305
Abused spouses, 257
see also Battered women
Accessibility, 81, 142, 236, 239, 248, 261
Accidental discovery, 14, 86
Acquaintances
see Sources of information
Adler, R., 100, 305
Adolescents
see Teenagers
Adults, 24, 33, 154, 166, 174, 215, 220, 269, 273, 276
Advertising, 7, 18, 19, 86–88, 168, 200–202, 262, 276, 295
African Americans, 182, 244, 249, 250, 283
Agada, J., 258, 268,269, 276, 305
Age
as demographic variable, 13, 119, 123, 175, 188, 197–199, 227–229, 270–274, 297, 302
Aged
See Elderly
Aguilar, F., 85, 248, 305
Ainslie, T., 25, 305
Ajzen, I., 145, 153, 314
Allen, B., 64, 74, 77, 84, 103, 257
Allen, D., 221, 256, 314, 324, 334
Allen, T., 85, 142, 221–223, 233, 234, 236, 237, 248, 249, 285, 305, 315
Allard, S., xvi
Allport, G., 73, 305
Altheide, D., 210, 305
Amazon.com, 187
Anderson, D., 146, 147, 148, 271
Anderson, P., 322

Animals, 10, 40, 56, 61, 85
Annual Review of Information Science and Technology (ARIST), 220–225, 230, 232, 284, 285
Anomie, 138
Anomolous State of Knowledge (ASK), 63, 70, 290
Antecedents to information seeking, 92, 130
Anthropology, 40, 132, 216, 242, 286, 299
Antal, D., 66, 320
Anwar, M., 234, 258, 278, 305, 321
Anxiety, 15, 32, 79, 80, 98–101, 109, 269, 283, 289
Apted, S., 85, 305
Arborelius, E., 245, 246, 331
Archives, 22, 174, 238, 270
Aronson, E., 305
Artandi, S., 51, 59, 305
Artists, 233, 253, 254
Assumptions about concepts and research, 8, 9, 45, 49, 58, 60, 71, 73, 103, 133–135, 143, 149, 154, 160–162, 216, 229, 289, 297
Atkin, C., 67, 69, 72, 76, 81, 95, 107, 198, 305, 326
Attorneys
see Lawyers
Atwood, R. 179, 195, 196, 198, 258, 274, 305
Auerbach, 220, 223, 306
Auster, E., 6, 192, 222, 227, 233, 248, 249, 258, 281, 306, 310
Australian, 247, 302
Avoidance, 5, 14, 15, 32, 79, 92–95, 265, 270, 284, 289
see also Selective exposure
Avoiding information
see Avoidance
Axiology, 133

Ayres, L., 220
Ayris, P., 85, 306

B ————————————————————

Babbie, E., 161, 175, 179, 191, 306
Backhouse, J., 65, 321
Bailey, C., 220, 223, 311, 312
Baker, T., 87, 135, 171, 258, 267, 278, 306
Balasubramanian, S., 188, 189, 310
Baldwin, N., 116, 233, 249, 255, 267, 268, 279, 306
Bandura, A., 153, 274, 306
Bankowitz, R., 243, 324
Barclay, R., 236, 325
Barnbaum, D., 176, 306
Barriers to seeking, 193, 196, 277
Barrow, L., 57, 333
Barry, C., 90, 235, 306
Bates, M., xvi, 87, 232, 233, 238, 271, 306, 319
Bateson, G., 40, 53, 225, 306
Bath, P., 266, 326
Batson, C., 100, 306
Battered women, 251
   see also Abused spouses
Baum, S., 267, 323
Baxter, G., 195, 321
Bebout, L., 238, 239, 306
Becker, H., 148, 306
Beheshti, J., 271, 321
Belk, R., 258, 264, 306
Belkin, N., 50, 53, 54, 59, 63, 69, 70, 81, 89, 90, 306
Benoît, G., 153, 306
Berger, C., 81, 147, 307
Berland, G., 267, 307
Berlo, D., 48, 52, 307
Berlyne, D., 73, 307
Berning, C., 101, 318
Bibliometrics, 234
Bichteler, J., 233, 235, 307
Bierbaum, 140, 307
Biesecker, A., 258, 273, 307
Biesecker, T., 258, 307
Billboards, 19, 294
Black
   see African American
Blind persons, 278
Bloch, P., 87, 108, 258, 262, 307
Blumenfeld, B., 243, 324

Blumer, H., 148, 307
Blumler, J., 143, 319, 322, 327
Blythe, J., 233, 247, 307
Bogart, L., 103, 105, 307
Books
   see Sources of information
Boredom, 84, 103, 106
Borgman, C., xvi, 24, 187, 228, 234, 236, 307, 326
Bosman, J., 73, 74, 147, 307
Bouazza, A., 50, 220, 232, 233, 239, 242, 307
Boulding, K., 53, 63, 307
Bourdieu, P., 82, 153, 276, 307
Bow, A., 269, 278, 333
Bowers, J., 56, 307
Bowes, J., 266, 276, 308
Bowler, S., 260, 308
Boyce, B., 85, 308
Bradac, J., 56, 308
Brands
   of products, 22, 177
Bray, K., 275, 329
Breivik, P., 100, 308
Breuleux, A., 271, 321
Brier, S., 49, 308
British, 247
Brittain, J., 67, 238, 308
Broder, A., 141, 308
Brooks, B.C., 69, 306
Brown, C., 194, 233, 235, 242, 308
Brown, J., 107, 308
Brown, J.S., 61, 308
Brown, W., 295, 260, 325
Browsing, 4, 7, 15, 23, 84–88, 94, 108, 151, 239, 254, 263, 264, 283, 295
   see also Discovering, Encountering, Foraging, Grazing, Navigating, Scanning, Zapping
Bruce, H., 90, 179, 194, 222, 308, 325
Brucks, M., 82, 308, 324
Bruner, J., 139, 146, 147, 308
Bruza, P., 86, 326
Bryant, J., 94, 101–103, 109, 151, 153, 308, 326, 327, 333
Buchanan, B., 65, 243, 314, 324
Buckland, M., xvi, 44, 45, 56, 57, 59, 140, 308, 323
Budd, J.,133, 308
Buhl, C., 200, 201, 205, 215, 263, 264, 323
Burch, R., 243, 278, 314
Burrell, G., 140, 154, 308

Burstein, P., 1114, 135, 329
Business, xv, 9, 14, 19, 45, 106, 139, 179, 196
Busse, T., 151, 321
Butterfield, E., 91, 320
Buying
    see Shopping
Byron, M., 176, 306

C

Cacioppo, J., 66, 308, 325
Campbell, D., 179, 180, 187, 207, 309, 310, 332
Campbell, J., 47, 309
Canadian, 45, 179, 248, 255, 71, 278, 279
Cancer, 17, 21–34, 123, 130, 266, 278, 294
Candidates
    political, 11–12, 99, 152
    see also Political information
Canter, D., 86, 309
Cappella, J., 114, 115, 309
Carlson, D., 105, 309
Carol, B., 90, 313
Cars, 10, 19–21, 183–188, 260
Carter, R., 59, 90, 146, 191, 309
Case, D., 153, 236, 238, 255, 258, 278, 309
Case studies, 163, 177–183
Casto, J., 234, 236, 319
Catalog
    Library, 7, 24, 187, 228
    see also Sources of information
Cedar, T., 247, 278, 327
Chaffee, S., 41, 42, 56, 59, 135, 309
Chang, S., 84–88, 222, 309
Channels
    of communication, 4–6, 14, 22, 42, 76, 87, 96, 103, 124, 125, 142, 171, 174, 182, 196–199, 212, 227–229, 237, 266, 267, 276–279, 290
Chard, F., 100, 306
Chatman, E., xvi, 95, 138, 139, 146, 153, 154, 179, 199, 200, 202, 255, 258, 266, 269, 276, 277
Cheatle, E., 253, 309
Chelton, M., 153, 309
Chemists, 13, 164, 234, 235, 240
Chen, C., 142, 258, 260, 262–264, 272, 310
Cherwitz, R., 57, 310
Chew, F., 93, 95, 179, 191, 192, 310
Childers, T., 97, 258, 310

Children, 19, 94, 96, 101, 107, 151, 164, 182, 258, 260, 270, 271, 274, 295
Chile, 294
Chiropody, 267
Choo, C., xvi, 86, 88, 192, 222, 226, 227, 233, 248, 249, 257, 281, 306, 310
Chu, C., 233, 240, 241, 255
Cicourel, A., 73, 310
Citizens, 10, 11, 104, 195, 210, 257–262, 270, 279
    see also Voters
Clarke, P., 258, 269, 271, 305, 310, 313
Clements, J., 107, 310
Clergy, 233, 354, 255
Cleveland, D., 48, 220, 329
Cleveland, Ohio, 276, 316
Cobbledick, S., 196, 233,253, 254, 310
Cohen, A., 66, 310
Cohen, S., 237, 305
Coke, J., 100, 306
Cole, C., xvi, 48, 54, 56, 179, 196, 233, 241, 252, 253, 269, 275, 310, 329
Cole, C.A., 187, 188, 310
Collins, P., 151, 308
Communication
    academic disipline of, xv, 14, 105, 139, 149, 154, 225, 238, 267, 289, 299
    mass, 6, 12, 65, 77, 88, 92, 101, 104, 109, 114, 138, 145–150, 196–199, 260, 270–276
    interpersonal, 120, 146, 147, 152, 234, 248, 255, 260, 268, 277, 298
Compaine, B., 290, 310
Comprehensive Model of Information Seeking (CMIS), 122–126
Computers, 4, 96, 185, 259, 272, 294
Conferences, 6, 224, 238
Connelly, D., 244, 310
Consumers, 11, 13, 18–21, 82, 101, 115, 118, 119, 139, 185–190, 197, 211, 215, 229, 232, 257–260
Content analysis, 15, 163, 186, 208–212, 267
Context
    definition of, 13, 108, 225–249
Conversation, 33, 74, 149, 293
Cook, K., 161, 176, 285, 319
Cook, T., 179, 184, 188, 213, 310
Cool, C., 222, 310
Coping, 17, 94, 105, 18, 149, 268, 269
Corcoran-Perry, S., 247, 310
Cornelius, I., 71, 153, 310

Costs and benefits, 100, 134, 143, 185, 197
Coughlin, C., 234, 324
Cove, J., 84, 87, 310
Covell, D., 179, 205, 214, 215, 244, 311
Cox, D., 235, 239, 240, 313
Craft-Rosenberg, M.,153, 269, 320
Crandall, R., 173, 312
Crane, D., 221, 223, 267, 285, 311
Crawford, S., 221, 223, 311
Creativity, 3, 108, 151, 254, 283, 290
Creelman, J., 258, 278, 311
Crime, 168, 262, 268, 274
Critical incident technique, 190, 205, 206
Critics
    literary, 240, 254, 279
Croft, B., 86, 331
Cronin, B., 88, 208, 234, 239, 311
Crosman, I., 153, 330
Crouch, W., 161, 176, 285, 319
Csikszentmihalyi, M., 146, 151, 179, 200, 206,
    311, 315, 320
Cuadra, C., 89, 305, 311, 317, 321, 322, 324
Culnan, M., 233, 248, 311
Curiosity, 31−34, 73, 119
Curley, S., 244, 310
Curry, A., 106, 311
Customers
    see Consumers
Cutler, N., 104, 144, 311
Cyert, R., 82, 311

D

Daft, R., 233, 248, 311
Dallas, Texas, 275
Daniels, P., 139, 311
Danish, 200−201, 264
Danowski, J., 104, 144, 311
Darnton, R., 179, 210, 311
Data
    definitions of, 41, 61−62
Databases, 7, 34, 98, 116, 229, 237, 245
Davis, D., 244, 311
Davis, J., 238, 239, 306
Davis, M., 103, 137, 311
Davis, R., 220, 223, 311, 312
Decisions
    see Decision making
Decision-making, 5, 8, 10−15, 18−21, 24−30,
    43, 51, 55, 62, 72, 79−83, 92, 108, 109,
    118, 122, 143, 270, 283, 290

Deduction, 165, 166, 174
Dee, C., 278, 311
DeMartini, 196, 255, 314
Demands
    for information, 66, 101, 117
    see also Needs
DeMey, M., 139, 311
Demerath, L., 236, 325
Demographic groups, 13, 15, 100, 115−120,
    171−174, 192, 197, 215, 220, 227−229,
    254−258
DeMoss, M., 263, 323
Denzin, N., 216, 318, 330
Derr, R., 57, 67, 311
Dervin, B., 7−9, 17, 31, 40, 43, 44, 67−72,
    78, 90, 95−97, 103, 105, 118, 122−125,
    132−135, 142, 146−148, 179, 191, 195,
    198, 210, 223, 225, 229, 230, 258−261,
    266, 268, 274, 288, 305, 312, 314, 316,
    320, 321, 324, 330, 333
DeSalvo, P., 99, 267, 325
Deutsch, K., 98, 312
Dewdney, P., 71, 278, 312, 317
DeWeese, L., 220, 312
Dewey, J., 75, 136, 139, 146, 147, 225, 312
Diaries, 15, 163, 177, 201, 208, 213, 250, 256
Diary method
    see Diaries
Dickson, P., 82, 331
Diener, E., 173, 312
Diffusion of Innovations
    Theory of, 138, 153, 154, 265
Digital Divide, 297
Dillman, D., 176, 249, 313
Discovering information, 87
    see also Browsing, Encountering, Foraging,
    Grazing, Navigating, Scanning,
    Zapping
Doctor
    see Physicians
Donnelly, W., 102, 313
Donohew, L., 17, 53, 80, 104, 115, 139, 225,
    313
Donohue, G., 95, 265, 312
Donovan, T., 260, 308
Doorstep interviews
    see Interviews
Door-to-door interviews
    see Interviews
Dordick, H., 259, 333
Dorsch, J., 141, 313

Dowd, P., 195, 260, 325
Downey, M., 254, 313
Doyal, L., 66, 313
Dozier, D., 104, 150, 154, 313
Dresang, E., 271, 313
Dretske, F., 58, 313
Driscoll, J., 73, 313
Drive reduction, 139
Drives
    instinctual, 73, 74, 150
Duffy, J., 150, 329
Duggan, L., 211, 224, 228, 230, 232, 319
Duguid, P., 61, 308
Duncan, R., 85, 313
Dunn, W., 153, 313
Durkheim, E., 103, 137, 138, 207, 313
Durrance, J., 142, 260, 313

E _____

Economics, 80, 137, 139
Economists, 81, 41
Edgar, T., 276, 315
Education, 106, 107, 119, 123, 139, 165, 188,
    189, 195, 198, 203, 227, 229, 232, 238,
    244–248, 21, 260, 267–270, 275–277,
    285, 295, 266
Eisenberg, M., 90, 313, 328
Eisenschitz, C., 214, 289, 321
Elderly, 7, 15, 32, 101, 146, 188, 189, 195,
    229, 256, 270, 272, 273, 297
Eliot, C., 220, 313
Ellis, B., 106, 313
Ellis, D., 115, 116, 196, 233, 235, 239, 240, 313
Ellyson, S., 260, 312
Ely, J., 243, 244, 278, 314
Email
    as source, 124, 141, 294, 301
    surveys using, 15, 173, 174, 190, 193, 194,
        302
    content analysis of, 179, 210, 211
Emotions, 21, 32, 71, 72, 77, 150, 187, 201,
    206, 261, 294
Encountering information, 5, 15, 86, 87, 108,
    147, 225, 284
    see also Browsing, Discovering, Foraging,
        Grazing, Navigating, Scanning,
        Zapping
Encyclopedias
    see Sources of information

Engineers, 7, 11, 15, 25, 45, 80, 142, 229,
    231–233, 236–238, 256, 286, 302
England, 208, 209, 226, 253
Enochsson, A., 271, 313
Entertainment, 74, 80, 102–108, 138,
    143–152, 199, 261, 274, 280–283, 290,
    293, 295
Entertainment Theory, 131, 140, 150, 151
    see also Play Theory
Entropy, 47–49
Epstein, B., 250, 314
Erdelez, S., 86, 153, 196, 272, 314
Ethics, 151, 160–164
Ethnicity, 13, 123, 195, 227, 297
    See also Ethnolinguisitic groups
Ethnographic method, 132, 163, 179, 211,
    212, 243, 263, 267, 277, 301
Ethnolinguistic groups, 248, 257, 270,
    274–276
    See also Ethnicity
Everyday life, 9, 11, 18–32, 70, 82, 101, 115,
    146, 188, 194–199, 228, 259–268,
    271–277
Everyday Life Information Seeking model
    (ELIS), 82
Expectancy-Value Theory, 145, 153
Experience Sampling Method, 15, 146, 206
Experiments
    field, 12, 15, 179, 188–190, 299
    laboratory, 12, 15, 179, 184–190
    quasi-, 184
Explication of concepts, 41, 42, 59, 163, 263

F _____

Fabritius, H., 179, 213, 233, 250, 251, 256,
    314
Fairthorne, R., 51, 314
Family members
    see Sources of information
Farace, V., 40, 314
Farmers, 255
Fatalism, 273, 276
Feedback, 82, 119, 126, 127
Feinstein, J., 66, 308
Fiction, 104–107, 146
Fidel, R., 222, 325
Fiji, 266
Fink, E., 196, 315
Finland, 226
Finn, S., 49, 104, 105, 139, 313, 314

Finnegan, J., 96, 265, 332
Finnish, 261
Fischer, D., 287, 314
Fish, S., 153, 314
Fishbein, M., 145, 153, 314
Fiske, M., 204, 323
Fitzmaurice, M., 196, 315
Fitzpatrick, M., 276, 315
Florio, E., 196, 255, 314
Flow,
  psychological state of, 207
  two-step, 267
Focus group interviews
  see Interviews
Folkman, S., 153, 314
Foraging, 15, 88, 108, 283
  See also Browsing, Discovering,
    Encountering, Grazing, Navigating,
    Scanning, Zapping
Ford, N., 196, 269, 314
Formal sources, 8, 12, 14, 22–24, 29–31, 34,
  43, 87, 91, 116, 122, 213, 235–255, 289,
  302
Forsythe, D., 65, 242, 314
Foucault, M., 132, 153, 314
Foulk, C., 52, 81, 334
Foulkes, D., 139, 319
Fox, C., 39, 51, 55, 59, 60, 314
Foxall, G., 263, 314
Freedman, J., 93, 328
Freimuth, V., 258, 267, 276, 277, 314, 315
Freud, S., 102, 136, 139, 144, 178, 315
Frey, D., 93, 315
Frické, M., 58, 315
Friends
  see Sources of information
Friestad, M., 96, 315
Fritz, R., 151, 315
Froelich, T., 90, 315
Furse, D., 189, 315

G

Gadamer, H., 135, 315
Galanter, E., 73, 98, 323
Gallup poll, 103, 315
Galtung, J., 66, 320
Gandy, O., 97, 315
Gantz, W., 179, 196–199, 315
Gap

knowledge, 5, 15, 70–75, 86, 91, 95–97,
  151, 196, 261–266, 274, 277, 283
Gardiner, J., 247, 330
Gardner, H., 132, 315
Garfinkel, H., 73, 148, 315
Garner, W., 49, 75, 99, 315
Garrison, B., 251, 315
Garvey, W., 221, 223, 241, 285, 315
Gatekeepers, 221, 229, 237, 239, 268, 276, 279
Gatz, M., 274, 331
Gaziano, C., 96, 265, 315
Geertz, C., 146, 315
Gelder, A., 253, 315
Gender, 13, 123, 166, 193, 197, 199, 226, 258,
  268–273, 297
Geographic location, 195, 269, 278, 279, 297
Gerstberger, P., 84, 233, 234, 236, 315
Gettier, E., 57, 315
Getzels, J., 151, 315
Ghiselin, B., 151, 315
Giddens, A., 135–137, 146, 316
Gill, G., 99, 267, 325
Glaser, B., 137, 165, 316
Glass, A., 91, 316
Glassman, N., 236, 325
Glazier, J., 154, 312
Goffman, E., 148, 153, 316
Golding, P., 97, 323
Goldman, A., 74, 316
Goldstein, W., 81, 316
Goren, D., 250, 251, 316
Gorman, P., 196, 233, 243–245, 256, 316
Goslee, S., 290, 316
Gough, I., 66, 313
Gould, C., 238, 239, 242, 316
Gourash, N., 258, 273, 276, 316
Graber, D., 100, 316
Gralewska-Vickery, A., 233, 316
Granovetter, M., 153, 316
Gratch, B., 140, 316
Gratifications
  see Uses and Gratifications
Graves, J., 247, 310
Grazing, 87
  See also Browsing, Discovering,
    Encountering, Foraging, Navigating,
    Scanning, Zapping
Great Britain, 145, 232
Green, A., 65, 66, 78, 316
Green Party, 278

Greenberg, B., 87, 266, 276, 288, 312, 316, 317
Grewal, D., 82, 324
Gross, B., 82, 329
Gross, P., 251, 330
Grossberg, B., 155, 316, 327
Grounded theory, 136, 165, 176
Grove, J., 207, 332
Grunig, J., 65, 317
Guagnano, G., 260, 312
Guba, E., 133, 321
Gugle, N., 150, 329
Gulf War, 192
Gundry, L., 258, 269, 317
Gurevitch, M., 143, 319, 322

H ——————————————

Haas, S., 238, 286, 322
Habermas, J., 136, 137, 146, 153, 246, 317
Habits, 6, 11, 82, 169, 173, 207, 236, 238, 240, 258, 261, 267, 274, 280, 288
Habitus, 82, 276
Hagen, I., 153, 317
Hainsworth, M., 233, 253, 317
Hall, K., 235, 239, 240, 313
Hampshire, S., 74, 317
Hancock-Beaulieu, M., 24, 317
Handler, G., 239, 316
Haney, R., 17, 313
Hardy, A., 140, 143, 317
Harman, R., 85, 324
Harris, R., 236, 258, 278, 312, 317
Harter, S., 74, 89, 90, 317
Haug, J., 179, 213, 216, 317
Hauser, J., 179, 184–187, 263, 317
Hawkes, G., 260, 312
Haynes, R., 244, 311
Hayes, R. 61, 317
Health, 6, 32, 34, 66, 70, 82, 99, 107, 123–125, 190, 202–205, 210, 242–247, 255, 260–279
Health care providers, 231, 233, 242–247
Heap, J., 290, 317
Heeter, C., 87, 317
Helfand, M., 196, 244, 316
Hempel, C., 59, 317
Henderson, C., 99, 267, 325
Henning, B., 94, 317
Hermeneutics, 207, 286
Herner, M., 221, 223, 284, 317

Herner, S., 85, 221, 223, 284, 317
Hernon, P., 116, 142, 221, 233, 239, 259–261, 272, 310, 317
Hersberger, J., 258, 269, 277, 317
Hert, C., 88, 311
Hertzum, M., 233, 236, 318
Hewins, E., 190, 221, 222, 318
Higgins, M., 40, 318
Hikins, J., 57, 310
Hindle, A., 140, 323
Hirschman, E., 74, 83, 318
Hirsh, S., 271, 318
Hispanics, 196, 274
    see also Mexican-Americans
Historians, 192, 212, 233, 234, 269
Hobbies, 85, 228, 261
Hogarth, R., 154, 312
Hogeweg-de-Haart, H., 221, 223, 238, 239, 318
Holbrook, M., 74, 83, 318
Holland, M., 233, 236, 237, 318
Hollander, S., 99, 267, 325
Holmöv, P., 104, 318
Holt, D., 263, 318
Holyoak, K., 91, 316
Homeless parents, 255, 277
Hornik, R., 96, 266, 318
Horse-racing, 25–28, 34
Horstmann, F., 259, 333
Howard, D., 90, 318
Hsia, H., 49, 258, 276
Huberman, B., 144, 318
Hugo, V., 55
Human subject committees, 171
Humanities scholars, 231, 233, 240–242
Hyman, H., 92, 93, 96, 265, 318

I ——————————————

Ideographic research, 202
Ignatieff, M., 67, 318
Ignorance, 51, 85, 96
Ignoring, 8, 14, 277, 289
    see also Avoidance, Selective exposure
Iivonen, M., 162, 318, 329
Image
    as information structure, 50, 53–56, 63, 79, 99
Indianapolis, Indiana, 277
Induction, 165, 166, 174

Informal sources of information, 8, 12, 13, 34, 43, 62, 117, 123, 237–239, 251, 260, 289
Information
definitions of, 8, 39, 41–55
behavior, definition of, 5, 75
campaigns, 7, 71, 99, 106, 265
need, definition of, 5, 65–68
poverty, 15, 79, 95, 96, 108, 266, 276, 283
retrieval, 7, 13, 77, 89–91, 138, 251
seeking, definition of, 5, 75
structure, 39, 50, 53–56
theory, 39, 46–51
use environments, 227
Information Science Abstracts, 224
Information Seeking In Context (ISIC)
conferences, 224, 226
Infomercial, 107
Infotainment, 103
Ingwersen, P., 116, 318
Intention, 7, 44, 54–56, 76, 135, 179, 215, 265
Intentionality
of communication, 39, 50, 56, 57
Internet, 12, 18, 20, 21, 32, 33, 66, 141, 174, 193, 194, 228, 229, 244, 251, 265, 296
see also Websites, World Wide Web
Internet Mailing List, 13, 174
Interviews
doorstep, 194–195
focus group, 15, 177, 190, 202–204, 211, 247, 262
long, 199–201
short, 194–198
Iser, W., 153, 318

J

Jacobson, T., 147, 228, 312, 318
Jacobvitz, R., 151, 305
Jacoby, J., 101, 318
Jaeckel, M., 275, 329
Jameson, A., 265, 266, 269, 329
Janes, J., 90, 318
Janesick, V., 159, 216, 318
Janitors, 13, 139, 145, 152, 200, 257
Järvelin, K., 178, 318
Jarvis, W., 66, 308
Jiao, Q., 100, 187, 258, 269, 319
Jobs, 7, 99, 180, 227, 229, 230, 259, 260, 276, 277

Johnson, J., xvi, 3, 40, 75, 92, 113–116, 122–126, 128–130, 258, 266, 273, 276, 283, 319
Johnson, M. 151, 319
Jones, H., 234, 236, 319
Jones, J., 86, 88, 328
Jones, S., 173, 319
Jones, W., 241, 242, 333
Journalists, 172, 231, 233, 249–251, 286, 302
Journals
see Sources of information
Joyce, J., 140
Julien, H., 179, 196, 211, 224, 228, 230, 232, 258, 269, 271, 319
Judges
court, 33, 252, 253
Just, W., 286, 287, 319

K

Kafai, J., 271, 319
Kahn, R., 99, 319
Kantor, P., 24, 328
Katter, R., 89, 311
Katz, D., 99, 319
Katz, E., 139, 143, 233, 249, 250, 319, 322, 327
Katzer, J., 161, 176, 285, 319
Kay, H., 150, 319
Kean, T., 267, 315
Keegan, W., 86, 319
Kefalas, A., 86, 319
Kellermann, K., 52, 81, 319
Kelly, G., 100, 138, 139, 147, 153, 319
Kelly, J., 244, 310
Kemp, D., 90, 319
Kendall, P., 204, 323
Kennedy assassination, 136
Kennedy, J., 236, 325
Kenner, H., 141, 319
Kerlinger, F., 135, 319
Keso, H., 113, 225, 230, 231, 330
Kiesler, S., 91, 319
King, D., 222, 233, 234, 236, 319
King Henry V, 209
Kintsch, W., 241, 332
Klapp, O., 49, 319
Klapper, J., 114, 319
Kleiber, C., 153, 269, 320
Knorr-Cetina, K., 234, 320

Knowledge
definitions of, 61
Koppelman, F., 87, 108, 327
Kozlowski, S., 269, 324
Kraft, D., 85, 308
Krikelas, J., 65, 75, 113, 115, 116, 119–122,
128, 129, 138, 283, 320
Krippendorff, K., 52, 179, 210
Krueger, R., 179, 203, 216
Krull, R., 48, 49, 332
Kubey, R., 151, 179, 206, 320
Kuhlthau, C., xvi, 52, 71, 78, 81, 100, 101,
115, 116, 138, 147, 153, 179, 181–183,
187, 196, 215, 233, 249, 252, 253, 255,
258, 269, 280, 310, 320
Kuhn, T., 134, 320
Kurds, 286

L

Lachman, J., 91, 320
Lachman, R., 91, 320
Lancaster, D., 247, 330
Lane, D., xvi
Langer, E., 82, 320
Lanzetta, J., 73, 313
Large, A., 271, 320
Larson, R., 151, 179, 206, 320
Lasch, C., 39, 320
Latour, B., 234, 320
Lawyers, 7, 29, 80, 231, 233, 249, 251–253,
260, 276, 278, 279, 302
Layne, S., 254, 320
Lazersfeld, P., 134, 320
Learning
theories of, 146–148
Least Effort
principle of, 131, 140–143, 154, 212, 214,
283, 289, 298,
Leckie, G., 113, 115, 116, 126–130, 233, 234,
247, 252, 255, 283, 320
Lederer, K., 66, 320
Lehmann, D., 263, 320
Leisure, 238, 247, 248. *See also* hobbies, play.
Lengel, R., 233, 248, 311
Lesbians, 278
Leung, L., 153, 321
Levi, A., 80, 91, 305
Levine, M., 84, 321
Levitan, K., 2, 321
Leviton, L., 213, 310

Levy, M., 104, 144, 321
Lewin, K., 267, 321
Leydesdorff, L., 208, 234, 321
Libraries
see Sources of information
Library Literature, 224
Liebnau, J., 65, 321
Lin, C., 114, 152, 221, 223, 321
Lin, N., 285, 316, 321
Lincoln, Y., 133, 216, 318, 321, 330
Lindlof, T., 216, 321
Line, M., 67, 321
Linguistics,
academic discipline of, 139
Linz, C., 105, 321
Lipetz, B., 221, 223, 285, 321
Listservers
see Internet Mailing Lists
Literary critics
see Critics
Littlejohn, S., 140, 321
Livingstone, S., 202, 321
Lloyd, B., 90, 327
Locus of control, 8
Longitudinal studies, 170
Losee, R., 47, 54, 55, 321
Louis, M., 269, 321
Luckmann, T., 148, 307
Lukose, R., 144, 318
Lunt, P., 202, 321

M

Machlup, F., 47, 51, 61, 321, 323
MacKay, D., 49, 54, 321
Maclean, M., 57, 333
Magazines
see Sources of information
Mail survey
see Survey methods
Mailer, N., 106
Majid, S., 234, 321
Management
academic discipline of, xv, 14, 99, 139, 249
Managers, 7, 14, 15, 80, 119, 227, 229, 231,
233, 248, 249, 302
Mann, T., 140, 321
Manning, P., 205, 214, 215, 243, 311
Mansfield, R., 151, 321
Mansfield, U., 47, 321, 323
Marcella, R., 179, 195, 321

March, J., 80, 83, 109, 322
Marchionini, G., 75, 116, 228, 322
Markets
  see Shopping
Marshall, J., 233, 243, 267, 322
Martyn, J., 221, 233, 284, 322
Marx, K., 103, 134, 137
Maslow, A., 3, 66, 99, 270, 322
Mass media
  see Sources of information
Masterman, M., 134, 135, 322
Matthew Effect, 141
McLuhan, M., 103
McCombs, M., 96, 322
McCracken, G., 263, 322
McCreadie, M., 44, 45, 273, 322
McGill, M., 142, 327
McKechnie, L., 136, 152, 287, 325
McKinley, W., 22–24
McKinney, R., 90, 318
McKinnie, A., 220
McPhee, R., 159–162, 177, 326
McQuail, D., 130, 139, 144, 148, 319, 322,
  326
Mead, M., 173
Meadow, C., 85, 236, 308, 309
Measurement
  of variables, 41, 162–171
Media Use as Social Action (MASA), 131, 140,
  148, 149, 283
Medical information, 8, 12, 31–34, 99,
  202–204, 242–247, 264–266
Medical Doctor (MD)
  see Physicians
Medicine
  academic discipline of, xvi, 14, 179, 242
Meho, L., 238, 286, 322
Meier, R., 100, 322
Mellon, C., 71, 100, 139, 187, 196, 258, 269,
  322
Memory
  human, 66, 75, 88, 120, 161
Mendelsohn, H., 96, 103, 150, 322
Menzel, H., 67, 116, 220, 223, 284, 322
Merton, R., 131, 135–138, 179, 204, 267,
  322, 323
Meta-analysis, 15, 163, 213, 214, 244
Methodology, 160–162, 178–215
Metoyer-Duran, C., 222, 237, 258, 268, 270,
  276, 323
Meyerowitz, B., 274, 331

Mexican-Americans, 276
  see also Hispanics
Mick, D., 179, 200, 201, 205, 215, 258, 263,
  264, 323
Middleberg, D., 251, 327
Miller, G.A., 40, 47, 73, 74, 98, 99, 139, 323
Miller, J.G., 98, 323
Miller, R., 65, 243, 314, 324
Miller, W., xvi
Mintzberg, H., 98, 323
Misinformation, 50, 54, 57, 58, 79, 270, 282
Mizzaro, S., 90, 323
Models
  for research, 46–50, 81, 113–130
Mokros, H., 179, 211, 323
Monge, P., 40, 314
Montgomery, L., 153, 269, 320
Mood Management Theory, 146, 148
Mooers' Law, 142
Mooers, C., 142
Morgan, M., 140, 154, 213, 276, 323
Morowitz, H., 47, 69, 323
Morris, R., 78, 323
Morrison, E., 258, 269, 323
Motivation, 65–73, 93, 101
Motives for seeking information
  see Motivation
Mulkay, M., 234, 320
Mullaly-Quijas, 179, 203, 204, 233, 247, 323
Mullins, N., 179, 211, 323
Multiple Sclerosis, 267
Murdock, G., 97, 323
Murray, A., 101, 272, 332
Music, 271
Mystification, 161
Myths about information behavior, 7, 8,
  288–290

N ——————————————————

Nair, M., 104, 139, 313
Napster, 295
Nauta, D., 51, 323
Navigating, 86, 114
  see also Browsing, Discovering,
    Encountering, Foraging, Scanning,
    Zapping
Needs
  basic human, 8, 65–67
  information, 5, 8–15, 65–76, 116–129,
    140–152

Neighbors
see Sources of information
Nelson, C., 234, 323, 324
Neveling, U., 42, 51, 332
New England, 260
New Zealand, 266
Newcomers, 269
Newhagen, J., 82, 179, 258, 274, 275, 280,
    323, 324
Newman, B., 82, 329
Newspapers
see Sources of information
Nicholas, D., 228, 233, 251, 324
Nilan, M., 52, 90, 146, 147, 221, 223, 230,
    285, 312, 328, 334
Nissenbaum, S., 241, 256, 324
Noble, 234, 324
Noise
in Information Theory, 46, 47
Norretranders, 45, 46, 49, 324
North American Aviation, 220, 324
Nurses, 130, 203, 233, 242, 247

O

O'Connor, B., 87, 324
O'Connor, J., 67, 324
O'Keefe, B., 155, 316, 327
O'Meara, J., 179, 199, 324
O'Reilly, C., 101, 324
Occupations, 13, 15, 117–119, 126, 127,
    232–255, 279, 283, 302
see also Jobs
Ocholla, D., 255, 324
OCLC, 224
Oddy, R., 69, 306
Oehlerts, D., 238, 239, 306
Olien, C., 95, 265, 331
Onwuegbuzie, A., 100, 187, 258, 269, 319
Operationalization
of measures, 59, 166
Opinion leader, 267, 269
Optimal Foraging Theory, 153, 154, 299
Orr, R., 116, 142, 324
Osheroff, J., 65, 223, 243, 244, 314, 324
Ostroff, C., 269, 324
Otike, J., 233, 253, 324
Overhage, C., 85, 324
Overload
of information, 15, 79, 80, 98–102, 108,
    265, 283, 289

Oxman, A., 244, 311
Ozanne, J., 82, 324

P

Packel, D., 264, 326
Paisley, W., 95, 98, 116, 220, 221, 223, 238,
    284, 324, 325
Palmer, J., 93, 95, 233–235, 325
Palmgreen, P., 144, 145, 325, 326
Palmour, V., 179, 195, 260, 325, 332
Papa, M., 153, 325
Paradigms
research, 14, 59, 132–134
Parents, 56, 173, 255, 259, 270, 271, 277
Park, T., 146, 325
Parks, D., 267, 325
Parks, R., 248, 311
Participant observation, 15, 179, 194, 212
Pascal, B., 102, 325
Passive acquisition
of information, 5, 14, 50, 75, 76, 143, 196,
    261
Paston, A., 208
Paston, J., 208
Pastors
see Clergy
Patients, 17, 211, 229, 232, 242–247, 257,
    259, 264–267
Pavitt, C., 133, 325
Pearlin, L., 94, 325
Pejtersen, A., 233, 236, 318
Pendleton, V., 95, 277, 309
Perrow, C., 94, 99, 100, 325
Perse, E., 87, 325
Personal construct, 154
Perspectives
research, 15, 132
Pertinence, 15, 79, 90, 91, 108, 283
see also Relevance, Salience
Pettigrew, K., 115, 116, 126–130, 136, 152,
    153, 222, 234, 236, 247, 267, 287, 320,
    325
Petty, R., 66, 308, 325
Pew Internet Project, 264, 265
Phenomenology, 132, 148, 200, 246, 263, 286
Philosophers, 242
Physicality
of information, 39, 50, 52, 53, 60
Physicians, 11, 15, 130, 203, 214, 233,
    242–247, 256, 260, 279, 302

Physicists, 235, 240
Piaget, 1139, 325
Pierce, C., 47
Pietiläinen, T., 113, 225, 230, 231, 330
Pifalo, 99, 141, 258, 267, 313, 325
Pinelli, T., 233, 236, 237, 249, 256, 325
Pirollis, P., 144, 318
Pitkow, J., 144, 318
Plato, 102
Play Theory, 129, 138, 145, 146, 148, 149, 256
Policy makers, 233, 255, 259
Political information, 6, 11, 71, 92, 98, 99,
    144, 197, 210, 239, 242, 261, 262, 267,
    274, 275, 280
Politics
    see Political information
Pollock, D., 234, 323, 324
Poole, H., 73, 140, 220, 326
Poole, M., 159–162, 177, 326
Popkin, S., 98, 99, 258, 260, 326
Popper, K., 43, 326
Post, J., 97, 310
Postal survey
    see Survey
Postman, N., 69, 271
Powell, C., 233, 236, 237, 318
Powell, R., 154, 312
Pratt, A., 53, 326
Pribram, K., 73, 98, 323
Price, D., 233, 236, 326
Priests, see Clergy
Problem-solving, 43, 79, 83, 84
    see also Decision making
Proper, H., 86, 326
Psychologists, 33, 66, 73, 74, 77, 80, 82, 85,
    91, 99, 239, 245, 302
Psychology
    discipline of, 14, 19, 67, 81, 85, 91, 118,
        132, 139, 154, 185, 264, 284, 299
Public health, xvi, 14, 243
Punj, G., 189, 315
Purchases, 11, 18–21, 174, 185, 262
    See also Shopping

Q

Qualitative methods, 81, 102, 132, 164–170,
    177, 179, 191, 202, 211, 216, 251, 256,
    261, 262, 286
Questionnaires, 163, 175, 191–194, 211, 236,
    246, 249, 270, 286

R

Race, 13, 195, 196, 198, 227, 274, 275
    see also Ethnicity, Ethnolinguistic groups
Radford, M., 153, 326
Radio
    see Sources
Radway, J., 103, 179, 202, 326
Rainie, L., 264, 326
Raitt, D., 233, 236, 326
Random alarm technique, 206
Rathbun, P., 195, 260, 325
Rayburn, J., 145, 326
Reader Response Theory, 153, 201, 299
Reagan, J., 93, 326
Reagan, R., 161
Reasoned Action
    theory of, 153, 154
Receiver
    in Information Theory, 46, 47
Recordings
    audiotape, 162, 202, 212, 248
    video tape, 121, 185, 203
Redundancy
    in Information Theory, 46, 47
Rees, A., 89, 326
Rees, C., 258, 266, 326
Reeves, B., 105, 326
Reis, H., 205, 333
Relevance, 15, 44, 78, 79, 88–92, 108, 124,
    190–193, 283
    see also Pertience, Salience
Reliability of measures, 166–169, 174, 195,
    235, 241, 249, 284
Renckstorf, K., 73, 74, 148, 149, 326, 332
Reneker, M., 179, 205, 224, 326
Rescher, N., 286, 326
Reynolds, P. 114, 136, 326
Reynolds, R., 52, 81, 319
Rice, R., xvi, 44, 45, 52, 84–88, 95, 104, 107,
    116, 150, 154, 187, 222, 249, 255,
    267–269, 279, 306, 313, 322, 326, 327
Rich, E., 244, 310
Richins, M., 87, 307
Richmond, C., 179, 208–210, 327
Ridgway, N., 87, 108, 263, 264, 307
Rifkin, J., 267, 327
Rioux, K., 272, 314
Ritchie, L., 48, 49, 88, 89, 327
Rivers, R., 86, 309
Roberts, R., 85, 327

Robertson, R., 47, 327
Robertson, S., 52, 53, 306
Roeh, I., 250, 327
Rogers, E., 40, 48, 51, 98, 134, 153, 255, 267, 278, 309, 325, 327
Rokeach, M., 74, 327
Roles
  see Social roles
Rosch, E., 90, 93, 315, 327
Rosenberg, V., 142, 237, 248, 269, 320, 327
Rosengren, K., 103, 140, 155, 327
Ross, C., 105, 106, 153, 327
Ross, S., 233, 251, 327
Rousseau, D., 258, 269, 317
Royle, J., 247, 307
Ruben, B., 43, 45, 309
Rubin, A., 87, 145, 327
Rubin, R., 105, 106, 327
Rural dwellers, 244, 247, 269, 278, 279, 297
Russell, B., 57, 327
Russell, H., 40, 314

S

Safety
  as a concern, 7, 252, 268, 273, 274
  as a basic human need, 270
Safire, W., 103
Salasin, J., 247, 278, 327
Salience, 79, 91, 92, 124
  see also Pertinence, Relevance
Salomon, L., 87, 108, 327
Salton, G., 142, 327
Salvage, A., 273, 331
Samoa, 266
Sampling, 15, 146, 172, 180, 195, 205, 206, 213, 214
Sandstrom, A., 133, 216, 328
Sandstrom, P., 87, 132, 133, 216, 328
Santa, J., 91, 316
Saracevic, T., 24, 89, 211, 323, 326, 328
Satisficing, 8, 34, 188
Saunders, C., 86, 88, 328
Savolainen, R., 70, 82, 116, 153, 225, 228, 255, 258, 261, 262, 280, 312, 314, 320, 328, 330, 331, 333
Scanning, 68, 72, 74, 85, 87, 222, 235, 248
  see also Browsing, Discovering, Encountering, Foraging, Navigating, Zapping
Schamber, L., 90, 328

Schauder, D., 269, 278, 333
Schement, J., 40, 42, 63, 328
Schiller, H., 97, 328
Schizophrenia, 98
Schmidt, J., 87, 328
Schmitt, K., 151, 305
Schoderbek, P., 86, 319
Schutt, R., 161, 180, 328
Schutz, A., 73, 149, 328
Schwartz, R., 207, 332
Scientists, 11, 14, 15, 20–24, 29–31, 34, 43, 60, 80, 83, 116, 151, 161, 207, 211, 229, 231–236, 248, 249, 253, 256
Scott, L., 1153, 201, 263, 328
Searle, J., 65, 328
Sears, D., 93, 328
Sechrest, L., 207, 332
Security analysts, 116, 181, 233, 249, 255, 279
Seldén, L., 196, 269, 328
Selective dissemination of information (SDI), 7
Selective exposure, 15, 80, 92, 93, 161, 283
  see also Avoidance, Ignorance, Ignoring
Self-efficacy, 164, 274, 275, 280
  see also Social Learning Theory
Sender
  in Information Theory, 46, 47
Senior citizens
  see Elderly
Sense-making, 6, 43, 60, 71, 75, 131, 140, 146–148, 178, 190, 211, 224, 246, 262, 281, 283, 288, 290, 303
Serendipity, 32, 82, 84–87
Sever, I., 269, 328
Shanahan, J., 140, 154, 213, 276, 323
Shannon, C., 46–50, 58, 69, 114, 115, 328, 332
Shapira, Z., 80, 322
Shapiro, G., 85, 328
Sharing of information, 210, 211, 271
Shaw, J., 24, 328
Sheatsley, P., 92, 93, 96, 265, 318
Shepherd, M., 150, 329
Shera, J., 48, 329
Sherrell, D., 87, 108, 263, 264, 307
Sherry, J., 258, 263, 264, 306, 329
Sheth, J., 82, 329
Shiffman, S.,153, 330
Shoemaker, P., 258, 267, 268, 329
Shopping, 5, 11, 12, 18–21, 34, 82, 101, 106, 186–190, 260–264
Shuchman, H., 2233, 236, 329

Shugan, S., 187, 329
Sidberry, G., 275, 329
Sievert, D., 242, 329
Sievert, M., 242, 329
Signal
  in Information Theory, 45–47
Simon, H., 82, 83, 305, 311, 329
Simon, J., 114, 135, 329
Situational relevance, 91, 92
  see also Pertience, Relevance, Salience
Situation
  definition of, 225, 226
  see also Context
Skinner, Q., 137, 329
Slater, M., 221, 233, 329
Slife, B., 133, 329
Sligo, F., 265, 266, 269, 329
Smith, D., 100, 306
Smith, E., 153, 329
Smith, K., 267, 323
Snipp, J., 260, 308
Social class
  see Socioeconomic status
Social construction, 234
Social Learning Theory, 118, 119
  see also Self-efficacy
Social network, 123, 153, 154, 237, 254
Social Network Theory, 153, 154, 254
Social roles, 14, 15, 119, 220, 227–229, 257,
  259, 277, 283
Social scientists, 13, 116, 231–235, 238–240,
  253
Social work
  academic discipline of, xvi
Socioeconomic status, 96, 225–227, 230, 257,
  265, 268, 275–277
Sociology, 81, 139, 154, 284, 299
Solomon, P., 179, 212, 213, 329
Sonnenwald, D., 162, 329
Sources of information
  academic journals, 6, 22, 23, 34, 122, 142,
    181, 205, 214, 226, 235–238,
    243–247, 254, 260, 267
  books, 6, 22–24, 34, 42, 69, 84, 87, 97,
    105, 106, 120, 145, 170, 187, 207, 214,
    238, 254, 260, 289, 294, 297
  encyclopedias, 12
  family members, 8, 12, 21, 29–31, 43, 95,
    106, 137, 152, 200, 211, 243, 260,
    268–274, 277, 289, 303

friends, 8, 12, 20, 21, 34, 43, 104, 142, 152,
  161, 185–187, 200, 243, 260, 261,
  268–271, 289
libraries, 6–9, 13, 22–24, 29–31, 34,
  66–69, 84–85, 90, 100, 106, 107,
  118–122, 146, 167, 168, 195, 196,
  202–206, 216, 227, 237, 239, 244,
  247, 254, 260, 267–271, 277, 278
magazines, 7, 19, 20, 144, 186, 192, 200,
  254, 260, 262
mass media , 6, 12, 87, 95, 103, 104, 109,
  125, 138, 141–145, 189, 196–199,
  261, 270–272, 289
neighbors, 200, 260, 261, 267
newspapers, 8, 15, 16, 66, 103, 107–111,
  141–146, 158, 180, 184–186, 194,
  228, 238, 243–251, 263
radio, 4, 12, 43, 47, 192, 200, 260, 271, 275,
  293
telephone, 4, 32, 123, 195, 196, 246, 260,
  267, 268
television, 7, 13, 18, 49, 70, 87, 94, 100,
  103–107, 143–152, 173, 186, 193,
  200, 206, 214, 260, 272, 275–277,
  290, 295
websites, 9, 33, 34, 42, 101, 114, 141, 169,
  170, 174, 187, 192
Sormunen, J., 248, 311
Spacks, P., 106, 329
Speller, D., 103, 318
Spencer, C., 179, 206, 329
Spencer, H. 137
Sperber, D., 83, 88, 89, 329
Spink, A., 82, 258, 275, 329
Spradley, J., 148, 329
Sproull, L., 91, 319
Stake, R., 179, 180, 216, 330
Stam, D., 233, 254, 330
Stanley, S., 180, 309
Stein, J., 267, 315
Steinbruner, J., 82, 330
Stephenson, W., 107, 149, 150, 154, 330
Stern, B., 153, 263, 330
Stewart, D., 189, 315
Stewart, J., 81, 134, 330
Stocking, H., 251, 330
Stone, A., 153, 330
Stone, S., 221, 233, 241, 330
Storrs, G., 86, 309
Stotland, E., 66, 310
Strauss, A., 137, 165, 316

Strength of Weak Ties, 153, 154
    see also Social Network Theory
Stress, 100, 118, 150, 182
Strother, E., 233, 247, 330
    students, 7, 13, 14, 22–24, 34, 99, 106, 122,
        196, 228, 229, 232, 241, 258, 269, 280,
        298
Suleiman, S., 153, 330
Supaat, H., 258, 278, 305
Survey methods
    email, 15, 173, 174, 190, 193, 194, 302
    mail, 15, 169, 190–193, 243, 265
Sutton, S., 2233, 251, 252, 330
Swanson, E., 233, 249, 330
Sweden, 326
Sylvain, C., 115, 116, 126–130, 234, 247, 252,
    320
Szilard, L., 47

T

Taliaferro, A., 100, 306
Talja, S., 113, 153, 225–227, 230, 231, 330
Tannenbaum, S., 244, 330
Tape recording
    see Recordings
Tapscott, D., 271, 330
Tarde, G., 265, 330
Taste
    Theory of, 153, 156
Taylor, R., 31, 68, 71, 76–78, 146, 227, 256,
    268, 330
Teachers, 239, 255, 259, 262, 270, 273
Teenagers, 7, 152, 269, 271
Telephone
    see Sources of information
Television
    see Sources of information
Tenopir, C., 222, 319
Ter Maat, J., 267, 323
Thayer, L., 63, 79, 93, 322, 330
Theories, 15, 114, 131–155, 161
Thompson, R., 53, 86, 331
Thomson, M., 244, 331
Thórsteinsdóttir, G., 269, 330
Tibbo, H., 222, 331
Tichenor, P., 95, 265, 322, 331
Timpka, T., 233, 245, 246, 331
Tinker, A., 258, 273, 331
Tipton, L., 17, 53, 80, 115, 225, 313
Todd, H., 258, 273, 331

Toms, E., 86, 150, 153
Tonga, 266
Törnudd, E., 220, 331
Trow, D., 82, 311
Truth, 39, 50, 57, 58, 67–69, 293
    see also Misinformation
Tufte, E., 107, 331
Tuominen, K., 153, 331
Turk-Charles, S., 274, 331

U

Uman, G., 179, 205, 214, 215, 244, 311
Uncertainty, 39, 50–52, 55, 60, 69–73, 76,
    77, 81, 83, 100, 104, 120, 138, 145, 180,
    248, 249, 281, 283, 295, 301
Units of analysis, 169, 170
Unobtrusive measures, 207
Urban dwellers, 13, 96, 185, 244, 258,
    267–269, 279, 288
Urban poor, 13, 268, 288
Urban, G., 184–187, 263, 317
Urbany, J., 82, 331
Urquhart, C., 233, 244, 246, 247, 331
Uses and gratifications, 86, 139, 143–146, 283
Utility
    of information, 50, 62, 74, 87, 106, 145,
        279, 288, 290

V

Vakkari, P., 6, 59, 178, 225, 312, 314, 320,
    328, 330, 331
Vale, M., 233, 253, 331
Validity
    of measures, 166–169, 173, 174, 214, 279,
        284
Van de Wijngaert, L., 64, 228, 331
Van der Rijt, G., 258, 273, 332
Van Dijk, T., 241, 332
Van Snippenburg, L., 153, 332
Varlejs, J., 177, 332
Vickery, A., 73, 89, 90, 233, 306, 316
Victims, 91, 269
Videotape, 121, 185, 203
Videotext, 146
Viewers
    television, 12, 101, 107, 153, 207, 272–277
Vignettes, 246, 247
Vinson, D., 243, 244, 278, 314
Viswanath, K., 96, 265, 332

Voigt, M., 116, 321, 332
  von Neuman, J., 47
Vorderer, P., 94, 317
Voters, 7, 11, 13, 99, 257–262
  see also Citizens, Political information

W

Wakeham, M., 233, 247, 332
Waldhart, E., 221, 332
Waldhart, T., 221, 332
Wallendorf, M., 263, 306, 322
Walsh, B., 84, 87, 310
Walsh, R., 84, 87, 253, 332
Walsh-Childers, K., 107, 308
Walter, V., 2258, 269, 270, 332
Walters, C., 115, 332
Ward, D., 179, 203, 204, 233, 247, 323
Ward, J., 267, 323
Ward, S., 78, 312
Warner, E., 260, 272, 332
Wartella, E., 155, 316, 327
Watson-Boone, R., 233, 242, 332
Watt, J., 48, 49, 332
Watters, C., 150, 329
Weaver, W., 46–50, 69, 328, 332
Webb, E., 207, 332
Weber, M., 103, 137, 138
Websites
  see Sources of information
Wei, R., 153, 321
Weick, K., xvi, 100, 155, 332
Weinberg, B., 184–187, 263, 317
Weisberg, R., 151, 332
Wellisch, H., 42, 332
Wersig, G., 42, 51, 285, 332, 333
Westley, B., 57, 333
Wheeler, L., 205, 333
White, H., 141, 333
White, M. 179, 187, 210, 211, 241, 267, 333
White, N., 260, 312
Whitt, A., 2258, 269, 278, 333
Wiberley, S., 233, 241, 333
Wicks, D., 153, 196, 233, 254, 255, 333
Wilkie, W., 82, 331
Williams, F., 134, 145, 260, 333
Williams, P., 228, 233, 251, 324

Williams, R., 133, 329
Williamson, K., 84, 146, 153, 258, 269, 272, 273, 278, 333
Wilson, D., 83, 88, 89, 329
Wilson, P., 57, 66, 79, 94–97, 104, 333
Wilson, T., xvi, 71, 73–75, 115–119, 128–130, 153, 219–221, 231, 234, 256, 281, 283, 285–288, 297, 314, 324, 333, 334
Windahl, S., 104, 130, 139, 144, 148, 321, 322
Windel, G., 285, 333
Winterhalder, B., 153, 329
Woefl, N., 179, 203, 204, 233, 247, 323
Wolf, F., 213, 334
Wolfe, D., 66, 310
Wolton, D., 250, 334
Woolgar, S., 234, 320
World Wide Web (WWW), xvi, 4, 7, 15, 101, 114, 169, 170, 187, 192, 229, 270, 290
  see also Sources of information
Wright, P., 96, 315
Wurman, R., 99, 109, 297

Y

Yin, R., 176, 179, 180
Yoon, K., 52, 334
Youth
  see Children, Teenagers
Yovits, M., 52, 81, 334

Z

Zapping, 87
  see also Browsing, Discovering, Encountering, Foraging, Navigating, Scanning
Zerbinos, E., 75, 146, 334
Zey, M., 80, 322, 329, 334
Zhang, Y., 179, 192–194, 334
Zillman, D., 94, 99, 101–103, 109, 151, 153, 308, 334
Ziman, J., 179, 210, 334
Zipf, G., 131, 140–143, 154, 298, 334
Zuckerman, H., 208, 334
Zunde, P., 46, 334
Zweizig, D., 138, 334

Library and Information Science

(Continued from page ii)

Lois Swan Jones and Sarah Scott Gibson
Art Libraries and Information Services

Nancy Jones Pruett
Scientific and Technical Libraries: Functions and Management
Volume 1 and Volume 2

Peter Judge and Brenda Gerrie
Small Bibliographic Databases

Dorothy B. Lilley and Ronald W. Trice
A History of Information Sciences 1945–1985

Elaine Svenonius
The Conceptual Foundations of Descriptive Cataloging

Robert M. Losee, Jr.
The Science of Information: Measurement and Applications

Irene P. Godden
Library Technical Services: Operations and Management, Second Edition

Donald H. Kraft and Bert R. Boyce
Operations Research for Libraries and Information Agencies: Techniques for the Evaluation of Management Decision Alternatives

James Cabeceiras
The Multimedia Library: Materials Selection and Use, Second Edition

Charles T. Meadow
Text Information Retrieval Systems, First Edition

Robert M. Losee, Jr., and Karen A. Worley
Research and Evaluation for Information Professionals

Carmel Maguire, Edward J. Kazlauskas, and Anthony D. Weir
Information Services for Innovative Organizations

Karen Markey Drabenstott and Diane Vizine-Goetz
Using Subject Headings for Online Retrieval

Bert R. Boyce, Charles T. Meadow, and Donald H. Kraft
Measurement in Information Science

John V. Richardson, Jr.
Knowledge-Based Systems for General Reference Work

John Tague-Sutcliffe
Measuring Information

Bryce L. Allen
Information Tasks: Toward a User-Centered Approach to
Information Systems

Peter Clayton
Implementation of Organizational Innovation: Studies of
Academic and Research Libraries

Harold Sackman
Biomedical Information Technology: Global Social
Responsibilities for the Democratic Information Age

V. Frants, J. Shapiro, and V. Votskunskii
Automated Information Retrieval: Theory and Methods

A. J. Meadows
Communicating Research

Charles T. Meadow, Bert R. Boyce, and Donald H. Kraft
Text Information Retrieval Systems, Second Edition

Robert M. Hayes
Models for Library Management, Decision Making, and Planning

Donald O. Case
Looking for Information: A Survey of Research on Information
Seeking, Needs, and Behavior